Freud Scientifically Reappraised

Freud Scientifically Reappraised

Testing the Theories and Therapy

SEYMOUR FISHER
&
ROGER P. GREENBERG

State University of New York
Health Science Center, Syracuse

John Wiley & Sons, Inc.
New York • Chichester • Brisbane • Toronto • Singapore

Library of Congress Cataloging-in-Publication Data:

Fisher, Seymour.
    Freud scientifically reappraised : testing the theories and
therapy / Seymour Fisher, Roger P. Greenberg.
       p.   cm.
    Includes bibliographical references and indexes.
    ISBN 0-471-57855-X (cloth : alk. paper)
    1. Freud, Sigmund, 1856–1939. 2. Psychoanalysis. I. Greenberg,
Roger P. II. Title.
BF173.F85F548   1996
150.19'52—dc20   95-8727

Preface

This book evolved from our continuing interest in finding out how well Freud's major ideas stand up to scientific appraisal. In 1977, we completed the *Scientific Credibility of Freud's Theories and Therapy*,[1] which was our first systematic attempt to ascertain the empirical soundness of Freud's formulations. At that time, we collected all the scientific publications in the world literature that even remotely touched on psychoanalytic concepts and used them to judge whether the fundamentals of Freud's theories are congruent with the accrued scientific data. One of the things we learned is that Freud's theories do not represent a unitary monolithic structure. They consist of a network of quasi-independent minitheories that vary in how well they are validated by reasonably controlled observations. Our critique of the cumulative evidence indicated that certain of Freud's ideas (e.g., Oedipal conflict, oral and anal personality types) were well supported and others (e.g., dream functions, superego formation) were not. We also found that although psychoanalytic therapy is more effective than no treatment, it is apparently not superior to other forms of psychotherapy.

Since the publication of our 1977 book, a stream of new pertinent research has appeared. Indeed, there has been an efflorescence of general interest in psychoanalysis. Large numbers of books and articles dealing with every conceivable dimension of psychoanalysis have poured forth. At the same time however, and somewhat paradoxically, explicit interest in psychoanalytic concepts has declined among those doing research in the areas of personality and psychopathology. There has been less research that formally announces it is testing this or that psychoanalytic proposition. Still, many studies are tackling issues relevant to Freud's classical propositions. For example, social

---

[1] Although the *Scientific Credibility of Freud's Theories and Therapy* was first published in 1977, we will reference it throughout in terms of the 1985 reissued version.

psychologists are assiduously dissecting depressive realism, a phenomenon that seriously intersects basic psychoanalytic assumptions about depression and the nature of psychopathology. And cognitive psychologists are increasingly interested in phenomena that relate to unconscious decision-making processes that lie at the very core of Freud's thinking. In other words, a good deal of the experimental work in progress does not bear a psychoanalytic stamp but actually falls within the psychoanalytic domain.

We decided it would be sensible to probe the pertinent research findings that have accumulated since the 1970s and to ascertain how they add or detract from our original conclusions about Freud's work. We have cast our nets widely into multiple literature pools and have assimilated observations from such diverse areas as social, clinical, cognitive, developmental, and physiological psychology and from multiple disciplines such as anthropology, sociology, psychiatry, and psychosomatic medicine. Much new information has become available, and we are now in an even better position than we were in the 1970s to appraise Freud's contributions. We would like to emphasize that we originally decided to evaluate Freud's formulations rather than derivatives and elaborations produced by his followers. Our position on this matter was as follows (Fisher & Greenberg, 1985):

> It was our decision to confine our assessments entirely to Freud's constructs, as he stated them. This was logical, first of all, because most scientific studies have actually focused their hypothesis-testing upon Freud's original models. Secondly, the diversity of the secondary elaborations of Freud's ideas is so Babel-like as to defy the derivation of sensible deductions that can be put to empirical test. Finally, there is no evidence that the secondary elaborations were produced in a fashion that would render them superior to the original forms from which they were derived. (p. 1x)

We continue this policy in presenting our updated material.

Although the present volume is an extension of our 1977 presentation, it is not simply a revision but represents a completely new effort incorporating schemata and perspectives previously unavailable to us. We can now adopt a broader approach that does not simply ask whether Freud's ideas are empirically supported but rather goes further to inquire whether clusters of exciting findings prominent in various lines of modern research have possible positive or negative relevance for his assertions. Indeed, we are perhaps more interested in reshaping Freud's formulations to reflect accumulated empirical research than in simplistically checking out whether they are "right" or "wrong." On the basis of our 1977 book, it was already obvious to us that so much new empirical information had accumulated—beyond anything Freud could have imagined—that most of his paradigms probably stand in need of some degree of revision or more elaborate specification.

SEYMOUR FISHER
ROGER P. GREENBERG

February 1996

Acknowledgments

The essence of this book is information–in great quantities. Fortunately, our library facilities at the State University of New York Health Science Center (Syracuse) are superb, and we were expeditiously supplied with even the most esoteric references.

We also have had first-class secretarial support, and we are grateful to both Sandra Stowell and Donna Vinch for their conscientious attention to apparently endless revisions.

One of our major assets was working in a department that provides a setting conducive to thoughtful detachment and the exploration of controversial issues.

We would particularly like to thank Dr. Joseph Masling for his expert critical advice in the preparation of Chapter 4, "The Oral Paradigm."

Contents

Part Three
Integration

Chapter 1

What Is Psychoanalytic Reality?

AMBIGUITY AND POLARIZATION

Those who consider themselves to be serious actors in psychoanalytic affairs continue to disagree about the nature of the psychoanalytic enterprise. Perhaps even more seriously, they are still debating how to ascertain what is factual or true or real within psychoanalytic borders. Edelson (1977) nicely portrays the confusing questions that persist in this area:

> Is psychoanalysis a radically different enterprise from other sciences? Are its methods of discovery different? Are its methods of confirmation different? Is it not . . . concerned with asserting true propositions about reality . . . ? (p. 2)

As is well known, there are those (e.g., Edelson, 1984; Fisher & Greenberg, 1985; Grunbaum, 1984; Kline, 1981; Masling & Schwartz, 1979; Wallerstein, 1986b) who advocate that psychoanalysis should be bound by the same scientific standards as all other disciplines aspiring to respectable empirical status. They take the position that the way to establish a "psychoanalytic fact" is to subject the data in question to the usual canons of scientific proof. At the other extreme, a fairly populous bloc is allied with various versions of the hermeneutic tradition. Advocates of this view (e.g., Habermas, 1971; Ricoeur, 1974; Spence, 1982a, 1982b) would banish scientific standards from the appraisal of psychoanalytic truth. They urge that psychoanalysis should be modeled after disciplines like history or literary criticism and adopt methods of inquiry akin to biblical exegetical interpretation. Criteria such as "coherence," "consistency," and "configuration" are to outweigh the usual empirical guidelines for specifying verity. In this vein, Spence (1982b)

1

conceptualizes psychoanalytic therapy as not being concerned with "historical truth":

> The analyst . . . commits himself to a belief in his hypothesis and is inclined to use it in a pragmatic fashion. He is less committed to a belief in its truth value . . . either because he has no clear way of knowing whether or not it actually occurred or because he is proposing something that has no clear correspondence with an event in the patient's life . . . we can hardly ask questions about its historical truth. The more appropriate question concerns what might be called its artistic truth, its significance as a kind of creative endeavor, a putting together of known facts about the patient in a new form that carries a high probability of something happening in the analytic space. (p. 275)

He adds with respect to psychoanalytic interpretations:

> They are designed to produce results rather than document the past; they are designed primarily to bring about a change in belief. . . . Once we conceive of interpretations as artistic creations that have the potential for producing an aesthetic response, we are . . . even less interested in the truth of the particular parts. (p. 276)

Thus, even if an interpretation comprises illusory elements, that is quite all right, as long as it offers presumed heuristic advantages.[1]

---

[1] Grunbaum (1984) has critiqued that hermeneutic position in depth and concludes that it is largely based on flawed assumptions. He forcefully states: "Once the hermeneutic construct is robbed of its scientophobic myths, its sterility for the constructive utilization of the Freudian legacy in psychology and psychiatry becomes apparent" (p. 93).

He notes that the concepts of the hermeneutic adherents are based "on profound misunderstandings of the very content and methods of the natural sciences" (p. 1).

He specifically attacks the hermeneutic presumptions about the uniqueness of causality as it applies in the psychoanalytic context and the uniqueness of the analysand's role in validating psychoanalytic hypotheses.

Wallace (1988) too is highly critical of the hermeneutic stance:

> The relativist-subjectivists inflate partial truths into a thesis as one-sided and erroneous as what they oppose. They alert us to the impact of theoretical presuppositions on the investigator's perceptions, while totally depreciating the contribution of the reality with which he or she interacts. They reason from the fact that perception can be unreliable or illusory to the conclusion that it is always so. That memory can be untrustworthy becomes "it is completely and invariably so." That recollections are subject to reinterpretation over time becomes "we can never approximate to the individual's representation of the event at the time it was experienced" . . . That psychical life is ambiguous becomes "the psyche is unknowable" . . . Clearly, such doctrines as those of Spence . . . are convenient for witch doctors, astrologers, chiropractors, and politicians—the notion, to put it bluntly, that no one can call us to account, that we can believe what we want as long as it is pretty and helps somebody. (pp. 141–142)

The marked polarity in conceptions of psychoanalytic "truth" just described actually mirrors Freud's original ambivalence in this respect (Breger, 1981). On the one hand, his early professional career was rooted in neurological research, medical-scientific training, and the rational-empirical spirit of the 19th-century image of reason. He was persistently pulled to maintain his connection with a scientific ideal and scientific respectability. At the same time, however, he was fascinated with the subjectivity and the intrigue of the irrationality he encountered in his clinical work. In this context, his thinking was often based on quick intuitions and the "feel" of things. He discerned much that could not at that time be checked out by conventional scientific methods, and therefore he came to ascribe great power and validity to the observations of the individual clinical expert. But even as Freud hailed the independent validity of the psychoanalytic method of observation, he tried valiantly to create a metapsychology (not to mention The Project) infused with a halo of scientific-sounding terms and schemata (e.g., the libidinal energy system).

Freud occasionally let it slip how pleased he was when experimental support surfaced for some of his ideas. For example, in *The Interpretation of Dreams* (Freud, 1900), he refers as follows to research by Schrotter that presumably reinforced the validity of dream symbolism: "The sexual symbolism of dreams has already been directly confirmed *by experiment* " (italics added; p. 384). In another instance (Freud, 1925), he complained that it was a "gross injustice that people have refused to treat psycho-analysis like any other science" (p. 58). In the end, Freud apparently convinced himself that what he did and learned in the context of psychoanalytic therapy was scientifically sound.[2]

Grunbaum (1984) has directly challenged Freud's position on this matter. As is well known, Grunbaum, while defending the potentiality of psychoanalysis to be a scientific enterprise, denies that

---

[2]Eckardt (1982) argues that Freud never actually took a scientific approach to the observations he made of his patients. She states:

> Freud seems to have believed that a theory could be justified solely on the basis of its explanatory power. . . . He typically proceeded in the following way: First, he starts from various background assumptions. . . . These, in conjunction with various observations, give rise to certain questions. Next, he attempts to formulate an answer to these questions, and this answer constitutes his tentative hypothesis. He then attempts to justify his hypothesis by seeking further observations explainable by the hypothesis. If he finds such additional observations, he takes the hypothesis to be confirmed. However, if he comes upon evidence that does not fit his hypothesis, then the original hypothesis is frequently revised. The revised version is then tentatively accepted until such time as further recalcitrant data are found. Note that at no time . . . is the tentatively accepted hypothesis . . . subjected to rigorous predictive tests. As long as it can *explain* all the relevant data at hand, Freud regards it as acceptable. (pp. 554–555)

psychoanalytic therapy can yield verifiable data. He considers that "epistemic contamination" reduces the truth value of clinical psychoanalytic observation to practically zero. His vigorously argued position in this respect was triggered by what he calls "Freud's Tally Argument," which is basically an assertion that the therapeutic interpretations of the analyst can be effective only if they "tally with what is real." Grunbaum states:

> It is of capital importance to appreciate that Freud is at pains to employ the Tally Argument in order to justify the following epistemological claim: actual *durable* therapeutic success guarantees not only that the pertinent analytic interpretations ring true or credible to the analysand *but also* that they *are* indeed veridical, or at least quite close to the mark. Freud then relies on this bold intermediate contention to conclude nothing less than the following: Collectively the successful outcomes of analyses do constitute *cogent* evidence for all that general psychoanalytic theory tells us about the influences of the unconscious dynamics of the mind on our lives. In short, psychoanalytic treatment successes as a whole vouch for the truth of the Freudian theory of personality, including its specific etiologies of the psychoneuroses and even its general theory of psychosexual development. (pp. 140–141)

Grunbaum cites multiple reasons for rejecting the Tally Argument and its associated implication that clinical data provide a source of scientific validation. Briefly, he argues that the responses of analysands to analysts' interpretations are influenced by a spectrum of variables that have little to do with the validity of such interpretations. Instead, the responses are shaped by numerous adventitious vectors, such as suggestions emanating from the analyst, the need of the analysand to comply with or resist the analyst, and the potential unreliability of the memories produced by the analysand about earlier life experiences.[3] He adds that because the Tally Argument assumes psychoanalytic therapy is uniquely effective (and uniquely anchored in psychoanalytic principles), it is confronted by the contradiction that many other forms of psychotherapy (based on very different rationales) are just as successful. Further, he notes the demonstrated roles

[3] Colby and Stoller (1988) would go even further than Grunbaum:

> The crucial problem is not that patient problems are influenced by the analyst and thus contaminated, as Grunbaum has argued . . . charitably (or naively), assuming fidelity of Freud's case reports, which, to those in the know, are simply stories endlessly told and retold around psychoanalytic campfires—but that the authenticity of agreed-on described observations does not exist. The public observation records in the literature consist of the clinician's unconstrained idiosyncratic selections, omissions, and paraphrasing. (p. 30)

of generalized variables such as placebo effects and expectancies (which have little to do with the psychoanalytic corpus) in producing positive therapy outcomes.

He is staunchly persuaded that the data flowing from the psychoanalytic dyad may be interesting but have no scientific currency. His sardonic stance is extreme and highlights the tendency for psychoanalytic issues to evoke strongly polarized reactions. In any case, Grunbaum's position goes too far. The plain fact is that clever researchers are able to distill scientifically reliable insights from the detailed protocols of psychoanalytic therapy sessions. Illustratively, Luborsky and Mintz (1974) demonstrated consistent statistically significant relationships between momentary forgetting by the analysand and certain parallel psychodynamic factors. Also, Luborsky and Crits-Christoph (1990) empirically verified from therapy protocols the basic core of the transference concept as Freud visualized it—that the patient's relationship with the therapist matches the patient's relationships with other people. By way of further illustration, Luborsky and Auerbach (1969) and Spence (1970) found significant regularities in a specific psychodynamic issue dealt with during a series of therapy sessions and the probability of specific localized bodily complaints (pain and discomfort) appearing at parallel points in the sessions. All the studies just enumerated are based on therapy data but represent good science.

Edelson (1984) has been in the forefront of those psychoanalysts disagreeing with Grunbaum's dismissal of the scientific probity of data derived from psychoanalytic therapy sessions. Although he agrees that few of his colleagues have conscientiously adopted the safeguards necessary to ensure scientific probity, he feels that such safeguards are reasonably within reach. He offers a long elaborate list of measures to enable the proper evaluation of hypotheses in the psychoanalytic situations. The list diversely includes such items as "seek falsifications rather than confirmations in case studies," "minimize suggestion," "predict responses by the analysand to an interpretation that has not previously been manifested," and "use causal modeling and statistical controls in order to be able to argue that a causal relation holds" (p. 158). The sheer length and the diversity of Edelson's list demonstrate that he is well aware how complex a process it is to extract reasonably scientific information from therapeutic transactions. It should be parenthetically noted that he is opposed to the typical clinical case history reports that abound in psychoanalytic journals. He feels that they are all too often selective anecdotes that simply reinforce existing theoretical biases and make no reasonable scientific contribution.

Interestingly, he regards Grunbaum's frontal attack on the scientific potential of data derived from the therapy context as one of the three major instances in which "the status of psychoanalysis as science has been called into question" (p. 1). Next, he mentions the original position of the logical positivists: "Psychoanalysis was infested with theoretical terms so vague, so unconnected to empirical procedures, its hypotheses could not be empirically verified or confirmed" (p. 1). Finally, he notes Popper's charge: "Psychoanalysis was incapable of meeting his criterion for demarcating science from nonscience, for its hypotheses could not be falsified by any empirical evidence" (p. 3). These criticisms have been broadly examined by Edelson and also Grunbaum (1984) and well confuted.

In this book, we wish to avoid the extremes that so often shadow appraisals of the psychoanalytic scene. Despite our own scientific perspective, we acknowledge the commonsense value in being free to adopt hermeneuticlike attitudes when conducting psychoanalytic therapy. Indeed, large segments of therapy are everywhere carried out in the "literary" spirit advocated by the hermeneuticists. Also, who can disagree with the hermeneutic position that it is important for the therapy process to produce a satisfying coherent narrative? We would not, however, go so far as to concede that efforts to nail down what "really" happened in the analysand's life should be abandoned. We assume that even the most extreme hermeneutic devotees entertain some secret concern about whether what they are hearing from the analysand is more than just fantasy.

By the same token, although we agree with Grunbaum that Freud's theories should be tested empirically, we favor a concept of empiricism that is flexible and not relentlessly supercritical. We consider that any observations made with roughly proper controls for dealing with bias and ensuring reliability are worth counting. We do not think it is the mission of one who reviews the scientific literature pertinent to Freud's work to be highly critical (as exemplified in the critiques by Kline, 1981) of every individual study (which any experienced researcher can easily manage), but rather to look at overall trends across multiple reports. True, gross errors in individual research designs should be spotted and described, but it is wasteful to comment on the endless relatively minor defects that trouble just about all studies. It is even less sensible to condemn the core data of a study because of peripheral deviations in design or procedure.

THE IMPACT OF PSYCHOANALYTIC THOUGHT

Those who for whatever reasons are uninterested in psychoanalytic ideas might wonder whether it is worthwhile investing time and energy in checking the empirical soundness of Freud's formulations. We would respond that Freud's ideas have penetrated into the matrix of modern psychology and continue to exert formidable influence. Shakow and Rapaport (1964) documented in detail how Freud sharply impacted early 20th-century American psychology. In their 1960s evaluation they concluded: "The ideas which demonstrably originated in the Freudian body of theory and observation have indeed permeated virtually the whole range of psychology. In fact, we have seen that with the cumulative growth of this influence, Freud has become the most prominent name in the history of psychology" (p. 191).

Shakow and Rapaport go on to specify: "Psychology has become pervaded by Freud's ideas of the role of the unconscious and its manifestations of motivation (particularly its goal-directedness), his idea of the genetic approach, and his principle of psychological determinism" (p. 193). After assiduously sorting through the literature of that period, they specify that Freud had "markedly affected" the following areas of psychology: abnormal, personality, developmental, industrial, social, and psychotherapy. They even feel that some areas of experimental psychology (e.g., learning, thinking, perception) had been noticeably "touched."

Are Freud's ideas still important and influential within psychology at the close of the 20th century? An examination of multiple issues of the *Psychological Abstracts* shows that the category "Psychoanalysis" is full to the brim with references. Many themes occur and recur in the stream of current psychological research that reflect basic Freudian notions. Consider the research concerned with subliminal and unconscious influences on thought, fantasy, and perception. In this regard, a 1992 issue of the *American Psychologist* (vol. 47, no. 6) devoted major attention to a series of articles by outstanding researchers who affirmed the scientific solidity of the construct of a functioning unconscious system involving perception, memory, and thinking. Consider the wide acceptance of the role of irrational motives in behavior. Consider the many studies focused on early influences of parents on personality development (e.g., Fisher & Greenberg, 1985). Consider the widely practiced psychodynamic psychotherapies, most of which use strategies based on free association and attaining insight. Consider the immense attention devoted to adaptation to stress, particularly as viewed through the lenses of the classical (Freudian) defense mechanisms. Consider the great outburst of research concerned with the influence of fantasy and feeling on somatic symptomatology (which obviously derives significantly from Freud's conversion hysteric model). Consider the widespread use of projective tests and research designs that utilize measures based on the projective principle (and which clearly mimic the model of free association).

In various other areas of work, psychoanalytic concepts are frequently introduced for explanatory or comparative purposes (e.g., etiology of depression, origins of homosexuality, the nature of the dream process, body-image phenomena, patterns of sexual behavior, development of the self-concept). If for no other reason, psychoanalytic paradigms must be regarded as influential simply because they consistently whisper that there are large areas of psychological functioning that need to be explored and explained even if they are not easily described in terms of overt behavior or are difficult to deal with in the laboratory. Friman, Allen, Kerwin, and Larzelere (1993) have actually analyzed the frequency of psychoanalytic citations in the psychological literature and concluded that although there has been a small decline, "the standing of psychoanalysis remains high in the social sciences and the humanities" (p. 662). They also note:

> Freud is still cited more than all other sources in history except Lenin, Shakespeare, the Bible and Plato. . . . The influence of psychoanalysis appears stronger than that of other areas of psychology. . . . Classic source items in psychoanalysis appear to be cited more than classic source items in behavioral and cognitive psychology. For example, in 1988 Sigmund Freud was cited almost five times as often as B.F. Skinner and four times as often as Herbert Simon. (p. 661)

Colby and Stoller (1988), who actually present a mordantly negative view of psychoanalysis as a science, felt that in all fairness they should also take stock of what has been positive about the psychoanalytic enterprise. They came up with numerous positive points.

They note first of all, that the psychoanalytic situation provides a special chance to examine the nature of subjective experience: "Never before has there been such an opportunity for collecting naturalistic information on subjective experience. To reduce their unhappiness people will talk about themselves: to an analyst for hours a week, for years. . . . They reveal their secrets, past and present. . . . They also tell more than they had intended and more than they know they are telling" (p. 35). Colby and Stoller add that no other field has immersed itself so deeply in the study of persons' subjectivity. They state: "No one before, other than a few poet-dramatists, was so respectful of, even enthralled with, the most minute details of subjective life-thoughts, feelings, memories, movements, daydreams, nightdreams" (p. 35).

Another positive feature of the psychoanalytic enterprise they enunciate is its devotion to understanding the "unconscious forces" in human behavior. They assert, "No other field has had the enthusiasm, nerve, arrogance, and, at times, courage to try to systematize these unconscious aspects of subjectivity" (p. 35).

Their positive list includes the unique appreciation of psychoanalysis for the role of infancy and childhood in shaping adult personality and psychopathology.

They comment too that "no other field has been so preoccupied with the ways and means that people falsify their integrity: the mechanisms of defense against one's inner truth . . ., the compromise formations that let self-deception flourish" (p. 36).

Other positive features of the psychoanalytic enterprise cited touch on such diverse themes as a special sensitive appreciation of how the observer influences the field of observation; a heightened awareness of the power of fantasy; and a willingness to fully acknowledge the intricate complexity of the "mind" and to dare to formulate rules that would make some sense of the "tangled mass."

Finally, Colby and Stoller comment: "Even those put off by psychoanalysis grant that it has provoked many long-lasting excitements in the world of ideas. It has not been easy to dismiss: some of those who disagree have been driven to fine work" (p. 37). But ultimately, they dismiss psychoanalysis as a "mess" having little if any scientific value. They rather condescendingly picture psychoanalysts as good-intentioned "artisans working to reduce mental suffering" (p. 34) but then ambivalently go on to say that analysts have the opportunity to observe, in their patients' lives, unexpected "natural experiments" that a "laboratory experimenter" would not dare to undertake. So, even though analysts are scientifically inept, they possess a valuable knowledgeable awareness of "what is there" (p. 34).

Undoubtedly, many psychoanalysts have resisted toeing the mark scientifically. This is in part, a consequence of the long years during which the psychoanalytic establishment was permitted to prosper and expand without much formal expectation that it would have to justify itself empirically. We suggest that a prime reason for the psychoanalytic resistance to scientific discipline is that it was embodied in a treatment procedure. Therapists who permit themselves to be uncertain or tentative in their commitment to their enterprise do not inspire confidence in those who come to them for treatment. Therapists have to be sure of themselves and to radiate confidence. Probably, they cannot entertain even significant private doubts and continue to function as convincing healers.

The stance of the practitioner therapist is antithetical to the ideals of scientific openness and readiness to change one's position as new data dictate. Had psychoanalysis penetrated into the United States purely as a series of theoretical statements, it would probably have shown loyalty to scientific principles early on. Of course, Freud's original inspiration came from observing distressed persons (including himself) in a therapeutic context, and he displayed considerable flexibility in altering his concepts as he gained more experience. However, when psychoanalysis became a therapeutic vocation for large numbers of practitioners, the original spontaneity dissipated and was typically replaced by a self-assured rigidity aimed at soothing potential patient consumers. We cannot help but wonder whether, if or when psychoanalysis as a therapy declines in prominence, its scientific credentials will so much the more prosper, as a function of greater receptivity to empirical input.

Amazingly, Freud's views originally swept large segments of the American scene and selective subgroups of the psychiatric and social science community without offering a shred of scientific evidence concerning their validity. Freud's ideas initially appeared in the United States during the first and second decades of the 20th century and made rapid headway. Shakow and Rapaport (1964) tried to explain why these ideas flourished so well:

> The American atmosphere of the first decades of the 1900s was a peculiarly favorable one for Freudian ideas. The muckrakers and early realists of the last decades of the nineteenth century had already laid the foundations for breaking down the "genteel" tradition of a primarily Puritan and Victorian culture. This trend was markedly accelerated by the literary realists, the social protesters, the feminists, and the Bohemians. . . . Freudian ideas were welcomed with open arms by the rebellious forces. . . . In fact, Freudian ideas became so integral a part of the *Zeitgeist* that this *Zeitgeist* became an indirect but major channel for Freud's influence on professional psychology. (p. 95)

They add: "Freud's influence was being inescapably forced upon psychology by various public and professional pressures in a period of great social and moral upheaval in the United States" (p. 97). The truth is that during this "introductory period" and for several subsequent decades the only empirical evidence for the efficacy of psychoanalytic therapy comprised a small number of published cases (especially Freud's) with indeterminate and frequently unsuccessful outcomes (Fisher & Greenberg, 1985).

Shakow and Rapaport comment that despite such negative factors, psychologists were really forced by cultural pressures to pay attention to psychoanalytic ideas and to ponder them. In many instances, they were intrigued by what they heard but, with a few exceptions, were repulsed by the lack of scientific purity in psychoanalytic methodology. Hornstein (1992) suggests that many psychologists were deeply threatened not only by the popularity of psychoanalysis but also by its willingness to tackle phenomena they had renounced as "too subjective." In this context, a number of psychologists began (perhaps defensively) to devise experiments to test the validity of Freud's formulations (and to resolve their own ambivalence). Many of these early studies were naive and based on grossly oversimplified notions of what Freud had actually said. However, they represented the beginning of a rapprochement that was to gain in strength. By 1942, Rapaport was in a position to analyze a series of studies bearing on repression. In 1943, Sears published his *Survey of Objective Studies of Psychoanalytic Concepts*, which contained accounts of about 150 studies touching on diverse aspects of Freud's ideas; and a decade later (1952), the respected experimentalist Hilgard put together a survey of numerous objective studies of psychoanalytic phenomena. Most of the reviews just cited were quite critical, but their very existence indicated that a serious process of scientific appraisal was underway.

Following the 1950s, a major extensive review of the scientific literature testing Freud's theories did not appear until Kline's 1972 volume, *Fact and Fantasy in Freudian Theory*, which appraised about 700 studies; and this was followed by our 1977 book (*The Scientific Credibility of Freud's Theories and Therapy*) that sifted though a reservoir of approximately 1,800 studies. The number 1,800 speaks for itself in highlighting the amount of research energy that had by that time been invested in scientifically checking out Freud's concepts.[4]

The question whether psychoanalytic propositions can be meaningfully tested within the confines of good scientific usage has already been functionally answered by the publications of numerous researchers. There are many studies in which investigators not only have displayed a full understanding of the complexity of the psychoanalytic hypotheses they were appraising but also have employed laboratory designs reasonably commensurate to the complexity. Commentators (e.g., Holt[5], 1991) who complain that the scientific efforts in this area are grossly inadequate or inconsequential have simply not done their homework. We suspect that in some instances because of their intense investment in a concept of psychoanalysis as being a superior aristocratic breed, they defensively demand a level of research testing excellence that is not consistently found anywhere in the behavioral science literature. From this superperfectionistic perspective, investigators would have to declare that no psychological theories have been adequately tested.

The new "biological psychiatry" movement largely assesses the level of explanation in Freud's formulations as trivial and inconsequential. Adherents of this biological approach aver that the etiologies

---

[4] Other major empirically evaluative efforts, although less comprehensively devoted to reviewing the scientific literature should be mentioned: Farrel's (1981) *The Standing of Psychoanalysis*; Macmillan's (1991) *Freud Evaluated*; Eysenck and Wilson's (1973) *The Experimental Study of Freudian Theories*; and Masling's series of edited books *Empirical Studies of Psychoanalytic Theories* (vols. 1, 1983a; 2, 1986; 3, 1990).

[5] Holt (1991), in a single sentence, casually and blithely, dismisses the entire scientific literature: "Results of recent surveys of the attempts to test and verify the clinical theory (e.g., Fisher & Greenberg, 1977) are about as mixed and spotty as those of Sear's (1943) original review" (p. 340).

of the major forms of psychological disturbance can be traced to biochemical (molecular) events and that there is no need for psychodynamic paradigms. They base their position on two lines of argument. First, they point to an apparently flourishing literature in which various forms of psychopathology (e.g., schizophrenia) seem to be linked to biological markers (e.g., brain defects). Second, they refer to the presumed success that has been attained in treating various psychiatric syndromes simply by administering a drug (as opposed to manipulating psychological variables).

Actually, the biological literature with reference to the etiology of psychiatric syndromes is in an unsettled, indecisive state. It is not even clear that the most severe syndrome, schizophrenia, is in any *general* sense typified by detectable quantified defects in brain structure or function (Fowles, 1992; Nasrallah & Weinberger, 1986; Straube & Oades, 1992). The evidence concerning the existence of such defects in the so-called affective and anxiety disorders is even more problematic (Depue & Iacono, 1989).

Further, the presumed success of drugs in alleviating psychiatric syndromes has been considerably inflated. The success rates of treatment drugs for schizophrenia are generally low and unpredictably variable (Karon, 1989). The true differences between the therapeutic powers of the antidepressants and antianxiolytic agents vis-à-vis placebos range closer to 20% or 30% than the often touted 40% or even greater percentages. It has also been shown that depressed or anxious individuals respond as well or better to forms of psychotherapy than to drugs; and the relapse rates for psychotherapeutic treatment are generally lower than for drugs (Fisher & Greenberg, 1989).

In fact, the scientific anlage for so-called biological psychiatry is tenuous. It is not clear that even if a molecular understanding of psychopathology could be achieved that this would negate the value of a level of discourse pitched in psychodynamic terms. It would be premature to translate the current wishful dreams of glory of biological psychiatry into an agenda that banishes psychodynamic schemata.

It is ironic that the biologically oriented critics of Freud are rarely aware of how deep was his investment in biological modes of explanation. The fact is that one can make out a good case that Freud often assigned more importance to biological than so-called psychodynamic factors. Repeatedly, he plays down the etiologic significance of individual differences in socialization and emphasizes instead the role of universal "hereditary" and "constitutional" variables.

Sjoback (1988) demonstrates in a painstaking analysis of Freud's theories of the etiology of neurosis that with the passage of time these theories actually became increasingly concerned with "constitutional factors." Freud basically attributed neurotic inclinations to difficulties in coping with childhood sexual impulses and ultimately defined the nature of these impulses in constitutional terms. He explicitly notes (1906):

> I think it is worthwhile emphasizing the fact that, whatever modifications my views on the aetiology of the psychoneuroses have passed through, there are two positions which I have never repudiated or abandoned—the importance of sexuality and of infantilism. Apart from this, accidental influences have been replaced by constitutional factors and "defence" in the purely psychological sense has been replaced by organic "sexual repression." (pp. 277–278)

Freud considered repression of infantile sexual impulses to be the major cause of psychoneuroses; but at the same time he viewed individual variations in repression to be predominantly intraorganismic, a function of the individual's constitutional and hereditary properties. Sjoback speculated why Freud so steadfastly highlighted the influence of hereditary factors in explaining behavior and concluded that this was a defensive strategy to ensure the idea of a ubiquitous, inevitable (not amenable to external, environmental influence) pattern of sexual impulses and wishes to which persons are universally subject. Sjoback notes that Freud would not budge from the position that "heredity exerts a prevailing influence on the fate of the individual" (p. 22).

EMPIRICALLY REVISING "PSYCHOANALYTIC REALITY"

The future power of Freud's psychoanlyatic formulations will depend on how permeable they are to new empirical input. We learned from our 1977 pantoscopic analysis of the research literature pertinent to Freud's basic ideas that an abundance of new information has become available that he could not have anticipated and that necessarily calls for reformulation and revisions. The revisions we finally proposed in 1977 brought Freud's concepts up-to-date with the then most trustworthy data in the literature. These suggested revisions were not peripheral or simply cosmetic in nature. A number were quite deep-going and demonstrated how fresh scientific inputs can enrich and expand psychoanalytic horizons.

We will convey the potentialities of a research pathway to revision by briefly reviewing several of the significant alterations of Freud's thinking that we concluded were justified on the basis of our empirical searches (Fisher & Greenberg, 1977).

We should first, however, affirm that we found the research literature supported a range of Freud's basic formulations to varying degrees. Thus, his concepts of both the oral and anal personality constellations were nicely in tune with a variety of research probes. Affirmation was also found, but with lesser power, for the following: his account of the role of Oedipal factors in certain aspects of male personality functioning; his formulation concerning the relatively greater concern about loss of love in the woman's as compared with the man's personality economy; and his views of the instigating effects of homosexual anxiety on paranoid delusion formation. There was also what appeared to be borderline support for his theory regarding the determinants of homosexuality. Still other of Freud's ideas were confirmed at least in part.

On the other hand, the research literature squarely contradicted Freud's portrayal of dreams as primarily containers of secret, unconscious wishes. We found that the so-called manifest content of the dream is not a mere camouflaging shell bereft of significant information about the psychological state of the dreamer. There is no convincing evidence that the dream is essentially a wishful core (nested in a defensive facade) that can be decoded only through the dreamer's free associations. The findings indicate, as Freud supposed, that dreams can sometimes provide outlets for venting tensions, but they probably serve numerous other functions, as do most forms of fantasy or thinking. Overall, the research literature demonstrated that Freud's concept of the dream was too simplistic, especially with reference to its dismissal of the manifest content as a form of defensive static. It did affirm that there is important information in dream productions which can be extracted less esoterically than Freud imagined.

Another substantial revision of Freud's theories came from the research literature concerned with the dynamics of male identification and conscience (superego) formation. Freud's scenario with respect to these processes first postulated that the vital force in the boy's giving up his Oedipal struggle with his father is fear of being retaliatorily attacked (castrated) by him. Freud proposed, too, that this fear basically stirs the boy to identify with (rather than oppose) father and in this context not only to take on a male role but to make father's moral concepts (superego) part of himself. However, we showed that the pertinent empirical studies contradicted Freud's emphasis on fear as the motivating element in the identification process and also in the formation of conscience (superego).

On the contrary, it appeared that it was father's warmth and nurturance that persuaded his son to be masculine like him and to acquiesce to his moral values. The Oedipal struggle seems primarily to be resolved not out of fear but rather out of a desire to join forces with a potentially supportive and friendly figure. This data-driven reshaping of a major aspect of Freud's developmental theory impressed us (Fisher & Greenberg, 1985) as providing the advantage that "one need no longer take the awkward position that the core of the average boy's identity is something alien that has been stamped into him through fear. The superego need no longer be portrayed as an entity that was imposed by psychological rape" (p. 405). We also uncovered data that contradicted Freud's rather constricted assumption that the boy's superego is almost entirely acquired during the limited time Oedipal conflicts are resolved and also that mother's standards contribute little to it. Overall, we empirically established that superego formation is more complex and multifaceted than Freud had pictured.

Consider a third illustration of how the empirical data we mustered led to recasting certain of Freud's notions. We were able to demonstrate that several of his concepts about the psychodynamics of women were inaccurate. The data did not support his views that females have more difficulty than males in arriving at an identification with the like-sex parent, that the feminine superego shapes up to be less severe or "strong" than that of the male, or that the female's arrival at mature sexuality requires her to shift her erogenicity from one body locale to another (clitoris to vagina). In brief, we conjured up an image of the female maturation process that is less radically different from the male pattern than Freud had envisaged.

The material just reviewed indicates that Freud's theories can be meaningfully reshaped on the basis of scientifically derived information. The alterations not only give the theories a more secure grounding in empirical observation but also may even broaden and enrich them. There are those who feel that the scientific testing of Freud's ideas must necessarily oversimplify them. We have established, however, that this is not the case. Indeed, we would anticipate that as the amount of scientific data in this area increases, the complexity of Freud's original conceptions will, pari passu, also expand. The chapters that follow offer reasonable support for this anticipation.

PART ONE

The Theories

Chapter 2

Freud's Understanding of Psychopathology

The Depression Formulation

Freud's theories concerning the etiology of psychopathology represent the very center of Freud's thinking about human behavior. Most of his salient psychological formulations derive from his experiences with psychological distress in himself and others. Because of the primacy of concepts based on psychopathology in his explanatory paradigms, we initiated our appraisal of his work by examining his major assertions concerning psychoneurosis and related maladaptive modes.

One of the first questions we confronted is whether it is possible to translate his general or overall formulations concerning psychopathology (in contrast to formulations dealing with specific syndromes) into testable statements. After considerable analysis, we emerged unconvinced that it can be done because, at the level of generality, it is all too frequently difficult to decide what Freud's final word is with respect to this or that etiologic variable. But further, even when one can specify that a particular variable plays a large role in producing psychopathology, that variable is often so vaguely defined as to defy functional replication. Others (e.g., Kline, 1981; Macmillan, 1991; Sjoback, 1988; Sulloway, 1979) have similarly been impressed with the difficulties in decoding and testing Freud's overall (diagnostically nonspecific) explanations of psychopathology.

Let us briefly scan Freud's (1906, 1917, 1926) generalized depictions of psychological disturbance. Broadly, he portrays psychopathology as resulting from the interaction of a number of factors. His account of the apparently most basic aspects of the psychopathology process can be roughly skeletonized as follows:

19

1. Representations of instinctual sexual drives press, from an early age, for expression or satisfaction, but various obstacles can block expression.

2. The obstacles are said to revolve largely about the individual's painful and unpleasant reactions to experiencing sexual arousal. Presumably, the negativity of the reactions requires banishing conscious awareness of the offensive impulses.

3. The negative responses of self to sexual arousal are variously attributed by Freud to phylogenetically transmitted disgust with aspects of sexuality and with having experienced sexual traumas (e.g., being seduced at an early age, witnessing parental intercourse).

4. The anxiety stirred by such traumatic factors is said to interfere with movement toward psychosexual maturity and to result in regression to, or fixations at, earlier immature phases of development.

5. A particularly salient crisis point in the individual's ability to cope with sexual impulses is presumed to occur when the Oedipal struggle peaks at about age 5. Oedipal dynamics (by intensifying the negativity of sexual wishes) are ascribed outstanding importance in the etiology of neuroses.

6. Another major mediating variable presumed to affect the likelihood of experiencing sexual arousal as threatening is a hereditary vulnerability to overly intense sexual impulses and deficient ego strength.

7. Sheer intensity of internal conflict is also referred to as a factor in the likelihood of developing neurotic symptoms. The conflict may be conceptualized as involving "ego instincts" versus "sexual instincts."

8. The repressed sexual impulses, which are described as having been immured in the unconscious, are portrayed as continuing to seek expression, but the individual must resort to irrational modes of defense or control to prevent them from again reaching conscious awareness where they would stir intense unpleasant emotions. The symptoms of psychoneurosis are said to be manifestations of the irrational defensive strategies that have been adopted.

9. However, psychoneurotic symptoms are further represented not only as being defensive strategies pressed into service to maintain repression of instinctual impulses, but also as being unconscious means for attaining satisfaction of the impulses. Psychoneurosis may be conceptualized, at one level, as responses to inability to satisfy a libidinal need.

This is a spare, stripped-down version of Freud's overall narrative concerning the general etiology of psychoneurotic phenomena. Although Freud referred to a few other pertinent variables (e.g., actual vs. fantasied experiences; mode of disposition of aggressive impulses), we have for reasons of simplicity not cited them.

In scanning the preceding variables that Freud considered to be central to the general process of developing psychoneurotic disturbance, it is easy to detect how vague and unquantifiable many of them are. Freud diversely assigns significance to phylogenetically transmitted inclinations, hereditary weaknesses, sexual traumas, Oedipal power struggles, and the general intensity of inner conflicts. It is noteworthy that the importance he ascribed to genetic, hereditary variables is far greater than usually recognized. Some investigators (e.g., Sjoback, 1988) concluded, after detailed analysis of Freud's writings, that he attributed far more causal power (for instigating psychoneurosis) to hereditary than environmental factors. In any case, it appears to us to be an impossible task to derive even a rough formulation of the relative weights Freud would have assigned to the various general etiologic sources of psychopathology.

We are, however, more optimistic about evaluating Freud's statements concerning certain specific psychopathological syndromes. When he focuses on particular forms of psychological disturbance, he often offers fairly unique etiologic formulations that should be possible to appraise empirically. He has presented rather distinctive accounts of the origins of such specific forms of disturbed behavior as depression and paranoia. It is true that he implicitly regards such specific psychodynamic factors as existing within the matrix of the general etiologic factors cited earlier, but only the individual specific formulations lend themselves to testing. We will, therefore, look at Freud's explicit descriptions of certain forms of psychopathology and ascertain how well they stand up to the scrutiny of pertinent scientific studies.

THE DYNAMIC FORMULATION OF DEPRESSION

What did Freud specifically propose with respect to the etiology of depression (melancholia)? His ideas are largely contained in *Mourning and Melancholia* (1917), *The Ego and the Id* (1923), *New Introductory Lectures* (1933), and *Civilization and Its Discontents* (1930).[1] Essentially, he theorized that depression is most likely to be triggered when persons suffer a specific type of trauma such as, the loss of a loved one or an

---

[1] Freud's depression theory takes on heightened interest in view of the reported surge of major depression in the 20th century throughout the world (Weissman, 1992).

"abstraction" (e.g., liberty, an ideal): Some major loss serves as the pre-cipitant. Freud suggested that having suffered losses early in life mag-nifies the likelihood of becoming depressed after experiencing loss as an adult. Incidentally, he specified that the loss in melancholia is more of an unconscious genre than that triggering normal grief. He states (1917):

> A loss . . . has occurred, but one cannot see clearly what it is that has been lost, and it is all the more reasonable to suppose that the patient cannot consciously perceive what he has lost either. This, indeed, might be so even if the patient is aware of the loss which has given rise to his melancholia, but only in the sense that he knows *whom* he has lost but not *what* he has lost in him. This would suggest that melancholia is in some way related to an object-loss which is withdrawn from conscious-ness, in contradistinction to mourning, in which there is nothing about the loss that is unconscious.[2] (p. 245)

The most original and complex aspect of Freud's depression for-mulation relates to his description of how lost objects are "intro-jected" and made a part of the individual's intrapsychic system. He indicated that the intense self-reproaches (self-attack) typical of de-pression are really directed at representations of the lost object that have been shifted on to the patient's own ego. He assumes that when loss occurs, "the free libido" is "withdrawn into the ego" and estab-lishes "an *identification* of the ego with the abandoned object." He con-tinues (1917):

> Thus the shadow of the object fell upon the ego, and the latter could henceforth be judged by a special agency, as though it were . . . the for-saken object. In this way an object-loss was transformed into an ego-loss and the conflict between the ego and the loved person into a cleavage between the critical activity of the ego and the ego as altered by identification. (p. 249)

---

[2] Freud (1917) suggested that normal healthy modes of mourning call for the realiza-tion that the "loved object no longer exists," and the requirement that "*all* libido shall be withdrawn from its attachment to that object" (p. 244). That is, he equated good adjustment to the capacity to give up any attachments to that which has been lost. However, Stroebe, Gergen, Gergen, and Stroebe (1992) have documented that the na-ture of normal mourning varies considerably from culture to culture. Although many cultures pretty much require as part of normality that one give up all ties to the lost one, other cultures (e.g., Japanese, Egyptian) define as normal a long-term commitment to remain highly aware of and devoted to the lost one. Stroebe et al. also point out that the modern Western rejection of maintaining ties to the lost object is quite counter to an opposite orientation that was common during the Romantic age, about a century ago.

In this formulation, depressed persons presumably react to the loss of a love-object by an act of narcissistic identification that converts the lost object into an internalized agent linked with the ego. Both the positive and negative aspects of the object are said to be "taken in" by this process. The depressed person "constructs" within the self an internal authority that can incite depression because of its hostile onslaughts against the ego (parts of which are equated with negative aspects of the lost object).

Freud (1917) emphasized that those susceptible to depression must have originally had a "strong fixation" on the lost object, but that paradoxically the "object cathexis proved to have little power of resistance" (p. 249). He explained this divergence as reflecting the impact of the original narcissistic flavor of the investment, which fairly easily permits withdrawal of interest from the object because such interest is readily transformable into self-centered forms. The transformation process presumably relies heavily on "introjective identification," which may metaphorically be described in terms of images of incorporating or "cannibalizing" the object. In addition, a narcissistic object choice is depicted as originally involving an object that was "adopted" because of its special resemblance to the self.

Freud assumed that certain personal predisposing variables play a notable role in a person's susceptibility to depression. He was particularly clear with respect to "oral fixation." He specifically identified an oral orientation (with the obvious connotations of possessing "oral character" traits) as increasing the probability of suffering significant depression subsequent to a loss. He also specifically highlighted the severity of the individual's superego (conscience, ego ideal) as basic to whether the self-attack typical of depression is likely to occur. In a less clearly defined way, he further referred to inclinations toward "narcissism" and "ambivalence" as predisposing factors.

The reference to a narcissistic orientation implies that those who are inclined to depression relate to persons in a way that magnifies self as compared with the other. Freud thought that frustrating experiences in the first year or so of life (plus a strong hereditary factor) mediated such a self-oriented style of attaching to others. Similarly, an inclination to be unusually ambivalent in relationships with others was said by Freud to stem from early frustrations that destabilize the individual's ability to maintain consistent attitudes toward love objects. He indicated that the person's relationship with his or her parents is the prototype of the ambivalent mode. Thus, individuals love and admire their parents but also entertain many negative feelings toward them because they have so often been sources of punishment and disappointment. It should be underscored that unusual degrees of "oral fixation," "ambivalence," and "narcissism," conceptualized as derivatives of early negative experiences, are regarded as necessary preconditions for depression to be triggered by losses in the adult years.

Freud's formulations of depression (melancholia) can be translated into the following potentially testable notions:

1. Freud indicated that depression is more likely to be triggered in those individuals who have experienced losses of significant persons, values, or roles. However, his ideas concerning this matter do not permit assigning greater or less weight to "early" versus "more recent" losses. He did suggest that current losses gain intensity by reviving memories of early childhood losses. In any case, it would appear to be quite possible to ascertain whether depressed persons and nondepressed controls differ in the quantity and patterning of their loss experiences.

2. Freud assumed that vulnerability to depression is increased if the individual's mode of relating to other persons (also other "objects") is unusually "introjective." The term introjective refers to a process that involves identifying with the object and merging it with the self. Depressive vulnerability would be increased to the degree that the individual does not clearly differentiate self from "lost" objects with personal value in his or her life. This was probably the most original of Freud's formulations concerning the etiology of depression. Actually, the depression associated with such introjection was considered to result from the fact that the object taken into the self in this fashion was simultaneously loved and hated (because of both past rewarding and frustration experiences with it.)[3] The hate directed at the object would also target the self (ego), presumably because of the confused inability of the individual to differentiate self from the introjected representation of the object. Freud intimated that the egotism involved in the introjective orientation was expressed at another level by the individual's tendency to choose love objects that in some way resemble the self.

3. A third depressive variable that Freud focused on was the severity of self-judging attitudes (conscience, superego, ego ideal). He stated that the harsher and tougher the person's superego modes were, the greater the likelihood for depression to be triggered when the proper background conditions were present. He identified the habitual tendency to be self-critical as a major factor in depression.

4. Freud (with prompting from Abraham) asserted that depression was more likely to gain dominance in those who could be classified as

---

[3] Sjoback (1988) reports a number of variables that encourage ambivalence: parental disagreement, parental inconsistency, and discrepancies between what parents say and do.

"oral character" types. This would lead one to expect that depression would relatively more frequently afflict those who manifest the following characteristics usually attributed to the oral character (Fisher & Greenberg, 1985):

- Preoccupation with issues of giving-taking (nurturance-succorance, generosity-avarice).
- Concern about dependence-independence and passivity-activity.
- Special attitudes about closeness and distance to others—being alone versus attachment to the group.

Freud's concept of the oral character has been well validated by a number of empirical studies (Fisher & Greenberg, 1985; Kline, 1981).

The ideal way to test Freud's depression formulation would be to monitor and measure the sequence of variables he considered salient in the development of, and susceptibility to, depression. Presumably, this would mean observing a series of individuals as they encounter serious losses and ascertaining whether certain phenomena (e.g., introjection of the lost object, focusing hostility inward, increased self-criticism) followed and whether they were predictive of the likelihood of developing depressive symptomatology. In addition, the researcher would determine whether certain presumably predisposing variables (e.g., early childhood losses, oral character traits, narcissistic or ambivalent style of object choice) predicted the probability of depression. This would be the optimal design for checking out Freud's statements concerning the etiology of depression (melancholia). However, there are no studies in the scientific literature that have fulfilled this paradigm. Instead, there are motley efforts that, by and large, look at only one or, at the most, a few of the supposedly pertinent depression variables at a time. Our strategy in this chapter will be to pull together all the available studies bearing on each of the areas Freud highlighted in his depression formulations.

LOSS

The first issue we will consider is whether Freud was correct when he stated that depression is usually preceded or triggered by loss experiences. Not surprisingly, to implement this objective is quite a complex enterprise. Specifying what to label as a loss is difficult. Loss experiences can variously range from the minor to the major variety; may involve early childhood events or those immediately preceding the initial manifestations of depression; may, in the case of parental loss, be due to death or some other variable such as divorce; and so forth. Recall too that Freud included under this rubric not only loss of persons but also of abstractions like "liberty" or an "ideal."

An examination of the pertinent literature shows that, with minor exceptions, researchers have chosen to define loss in terms of loss of significant family figures (primarily parents), usually due to death. Up to 1980, almost all the studies in this area were based on a design that involved depressed adults recalling the parental losses (usually due to death) they had suffered in childhood and comparing their recall with that of nondepressed subjects. Crook and Eliot (1980) found 20 such studies that were sufficiently controlled to include in a scientific survey of the literature. One of the purposes of their review was to evaluate Freud's notion that depression is a reaction to a loss that "reactivates" depressive affects linked with the loss of a parent (or other loved object) during childhood. They concluded, "There is no sound base of empirical data to support the theorized relationship between parental death during childhood and adult depression . . ." (p. 258). In actuality, they finally subscribed to a more modest statement: "We do not conclude from the review that parental death during childhood and adult depression are unrelated, but we suggest that the overwhelming etiological significance attached to the event by many writers is unwarranted" (p. 258). They insist that all the studies which have claimed to link depression with early loss of parents are methodologically flawed. A frequently noted flaw was the failure to equate for age differences between depressed and nondepressed control samples. Because of recent advances in health care, older individuals are significantly more likely to have had parents who died early than would be the case for younger persons. Another common design defect resulted from not equating socioeconomic levels of the depressed and control samples. As is well documented, death rates are relatively higher in lower socioeconomic individuals.

On the basis of a broad literature review, Tennant, Bebbington, and Hurry (1980) too arrived at a negative conclusion concerning a possible correlation between loss of parents during childhood and adult probability of becoming depressed. Even in studies that have reported significant correlations between adult depression and the occurrence of childhood losses, one still finds that in terms of absolute numbers the majority of those labeled as depressed do not recall any serious childhood losses. It is also parenthetically noteworthy that Tennant, Smith, Bebbington, and Hurry (1981), in their survey of the research up to 1981 concerned with the relationship of psychiatric disturbance in general (rather than depression specifically) to early parental loss, judged that no consistent tie exists.

The findings up to 1980 were not encouraging with respect to the parental loss-depression connection. However, an interesting study by

O'Neill, Lancee, and Freeman appeared in 1987 that raises questions about the appropriateness of testing Freud's loss concept simply by correlating childhood loss with adult depressive symptomatology. They indicated that an important aspect of Freud's original theory "is that it assumes that the effect of earlier loss on depression is partly conditional on the presence of a current loss" (p. 354). They observed too that previous studies by Sethi (1964) and Surtees (1984) provided preliminary support for the importance of considering the interaction between early and current loss in this respect. In their own research, O'Neill et al. measured levels of depression in a large sample of college students and also ascertained the frequency of "early loss," which was defined as a "loss, for any reason, of a person who was very important and close to you, such as a parent, brother, sister, friend or relative"(p. 355). In addition, there was a measure of frequency of "recent loss," which was defined as follows: "In the past year or so, have you experienced any major life event or transition in your personal life that has made a major impact on you (e.g., serious illness, financial crisis, illness or death of a family member . . ." (p. 355). It was found that degree of depression was significantly positively related to "early loss" and also "recent loss." In addition though, an interaction was significantly demonstrated between these two loss categories, such that the greatest degree of depression characterized those who had experienced both current and early losses.

In an earlier study, O'Neill et al. (1987) probed the relationships between intensity of depression (in a large sample of American college students) and amount of both early and recent loss experiences. Recent, but not early, loss proved to be positively and significantly linked to the index of depression. The group most likely to be depressed, however, comprised those individuals who had suffered both recent and past losses. Although these few studies just cited are certainly not definitive, they mesh with Freud's original formulation in this area. They raise the possibility that investigators who simply look at childhood or recent losses separately may not be fairly testing Freud's version of the role of loss in depression.

Actually, one can ask whether the conditions that trigger depression can largely be defined in terms of the specific concept of loss. Many studies, in fact, (Blaney, 1985; Hammen, Mayol, deMayo, & Marks, 1986), have suggested that other stress variables besides loss may initiate depressive symptomatology. Simply knowing that individuals have experienced a high density of diverse negative life events (irrespective of whether they involve loss) significantly predicts depression. However, the magnitude of the relationship is low and not much more impressive than the generally disappointing findings concerning the link between early loss experiences and depression. In a related vein, a number of investigators (e.g., Coplin & Gorman, 1990;

Maser & Cloninger, 1990) have concluded that it is sometimes difficult to differentiate depression from anxiety and that a substantial positive correlation often exists between the occurrence of these two affect states. It has been suggested that what we label as depression may be part of a larger "negative affect" reaction to disturbing events (Watson & Clark, 1984).

However, this view has been disputed. Thus, Kendall, Kortlander, Chansky, and Brady (1992) concluded, "Depression involves the combination of high negative affectivity and low positive affectivity; anxiety involves high negative affectivity, with positive affectivity failing to play a salient role . . ." (p. 869). Correspondingly, Monroe and Simms (1991) stated on the basis of their analysis of the pertinent literature, that events signifying "loss or exits from one's social field" (p. 407) do initiate depression, whereas those signifying danger (but not loss) precede anxiety symptomatology. Thus, they consider depression and anxiety to be differentiable entities. This remains an area of some dispute.

The basic assumption that loss necessarily instigates persistent depressive affect has also been attacked. Wortman and Silver (1992) describe two studies in which they interviewed and administered questionnaires to individuals who had suffered severe loss (either sudden death of an infant or a grossly disabling accident). Such individuals were followed up with repeat interviews, in some instances for as long as 18 months. Degree of depression was one of the major variables evaluated. Surprisingly, Wortman and Silver discovered that persons who had severe injuries (usually involving the spinal cord) had by the 3-week point after the accident "reported happiness more frequently than anxiety, depression or anger, and it continued to be the most frequently reported emotion at the 8-week interview" (pp. 351–352). Similarly, when persons who had suffered the loss of a child were evaluated, the researchers found, "By the second interview, conducted 3 months after the infant's death, positive affect was more prevalent than negative affect, and this continued to be the case at the third interview, 18 months after the loss" (p. 353). Wortman and Silver learned too that 26% of these individuals did not evidence any signs at all of intense depression. They cite a number of other studies with similar observations. For example, Clayton, Halikas, and Maurice (1972) interviewed widows and widowers shortly after losing their spouse and found that only 35% could be classified as definitely or probably depressed. Similarly, Lund, Caserta, and Dimond (1986) noted that only about 15% of men and 19% of women they studied postloss of a spouse evidenced "at least mild" depression.

Such findings raise all kinds of questions concerning the idea that depressive symptoms are focally tied to loss experiences. It would appear that the issue is considerably more complex than Freud and others envisioned. First of all, depression can be triggered by various types of stress that do not have conventional loss connotations. Further, depressive symptomatology cannot, in the majority of cases, be reliably traced to a specific, definable loss, either currently or during childhood. We learn too, that the presumed special tie between loss and depressive symptoms can be diluted because anxiety symptoms may be just as correlatively prominent in such a context. We even learn from the Wortman and Silver (1992) data that a sizable percentage of individuals who suffer severe loss are, within a relatively brief time, manifesting more positive than negative affects. This surprising report is puzzling, but it suggests the workings of a compensatory, illusion-construction process. As will be described later, positive illusions help to defend against depression; and the postloss "elation" observed by Wortman and Silver may have analogous buffering intent.

The empirical data most in tune with Freud's original statements concerning the loss issue may, as already noted, be found in the research (O'Neill et al., 1987) indicating that depression selectively characterizes persons who not only have experienced an early childhood loss but also a current one. What Freud highlighted was that a current loss takes on exaggerated significance if there is already an anlage of significant childhood loss. Another way to state the matter is to say that Freud assumed that a certain class of childhood trauma induces heightened vulnerability to the trauma of later disappointments. The scientific findings supportive of this concept, although promising, are of a preliminary character. Nevertheless, it may be pertinent to add that we will shortly demonstrate that certain types of childhood experiences do, indeed, increase a person's likelihood of becoming depressed as an adult.

Overall, it has been difficult to demonstrate a clear, consistent link between depression and loss experiences. The symptoms of a major segment of those who become clinically depressed have not, in any empirical fashion, been shown to have been triggered by a loss, as such. In most instances, losses do not produce significant depression; and most instances of depression cannot be traced to a loss. So, the concept of loss vis-à-vis depression is really of limited utility. We need to look elsewhere in Freud's formulations concerning the dynamics of depression for possible explanatory power.

INFLUENCE OF PARENTS

Freud's model of depression assumes that certain early socialization experiences (plus genetic factors) predispose individuals to becoming depressed if losses occur in later years. We have already examined the data pertinent to his view that a childhood experience of loss (e.g., death of a parent) may induce a vulnerability to later difficulties. He was not really explicit about the specific nature of childrens' interactions with their parents that would render them susceptible to depression. In his various formulations concerning depression, however, he enumerated a number of mechanisms that probably would, within his theoretical paradigm, be mediated by parent-child transactions. Just to name a few, this would apply to the presumed vulnerability to depression linked to severity of conscience (superego) or the degree of inclination to form ambivalent relationships with "love objects" or the intensity of dependent wishes.

What can we learn from the empirical literature concerning a possible nexus between childhood socialization variables and a diathesis for depression? How does this literature mesh with Freud's ideas about the nature of depression? If, as his theories suggest, early socialization differences result in variable susceptibilities to depression, should researchers not be able to discern such differences when comparing the depressed and nondepressed?

An array of studies pertinent to this question has accumulated. Let us first consider those based on asking adults to recall retrospectively how they were treated by their parents during the childhood years. Most of this literature has been analyzed in two review papers (Blatt & Homann, 1992; Burbach & Borduin, 1986). We also will cite a number of studies not included in these reviews.

The investigatory design typifying this area of research involves determining levels of depression in individuals and then securing accounts of how they recall their parents treating them during childhood. These accounts may be in the form of spontaneous descriptions or responses to questionnaires. The measurement of depression may be based on standard self-evaluations (e.g., Beck, 1967) or clinical ratings by others (e.g., Hamilton, 1967). In their 1986 review, Burbach and Borduin examined 14 studies. They observed that although the assessment methods and settings of these studies varied a good deal, there was a common core of findings. In general, those individuals typified by depression exceeded nondepressed controls in the degree to which they perceived their parents as having provided low maternal and paternal support, utilized negative/punitive child-rearing strategies, restricted nurturance, and communicated negative evaluations. There was also a surprising paradoxical trend for the parents (especially mother) to be described as overprotective (and even too permissive).

Despite the apparent unanimity of the findings, Burbach and Borduin were critical of the methodologies employed. They zeroed in on the relative absence of nondepressed psychiatric controls, the unreliability of retrospective reports, the possible distorting impact of depression itself on the recall process, and the fact that evaluations of the retrospective descriptions of parents were rarely made blindly.

A subsequent more extensive analysis by Blatt and Homann (1992) of the literature (through 1990) bearing on the relationship between depression and retrospective descriptions of one's parents largely matched the Burback and Borduin depiction of depressogenic parents as difficult and negative. The analysis concluded: "Data from retrospective accounts suggest that experiences of parental lack of care, nurturance or support, and excessive parental authority, control, criticism, and disapproval are associated with the later development of depression" (p. 76).[4]

In this review and also the Burbach and Borduin (1986) paper, a spectrum of studies was analyzed that looked at the parents (primarily mother) of depressed children and also the effects of depressed mothers on their children. The findings were considered to be congruent with the data obtained from the retrospective descriptions of one's parents. Depressed children were likely to have unfriendly parents and depressed mothers were inclined to be nonnurturant toward their offspring.

As already mentioned, the negativity of retrospective reports by depressed adults about their parents has been questioned as possibly simply reflecting the negativity associated with being in a depressed mood. Brewin, Andrews, and Gotlib (1993) thoroughly reviewed the extensive research literature bearing on this point and concluded there was not much evidence for it. They state:

> The studies reviewed . . . offer little support for the claim that recall of childhood experiences is distorted by depressed mood. Both experimental and naturalistic studies reveal high stability in recall, even with changes in mood or clinical status. . . . Furthermore, patients' memories are in as much agreement with external criteria as are controls', whether the criteria be siblings' memories or independent records. (p. 91)

---

[4] The concept that negative parental behaviors set up the potential for depression in offspring is particularly strongly supported in a report by Whitbeck et al. (1992). They observed and interviewed the members of 451 families, and evaluated multiple aspects of their behaviors. Quite repetitively over successive generations, they could see how parental disturbance led to rejecting behaviors that, in turn, induced depressed affect in offspring. The general depressogenic impact of such rejecting behaviors, emanating from either mother or father, was more clearly patterned for women than for men.

The authors take the position that the collective data in the literature concerning the recall of parent attributes by troubled individuals justify saying that such individuals "with a history of anxiety or depression are more likely than others to report early relationships characterized by low care, high overprotection, and hostile and abusive behaviors" (p. 83).[5, 6] Persons with anxiety symptoms are included in the same category as those with depressive symptoms. Considering the difficulties in differentiating anxiety and depression (e.g. Dobson, 1985), this should not be surprising. Indeed, it is still unclear whether any of the individual psychopathological symptom categories can be distinguished in terms of the specific character of presumably etiologic early parent-child interactions. Skepticism is encouraged by the Bornstein and O'Neill (1992) report that spontaneous descriptions of parental attributes do not differ significantly among various categories of psychiatric patients (e.g., depressed, schizophrenic). However, the patients' descriptions depict parents more negatively than do those of normal controls.

Another theme in the literature is concerned with the link between depression and the child-rearing practices of one's parents. Accounts of a noteworthy series of studies (Gotlib, Mount, Cordy, & Whiffen, 1988; Jacobsson, Fasman, & DiMascio, 1975; Lefkowitz & Tesiny, 1984; Mastussek, Molitor, & Seibt, 1985; Parker, 1979, 1984; Parker, Tripling, & Brown, 1979; Richman & Flaherty, 1986, 1987) indicate that parents of adult depressives are perceived not only as negative and nonnurturant but also surprisingly as overprotective. Various measures have been employed in such studies to obtain ratings of the degree to which individuals recall their parents as having been too closely supervisory, too intrusive, too disapproving of independence. They demonstrate a definite trend for the very same depressogenic parents who are nonnurturant to display also an overly "close" and "overprotective" attitude. A few reports (Crook, Gerlsma, Emmelkamp, & Arrindell, 1990; Crook, Raskin, & Eliot, 1981; Lewinsohn & Rosenbaum, 1987) have not supported this trend, but the accumulation of positive findings is still impressive.

If we take the positive findings seriously, they suggest that depressogenic parents behave ambivalently or contradictorily vis-à-vis

---

[5] The question has also been raised whether the early negative behavior of the parents of depressed adults is not so much the cause of their offspring's depression as a reaction to a child who is, for various reasons (e.g., genetic), already depressed and difficult to deal with.

[6] Several studies (e.g., Crook, Raskin, & Eliot, 1981; Parker, 1984) have compared depressed individuals' recall of their parents' attributes with evaluations by observers who had direct contact with the parents and concluded there is significant congruence.

their children. On the one hand, they are distant in the sense that they are unfriendly and nonnurturant; but on the other hand, they are overly close insofar as they maintain the sort of intimate surveillance required to control their children and restrict their autonomy. Conceivably, this might foster the ambivalent style of attachment in their children that Freud thought typical of individuals inclined to depression. He (1917) specifically referred to confusing or antithetical parental behaviors as shaping children to be unusually ambivalent toward their parents (and other love objects) and in so doing to render them susceptible to depression when losses are experienced. Presumably, ambivalence introduces a sense of heightened instability or lack of dependability concerning basic relationships and, therefore, magnifies the negative impact of subsequent losses. Two studies (King & Emmons, 1990; Raulin, 1984) have applied formal empirical measures of ambivalence to a variety of diagnostic groups and normal controls and discovered that ambivalence scores are selectively elevated in the depressed. In one of the studies (Raulin, 1984), it had been predicted [on the basis of Meehl's (1962) theory of schizophrenia] that schizophrenics would have higher ambivalence scores than any other diagnostic group, but quite unexpectedly the depressives proved to be the highest. Also, a study by Schwarz and Zuroff (1979) showed that degree of depression in female college students was positively and significantly related to how inconsistent they recalled their parents to have been. Such data provide an interesting element of support for Freud's notions about the importance of ambivalence in depressive dynamics.

We cannot underscore too much that Freud considered ambivalence to be a major "precondition" for the development of melancholia. In fact, ambivalence played a key role in his conceptualization of how introjection of the lost object initiated the depressive process. Presumably, the positive feeling toward the object motivates the oral identification maneuver referred to as introjection, but the hostility felt toward the object, which is the other side of the ambivalence, sets the stage for aggressing against what has become part of one's own territory. With respect to this matter, Freud (1917) commented:

> If the love for the object—a love which cannot be given up though the object itself is given up—takes refuge in narcissistic identification, then the hate comes into operation on this substitutive object, abusing it, debasing it, making it suffer and deriving sadistic satisfaction from its suffering" (p. 251). He states further: "The melancholic's erotic cathexis in regard to his object has thus undergone a double vicissitude: part of it has regressed to identification but the other part, under the influence of the conflict due to ambivalence, has been carried back to the stage of sadism which is nearer to that conflict. (pp. 251–252)

PASSIVITY, HELPLESSNESS, DEPENDENCE, ORALITY

As already indicated, Freud (1917) linked susceptibility to melancholia with being fixated at or regressed to an oral level. His formulation concerning the role of introjection of the lost object in depressive dynamics was fundamentally stated in oral terms and metaphors. In an earlier publication (Fisher & Greenberg, 1985), we reported that among the empirical studies available up to 1976 there were eight that had found significant positive relationships between possessing "oral character" attributes and being pessimistically oriented. More recently, Bornstein, Poynton, and Masling (1985) measured, in two separate normal male samples, degree of orality (as defined by a Rorschach index) and also degree of depression. The orality index was objectively determined from the frequency with which inkblot responses contain oral references (e.g., food, nurturant figures). Previous studies have demonstrated that this orality index is elevated in persons who are alcoholic (Weiss & Masling, 1970), who are quick to yield (Masling, Weiss, & Rothschild, 1968), and who are likely to be upset by being alone (Masling, Price, Goldband, & Katkin, 1981). The data indicated that the orality scores were positively and significantly correlated with self-reported amount of depression in both samples. Although these correlations were significant, they were of relatively low magnitude (.17, .25). In another investigation, O'Neill and Bornstein (1990) examined the correlations of the Rorschach orality index with self-reported levels of depression in male and female psychiatric inpatients. In the male sample, the correlations were significantly positive, but not so in the female sample. Such findings when viewed in the context of the earlier studies reporting positive correlations between various measures of orality and "pessimism," provide support for Freud's view that oral fixation renders the individual vulnerable to depression. However, it should be noted that all the post-1977 significant results occurred only in male samples.

Being passive and dependent has been a core quality associated with an oral orientation; and the literature reflects a good deal of effort devoted to testing the proposition that passive-dependence is characteristic of those subject to depression. Even the widely influential "learned helplessness" theory of depression (Seligman, 1975), which is of nonpsychoanalytic origin, basically states that depression is triggered when individuals come to feel that their efforts lack efficacy and therefore lapse into a negatively toned passivity. It derived from a variety of experiments (involving animals and humans) in which exposure to uncontrollable aversive stimuli apparently interfered with subsequent adaptive, escape-avoidance learning. Eventually, serious questions were raised about the theory. For example, Silver and Wortman

(1980) commented: "When investigators began testing the model on human subjects . . . the findings were inconsistent. Exposure to insoluble problems or uncontrollable noise bursts or shocks did not always result in passivity, performance decrements, or depressed mood, as the model would predict . . ." (p. 286). Despite its defects, the learned helplessness paradigm, with its major focus on passivity, continues to influence thinking about the etiology of depression.[7]

The prominence of oral and dependent themes in psychoanalytically inspired accounts of the etiology of depression is mirrored in myriad studies that have found either significant or borderline positive relationships between measures of dependence and depression in either normal or clinically depressed samples (e.g., Birtchnell & Kennard, 1983; Brewin & Furnham, 1987; Cofer & Wittenborn, 1980; Dobson & Shaw, 1986; Greenberg & Bornstein, 1988; Hirschfeld & Klerman, 1979; Hirschfeld, Klerman, Clayton, & Keller, 1983; Hirschfeld, Klerman, Gough, Barrett, Korchin, & Chodoff, 1977; Hirschfeld, Klerman, Lavori, Keller, Griffith, & Coryell, 1989; Klein, 1989; Matussek et al., 1985; Paykel, Klerman, & Prusoff, 1976; Pilowsky, 1979; Reich, Noyes, Hirschfeld, Coryell, & O'Gorman, 1987; Richman & Flaherty, 1985; Warren & McEachren, 1983; Whiffen & Sasseville, 1991). Overholser, Kabakoff, and Norman (1989) also review several studies demonstrating frequent association of depression with a diagnosis of dependent personality disorder. Two studies have come up with clearly negative results (Andrews & Brown, 1988; Pilowsky & Katsikitis, 1983) with respect to the passivity issue. Others (Hirschfeld, Klerman, Clayton, Keller, McDonald-Scott, & Larkin, 1983; Joffe & Regan, 1988; Katz & McGuffin, 1987; Klein, Kupfer, & Shea, 1993) have demonstrated that measures of dependency are influenced by the presence of depression, as such; and therefore have suggested that an adequate design necessarily calls for using subjects who are currently in remission from their depressive symptoms. Actually, a number of the studies (e.g., Cofer & Wittenborn, 1980; Hirschfeld & Klerman, 1979; Hirschfeld, Klerman, Clayton, & Keller, 1983; Hirschfeld, Klerman, Clayton, Keller, McDonald-Scott, & Larkin, 1983; Hirschfeld et al., 1989; Paykel et al., 1976; Reich et al., 1987) reporting significant positive relationships between dependence and depression did use patients in remission. Barnett and Gotlib (1988), however, suggest that in many instances dependency is not a causal factor but rather a residual of previous depressive episodes.

---

[7] The inadequacies of the learned helplessness model led to a reformulation (Abramson, Garber, & Seligman, 1980; Abramson, Seligman, & Teasdale, 1978) in which the likelihood of "learned helplessness" developing was mediated by the degree to which causality for negative events was attributed to self and further mediated by how stable and universal such attribution was.

A particularly focused test of whether dependence and depression are linked is provided in a study by Hirschfeld et al. (1989) that looked at the power of dependence, as a trait, to predict the development of depression in a stressful context. This study examined the mediating contribution of dependence to the development of depression in a sample of high-risk individuals. The subjects were first-degree relatives and spouses of patients with affective symptoms. These individuals were followed for 6 years. A variety of self-report inventories were administered at base line, among which were measures of dependency. Separate analyses were done for younger (ages 17–30) and older (ages 31–41) individuals. Although dependency did not predict depressive symptomatology in the younger sample, it did so significantly in the older group. Those developing depression were significantly more dependent. Dependency did not predict depression in the total combined sample. In attempting to explain why dependency predicted better in the older than the younger samples, Hirschfeld et al. wondered whether age cohort effects might reflect the differential socialization experiences of each age group.

Despite exceptions and limitations, a significant trend exists in the studies reviewed for persons vulnerable to depression to show elevated levels of dependency. Dependency scores seem to account for 10% to 20% of the variance in depression measures. Bornstein (1993), after analyzing the literature in this area, pointed out how consistently relationships have been found between dependency and depression across various groups. He notes:

> Specifically, the dependency-depression relationship is found in nonclinical subjects . . . , in members of clinical . . . populations, and in samples of hospitalized medical patients. . . . Moreover, comparable dependency-depression relationships are found in children . . . and adults. . . . Finally, the dependency-depression relationship is found in both women and men. However, the magnitude of the dependency-depression relationship is somewhat stronger in men than in women. . . . (p. 93)

THE ANACLITIC-INTROJECTIVE DICHOTOMY

The work of Blatt and his associates helps to clarify some of the problems involved in straightforwardly demonstrating a nexus between depression and dependency (orality). On the basis of both clinical and research data, Blatt concluded there are two major types of depression: anaclitic and introjective. He (Blatt, D'Afflitti, & Quinlan, 1976) defines the anaclitic as "characterized by feelings of helplessness and weakness, by fears of being abandoned, and by wishes to be cared for, loved, and protected"; whereas the introjective is "developmentally more advanced and characterized by intense feelings of inferiority, guilt, and worthlessness and by a sense that one has failed to live up to expectations and standards" (pp. 383–384). Blatt (1974) noted further that the anaclitic type involves an "infantile type of object choice in which the mother is sought to soothe and provide comfort and care" and "results from early disruption of the basic relationship with the primary object and can be distinguished from an 'introjective' depression, which results from a harsh, primitive, unrelenting superego that creates intense feelings of inferiority, worthlessness, guilt, and a wish for atonement" (pp. 114–115). Blatt (1974) describes the major defense of the anaclitic as "denial" and that of the introjective as "identification with the aggressor" (which reinforces being critical of the self). Obviously, the introjective concept resembles a number of previous formulations (e.g., by Freud, 1917) that have attributed depression to turning hostility inward. Also, others (e.g., Beck, 1983; Freud, 1917) besides Blatt have conceptualized relatively distinct dependency and self-critical etiologic mediators of depression.

If Blatt's proposed dichotomy were sound, it would mean that probing the relationship between depression and dependency would be a more complicated matter than immediately envisioned. One would really expect the link between depression and dependency to be manifest in the anaclitic rather than introjective categories. Failure to detect a correlation between dependence and depression in a sample might simply be due to the presence of a preponderance of introjective subjects. The following findings bear on Blatt's dichotomous schema and their particular pertinence to the dependence-depression connection.

In pursuit of his two-pronged view of the etiology of depression, Blatt and his associates (Blatt et al., 1976) constructed the Depressive Experiences Questionnaire (DEQ) to "assess a wide range of experiences that, though not direct symptoms of depression, are frequently associated with depression" (p. 383). Factor analysis of the items, as responded to by normal subjects, revealed three stable factors:

1. Themes of being concerned with feeling helpless and wanting to be dependent on others.
2. Concerns about feeling guilty, having failed to attain expectations, and being critical of self.
3. A sense of confidence and pride in one's effectiveness.

The first two of these factors correspond to the anaclitic and introjective categories respectively. Blatt, Quinlan, Chevron, McDonald, and Zuroff (1982) have shown that Factors 1 and 2 also meaningfully differentiate

depressed psychiatric patients. Thus, judges using independently written clinical case records were significantly able to distinguish patients
high on dependency from those high on self-criticism as defined by the
DEQ. It is particularly striking that those patients classified as dependent were typified by specific "oral excesses" (e.g., alcohol, food, drug
abuse).

The availability of an instrument like the DEQ that can apparently differentiate anaclitic and introjective depressive vulnerability
modes has encouraged a number of informative investigations. They
have in common that they often find different patterns of correlates for
the anaclitic as compared with the introjective dimensions. In so
doing, they support Blatt's notion that each of the dimensions is
distinctive.

Several studies have asked whether there are differences in
parental imagery between the anaclitically and introjectively oriented.
Blatt, Wein, Chevron, and Quinlan (1979) found in one of their studies
of normal college students that introjectives produced descriptions of
their parents suggesting lack of warmth, nurturance, and affection;
but the anaclitics' descriptions were uncorrelated with such perceptions. Further, the introjective parental descriptions were significantly
more conceptually mature (as defined by Piagetian criteria pertaining
to generality and complexity) than were those of anaclitics. This was
predicted on the basis of the assumption that the anaclitic operates at a
less mature level than the introjective. In an Israeli sample, however,
Sadeh, Rubin, and Berman (1993) were unable to duplicate the Blatt
et al. findings. They did report that the anaclitic attitude was significantly positively correlated with descriptions of mothers as being
warm and positive but negatively with these qualities in fathers. Also,
the introjective attitude was observed to be positively related to degree
of conflict contained in father descriptions. In explaining these findings, Sadeh et al. state:

> This parent-specific pattern of results supports theories on the comple-
> mentary role of each parent in the developmental process. . . . The
> mother, representing the prime object of the early relationship, creates
> strong nurturant ties to the child. These serve as models for anaclitic-
> dependent representation of object relations with mothers. It has been
> hypothesized that the fathers as the second significant other support
> the resolution of this early mother-child anaclitic matrix, leading to a
> more separate representation of the self and other. The father, the sec-
> ond significant other distinct from the undifferentiated mother-child
> matrix, represents the demands of external reality or the precursors
> of the superego and may thus be associated with introjective experi-
> ences. . . . (pp. 202–203)

McCranie and Bass (1984) hypothesized that a dependent attitude (anaclitic) is more likely to evolve in those who are reared in a mother-dominant family. They reasoned:

> Dependency proneness is more likely to emerge when the mother plays a more influential role than the father in the family decision making and child rearing, dominating the child and demanding submission and conformity as conditions of acceptance. As a consequence, the child becomes obedient and passive and achieves little separation-individuation from parents. (p. 4)

But, by way of contrast, they conjectured that proneness to a self-critical (introjective) stance

> . . . is more likely to develop when the father dominates family decision making and participates more actively with the mother in child rearing, resulting in the child achieving a somewhat greater degree of separation-individuation . . . Instead of submission and passivity both parents demand achievement and success as conditions of acceptance, with the child reacting by striving to win their approval through performance. (pp. 4–5)

These hypotheses were tested in a sample of normal female nursing students who not only responded to the Depressive Experiences Inventory but also self-report questionnaires concerning their retrospective perceptions of their parents. The data obtained significantly supported the hypotheses. Rosenfarb, Becker, Khan, and Mintz (1994) also found some borderline evidence that self-critical women tend to perceive their father as powerful, demanding, and controlling. These are promising exploratory findings.

Although Smith, O'Keefe, and Jenkins (1988) reported that the introjective orientation was more consistently correlated than the anaclitic with overall intensity of depression, a later analysis by Nietzel and Harris (1990) came to a different conclusion. Nietzel and Harris performed a meta-analysis of all studies (appearing between 1976 and 1989) that, like the Depressive Experiences Questionnaire (DEQ), measured both dependency and/or autonomy/achievement depression-vulnerability variables and related them to standardized measures of depression. The vulnerability measures surveyed included not only the DEQ, but also comparable ones such as the Interpersonal Dependency Inventory (Hirschfeld et al., 1977) and the Beck (1983) Sociotropy-Autonomy Scale. The meta-analysis indicated that both the anaclitic and introjective dimensions were modestly but significantly (positively) related to depression. The mean effect size for the relationship between dependency (anaclitic) and depression was $r = .28$ and for the relationship between autonomy (introjective) and depression, .31. These coefficients do not differ significantly. There were also no significant sex differences. The findings add weight to Blatt's view that both vulnerability variables must be considered.

The most finely tuned efforts to test the soundness of the anaclitic-introjective distinction have revolved around specifying that stresses involving loss of relationships would be particularly depressogenic for those who are anaclitically (sociotropic) oriented, whereas stresses challenging one's autonomy and self-boundaries (e.g., failure) would selectively disturb the introjectively (autonomously) inclined. That is, a specific interaction between category of stress and type of vulnerability was predicted. A number of studies have been initiated within this framework.

Robins and Block (1988) were interested in whether two different vulnerability factors derived from Beck's (1983) theory of depression (and which parallel Blatt's dichotomy) would correlate differentially with reports of negative life events that had been classified as being specifically pertinent to each of the vulnerability factors. These factors were labeled as either sociotropic or autonomous, with the former equated with "social dependency" and the latter with "individuality." Male and female college students were asked to report their levels of depression by means of the Beck (1967) Depression Inventory, their relative degrees of sociotropy versus autonomy (Sociotropy-Autonomy Scales), and their experiences of positive and negative life events in the 3 months preceding the time of the study. It was found that subjects who reported a relatively high frequency of negative social events (e.g., breakup of a relationship) were particularly likely to have more symptoms of depression if they were also high in sociotropy. In addition though, sociotropy proved to be a significant vulnerability factor for depression among subjects who reported an unusually high number of negative autonomous events (e.g., academic problems). The autonomy vulnerability factor failed to mediate level of depression selectively. Basically, then, the findings indicated that those individuals who were most dependently oriented were particularly likely to experience higher levels of depression when exposed to any of a variety of negative life events. The specificity of the Beck and also the related Blatt model were not supported by the findings.

Zuroff and Mongrain (1987) describe a well-designed investigation that also appraised the interactions between specific stress inputs and anaclitic versus introjective vulnerabilities. The subjects were three samples of female college students: (a) high anaclitic-low introjective (as defined by the DEQ), (b) high introjective-low anaclitic, (c) low anaclitic-low introjective (controls). They were exposed to tapes presenting either an anaclitic theme (loss) or an introjective theme (failure) and were asked to describe their (depressive) reactions by means of adjectives with anaclitic versus introjective connotations. Essentially, the results indicated that anaclitic individuals responded selectively by displaying greater anaclitic depression to the anaclitic theme than was true of the other two samples, but they did not differ from the other groups in the amount of introjective depression aroused by the introjective theme. However, such specificity did not characterize the high introjective individuals. They reacted with more introjective depression than the other samples to *both* the anaclitic and introjective themes.

Zuroff and Mongrain point out that Hammen, Marks, Mayol, and deMayo (1985) observed a similar pattern in a naturalistic longitudinal study of the relationship between depression and life events in dependent and self-critical college students. The dependent proved to be selectively vulnerable to "negative interpersonal" events; but the self-critical were not selectively vulnerable to "negative achievement" events. Apropos of such findings concerning differential response of the anaclitically versus introjectively oriented to a theme, Dauber (1984) found that female college students who are introjectively inclined, as defined by the DEQ, are selectively likely to respond with increased depression to a subliminal theme ("Leaving mom is wrong") (presented tachistoscopically) that was designed to intensify guilt about wanting to be autonomous.

In a subsequent paper, Mongrain and Zuroff (1989) examined four groups of female college students (high dependency-low self-criticism; high self-criticism-low dependency; high dependency-high self-criticism; low dependency-low self-criticism) who had been classified in terms of their DEQ scores. These subjects also rated how upsetting a series of hypothetical life events (classifiable as having dependent versus self-critical significance) were. Other measures were obtained of degree of depression and inclinations toward "dysfunctional" depressogenic attitudes (differentiated with respect to dependent vs. self-critical content). The findings that emerged were summarized by Mongrain and Zuroff as follows:

> As predicted, Dependency was associated with significantly higher levels of perceived stress for hypothetical interpersonal events and was unrelated to achievement-failure events. For self-criticism, a relation approaching significance ($p = .08$) was obtained for achievement-related events but not for interpersonal events. . . . Anaclitic dysfunctional attitudes were related to the perception of concordant life events as stressful, and introjective attitudes tended to predict perception of concordant events. This was true independent of current mood state. (p. 249)

Several investigations have explored the specificity paradigm in the context of the behavior of persons who have been diagnosed as clinically depressed. Hammen, Ellicott, Gitlin, and Jamison (1989) outline a study of a sample of unipolar patients and another sample of bipolars. The patients were admitted to the study only after they demonstrated clear recovery from a recent depressive episode. They completed the Beck (1983) Sociotropy/Autonomy Scale, which permitted classifying them according to the dichotomous Beck depressive vulnerability schema—sociotropy (dependent) or autonomy (self-critical, concerned about failure). In addition, reports were secured during a subsequent 6-month period regarding what forms of stress (classified with reference to sociotropic or autonomous significance) were experienced and also what depressive symptoms recurred. There was a statistically significant trend for the unipolar individuals to show a specific susceptibility to stressful events that were congruent with their relative sociotropic versus autonomous vulnerabilities. However, such congruence could not be demonstrated for the bipolars. Hammen et al. did not have a focused explanation as to why the specificity hypothesis was supported in the unipolar but not bipolar groups.

Segal, Shaw, Vella, and Katz (1992) recruited individuals who had recovered from a depressive episode and then followed them for a year to determine who would relapse. These individuals had been initially classified as affiliative (dependent) versus achievement (self-critical) oriented by means of the Weissman and Beck (1978) Dysfunctional Attitudes Scale. During the year of follow-up, they periodically reported their major life experiences (which were classified as having either dependent or self-critical implications). The specificity hypothesis was significantly affirmed insofar as self-critical subjects relapsed more frequently after achievement-pertinent stresses than after interpersonal-related ones. However, the specificity hypothesis did not hold up with respect to the affiliative (dependent) dimension.

This pattern of findings represented a reversal of an earlier study by Segal, Shaw, and Vella (1989). They followed remitted unipolar depressed patients for 6 months and assessed the occurrence of category-specific life events (classified in terms of pertinence to dependent vs. self-critical issues). The patients had initially been evaluated by means of the Dysfunctional Attitude Scale (Weissman & Beck, 1978) with respect to their dependent versus self-critical orientation. Levels of depression and symptoms of relapse were monitored during the 6-month period of observation. The data indicated a significant trend for the dependent patients to experience more intense depression or risk of relapse following exposure to interpersonal rather than achievement events. Comparable specificity was not shown for the self-critical variable.

In another study involving clinically depressed patients, Robins (1990) administered the Beck Sociotropy/Autonomy Scale and an inventory of major life events that had occurred the previous year and categorized with reference to dependency or achievement (failure) vulnerability connotations. The congruence hypothesis was significantly supported for the depressed patients with a presumed sociotropy vulnerability, but it was not supported for those classified as autonomy-vulnerable. A control sample of nondepressed schizophrenic patients did not manifest a significant trend for specificity in the interaction of life events and vulnerabilities (classified as a sociotropic versus autonomous) to predict depressive symptomatology. In a further study, Robins probed the specificity hypothesis in a sample of normal college students whose level of depression was measured with the Beck (1967) Depression Inventory. Also, the same measures of life experiences were secured as in the previous phase of the study. In neither the dysphoric nor nondysphoric subgroups of this student sample was the specificity hypothesis affirmed.

Klein, Harding, Taylor, and Dickstein (1988) administered the DEQ to a sample of depressed psychiatric outpatients and ascertained their degree of dependent versus self-critical orientation. The specificity of this distinction was explored by relating it to a multitude of clinical, family history, and short-term outcome variables. No distinctive patterns of relationships of the dependent versus self-critical categories with the multiple variables emerged. Klein et al. concluded that their findings "provided little support for Blatt's . . . model" (p. 399).[8]

The various studies just reviewed have come up with patchy results. It is promising that anaclitic (sociotropic) vulnerability demonstrated the predicted specificity in three of the six studies involving normal individuals (Hammen et al., 1985; Mongrain & Zuroff, 1989; Zuroff & Mongrain, 1987). However, such specificity held true for only two of the five studies based on clinically depressed persons (Hammen, Ellicott, & Gitlin, 1989; Hammen, Ellicott, Gitlin, & Jamison, 1989; Robins, 1990). It is not evident why the findings are more supportive in the normal than psychiatric samples. Overall, considering the difficulties and complications that attend any extended series of validation efforts, it seems worthwhile to take seriously the specificity hypothesis

---

[8] Smith, O'Keefe, and Jenkins (1988) mention (in a footnote) that in their study of male and female college students, who responded to the DEQ, self-report measures of depression, and a measure of one's experience with various positive and negative life events, no evidence was detected for "event-type-personality type matching in predicting depression" (p. 168). They did caution that the measure of life events employed was relatively abbreviated. However, this report was probably not supportive of the specificity paradigm.

in relation to the anaclitic dimension and to explore further the differences between the supportive and nonsupportive studies.

An appraisal of the findings in normal individuals pertinent to the introjective (autonomous) dimension shows that only one study of six (Mongrain & Zuroff, 1989) demonstrated the specificity pattern. But three of the five studies based on clinically depressed patients did observe a significant specificity effect (Hammen, Elliott, & Gitlin, 1989; Hammen, Ellicott, Gitlin, & Jamison, 1989; Segal et al., 1992). These encouraging results contrast with those linked with the normal samples. Again, no ready explanation for the difference is apparent, giving the impression that the data justify additional exploration.[9]

The multiple investigations inspired by the anaclitic-introjective (sociotropic-autonomous; dependent-self-critical) distinction have shown, first of all, that depression cannot be linked to any one overall etiologic variable. Second, they have highlighted both dependence and self-criticism as probable major personality contributors to the development of depression. Third, they have reinforced the notion that personal attributes can render an individual more or less vulnerable to the depressogenic impact of negative life events, perhaps even specific classes of such events.

If the findings concerning the anaclitic (sociotropic) dimension are combined with the earlier cited data derived from multiple studies of the tie between depression and dependence (orality), it seems reasonable to conclude that dependence is a basic element in any equation defining diathesis for depression. Freud's original formulations about this matter are rather well supported. More will be said about this matter at a later point. The observations concerning the role of the introjective (self-critical) variable are also promising. They mirror the importance that Freud ascribed to the turning of hostility inward toward the self (against the introjected lost object) as a cause of depression.

---

[9] Other approaches to predicting specificity in the interactions of vulnerabilities and particular classes of negative events may be found in the literature. For example, Hewitt and Flett (1993) noted that self-perfectionism is a specific vulnerability factor in the context of daily hassles with achievement connotations. The perfectionism variable closely resembles the Blatt et al. (1976) self-criticism (introjective) variable. Therefore, that it manifested selective vulnerability in relation to achievement (but not nonachievement) hassles provides indirect support for the specificity of the self-criticism factor.

Another example depicting specificity is provided by Olinger, Kuiper, and Shaw (1987), who found that persons who are cognitively vulnerable to depression because of excessively rigid attitudes about what is required for self-worth or happiness are particularly likely to develop depression if they encounter negative events pertinent to that form of rigidity.

Although Blatt et al. (1976) reported that the anaclitic and intro-jective dimensions are independent factors, some studies (e.g., Blatt et al., 1982; Hewitt & Flett, 1993; Ouimette & Klein, 1993) have detected significant positive correlations between them. Ouimette and Klein (1993) have also explored (in normal and clinical samples) whether specific forms of depressive symptomatology are selectively associated with the anaclitic versus introjective measures and concluded that such is not the case. On the basis of their literature review, they consider that both measures may be sensitive not only to depression but also to anxiety and multiple forms of psychopathology. Because of such observations, they question the specificity features of the Blatt and Beck models of depression. The highest levels of depression have been observed in those with both elevated anaclitic and introjective scores. With respect to specificity, Bornstein, Greenberg, Leone, and Galley (1990) observed in two different samples that dependency (analogous to the anaclitic mode) was positively and significantly correlated with the use of "turning against self" (analogous to the introjective mode) defense mechanisms. Levit (1991) arrived at similar findings in another study.

CHANNELING OF HOSTILITY

Enormous energy has been devoted to checking the hypothesis that intropunitive hostility plays a significant role in the development of depression. We have filtered out more than 50 research studies that directly or indirectly ascribe some importance to this issue. These studies may be roughly grouped into those based on responses to self-report questionnaires designed to measure how one typically experiences or expresses hostility and those based on more indirect or concealed (e.g., projective, subliminal) approaches to evaluating characteristic hostility patterns.

Self-Report Approach

The following studies were found that utilized self-report questionnaires to explore the relationships between hostility modes and depression:

Altman & Wittenborn, 1980

Atkinson & Polivy, 1976

Becker & Lesiak, 1977

Biaggio & Godwin, 1987

Blackburn, 1974

Blackburn, Lyketsos, & Tsiantis, 1979

Caine, 1970

Fava, Kellner, Lisansky, Park, Perini, & Zielezug, 1986

Fava, Kellner, Munari, Pavan, & Pesarin, 1982

Fernando, 1977

Foulds, 1965

Friedman, 1970

Hayworth et al., 1980

Kendell, 1970

Lemaire & Clopton, 1981

Lyketsos, Blackburn, & Tsiantis, 1978

Matussek & Feil, 1983

Mayo, 1967

Moore & Paolillo, 1984

Moreno, Fuhriman, & Selby, 1993

Paykel, Weissman, Prusoff, & Tonks, 1971

Perris, Eisemann, Eriksson, Jacobsson, Knorring, & Peris, 1979

Philip, 1971

Pilowsky, 1979

Pilowsky & Spence, 1975

Riley et al., 1989

Schless et al., 1974

Weissman, Fox, & Klerman, 1973

Weissman, Klerman, & Paykel, 1971

Wittenborn & Maurer, 1977

Yesavaqe, 1983

Zuckerman et al., 1967

The self-report measures diversely involve such instruments as the Multidimensional Anger Inventory (Siegel, 1985), the Buss-Durkee (Buss & Durkee, 1957) Inventory, the Hostility and Direction of Hostility Questionnaire (Foulds, 1965), the Freiburg Aggression Questionnaire (Hampel & Selg, 1975), and the State-Trait Anger Scale (Spielberger, Jacobs, Russell, & Crane, 1983). These instruments typically call for persons' judgments as to how they usually express their anger (e.g., being self-critical, aggressing against others, verbally, motorically). The research designs in which the self-report questionnaire are applied are also quite diverse. The following is a brief overview of the designs:

1. Modes of hostility expression (e.g., inward vs. outward directed) in depressed individuals are compared with the modes of normal and other nondepressed psychiatric samples (e.g., Riley, Treiber, & Woods, 1989).

2. Hostility measures are related to measures of degree of depression (e.g., Schless, Mendels, Kipperman, & Cochrane, 1974).

3. Changes in depression levels are measured in depressed patients when they have completed treatment programs (e.g., Blackburn, 1974) and such changes are related to shifts in hostility measures.

4. Persons are exposed to hostile conditions and the consequent alterations in their hostility modes are then correlated with shifts in depression that occur (e.g., Atkinson & Polivy, 1976; Philip, 1971).

5. Baseline measures of hostility are used to predict the development of depression in future stress situations (e.g., Hayworth et al., 1980).

The multiple findings emerging from the questionnaire studies do not lend themselves to easy summary. They are diverse and often contradictory. Roughly 44% of the published papers do indicate in one way or another that the amount of hostility directed inwardly is either higher in the depressed or predicts shifts in levels of depression. Another 24% clearly contradict the hostility-inward hypothesis; and 32% obtained indeterminate results that cannot be interpreted as either affirming or negating the hypothesis. A detailed critique of the studies in these three categories did not uncover any variables that would consistently account for the differences in results. The differences could not be explained in terms of the populations studied, the specific questionnaires utilized, the gender of the subjects, or the research designs.

Nonquestionnaire Approaches

The following studies were located that used projective or other (nonquestionnaire) techniques for exploring the hostility-inward hypothesis:

Barrett & Loeffler, 1992

Beck & Hurwich, 1959

Blackburn & Eunson, 1989

Block, Gjerde, & Block, 1991

Bulatao, 1961

Cochrane, 1975

Cochrane & Neilson, 1977

Cox, 1974

Dammann, 1993

Forrest & Hokanson, 1975

Gershon, Cromer, & Klerman, 1968

Gleser & Sacks, 1973

Gordon & Brackney, 1979

Gottschalk, Gleser, & Springer, 1963

Gottschalk, Hoigaard, Birch, & Rickels, 1979

Kumari & Blackburn, 1992

Lemaire & Clopton, 1981

Miller, 1973

Nelson & Craighead, 1977

Newman & Hirt, 1983

Oliver & Burkham, 1982

Perry & Cooper, 1989

Peterson, Luborsky, & Seligman, 1983

Rizley, 1978

Rubin, 1986

Rutstein & Goldberger, 1973

Schofer, Koch, & Balck, 1979

Smyth, 1982

Swann, Wenzlaff, Krull, & Pelham, 1992

Vaillant, 1986

Varga, 1973

Wenzlaff & Grozier, 1988

Wessman, Ricks, & Tyl, 1960

A sharper picture emerged from an analysis of these investigations, which were based not on questionnaire responses but on more perceptual, projective, and behavioral modes. Thus, 72% supported the hostility-inward hypothesis; 15% contradicted it; and 13% were indeterminate. It is intriguing to contemplate the range of esoteric strategies contrived to probe, the connection between depression and directionality of hostility. Consider the following:

1. Several studies have measured directionality of hostility in depressed and control subjects in terms of projective or semi-projective responses (e.g., Cochrane, 1975; Wessman et al., 1960).

2. A number of efforts have examined the impact of subliminally delivered hostile stimuli on depression indicators (e.g., Cox, 1974; Newman & Hirt, 1983; Silverman, Lachman, & Milich, 1982; Slipp & Nissenfeld, 1981).

3. A relatively popular approach has involved analyzing samples of speech and thought in various experimental and control groups for the presence of themes indicative of specific directionalities in the channeling of hostility (e.g., Blackburn & Eunson, 1989; Gottschalk et al., 1963).

4. Another approach has called for measuring the defense mechanisms employed by the depressed versus nondepressed, with a particular focus on those defense strategies related to the expression of anger (e.g., Gordon & Brackney, 1979; Perry & Cooper, 1989).

5. One of the more unique approaches has involved exposing depressed and nondepressed subjects to frustrating conditions and then providing them with self-punitive versus other-punitive means for venting their tensions (e.g., Forrest & Hokanson, 1975; Nelson & Craighead, 1977).

Other miscellaneous approaches diversely include the contents of psychotherapy sessions (Peterson et al., 1983), naturalistic longitudinal developments (Block, Gjerde, & Block, 1991), and styles of relating to others (Swann et al., 1992).

Overall, the nonquestionnaire approaches have largely supported the concept of depression as linked with the channeling of hostility against self.

The entire literature (e.g., Abramson et al., 1978; Abramson et al., 1980) concerned with the role in depression of negative, stable, and universal attributions to self for adverse events is at least implicitly a declaration that self-directed hostility is a significant etiologic factor in becoming depressed. This represents another form of support for the self-attack hypothesis.

At this point, we will cite in more detail several studies that specifically bear on Freud's hostility-inward formulation. We selected these studies because of their unique designs or sources of data.

A rare longitudinal investigation by Block, Gjerde, and Block (1991) followed boys and girls from nursery school through high school and obtained an enormous amount of data concerning many aspects of their personalities and behaviors. The major analysis was directed at using measures from the early years to predict the development of depressive symptomatology at age 18. Early personality characteristics were defined by multiple teachers' and psychologists' judgments (as expressed in the vocabulary of Q-sets). Depression at age 18 was measured by means of a standardized self-report questionnaire. The depression scores were statistically corrected to remove any contributions by anxiety (as defined by a self-report questionnaire). Analysis of the results indicated different patterns in the boys and girls appraised. In the female sample, depressive symptoms were predicted by childhood personality attributes that are summarized by the terms "oversocialized, intropunitive" (p. 733). Prior to becoming depressed, girls who are particularly susceptible are likely to be described as shy, obedient, and overcontrolled. Block et al. conclude that depression-prone girls tend to be "passive, autocentric, and self-devaluing" (p. 735). They refer to them as "internalizers."

However, this picture contrasts with that which emerged for the male sample. The significant childhood predictors of depression in boys indicated that the susceptible were "active, allocentric, and extrapunitive" (p. 735). They were further depicted as "unsocialized, aggressive, self-aggrandizing" (p. 733). Their style was conceptualized as "externalizing."

Block et al. indicate that findings by Nolen-Hoeksema (1987) support such sex differences. They state:

> She describes depressed boys as endorsing antisocial items, such as "I never do what I am told," "I do bad things," "I get into fights all the time"; whereas depressed girls, by contrast, endorse items indicative of self-evaluation, self-preoccupation, and loneliness, such as "I hate myself," "I will never be as good as others" . . . . (p. 735)

The longitudinal data of Block et al. are unique and therefore deserve thoughtful consideration. They affirm Freud's self-attack hypothesis in the case of females, but contradict it with respect to males. Males susceptible to depression appeared to channel hostility outward rather than against self. Therefore, it may be that Freud's formulation applies to females but not males. Keep in mind, however, that many previous studies of the channeling of hostility in relation to depression have not detected consistent sex differences.

A second particularly pertinent study was carried out by Forrest and Hokanson (1975). We focus on it because of the unusually direct fashion in which masochistic behavior was shown to typify the depressive approach. The design of the study involved subjects (college students) with high or low depression scores, as defined by the Beck (1967) Depression Inventory and the Minnesota Multiphasic Personality Inventory (MMPI) Depression scale (Dahlstrom & Welch, 1960), who individually interacted with another person (introduced as a subject but actually a confederate of the experimenter). The interaction called for a series of apparent exchanges between the subject and the confederate. The subjects were told:

> This experiment is designed to investigate the way people behave with one another. In real life situations people can choose a variety of ways to respond to other people. They can behave in an aggressive fashion, a friendly fashion or in a self-blame fashion. This experiment is designed to give you that choice. (p. 349)

They were then instructed to examine a panel on which there were three buttons labeled "shock," "reward," and "self-shock" respectively. Pressing the "shock" button would presumably cause the other subject (confederate) to receive a painful shock. They were further told:

> The red light in the middle of the panel is a "shock warning" light. When this lights up, it indicates that the person in the next booth has pressed his shock button, and you will receive a painful shock in five seconds. When you press the reward button, your partner will receive a reward signaled by the "reward" light flashing on. When you press the self-shock button, you will receive a shock yourself. . . . When the green light labeled "respond" comes on, you are to decide which of the three buttons you want to press. (p. 349)

The experimental session was divided into baseline, contingent, and extinction phases. During each phase, the subject received a stimulus (shock signal followed by a shock, friendly gesture, or nothing). Shortly afterward, the respond signal illuminated and the subject was to counterrespond. During the contingent phase, the confederate's behavior reinforced self-punitive behavior in the subject. A plethysmograph recorded peripheral vasodilation and constriction during specific phases of the experiment.

The results indicated that across conditions the depressed subjects exhibited a higher rate of self-punitive responses than did the nondepressed. Basically, the depressed utilized the self-punitive mode to a significantly greater extent than the nondepressed when confronted with their partner's aggressive behavior. Interestingly, the higher the voltage of the self-punitive shock, the greater the probability that the depressed subjects would choose the self-punitive response.

The data derived from the plethysmographic recordings indicated a significant trend for the depressed to manifest a greater reduction in autonomic arousal than the nondepressed after a self-punitive response. The nondepressed showed a greater reduction after an aggressive response. Overall, it was concluded that "self-punitive (masochistic) behaviors and their associated autonomic tension-reduction properties may be acquired in a unique learning history in which these self-harming behaviors were instrumental in lessening threat or aversiveness from others" (p. 356). This is one of the most direct and dramatic empirical demonstrations of the nexus between depressive tendencies and being attracted to self-attack forms of behavior. The design is a clever marriage of psychodynamic theorizing and a relatively simple laboratory-based mode of measuring directionality of hostility.[10]

In an investigation by Peterson, Luborsky, and Seligman (1983), an elaborate analysis was undertaken of attributions preceding depressive mood shifts of an individual during a sequence of psychotherapy sessions. Using a transcript of the therapy productions, judges identified each instance in which the patient expressed either an increase or decrease in depressive affect. Further, judges examined the 400 words preceding and following each instance of an affect shift and rated the degree to which there were internal (self-blame) or external attributions for any bad or negative events mentioned. There were also ratings of how stable and universal the attributions were. It was significantly demonstrated that increases in depression were particularly likely to be anticipated by negative self-attributions. Such attributions have obvious self-attack connotations. Although this study is based on data from only one patient, it deserves special consideration because of its ingenious quantification of intricate psychotherapy transactions. It is striking to find in such spontaneous material the anticipated sequence of self-attack followed by increase in depression.

Our final example derives from the work of Swann et al. (1992). They conjectured:

> People with negative self-views (persons who are depressed or suffering from low self-esteem) tend to create and embrace rejecting social worlds. . . . That is, we hold that people who possess negative self-views prefer rejecting social worlds because such worlds have become familiar and predictable to them. As a result, although they may recoil at the prospect of being rejected, they are simultaneously drawn to

---

[10] In an earlier study, with a similar methodology, Stone and Hokanson (1969) demonstrated how persons could learn to cope with the tensions aroused by aggression from others by responding intropunitively.

unfavorable feedback because it engenders a feeling of existential security and control. (p. 293)

Swann et al. performed a series of studies in which they showed that depressed college students (compared with nondepressed) preferred interaction partners who evaluated them unfavorably; preferred friends or dating partners who viewed them unfavorably; and preferentially sought unfavorable feedback (even though it made them feel more unhappy). Although Swann et al. argue that such behavior is motivated by a need for self-verification rather than masochism, we are still impressed with the basic fact that the depressed sought relationships that would expose them to negative, depreciating input. The underlying masochistic tenor of such behavior is unmistakable.[11]

The several examples from the literature concerned with self-directed hostility in the depressed highlight the range of contexts in which such self-attack has been detected. They demonstrate also the wide span of unique methodologies that have been mutually supportive in this respect.

Self-Focus of Attention

A relatively new major line of research concerned with self-awareness bears directly on the relationship between being intropunitive and being depressed. A considerable number of studies (Ingram, 1990a, 1990b) have found that self-awareness and depression are positively correlated. Augmented self-awareness, however, has also been observed in other forms of psychopathology, such as anxiety states, alcoholism, and schizophrenia (Ingram, 1990). But with reference to depression, some studies indicate that exposing individuals with psychiatric diagnoses to stimuli that magnify self-awareness will increase depressive affects as well as anxiety and irritability (e.g., Gibbons, Smith, Ingram, Pearce, Brehm, & Schroeder, 1985). This apparently does not occur in control groups of nonpsychiatric, nondepressed persons, except in special stress situations. Some theorists (e.g., Pyszczynski & Greenberg, 1987; Pyszczynski, Hamilton, Herring, & Greenberg, 1989; Pyszczynski, Holt, & Greenberg, 1987) have assigned central importance to the role of self-focused attention in instigating and maintaining depressive symptomatology. The focusing of attention on the self is depicted (Pyszczynski & Greenberg, 1987) as instigating a self-evaluative, judgmental process in which the individual critically compares his or her standing on some self-relevant dimension with an expected or idealized standard. The authors note: "When one falls short of the standard . . . self-focus produces

---

[11] Hooley and Richters (1992) criticized the Swann et al. (1992) observations for various presumed methodological defects, but we still find them worthy of consideration.

negative affect" (p. 125). This presumably results in efforts to correct the discrepancy. The following is a formal statement by Pyszczynski and Greenberg concerning their theory of how self-focus mediates the development of depression:

> We propose that depression occurs after the loss of an important source of self-worth when an individual becomes stuck in a self-regulatory cycle in which no responses to reduce the discrepancy between actual and desired states are available. Consequently, the individual falls into a pattern of virtually constant self-focus, resulting in intensified negative affect, self-derogation, further negative outcomes. . . . Eventually, these factors lead to a negative self-image, which may take on value by providing an explanation for the individual's plight and by helping the individual avoid further disappointments. The depressive self-focusing style then maintains and exacerbates the depressive disorder. (p. 122)

Apparently, then, a salient function of self-awareness (in the context just described) is to heighten self-criticism and self-disapproval. Our interpretation is that such self-focus, by emphasizing discrepancies between actuality and the ideal, increases the probability of putting self in a negative light and, therefore, of attacking self. That much of the literature links depression with magnified self-awareness is congruent with the basic notion of a connection between self-attack and being depressed. Although it is ambiguous (as in all studies of depression) whether the depression is a cause or consequence of magnified self-awareness, the possible etiologic role of self-awareness is affirmed by the kind of data provided by Gibbons et al. (1985), which showed that persons who are already depressed become more so if their attention to self is increased. In a related vein, Pyszczynski et al. (1989) demonstrated that subclinically depressed college students could be induced to become less negative about their experiences by diverting their attention from self to others.

SUMMARY OF INTROPUNITIVE FINDINGS

We have sifted through a good deal of material in testing Freud's formulation of intropunitive channeling in the etiology of depression. By and large, the data have favored the formulation. We have seen four levels of affirmation. First, the multiple studies attempting to validate the concept of a self-critical (introjective) form of depression, as defined by Blatt et al. (1976) and Beck (1983), have, for the most part, been successful. Second, there has been considerable work demonstrating the role of internal (stable, universal) attributions for failure in depression. Third, although questionnaire measures of intropunitive inclinations have not satisfactorily distinguished depressed and nondepressed groups, a clear significant distinction in the expected direction has emerged from studies using projective or specialized laboratory tasks. Finally, there is the indirect support provided by the positive correlation of self-focused attention (which tends to induce a self-critical orientation) with degree of depression. The findings have largely held true not only in clinically depressed samples, but also for normally functioning individuals who report elevated feelings of depression.

OVERVIEW

Generally speaking, how well do the data we have processed match with Freud's understanding of the etiology of depression? The match is often quite good. It is true that the research evidence does not support Freud's idea that early loss, as such, is the anlage for depression. However, as Freud more specifically suggested, some evidence does exist of an interaction, such that present loss in the context of significant early loss increases the probability of becoming depressed.

Also, Freud's model, which implicates orality (dependence) and self-criticism (turning hostility against self) as important factors in vulnerability to depression, has been surprisingly consistently validated, especially in the extensive work inspired by Blatt et al. (1976) and Beck (1983). These investigations were concerned with predicting that specific types of stress selectively trigger depressive responses as a function of whether the individual is inclined to be introjective (self-critical) or anaclitic (dependent). Life events with dependent connotations were particularly likely to trigger depressive affect in the anaclitically inclined; whereas events with self-critical significance selectively increased depression in those introjectively oriented. The findings did not consistently conform to prediction, but were promising. They are impressive because they derive from pinpointed hypotheses about the interactions of defined stress events and selective vulnerability factors. Because the hypotheses revolve around dependency and self-criticism, they add a special note of support to Freud's emphasis on the importance of these two variables in the etiology of depression. Freud's emphasis in this respect is interestingly paralleled by the association of depression with having been socialized by harsh dominating parents and the fact that both dependence and self-criticism have been linked with similar parental behaviors (Bornstein, 1993; Koestner, Zuroff, & Powers, 1991).

As noted earlier, one of the most novel and complex aspects of this model relates to Freud's assumption of a basic ambivalence toward the lost object, which motivates both the positive taking in of (identification with) that object and the subsequent attack on it after it has become part of the self-territory. The importance that Freud (1917) assigned to the ambivalence factor is conveyed by a statement he made to the effect that ambivalence is one of three prime "preconditions" for the development of depression. The other two are "loss of the object" and "regression of libido into the ego" (p. 258). The work of such researchers as King and Emmons (1990) and Raulin (1984) demonstrating that the depressively inclined are typified by an unusual amount of ambivalence represents a striking match with the ambivalence concept, which is a key feature of the introjection sequence leading up to depression as Freud envisioned it. Freud stated that depression is encouraged in those who simultaneously love and hate objects that may be potentially introjected when they are lost. Presumably, the introjection is an attempt to preserve the loved aspects of the object, but the hated features are said to attract hostility when the object is made part of the ego; and thereby to set in motion the depression sequence. We do not see that any of the other major theories of depression can, as adequately as Freud's theory, account for the ambivalence associated with being depressed.

With reference to the introjection formulation, we do not as yet have any data concerning whether there is an underlying process analogous to establishing "an identification of the ego with the abandoned object." We also do not know whether those persons subject to depression have, as Freud stated, particular difficulty in differentiating self from love objects.

There is an interesting parallel between Freud's concept of the introjected object becoming part of the ego structure and the widespread use of the self-schema concept to represent the depressed (and also non-depressed) individual's sense of self. Many researchers concerned with analyzing what is distinctive about the self-attitudes of the depressed have appealed to the notion of an internalized self-representation containing both negative and positive elements and serving as a framework for selectively processing information (e.g., Derry & Kuiper, 1981; Hewitt & Genest, 1990; Ingram, 1990). The self-schema has been portrayed as diversely modulating memory, perceptual, and decision processes. Fairly explicitly, the schema is represented as a composite structure built up out of experiences and relationships. It may contain both congruent and conflictual elements. It is not a large leap to regard Freud's depiction of the introjected object taking up residence in the ego, and thereby influencing feelings about self, as analogous to the picture often presented of the self-schema. Freud's imagery and vocabulary have a more esoteric ring than the equivalents in the self-schema literature, but there are clear underlying parallels.

If we pull together those aspects of Freud's depression formulation that seem to be at least moderately well supported by the research literature, what sort of picture emerges? It seems reasonable to assert that depression is a state, sometimes triggered by a current loss (stress), in those who are selectively vulnerable because of early socialization experiences that involved loss of parents or dealings with parents who were somehow both nonnurturant and restrictively overprotective. Such experiences apparently induce strong unsatisfied wishes for nurturance and dependent ties that may be labeled as oral in nature. They also induce a self-critical, self-depreciating orientation. Either the oral or self-critical modes may be dominant, depending on the degree to which parents stimulated dependence or an aspiring, self-exacting orientation. Blatt and Homann (1992) present data suggesting that the self-critical (introjective) mode may be developmentally more mature than the oral (anaclitic) mode. Because the early socialization experiences of those vulnerable to depression are simultaneously of a nonnurturant and overprotective nature, they seem to stimulate a tendency to relate to others ambivalently. There is an impressive fit between such ambivalence and Freud's depiction of ambivalence as providing the basis for the positive maneuver of introjecting the lost object and the more negative one of attacking the object after it has become part of the ego or self-structure. It is noteworthy that Freud's theory of depression has received empirical support even though he (1917) originally presented it in the following tentative tone: "Our material, apart from such impressions as are open to every observer, is limited to a small number of cases. . . . We shall, therefore, from the outset drop all claim to general validity for our conclusions. . . ." (p. 243).

Freud, did not, of course, formally anticipate a number of other mediating variables that have turned up prominently in the empirical depression literature. He had relatively little to say about variables like learned helplessness, automatic thoughts, selective recall of information about self and others, and attribution styles. He did, however, formally attach considerable importance to so-called biological influences that have been more recently highlighted by investigators.

Depression is far too complex a phenomenon to be encompassed by any one theoretical formulation, neither Freud's nor any of the other multiple theories that have been offered. The variables that contribute to and mediate depression have been shown to cover a wide range. Indeed, there may be multiple species of depression. At the same time, however, Freud did make a contribution insofar as his formulation applies meaningfully to a spectrum of those labeled as depressed.

The question remains, though, as to whether his formulation is unique to the realm of depression. He did, in fact, intimate that some of the dynamics characteristic of depression might apply, in part, to other forms of psychopathology (e.g., obsessive-compulsive). Considering that the empirical literature (e.g., Eysenck, Wakefield, & Friedman, 1983; Fisher & Fisher, 1993; Kirk & Kutchins, 1992) continues to pile up evidence that many diagnostic categories cannot be reliably distinguished and that a surprisingly large proportion of disturbed individuals can be reasonably labeled with multiple diagnoses, one must be skeptical that unique causal agents for specific classes of symptomatology will prevail in the long run. We can envision some specificity but also a good deal of overlap. The entire literature on negative affectivity (Fisher & Fisher, 1993; Watson & Clark, 1984) tells us that many different measures of psychopathology are strongly intercorrelated and probably refer to the same basic tendency to have a low threshold for distress and discomfort.

The limited reliability and validity of most of the major psychiatric diagnostic categories (including "major depression") necessarily impose boundaries on the potential powers of any attempt to arrive at psychodynamic formulations that differentiate apparent groupings (e.g., depressive, paranoid, obsessive-compulsive) of symptoms. In view of our present knowledge, Freud's efforts to isolate focused psychodynamic etiologies for major "psychoneurotic" syndromes cannot be expected to have more than modest success.[12] We have already noted the difficulty in distinguishing depression from anxiety. In addition, negative parental behaviors that apparently mediate offspring's vulnerability to depression may be etiologically contributory to other classes of symptoms.

DEPRESSIVE REALISM

A relatively new current of research concerned with "depressive realism" has appeared that may have provocative implications with respect to Freud's analysis of the nature of depression. Largely, but not entirely, derivative of probings by social psychologists (e.g., Alloy & Abramson, 1988; Alloy & Clements, 1992; Crocker, Alloy, & Kayne, 1988; Sackeim & Gur, 1979; Taylor & Brown, 1988; Tennen & Herzberger, 1987), the depressive realism findings have raised the serious possibility that depressed persons may be more realistic in a range of their perceptions and judgments than are the nondepressed. Many prominent theorists (e.g., Beck, 1967; Seligman, 1975) depict depression as deriving from persistent biased distortions concerning the

[12] Note, for example, that dependence generally accounts for only about 10% to 20% of the variance in depression scores (Bornstein, 1993).

meanings of events. Presumably, the depressed are typified by such distortions as underestimating their own ability to influence outcomes or magnifying the probability of unpleasant negative events. However, this view is contradicted by a variety of studies showing that depressed persons may actually be seeing things more "truthfully" than do the nondepressed, who are inclined to impart an illusory glow of optimism to their interpretations.

Several studies illustrate certain forms of superior realism characterizing the depressed. Langer (1975) observed that when subjects are called on to perform tasks with a chance probability of success, they can fairly easily be deceived into believing they exercise control over the probabilities. Thus, if they are asked to draw cards from a deck to obtain higher cards than those of a competitor, most can, after brief experiential manipulations, be convinced that a certain amount of personal influence mediates the cards drawn. Alloy and Abramson (1979) were able to demonstrate that depressed individuals are less prone than the nondepressed to such an illusion.

In another context, Alloy and Abramson (1979) asked depressed and nondepressed college students to respond to a situation in which they were given the impression they could control whether a light would go on or off by either pressing or not pressing a button. A sequence of trials was run, and the button-pressing procedure was controlled so that subjects obtained only chance success. Subjects judged the amount of control they thought their button pressing gave them over the light. The results indicated:

> Depressed students' judgments of contingency were surprisingly accurate. . . . Nondepressed students, on the other hand, overestimated the degree of contingency between their responses and outcome when noncontingent outcomes were frequent and/or desired and underestimated the degree of contingency when contingent outcomes were undesired. (p. 441)

Relatedly, Alloy, Abramson, and Viscusi (1981) reported that if depressed and nondepressed individuals are influenced so that their moods are transiently reversed, susceptibility to the illusion of control shifts accordingly. Depressed persons were exposed to statements that rendered them more elated and nondepressed persons were targeted with statements that caused them to feel more depressed. While influenced by such moods, the subjects participated in the previously mentioned "press button-light on or off" procedure and evaluated the amount of control they had over the on-off fluctuations of the light. The data demonstrated that "naturally nondepressed women made temporarily depressed gave accurate judgments of control while naturally depressed women made temporarily elated showed an illusion of control and overestimated their impact on an objectively uncontrollable outcome" (p. 1129).

After a survey of the literature, Alloy, Albright, Abramson, and Dykman (1990) state that the multiple experimental explorations of depressive realism and nondepressive optimistic biases have documented these phenomena with reference to the following: judgment of control, prediction of future positive and negative events, expectancy of success, perception and recall of performance and personality feedback, and self-evaluation.

Layne (1983) concluded an overview of the literature concerned with depressive realism as follows: "The major implication of the empirical literature is that depressives' thoughts are painfully truthful, whereas nondepressives' thoughts are unrealistically positive" (pp. 851–852).

However, as more research accumulates, questions have arisen concerning the generality of depressive realism. For example, Campbell and Fehr (1990) could not corroborate that amount of depression is correlated with accuracy in persons' judgments of how others perceive them. Dunning and Story (1991) failed to establish that mildly depressed college students are more realistic than the nondepressed in predicting certain of their future behaviors. Further, Alloy and Abramson (1988), after sifting through the pertinent literature, indicated that the issue of depressives being more realistic than nondepressives is probably more complex than initially presumed. They concluded that the greater accuracy of depressives may apply more when judgments of self are involved than when judgments about others are called for. They noted too that the relative accuracy of depressives and nondepressives may depend on whether judgments take place in private versus public contexts and also whether the data provided for the judgments are ambiguous. Despite such complexities, a substantial bloc of studies documents that depressives tend to be more accurate than nondepressives in a number of contexts. The nondepressed more often resort to illusory optimism as a coping strategy. Depressive realism is a substantial phenomenon that cannot be ignored.

It is a dramatic reflection of Freud's astuteness that he actually sensed certain elements of this realism, as shown in the following quote (Freud, 1917):

> The patient represents his ego as worthless, incapable of any achievement and morally despicable; he reproaches himself, vilifies himself and expects to be cast out and punished. He abases himself before everyone and commiserates with his own relatives for being connected with anyone so unworthy. . . . It would be equally fruitless from a scientific and a therapeutic point of view to contradict a patient who brings these accusations against his ego. He must surely be right in some way and be describing something that is as it seems to him to be. Indeed, we

must at once confirm some of his statements without reservation. He really is as lacking in interest and as incapable of love and achievement as he says. . . . He also seems to us justified in certain other self-accusations; it is merely that he has a keener eye for the truth than other people who are not melancholic. When in his heightened self-criticism he describes himself as petty, egoistic, dishonest, lacking in independence, one whose sole aim has been to hide the weaknesses of his own nature, it may be, so far as we know, that he has come pretty near to understanding himself; we only wonder why a man has to be ill before he can be accessible to a truth of this kind. (p. 246)

However, Freud's glimpse of depressive realism was somewhat peripheral and parenthetical. He seems not to have grasped the larger implications of this glimpse. His own psychodynamic schema about depression was based on the general psychoanalytic principle that any form of psychopathology is the result of defenses that shut out or selectively distort internalized information. In explaining the causes of depression, he focused particularly on an inability of the depressed rationally to give up attachments to the lost object. He indicated that they lose the power to recognize realistically the significance of their loss. He states (1917): "Melancholia is in some way related to an object-loss which is withdrawn from consciousness" (p. 245). Further, the depressive symptomatology is presumably initiated by an unrealistic attack on self as a function of having "introjected" into one's self-structure (ego) the highly ambivalently regarded lost object. In addition, Freud considered that vulnerability to depression could be traced back to such variables as regression to or fixation at an oral level, heightened narcissism, and overly severe (superego) standards. Generally, then, Freud portrayed depressed persons as caught up with both past and current distorted ideas and modes of interpreting events.

The data concerning depressive realism and nondepressive illusory optimism seem directly to challenge Freud's portrayal. In multiple contexts, it is the nondepressed who turn out to be most drawn to defensive illusory strategies. How can we reconcile such observations with Freud's formulations concerning depression? We must, from the outset, recognize that the depressive realism concept does contradict Freud's original assumption that psychopathology flourishes best where the truth is denied or distorted. Freud repeatedly made the point that the task of psychoanalysis is to seek out patients' distortions and inconsistencies to render them more realistic. He did not see that illusory images and ideas may provide a satisfactory shield against stresses that can disrupt personality functioning. Baumeister (1991), Fisher and Fisher (1993), and Taylor (1989) have all presented evidence that illusion, and more specifically illusory optimism, may limit or prevent psychopathology. A self-deceptive attitude that reassures oneself that all is well and under control has been shown (e.g., Taylor, 1989) to defend against depression, anxiety, and even some forms of somatic pathology.

Although there is a contradiction between Freud's concept of the nature of psychopathology and the concept implicit in the phenomenon of depressive realism, a potential reconciliation is apparent between his theory of depression and what has been learned about depressive realism. In essence, "depressive realism" is a term applied to the contrast between the nondepressive's inclination to see life through illusory, positively toned, optimistic lenses and the depressive's inability to utilize such illusion. The major components of Freud's theory, which we have shown to be moderately well supported by empirical findings, depict variables and conditions that would probably interfere with positive illusion formation. Thus, Freud presumed that depressed individuals are those particularly vulnerable to the impact of loss because of early depriving, depreciating, and ambivalent relationships with their parents.

It has, in fact, turned out that persons subject to depression tend to be socialized by parents who behave in unusually negative and nonnurturant ways. Such parents apparently create an unfriendly, not very promising ambience; and in so doing would discourage the kinds of expectations that contribute to feeling optimistic. In short, harsh parents would interfere with positive illusion formation. Just so, have Layne (1983) and Taylor (1989)[13] interpreted the literature bearing on this point. The conditions Freud associated with the process of becoming vulnerable to depression would knock out any early beliefs that all will turn out well in life.[14]

---

[13] Taylor (1989) succinctly summarizes some of the major differences between the depressed and nondepressed with reference to defensive use of illusion: "Normal people exaggerate how competent and well liked they are. Depressed people do not. Normal people remember their past behavior with a rosy glow. Depressed people are more evenhanded in recalling their successes and failures. Normal people describe themselves primarily positively. Depressed people describe both their positive and negative qualities. Normal people take credit for successful outcomes and tend to deny any responsibility for failure" (p. 214).

[14] The ability to utilize fantasy to comfort oneself may depend in part on having learned specific skills basic to constructing fantasies and pretend scenarios. In reviewing the literature concerned with such skills, Fisher and Fisher (1993) concluded: "The children most likely to engage in pretend play have a good deal of contact with their parents and come from families with minimal physical punishment and relatively little marital discord. . . . Such data suggest that make-believe is practiced most by children from families in which socialization has been relatively smooth and effective" (p. 98). From this perspective, the depressogenic family with its apparent tendency to treat children harshly and nonnurturantly, would not encourage the development of expertise in fantasy and pretense.

Chapter 3

The Paranoid Formulation

Freud's formulation concerning the nature and origin of paranoid psychopathology is almost unique in its apparent specificity (Freud, 1911). By and large, he depicted paranoid distortions and delusions as defensive attempts to contain and deny unacceptable homosexual impulses. There is no need to repeat in any detail the story of how he derived the paranoid formulation from analyzing an autobiographical account by a German jurist, Daniel Paul Schreber, of his experiences during a schizophrenic breakdown. Schreber described his feelings, fantasies, and flamboyant delusions, which were vividly paranoid. He also detailed his feelings toward the psychiatrist (Dr. Flechsig) who had treated him over a period of time for a variety of symptoms. It was his conviction that this psychiatrist was engaged in a plot to change him into a woman and to abuse him sexually.

Freud concluded that Schreber's paranoid delusions resulted from highly unacceptable homosexual feelings he had developed toward the psychiatrist, which actually represented long unconscious feelings toward his father. More generally, Freud portrayed the male paranoid as having had a disturbed pattern of relationship with his father, rooted in Oedipal conflict and pervaded by fear of castration. This presumably caused fixation at a passive level calling for submission to father. Conceptually, the paranoid individual was, as a result of Oedipal conflict, socialized to be fearful of father and of the consequences of relating sexually to a woman; and therefore had to retreat defensively to father as a love object. However, said Freud, the attraction to father was painfully unacceptable and tightly repressed. Later traumatic events could revive and intensify the fantasied need for a homosexual relationship with father producing anxiety of such catastrophic proportions as to trigger a defensively denying paranoid reconstruction of the world. Freud (1911) formulated this defensive process as follows:

> It is a remarkable fact that the familiar principal forms of paranoia can be represented as contradictions of the single proposition:
>
>> "I (a man) love him" is contradicted by: (a) Delusions of *persecution;* for they loudly assert "I do not love him—I *hate* him." This contradiction . . . cannot become conscious to a paranoic in this form. The mechanism of symptom formation in paranoia requires that internal perceptions—feelings—shall be replaced by external perceptions. Consequently, the proposition "I hate him" becomes transformed by *projection* into another one: "He *hates* (persecutes) *me,* which will justify me in hating him." (p. 63)

Freud linked the same etiologic pattern to the development of paranoia in women. He translated the process into a sequence in which the female child had Oedipal experiences that made heterosexual object—choice unacceptable and stimulated an homosexual attachment to mother, which in turn had to be repressed and ultimately to be contained by a regressive paranoid reconstruction.[1]

PREVIOUS PERTINENT FINDINGS

In 1977, we assembled all the existing empirical research related to the validity of Freud's theory of paranoia. The research fell into two domains. Thus, a number of clinical studies attempted to determine how frequently homosexual conflicts were selectively present in paranoid schizophrenics. Also, a cluster of experimental investigations explored whether paranoid schizophrenics displayed a special sensitivity to stimuli with homosexual connotations.

We concluded that the clinical studies were of an uneven quality. We noted (Fisher & Greenberg, 1985): "In any case, it would be fair to say that the clinical studies have been plagued by so many methodological problems and are so divergent in their findings that they throw no real light on the validity of Freud's paranoia theory" (p. 259).

However, the data harvested by the experimental studies were more promising. Several of these studies were ingeniously designed and relied heavily on monitoring individuals' reactions when they

---

[1] Blum (1980) considers that the repressed homosexuality aspect of Freud's paranoia formulation has been too exclusively emphasized. He feels that, in other contexts, Freud (1919, 1923, 1933) indicated that factors such as aggression, masochism, and preoedipal fixations could play a role in the etiology of paranoia.

were exposed to visual images depicting homosexual themes. The images were variously introduced by ordinary pictures, tachistoscopic exposures, paired stereoscopic presentations, projected slides, and photographs in unique unstructured spatial contexts. Reactions to the images were variously measured in terms of amount of attention focused on specific target features, pupillary diameter, judgments of spatial position, and thresholds for tachistoscopic recognition. We (Fisher & Greenberg, 1985) summarized the findings from these procedures as follows:

> In numerous ways it has been shown that paranoids and nonparanoids respond significantly differently to stimuli with homosexual connotations. It is a fact that the majority of the experimental studies have demonstrated that the paranoid has a unique pattern of reaction to anything that has the potential for conjuring up homosexual images. Since most of the studies have devoted care to equating the paranoids and nonparanoids for variables such as age, chronicity, cooperativeness, and socioeconomic states, there is persuasive reason to conclude that the two classes of schizophrenics do differ in their orientation toward homosexual themes . . . a number of the studies where the results have not fallen in the predicted direction can reasonably be reinterpreted as reflecting the defensive maneuver of the paranoid when he feels threatened with the potential exposure of his underlying homosexual orientation.[2] (p. 268)

It should be emphasized that with only one exception, all the studies testing Freud's proposition involved males. So, the findings did not shed any light on how well the proposition applied to women.

MORE RECENT FINDINGS

Since 1977, few studies have been published that straightforwardly test Freud's paranoia theory.[3] We located only two such efforts, but they are well constructed and deserve detailed consideration.

---

[2] We also reviewed a number of studies (Fisher & Greenberg, 1985) that probed the degree to which paranoids and nonparanoids differ in their projection of homosexual themes and sexual confusion when responding to the Rorschach Inkblot Test, the Thematic Apperception Test, the Draw-A-Person Test, and the Franck-Rosen (Franck & Rosen, 1949) Test (which is based on whether persons complete a series of drawings with masculine or feminine configurations). Although the results of these various approaches were mixed and at times confusing, they are mildly supportive of Freud's formulation.

[3] Controversy still prevails as to whether projection, as Freud defined it, has ever been experimentally demonstrated. Freud's definition of projection originally meant the

We begin with an experiment carried out by Foster (1981), who was interested in whether subliminal exposure to a homosexual theme would produce more "cognitive psychopathology" in paranoid than nonparanoid schizophrenics. Presumably, paranoids would, because of their homosexual conflicts, be unusually vulnerable to disruption by a stimulus touching on such conflicts. Interestingly, Foster also intended to test an alternative to Freud's homosexual hypothesis by predicting that paranoid schizophrenics exposed to a subliminal stimulus would evidence more cognitive pathology than those exposed to a "shame stimulus." This alternative test was derived from the theorizing of Colby (1977) who related the paranoid mechanism to individuals' basic beliefs that they are inadequate and who therefore, when stress activates their sense of inadequacy, try to forestall their humiliation by transferring their negative self-critical feelings, utilizing the strategy of "blaming others for wronging the self" (p. 56). The study involved 24 paranoid schizophrenics, 24 nonparanoid schizophrenics, and 24 normal controls. Equal numbers of males and females participated in each category. All subjects were subliminally exposed (tachistoscopically) to four stimulus pictures, each focusing on a specific theme. Each set of pictures was sex appropriate. The homosexual-submission-to-same-sexed parent conflict was represented by a drawing of two nude males or females. There was a caption below each. For the males, the caption read "Fuck with Dad," and for the females, "Fuck with Mom."

The shame-humiliation hypothesis was tested with a picture of two parental figures pointing an accusatory finger at a boy or girl and was accompanied by the caption, "You Are No Good."

A third stimulus picture highlighting aggression portrayed an angry male or female with teeth bared and pointing a dagger at a maternal figure. The caption read "Argument." It was introduced as a "methodological control" because so many past studies have

---

attribution to a dissimilar target of a negative trait characterizing self, but of which one is not consciously aware. Holmes (1968, 1978, 1981) reviewed the pertinent literature in some detail and concluded that no one has convincingly supported Freud's version of projection as a defense strategy. Others (e.g., Sherwood, 1979, 1982) have disputed Holmes's position and offered what they consider to be convincing evidence of "classical projection." Meanwhile, a number of instruments have been developed that presumably measure projection as a defense mechanism. These have resulted in a network of studies moderately supportive of the underlying assumptions concerning the projection defenses (e.g., Ihilevich & Gleser, 1986; Vaillant, 1977, 1986). In particular, Bornstein, Scanlon, and Beardslee (1989) demonstrated that individuals who are inclined to use projective defenses (as defined by Ihilevich & Gleser, 1986) show heightened suspiciousness when they feel they are being observed.

demonstrated that this stimulus produces thought pathology in schizophrenic individuals.

Finally, there was a neutral picture of a man or woman walking, with the caption "Person Walking."

All subjects were seen individually for two separate experimental sessions. During each session, two experimental stimulus conditions were administered. The order of the four experimental stimuli (homosexual, shame, aggressive, neutral) across the two experimental days was counterbalanced among the 72 subjects. In each instance, the basic procedure involved first exposing subjects to a prestimulation neutral stimulus subliminally; then asking them to respond to a word-association test and a proverb test (to measure baseline cognitive functioning). The critical stimulus (e.g., homosexual theme) was then shown subliminally for several exposures (with the experimenter blind as to which picture was being presented). A second series of proverbs and word-association tasks followed to measure the impact of the critical stimulus. After an intermission, this procedure was repeated for the second critical stimulus. In a second session, the third and fourth experimental stimuli were analogously presented.

As mentioned, one of the measures of cognitive disturbance was a word-association task. Disturbance was evaluated in terms of such criteria as "loose associations," "clang associations," "associational failure," and "blocking." The proverb measure of disturbance appraised the degree to which a series of proverbs was interpreted "concretely" rather than "abstractly."

Analysis of the data indicated that the homosexual theme, as predicted, significantly increased the amount of concrete thinking (as defined by proverb interpretations) in both the male and female paranoid schizophrenic groups. As expected, this was not true for either the nonparanoids or the normal controls. Only one of the measures of cognitive disturbance based on word associations increased significantly in the paranoid group (only for males) after exposure to the homosexual stimulus.

No significant effects were found in the paranoid sample after exposure to the shame-humiliation picture or, as expected, to the neutral picture.

Foster concluded: "The data force us to conclude that the psychoanalytic viewpoint originally elaborated by Freud (1911) of a paranoid-specific homosexual fear of submission to the same-sexed parent—the man's wish to love a man, and the woman's wish to love a woman—has some validity" (p. 77). Foster was particularly impressed that the homosexual stimuli increased "concrete thinking" in both the male and female samples and considered that this rendered the findings especially "robust." It is also impressive that Freud's hypothesis proved superior when it was matched against an alternate explanatory hypothesis (Colby's shame-humiliation concept).[4]

Finally, it is noteworthy that Freud's formulation was supported for the female paranoids because so few findings available in this area have been pertinent to women.

The significance of the Foster findings depends on the validity of the subliminal activation technique. There has been a good deal of dispute about the matter. However, two publications (Bornstein & Pittman, 1992; Hardaway, 1990) that have extensively reviewed various aspects of the dispute have concluded that overall the literature supporting the power of subliminal stimuli is convincing.

Another study was actually carried out by Hoffman (1975) to assess specifically whether Freud's theory concerning the relationship between homosexual wishes and paranoia holds true for women. They recruited 53 female hospitalized psychiatric patients who were classified as paranoid or nonparanoid on the basis of their scores derived from the Paranoia scale of the Minnesota Multiphasic Personality Inventory (MMPI) and formal rating scales concerned with amount of paranoid projection and grandiosity displayed. All the subjects were asked to respond to the Rorschach Inkblot and Thematic Apperception tests. It was predicted that the paranoids would give a greater number of "homosexual signs" than the nonparanoids in their responses to both of the projective tests. Homosexual signs were blindly scored for the Rorschach in terms of criteria developed by Wheeler (1949) as the result of his investigation of the relationship between "repressed homosexuality" (as judged by therapists) and various types of Rorschach imagery. Wheeler's signs were originally based on males and therefore were modified to be applicable to females. The blind scoring of the Thematic Apperception stories for homosexual signs was based on criteria derived by Lindzey, Tehessy, and Zamansky (1958) from a study comparing the story imagery of overt homosexuals and normals.

When the subjects were stringently divided into paranoid and nonparanoid categories on the basis of the MMPI and ratings of degree of paranoid projection and grandiosity displayed, 11 patients met the paranoid criteria and 11, the nonparanoid criteria. The data indicated that, as predicted, the paranoids produced significantly more Rorschach

[4] Freud's original assumption that repression of homosexual impulses is basic to paranoia also presupposed that anal fixations typified those who were struggling with homosexual anxieties and who came to depend on paranoid defenses. Bornstein et al. (1989), however, did not find a significant relationship between a measure of suspiciousness and a questionnaire measure of anal traits.

and Thematic Apperception homosexual signs than the nonparanoids. Analogous significant differences were obtained when the patients were categorized as paranoid ($N = 36$) versus nonparanoid ($N = 17$) solely on the basis of the MMPI. Hoffman commented that the stricter the criteria used to classify subjects as paranoid or nonparanoid, the more significantly did the two groups differ in both their Rorschach and Thematic Apperception homosexual signs. He concluded that the findings convincingly supported Freud's theory of the etiology of paranoia in women.

As already described, Hoffman's research strategy, which focuses on the relationship between projective images said to be indicative of anxiety about homosexual wishes and paranoia, has been applied by a number of earlier investigators (Fisher & Greenberg, 1985). These previous studies primarily involved male subjects and gave mixed results, with a mild trend favoring Freud's formulation. It is noteworthy that Hoffman was able to distinguish the paranoids and nonparanoids with such targeted images, presumably representative of homosexual concerns, derived not only from one but two different types of projective tests. A basic question about Hoffman's approach relates to the validity and meaning of the so-called homosexual signs derived for the Rorschach and Thematic Apperception tests. Goldfried, Stricker, and Weiner (1971) reviewed the literature pertaining to the Rorschach Wheeler signs in some depth and concluded that a majority of these signs (which were used by Hoffman) had been adequately validated as indicators of homosexual anxiety. As far as we can ascertain, there has not been an equivalent verification of the homosexual signs offered by Lindzey et al. (1958) with respect to the Thematic Apperception Test.

It is fortunate that the two studies just reviewed both involved women. When, in 1977, we offered an overview of the available empirical data bearing on Freud's paranoia formulation, we commented particularly that although the results were supportive of Freud, they could not be generalized to women because, with minor exceptions, the experimental work had been restricted to samples of males. We can now assert with greater assurance that Freud's formulation has received some support not only for males but also females.

Just as we did in our original evaluation (Fisher & Greenberg, 1985) of Freud's paranoia formulation, we must question whether repressed homosexuality is the major cause of paranoid delusions. There are various reports in the literature of other conditions or factors that apparently contribute to a paranoid perspective. Illustratively Mirowsky and Ross (1983) document that simply being in a powerless status (e.g., as a result of poverty or membership in a rejected ethnic minority), which renders one vulnerable to victimization, encourages mistrust and related paranoid attitudes. Several reports (e.g., Fenig-stein & Vanable, 1992) indicate that intensifying self-awareness can trigger paranoid sensitivity; and it has been shown experimentally (Duval & Wicklund, 1972) that a range of conditions can magnify such awareness. Another study (Sands, 1981) suggests that experiencing early maternal overprotection typifies paranoid more than nonpara-noid schizophrenics. These illustrations open the door to the possibil-ity of paranoia deriving from other etiologic factors besides repressed homosexuality, as such.

This point raises the general issue of how far any psychodynamic formulation can account for specific forms of psychopathology. Psy-chodynamic statements usually crystallize patterns of coping or de-fense that persons have learned as the result of having been socialized in families with certain patterns of conflict and modes of buffering conflict. However, larger influences within a culture (e.g., poverty, eth-nic isolation, exposure to war conditions, disease epidemics, absence of adequately supportive religious or world views) may stir up various species of distress and alarm. It is even possible that most of the psychopathology in cultures stems from such larger conditions rather than from the modal forms of psychodynamics. Freud was obviously aware of such *general* etiologic factors when he repeatedly referred to "innate" genetically determined predispositions to this or that form of psychopathology or when he (Freud, 1927, 1930) pondered the overall power of disillusionment and the "superior power" of nature in pro-ducing psychological disturbance. As far as we can determine, he never spelled out the relative weights to be assigned to specific psychody-namic variables compared with *general* cultural conditions in deter-mining specific types of psychopathology.

Another limitation to ponder in applying the repressed homosex-uality formulation of paranoia is that there may be subcategories of paranoids who differ in their psychodynamics. For example, Heilbrun, Blum, and Goldreyer (1985) presented provocative data suggesting that defensive projection may characterize some paranoid schizophrenics more than others. They divided a sample of paranoid schizophrenics into either "process" or "reactive" categories. "Process" and "reactive" individuals were distinguished by the latters' "better premorbid his-tory." For this reason, they were assumed to be more likely to be sensi-tive to the social environment for standards of comparison and therefore to use distortions in the social comparison process (equiva-lent to the process of defensive projection) as a protective strategy when threatened by confronting their own negative qualities. This assump-tion was supported by the results of a laboratory task that measured the relative degree to which individuals ascribe negative or positive attri-butes to self versus others.

In any case, how should we summarize the status of Freud's repressed homosexuality model of paranoia? We would propose the following:

1. The majority of the better controlled experimental tests of the theory have supported its validity.

2. The supportive studies previously embraced only men, but promising findings have now emerged from investigations involving women.

3. It is impressive that no other theory of paranoia has so consistently been empirically affirmed; and one cannot see that the other theories could readily incorporate the apparent importance of the homosexual factor.

4. However, we must continue to be cautious about the generality of the repressed homosexuality formulation because it is known that other variables (e.g., powerless status) may play an etiologic role. Broad cultural and environmental factors may be involved that simply fall outside the bounds of a psychodynamic model of paranoia. Finally, keep in mind that Freud (e.g., 1923) himself eventually considered the possibility that other variables besides repressed homosexuality (e.g., unresolved hostility) could produce paranoia.

In closing this chapter, we regret to say that we have not found it possible to evaluate Freud's formulations of any other psychopathological syndromes besides the two (depression, paranoia) that we have examined here and in the preceding chapter. Freud's theories concerning other forms of disturbance (obsessive-compulsive, phobic, conversion) have simply not stimulated sufficient scientific research to permit meaningful tests of their validity.

Chapter 4

The Oral Paradigm

FREUD'S THOUGHTS ABOUT CHARACTER

In this chapter and in Chapter 5 we enter the territory embracing Freud's ideas about character types and the origins of personality consistencies. Freud developed concepts concerning character slowly and sporadically, and never really put them together in a finalized fashion. His character formulations are most widely known in terms of the oral and anal character paradigms. One of his first serious documentations of the character notion emerged in his 1908 paper dealing with anal eroticism and the anal character. But the oral character concept was actually not authored by Freud. It was Abraham (1927) who designed and worked out the details of this concept. We know, however, that Abraham derived the oral character formulation by direct analogy with Freud's model of the anal character; and we know, too, that Freud (1905) approved of Abraham's derivation. For these reasons, we will depart in this chapter from our originally stated intention to appraise only those theories that Freud himself developed. In fact, the notion of the oral character has been widely accepted as a constituent of the original corpus of psychoanalysis.

As mentioned, Freud first seriously came to grips with the character construct in his analysis of the consequences of defending against unacceptable anal impulses. He outlined how instincts and impulses that have been transformed by processes such as reaction formation and sublimation shape character traits. In essence, he proposed that how persons deal with problems associated with specific developmental stages determines their personality defenses and lifestyles. Presumably, if they fail to cope with the demands of a given phase, they become "fixated" at that stage and cannot advance further toward more mature levels. Or they may, after moving on to a more mature phase, discover they cannot cope with its new demands and consequently they "regress" back to the preceding (less mature) one. Freud theorized that behaviors are shaped by the levels at which persons get fixated. Basically, said Freud, individuals evolve traits that help them to manage conflicts linked with the roles that particular zones of their bodies play in their lives.

He conceived adult character structures as classifiable within the following types: oral, anal, phallic, or genital. He asserted that each child moves developmentally through a sequence of stages during which specific body regions are focused on, become highly sensitive foci of gratification, and are magnified as channels for conducting relationships. He indicated that during the first year of life the mouth is the primary zone of gratification; from 1 to 3, it is the anal region; and from 3 to 5, the genitals. The genital phase is also described as the time of maximum Oedipal conflict. From 5 to prepuberty is depicted as the "latency period," during which genital urges are said to be highly repressed. Then, at puberty, the genitals reassert themselves as the dominant erogenous zone. During each of these phases, there is said to be a pull toward activities that gratify the dominant erogenous region.

Baudry (1983) has examined in detail Freud's concern with character concepts throughout his published works. He points out that at various times Freud speculated about other factors, besides defensive maneuvers for coping with erogenous impulses, that may enter into character formation. Illustratively, Freud refers to constitutional determinants of the capacity to sublimate that are basic to character constructions and describes strategies employed to deal with traumatic experiences that are incorporated into the ego. Further, he (1923) explicitly refers to character-building processes based on identification with parental figures. He notes that identifications have "a great share in determining the form taken by the ego and . . . make an essential contribution toward building up what is called . . . 'character'" (p. 28). The following passage by Freud (1933) provides a bit more detail about this issue:

> We have . . . made out a little of what it is that creates character. First and foremost, there is the incorporation of the former parental agency as a super-ego, which is no doubt its most important and decisive portion, and further, identifications with the two parents . . . and with other influential figures, and similar identifications formed as precipitates of abandoned object-relations. And we may now add as contributions to the construction of character which are never absent, the reaction-formations which the ego acquires—to begin with in making its repressions and later, by a more normal method, when it rejects unwished-for instinctual impulses. (p. 91)

In this brief review of Freud's thinking about character, it is also worthwhile citing what he (Freud, 1913) had to say about the distinction between character formation and symptom formation:

> In the field of development of *character* we are bound to meet with the same instinctual forces which we have found at work in the neuroses. But a sharp theoretical distinction between the two is necessitated by the single fact that the failure of repression and the return of the repressed—which are peculiar to the mechanism of neuroses—are absent in the formation of character. In the latter, repression either does not come into action or smoothly achieves its aim of replacing the repressed by reaction formations and sublimations. Hence, the processes of the formation of character are more obscure and less accessible to analysis than neurotic ones. (p. 323)

The preceding material indicates that Freud did not take a simplistic position with respect to the variables shaping character structure. He was aware of multiple influences, such as genetic inclinations, defense modes, personal identifications, and the residuals of responses to traumas. Therefore, to look only at his statements pertinent to the etiologies of the oral and anal characters, with their emphasis on the role of repression and reaction formation, would be to miss the complexity of his thinking.

THE ORAL CHARACTER FORMULATION

The oral character was conceptualized as one who had, for various reasons, been unable to master the problems of the oral stage and who was, therefore, fixated on issues more pertinent to the oral phase than to those of genital maturity. Presumably, the persistence of unsatisfied oral drives and wishes shaped a character structure that provided indirect (concealed) modes for releasing oral tensions and also repressive defenses for denying them. Abraham theorized that persons could be fixated either in the early or late oral stages. The earlier is characterized by pleasure in sucking and the later by satisfaction in biting.

In our 1977 review of the major aspects of the oral character concept (as defined by Abraham), we identified the following as most basic:

1. With respect to etiology, it was theorized that events in the first year or so of life determine the probability of developing oral character traits. Further, it was presumed that a major determinant is the parental inclination to be either too frustrating or overgratifying of the child's oral needs.

2. Overgratification was regarded as likely to foster an optimistic ("I will always be well fed") view of the future; whereas poor gratification would result in a pessimistic outlook ("I will never get fed").

3. The oral character was depicted as unusually concerned with issues of dependence-independence and passivity-activity as shown in behavior and fantasies indicating a heightened preoccupation with being supported, nurtured, and cared for.

4. Abraham (1927) suggested that ambivalence would be a prominent attribute of the oral character. He indicated: "In the child who has been disappointed or over-indulged in the sucking period the pleasure in biting, which is the most primitive form of sadism, will be especially emphasized. Thus, the formation of character in such a child begins under the influence of an abnormally pronounced ambivalence of feeling" (p. 398).

5. Abraham also speculated that the oral character is especially open to novel experiences and manifests a high level of curiosity. He considered this to be a displacement to the intellectual sphere of the infantile pleasure in sucking, which is conceptualized as a manifestation of the desire to be "fed" a stream of new events.

6. One of Abraham's particularly interesting formulations was that the oral character's unresolved oral wishes would result during adulthood in exaggerated oral forms of gratification and expression (e.g., smoking, overeating, oral forms of sexual gratification).

To summarize, the oral character (whose oral needs were presumably either frustrated or overindulged) would be typified by the following:

- Heightened concern with issues of giving-taking (nurturance-succorance.)
- Conflict and tension about dependence-independence and passivity-activity.
- Special preoccupation with matters of closeness-distance (being alone versus attaching).
- Inclination to be either unusually pessimistic or optimistic.
- Persistent need to use oral channels for gratification or compensatory denial (e.g., excessive or minimal eating, smoking).

When, in 1977, we completed our exploration of the multiple strands of research pertinent to the oral character model, we highlighted several conclusions:

1. The major traits attributed to the oral character appeared to cluster together meaningfully, as defined by factor analyses. The qualities ascribed to the oral character, such as the need to affiliate with others, pessimism, and passivity, were found, as predicted, by the oral character paradigm, to occur together in individuals.

2. Convincing support was observed for the hypothesis that the oral character is particularly preoccupied with issues related to whether one seeks gratification through one's own efforts or is motivated to get others to provide care and comfort. The oral character is caught up with such related themes as dependence-independence, activity-passivity, and closeness-distance. We (1985) summarized the data pertinent to this hypothesis as follows:

   The empirical research findings are quite convincing in their support. . . . First of all, persons identified as orally oriented have shown themselves to be unusually susceptible to the effects of being approved by those they consider significant. They seek experiences that assure them they are in the good graces of persons who have power. . . . They cultivate skills enabling them to be especially sensitive to the motives and intents of others, presumably so that they can maintain ties and contacts. Also, there is adequate evidence that under stress they are particularly anxious to be *with people* rather than apart from them. (p. 133)

3. Excellent data emerged congruent with the view that the orally oriented are inclined to be depressed and to feel pessimistic about getting what they want.

4. Observations affirmed that oral characters make unusual use of oral modes of gratification (e.g., smoking, overeating, ingesting large amounts of alcohol).

5. The evidence pertinent to whether the oral character is particularly curious and open to new experiences was too sparse to provide definitive answers, as was the evidence concerning whether the oral character manifests heightened ambivalence.

6. Some encouraging evidence was found that disturbance in the child's early eating and nurturance relationships with parents, especially mothers, plays a role in "oral fixation." However, such evidence was generally still quite crude and fragmentary.

Our overall judgment was that major elements of the oral character concept had scientific substance. However, we remained uncertain about the presumed etiologic aspects of the concept.

MORE RECENT OBSERVATIONS

The Oral Character Cluster

We (Fisher & Greenberg, 1985) originally located 17 studies published prior to 1977 that related to the question whether the characteristics ascribed to the oral character do, as defined by factor analytic techniques, constitute an identifiable cluster. The majority of these studies supported the existence of such a cluster.

In our renewed search of the literature, we have found several reports that reaffirm the existence of an oral character cluster (Bromley & Lewis, 1976; Kline & Storey, 1977; O'Dell, 1980; Stone & Gottheil, 1975;[1] Torgersen, 1980).[2] These additional citations further support the notion of an oral character constellation. However, the 1977 paper by Kline and Storey critiqued the previous studies of orality and observed that "none of the existing oral scales was satisfactory as a reliable valid measure of oral characteristics" (p. 310). They decided to construct new measures of oral characteristics and to validate them with factor analysis that included a number of major personality inventories and other measures of oral attributes. The data they obtained indicated the need for two separate measures of orality, oral optimism and oral pessimism. These two measures were considered to parallel the theoretical distinction between being fixated at the oral sucking stage versus being fixated at the oral sadistic (biting) stage. The oral optimism scale contained items referring to optimism, dependence, fluency in words and ideas, giving, liking for the novel, sociability, and liking for relaxation. The oral pessimism scale comprised items pertaining to pessimism, independence, verbal aggression, envy, coldness and hostility,

---

[1] Although this study was published prior to 1977, we are citing it because we missed it in our original literature review.

[2] However, questions have been raised by a few studies with possible negative implications. Thus, Kline and Storey (1978a) failed to verify the existence of an oral factor in the Dynamic Personality Inventory (Grygier, 1961), which has been widely assumed to measure all the basic psychosexual stages and, in that sense, to support Freud's developmental theory. In addition, Howarth (1980, 1982) has shown that some scales purporting to measure orality (e.g., Kline & Storey, 1977) correlate significantly with Eysenck's "superfactors" that presumably have high heritability coefficients and this, says Howarth, might render "Freudian explanations . . . invalid" (p. 178).

ambition, malice, and impatience. Kline and Storey concluded from their analysis of their data that the oral optimist is "gregarious, talkative, adventurous, dependent, cheerful, confident, and likes admiration" (p. 324). They depicted the oral pessimist as verbally aggressive, anxious, frustrated, pessimistic, and inclined to use projection.

Abraham (1927) made much of the idea that there were two oral stages. We (Fisher & Greenberg, 1985) originally noted that there were scattered findings congruent with the two-stage concept. Previous factor analyses isolated such separate factors. Relatedly, oral-receptive inkblot images have been observed by several investigators to predict different aspects of behavior than do oral-sadistic images. For example, Weiss and Masling (1970) reported that oral-receptive inkblot responses distinguish alcoholics and others with oral symptoms, but oral-sadistic responses do not. The importance that Kline and Story attach to the oral-receptive versus oral-sadistic distinction intersects well with our (Fisher & Greenberg, 1985) original statement: "A sufficient number of persuasive clues have been uncovered to warrant our considering with further interest the oral-receptive versus oral-sadistic as a meaningful dimension" (p. 137). In any case, the Kline and Storey observations suggest the need for further systematic efforts to establish whether all measures of orality should attempt to capture both of these dimensions.

Problems in Measuring Oral Character Attributes

As Bornstein (1993) has documented, multiple strategies have been employed to appraise variables pertinent to the oral character concept. He enumerated 12 frequently used measures, ranging from projective types (e.g., the Masling, Rabie, & Blondheim, 1967, Rorschach Oral Dependency Scale) to paper-and-pencil questionnaires (e.g., the Hirschfeld et al., 1977, Measure of Interpersonal Dependency). He also cited multiple other less frequently used techniques. The measures vary not only in whether they are projective or nonprojective, but also in whether they are self-reported or based on interviews or derived from other behavioral observations. Further, they differ in the degree to which they are defined by behaviors or fantasies that specifically involve oral activities (e.g., eating) compared with attributes related to being dependent or passive. Measures derived from direct oral indicators, such as frequency of mouth-related activities or fantasies, can most easily be linked with the original body-oriented language of the oral character formulation; whereas measures that tap into variables like dependence are less straightforwardly tied in with such language.

The central question concerning the diversity of measures is whether there is significant overlap. Bornstein indicated, after analyzing the relevant literature, that correlations between projective and objective measures of dependency "are generally statistically significant and in the predicted direction" (p. 32). The correlations average in the .30–.40 range. Bornstein reported that for dependency measures based on tests within a particular category (e.g., objective or projective) scores are correlated in the .60–.80 range. He concluded that the literature supports the convergent validity of the multiple measures of dependent attributes.[3]

However, we see a more obscure picture when looking at the relationships of measures that literally focus on oral activities and measures based on dependent attitudes and behaviors. It is true some studies have found significant correlations between food-and-mouth-related activities and degree of dependency (Beller, 1957; Jamison & Comrey, 1968; Mills & Cunningham, 1988). Other studies, however, have failed to detect analogous correlations (e.g., Bornstein & Greenberg, 1991; Kline & Storey, 1980; Shilkret & Masling, 1981).[4] At this point, it would not be a sound practice to use terms such as "dependent" and "orally oriented" interchangeably. It is likely, though, that they have converging meanings; and Bornstein (1993) has been impressed with the similarities in results from heterogeneous studies using different dependency measures (including those based on oral

[3] Bornstein (1993) describes an interesting pattern of sex differences in relation to whether objective or projective measures of dependency are involved. He notes: "When self-report measures of dependency are used, the vast majority of studies examining gender differences in adult dependency have found significantly higher levels of dependency in women than in men . . ." (p. 46). He adds: "In contrast, when projective measures of dependency are employed, researchers typically find that men and women (and boys and girls) show similar levels of dependency . . ." (p. 47). Bornstein speculates that this pattern of gender differences occurs because men are less likely than women to acknowledge openly that they have dependent traits and feelings. Thus, they respond to self-report measures in a more guarded fashion. When responding to projective measures of dependency, however, there is less ability to employ disguising or defensive strategies.

[4] Von der Lippe and Torgersen (1984) demonstrated that persons who obtain high "oral character" scores on a self-report questionnaire based on such subscales as self-doubt, dependence, compliance, and sensitivity are typified by an unusual sensitivity to an oral stimulus (baby nursing) presented tachistoscopically. The relationship was especially strong in relation to the dependence subscale score. This represents an encouraging illustration of a link between dependence and an orality variable. Relatedly, Bornstein, Manning, Krukonis, Rossner, and Mastrosimone (1993), in relating self-report dependency scores to Rorschach indexes of orality and dependence, found that the highest correlation ($r = .50$) was between the self-report subscale called Emotional Reliance on Others and the Rorschach scale based on food/mouth-related imagery.

Juni and Frenz (1981) did not find a significant relationship between a modified version of the Masling (1983b) Rorschach orality index and selective response to tachistoscopically presented oral words.

references vs. those defined in terms of dependent behaviors) to investigate such diverse phenomena as suggestibility, depression, parenting style, and alcoholism.

THE DEPENDENCE-INDEPENDENCE DIMENSION

As already noted, the core of the oral character formulation relates to the idea that persons strongly under the influence of oral wishes or fantasies have as one of their major goals establishing relationships that will permit them to obtain support and nurturance from others. A large part of the empirical research published since 1977 dealing with this matter has evolved from the work of Masling (1986) and his colleagues. Masling starts with the assumption that the oral perspective pictures "the world (as) manageable only through the protection and support offered by others; the fear that 'I am alone and unable to cope' represents a key threat to the sense of well-being" (p. 75). He devised a technique for measuring degree of oral orientation based on the frequency with which individuals give "oral" and "dependent" responses to the Rorschach blots. Oral responses diversely embrace references to food, eating, drinking, food organs (e.g., mouth, stomach), and food providers. Dependent responses variously involve references to passivity and helplessness, gifts and gift givers, baby talk (e.g., "teeny-weeny person"), and nurturers (e.g., parent, God). It has been shown that this scoring system can be applied objectively. Masling (1986) considers that his Rorschach-derived score measures the degree to which individuals fall within the category of the "oral personality." He and his associates have assiduously examined the relationship of this score with central aspects of the dependency agenda. Their findings are, by and large, consistent and supportive of theoretical expectations.

Several of their studies simply tested whether the Rorschach orality score could predict the occurrence of dependent behaviors. Durberstein and Talbot (1993) explored the orality-dependency connection by relating individuals' Rorschach Oral Dependent scores to their responses to a questionnaire measuring degree of security about one's attachment to others. They found that "as predicted, a greater proportion of high-oral than low-oral subjects perceived themselves as interpersonally insecure" (p. 307). They anticipated this result on the basis of the assumption that high-orals are "preoccupied with themes of abandonment and loss," in part as the result of feeling "powerless" unless assured of the "guidance and protection of others" (p. 298). Relatedly, Bornstein, Leone, and Galley (1986) observed that high-oral males (as defined by Rorschach oral images) more often represent themselves in self-descriptions as weak and unassertive than do low-orals. This did not hold true in a female sample.

Shilkret and Masling (1981) created a laboratory situation in which male and female college students were asked to solve a series of difficult puzzles (in the presence of either a male or female experimenter) and were instructed that they could obtain as much help as they wanted. The amount of help they requested was recorded, and as predicted, it was found that for male subjects, there was a significant positive link between the Rorschach orality scores and the amount of advice sought, no matter whether the experimenter was male or female. For female subjects, however, the results were in the expected direction when the experimenter was female; whereas they were significantly in the opposite (nonpredicted) direction when the experimenter was male. Breaking the Rorschach scores down into their oral (food, mouth) and dependent components shows that the dependent elements were significantly and positively correlated with the amount of help asked for by males, both in the presence of male or female experimenters; whereas for females the relationship was positive only in the presence of a female experimenter. Rorschach scores based simply on the oral components were not significantly related to help seeking for either sex. But when the criterion for seeking help was defined in terms of subjects making eye contact with the experimenter, the link between Rorschach orality scores and seeking help was significantly positive for both sexes. Although these findings are largely supportive of the oral paradigm, there are some puzzling exceptions. Why did high-oral women in the presence of a male experimenter actually display less help-seeking behavior than did low-oral women? Also, why was the orality component of the Rorschach score so much less predictive of help seeking than the dependent component?

O'Neill and Bornstein (1990) specifically evaluated the hypothesis that an oral orientation is positively associated with a help-seeking attitude. Their subjects were male and female psychiatric inpatients. The MMPI was used to measure how strongly they were help seeking in their stance toward the world. More specifically, the F minus K index, which has been validated as a help-seeking indicator, was employed. The findings significantly supported the original hypothesis. Indeed, other analyses indicated that high-orals were likely to exaggerate their psychopathology when responding to the MMPI, as part of a "plea for help" (p. 36).

Several studies have focused on the oral's concern with pleasing and winning the approval of authority figures. Two investigations (Bornstein & Masling, 1985; Masling, O'Neill, & Jayne, 1981) analyzed the relationship between Rorschach orality scores and response to authority figures' requests. The requests had to do with a notice issued to students in introductory psychology classes calling on them, as part of a course requirement, to volunteer to participate in psychological experiments. In both studies, it was shown, as predicted, that the higher the individuals' orality scores the earlier they volunteered to participate—the high-orals were more compliant in their response. It is apropos that Weiss (1969) analogously reported earlier that high-orals complied with experimenter expectations to a greater degree than did other subjects.[5]

Juni and Fischer (1986), employing a Rorschach measure of orality quite similar to the Masling (1986) approach previously described, predicted that high-orals would, because of their need for "nurturance from an omnipotent benefactor" (p. 27), be characterized by heightened beliefs in deity and afterlife. Both male and female college students were evaluated. The data indicated that in the male sample (but not for females) the orality score was positively and significantly correlated with belief in God. However, orality correlated positively and significantly with belief in afterlife only in the female sample. Orality was not correlated with church attendance in either males or females. Juni and Fischer concluded that the overall results were supportive of their prediction.

In a cleverly contrived experiment, Juni (1981b) further pursued the issue of the orals' tie to potentially nurturant authority figures. He administered a group Rorschach to male and female college students and the protocols were subsequently scored for orality in terms of criteria fairly similar to Masling's (1983b). On completion of the Rorschach testing, the subjects were told that if they wanted feedback about their performance, they were to write their names and Social Security numbers on the test booklets and indicate that they wished to learn about the results. If not interested, they were not to identify themselves. It was theorized that high-orals would, because of a need to have connections with sources of power and nurturance, be especially motivated to ask for feedback. This proved to be significantly true.

The apparent need of orals to feel connected to potentially nurturant authority figures raised the possibility (Masling, Shiffner, & Shenfeld, 1980) that they would have a need to be able to relate to such figures with an enhanced degree of empathy and expertise that would guarantee being on the right side of them. Masling et al. reasoned that without the ability to tune in accurately to authority figures, orals

---

[5] Relatedly, Feldman (1978) reported that high-orals, after participation in a Gestalt workshop, were significantly more likely to describe the leader favorably than were low-orals. This was interpreted by Masling (1983b) as evidence that an oral orientation inclines the individual to take an ingratiating attitude toward authority figures.

would be more likely to find their dependent aims thwarted. They probed the validity of this proposition by studying persons receiving psychotherapy in a university psychology clinic. They obtained orality measures from male and female college students with the usual Rorschach protocols. Further, they measured how accurately the persons in therapy perceived the characteristics of their therapists by asking them to fill out questionnaires about various attributes of the therapist. They then compared their answers with the self-descriptions of the therapists when responding to the same questionnaires. Both a pilot study and a subsequent larger one were carried out with this design. The results from the pilot data indicated a nonsignificant trend for orality scores to be positively correlated with degree of accuracy displayed in sizing up one's therapist; the results from the larger study were in the same direction and statistically significant. The findings supported the hypothesis of the study.

In a related undertaking, Juni and Semel (1982) looked at the relationship of individuals' Rorschach orality scores to their ability to predict accurately the attitudes (e.g., toward abortion, welfare, owning pets) of a group discussion leader. The same questionnaire was used for this purpose as was employed in the Masling et al. (1980) study just described. Both male and female college students served as subjects. The data obtained indicated that in the female sample degree of orality significantly predicted accuracy in sizing up the group leader. However, this was not true in the male sample. Such a sex difference was not observed in the Masling et al. (1980) investigation. In any case, the combined findings from the two studies are moderately supportive of the proposition that high-orals maximize their skills for dealing with potential nurturant allies. Juni and Semel summarized the underlying principle as follows: "The oral personality . . . is eager to insure a nurturing environment, and thus is expected to attempt to understand and anticipate the behavior of potential sources of gratification" (p. 100).[6]

The oral inclination to be in close communication or contact with others has been explored at the literal level of skin touching. Juni, Masling, and Brannon (1979) were impressed with an earlier study (Hollander, Luborsky, & Harvey, 1970) that had shown that high-oral female psychiatric patients were more likely than low-orals to seek

---

[6] Studies in the 1970s had already shown that orality is linked with the accurate prediction of the personality test responses of others (Masling, Johnson, & Saturansky, 1974) and ability to remember the names of others (Feldman, 1978). Juni and LoCascio (1985) also demonstrated that orals selectively preferred forms of psychotherapeutic treatment in which there was intimate, personal interaction with the therapist rather than the cooler cognitive-behavioral mode.

being held and cuddled. Juni et al. hypothesized that the oral orientation would be typified by a special interest in, and willingness to touch, the skin of another person. They appraised male and female college students who were brought into a room with a maze and introduced to a blindfolded individual (confederate of the experimenter) whom they were to help "pass through" the maze. The blindfolded partner wore short sleeves so that any touching below the upper arm had to be on skin. The frequency and duration of touching of the skin of the confederate were recorded. The touch scores of subjects were then related to their Rorschach oral scores. As anticipated, there proved to be a significant positive correlation between number of Rorschach oral images and the relative amount of time spent touching the skin of the confederate. Juni et al. concluded: "orals prefer 'close encounters of the skin kind'" (p. 237).

It was not a large leap from such data to conclude that orals want to avoid being alone and find the presence of others reduces their anxiety level. Two studies (Masling, O'Neill, & Katkin, 1982; Masling, Price, Goldband, & Katkin, 1981) probed this matter by measuring spontaneous electrodermal responses in persons (male college students varying in their Rorschach oral scores) who were placed in a soundproof chamber and exposed to a range of special conditions. In the Masling et al. 1981 study, the subjects were either alone and not performing a task; alone and working on a clerical task; or together with a male confederate, with both working independently on a clerical task. It was found that the high-orals, when placed in the chamber with a confederate, showed fewer electrodermal increases over time than high-orals sitting alone or low-orals either alone or with a confederate. This pattern was interpreted to mean:

> The mere physical presence of another person who did not look, talk, or relate to the subject . . . alleviated the stress for the orals. Non-oral subjects, without the need to depend on others and without the history of finding satisfaction from others, apparently could not obtain such comfort from the presence of the confederate. (p. 399)

In the subsequent Masling et al. (1982) investigation, high- and low-orals' electrodermal responses were recorded both before and after they (male college students) had either a warm, friendly interaction or a cold, unfriendly interaction with a confederate. The data indicated that three of the experimental groups (low-orals in either condition and high-orals in the cold condition) increased in physiological arousal over time. Only the high-orals interacting with a warm confederate demonstrated no such increase in arousal. This was considered to reflect the special reassuring impact of the warm others on the high-orals. The results from the two studies just reviewed affirmed a selective effect of closeness to another on the level of autonomic arousal of high- versus low-orals.[7]

The presumed need of orals to find favor with others has been offered as an explanation why several previous studies found them to be easily persuaded and influenced. These studies (e.g., Masling, Weiss, & Rothschild, 1968; Tribich & Messer, 1974) have typically involved exposing individuals to a laboratory situation in which accomplices of the experimenter unanimously announce a blatantly incorrect answer to a problem and the subject is then given the opportunity to conform with this answer or to disagree. Orals have shown a special propensity to yield to the incorrect assertions.

As a follow-up to this work, Bornstein, Masling, and Poynton (1987) carried out studies in two samples in which pairs of college students (one high and one low in Rorschach orality) were individually requested to read a number of poems and to decide the sex of each of the poets. The two students were then asked to jointly discuss several instances in which their judgments disagreed and to reach mutual agreement. Their interactions were recorded. The data from both studies showed, surprisingly, that the low-rather than high-orals were more likely (significantly in the second sample) to yield to the other during the discussion of the disagreements.

Interestingly, though, in both studies the high-orals significantly more often asked for suggestions from the other. After pondering the nonpredicted trend for high-orals to be less yielding than low-orals, Bornstein et al. could not really offer a satisfying explanation. They did note that because the interaction was obviously being recorded some subjects might have construed the "field" to include unseen observing faculty members and therefore would not have wanted to appear weak or ignorant in their eyes. Bornstein et al. noted: "Perhaps the need to please the faculty member had greater salience than the need to conform to the other subject in the room" (p. 168). But overall, they were impressed with the complexity of the matter and the fact that orality may be a "strength rather than a deficit in certain situations" (p. 169). They pointed out that whether orality predicted yielding, as in the original Masling et al. (1968) and Tribich and Messer (1974)

---

[7] Juni, Nelson, and Brannon (1987) decided on the basis of the literature concerned with the affective connotations of musical tonality that "preference for minor (as opposed to major) tonality . . . relates to a stance of beseeching and need" (p. 229). They, therefore, hypothesized that persons with an oral orientation would show a preference for musical passages played in a minor rather than major tonality. Orality was defined in terms of oral images given in response to inkblot stimuli. The findings significantly supported the hypothesis.

studies, or nonyielding (as in the present study), it was in both contexts a significant determining variable.[8]

Despite complications and gaps related to sex differences and measurement issues, it is impressive to follow the trail of studies since 1977 that have examined different aspects of the nexus between orality and the dependence-independence dimension. Almost all these studies have supported the original formulation that the oral character placed high priority on establishing relationships that facilitate obtaining nurturance from others. The research support has come in both direct and indirect forms. It has, on the one hand, been shown that orality is positively correlated with such directly relevant indicators as insecurity about relationships, the need to ask for help, and the desire to obtain feedback from authority figures. On the other hand, of more indirect relevance is that orality has proven to be positively related to superior empathy with authority figures, greater belief in religious deities, enhanced likelihood of touching other persons, and differential autonomic response as a function of whether one is alone or with someone else. Both classes of data converge in reinforcing the notion of dependence as a prime feature of an oral orientation. Because the post-1977 findings are strongly congruent with similar pre-1977 reports (Fisher & Greenberg, 1985), the totality looks convincing. The full range of the pertinent literature documents that an oral orientation is linked with dependency not only in the several forms just enumerated, but also in such other forms as heightened conditioned responses when reinforced by approval from an authority figure (Noblin, Timmons, & Kael, 1966), selective preferences for being with others when oral anxieties are aroused (Rapaport, 1963), and the deriving of special benefit from brief interactions with a psychotherapist (Gottschalk, 1968).[9]

IS THE ORAL CHARACTER MORE VULNERABLE TO DEPRESSION?

The original view that oral characters are inclined to be pessimistic and depressed (because, in part, they feel chronically deprived) was

---

[8] A number of attempts (e.g., Feldman, 1978; Johnson, 1973; O'Neill, Greenberg, & Fisher, 1984) have been made to relate orality to field dependence (Witkin, Lewis, Hertzman, Machover, Meissner, & Wapner, 1954), but the results have not been consistent.

[9] Gordon and Tegtmeyer (1983) reported that in a population of normal children (mean age = 10.4 years) an index of orality derived from Rorschach responses (Masling, 1986) had only chance correlations with self-report measures of dependence.

supported by the pre-1977 literature and has been further affirmed by the post-1977 findings. The studies pertinent to this matter are described in the earlier chapter dealing with depression. An excellent analysis of the data bearing on this issue may also be found in Bornstein (1993).[10]

DO ORAL CHARACTERS MAKE UNUSUAL USES OF ORAL MODES OF GRATIFICATION?

Presumably because oral characters are in a chronic state of feeling orally deprived, they are unconsciously motivated to find compensatory gratification through such oral modes as eating, drinking, alcohol, and smoking. In our perusal of the pre-1977 literature (Fisher & Greenberg, 1985), we found moderate support for this proposition. Thus, a number of studies affirmed that obese individuals tend to produce an unusual amount of, or selectively focus on, oral imagery when responding to projective stimuli (e.g., inkblots). A similar selectivity was reported in a number of studies dealing with the relationship between orality and both alcoholism and smoking. We concluded:

> Particularly good support has emerged from empirical studies for the hypothesis that the orally oriented continue to make unusual use of oral channels of gratification. From diverse perspectives it has been shown that the oral character is inclined to such behaviors as overeating, consuming large amounts of alcohol, and smoking. (pp. 133–134)

Few empirical efforts in the post-1977 literature directly test the link between an oral orientation and eating behavior. One of the few examples is reported by Mills and Cunningham (1988) who administered one card (depicting the dog Blacky nursing from the mother dog) of the Blacky test to male and female college students. The Blacky test (Blum, 1949) was originally devised to detect conflicts central to the various developmental levels conceptualized by psychoanalytic theory. Scores are computed in terms of multiple-choice responses concerning possible interpretations of the pictures. It was anticipated that the greater the conflict exhibited by subjects in reacting to the Blacky

---

[10] In view of previously cited reports linking depression with the turning of hostility inward against the self, it is interesting that Bornstein, Greenberg, Leone, and Galley (1990) found the Masling (1986) Rorschach orality index to be positively and significantly correlated in male college students with the use of Turning Hostility Against Self defense mechanisms and negatively so with the use of Turning Hostility Against Others mechanisms. However, such relationships did not attain significance in a female sample.

orality theme, the more deviant they would be with respect to certain indexes reflecting eating behaviors.

It was found at a significant level that the greater their oral conflict, the more likely the subjects were to be either underweight or overweight and also the greater was their variability in weight over time. Other findings indicated at a significant level that individuals who were most orally conflicted also rated food as being of heightened importance to them and indicated an increased frequency of eating. No relation was observed between oral conflict and frequency of thinking about food. It was considered that the data were congruent with psychoanalytic theory concerning the likelihood of unusual eating behaviors in those who are orally oriented.[11] Kline and Storey (1980) administered self-report measures of oral optimism and oral pessimism to male college students and detected a significant trend for oral optimism to be positively correlated with a preference for milky warm foods and oral pessimism with a preference for bitter foods.

The other studies in the literature that are even remotely pertinent demonstrate variously that subliminal messages about loss can affect consumption of crackers (Patton, 1992; Talbot, Duberstein, & Scott, 1991) in a laboratory context; that eating-disordered patients produce more dependent (but not oral) Rorschach responses than do obese or normal-weight psychiatric patients (Bornstein & Greenberg, 1991); and that eating-disordered patients over a range of studies, exhibit elevated levels of dependency as defined by self-report measures (Bornstein, 1993). These scattered findings concerning eating behavior do not add much to the pre-1977 studies in this area.

In scanning the post-1977 findings concerning the relationship of an oral orientation to smoking behavior, we located only three directly pertinent studies. Howe and Summerfeld (1979) administered (to male and female college students) a questionnaire tapping into various forms of oral behavior (pencil-sucking, cigarette-sucking, childhood sweet-eating, food-chewing, nail-biting, and thumb-sucking). The orality indexes were then related to various aspects of smoking behavior. Surprisingly, none of the indexes (except, of course, cigarette-sucking)

---

[11] Juni (1983) reported that number of oral Rorschach responses was significantly positively correlated (in male and female college students) with the degree to which male subjects (but not female) preferred bland, soft, sweet foods to spicy, sour, and hard foods. This partially supported the hypothesis that an oral-dependent orientation should be linked with a preference for the softer, blander foods. However, a sadism score derived from the Rorschach did not (contrary to prediction) correlate with a preference for hard, spicy foods.

Apropos of this last finding, Gilleard, Eskin, and Savasir (1988) reported (in a Turkish sample of college students) that oral aggression (as defined by a self-report questionnaire) was positively and significantly correlated with frequency of nail-biting.

significantly distinguished smokers from nonsmokers. However, "continuous smokers" (those who had only occasionally given smoking up) were significantly distinguished from "intermittent smokers" (had given it up for at least a year) by higher scores on cigarette-sucking, adult pencil-sucking, and nail-biting. Also, those who smoked for psychological reasons (e.g., to relieve personal tensions) differed significantly from those who smoked for social reasons (e.g., because offered cigarettes by others) in scoring higher on cigarette-sucking and adult pencil-sucking. Howe and Summerfeld suggested that the overall lack of difference in orality scores between smokers and nonsmokers was because "the smoker group includes different kinds of smokers such as social smokers and occasional smokers" (p. 87). They concluded: "Those smokers for whom the habit is strong show significant orality" (p. 87). Although this conclusion seems moderately affirmed by the data, the explanation for the overall lack of differentiation between smokers and nonsmokers is not impressive.

Also, Kline and Storey (1978b, 1980) administered the Oral Pessimism and Oral Optimism Questionnaires to male and female college students who included smokers and nonsmokers. There proved to be a significant positive correlation between Oral Pessimism scores and being a smoker rather than a nonsmoker. This did not hold true for Oral Optimism scores. In a subsequent sample, these findings were essentially duplicated.

In an investigation we inadvertently omitted from our original review of the pre-1977 literature, Fisher and Fisher (1975) exposed heavy smokers (male and female) to a 2-hour period of smoking deprivation and obtained pre- and postmeasures of orality (based on responses to inkblots) and also the numbers of both somatic and body image complaints. Members of a control group went through the same procedure, except that they smoked throughout the 2-hour period. The data demonstrated that the greater the orality of the experimental subjects, the greater the number of somatic symptoms and body image distortions they experienced following smoking deprivation. Such relationships were absent in the control group indicating that being orally oriented increased the stress effects of the period of oral deprivation.

The several studies just cited with reference to smoking behavior provide a small additional amount of support for the orality-smoking formulation.

The yield was sparse from the post-1977 literature concerned with the possible connection between orality and alcoholism. In sifting through the publications concerned with the variables contributing to alcoholism, we are impressed with the complexity and multiplicity of the etiologic factors. It is difficult to find any individual variables that consistently relate to amount of alcohol consumed (e.g., Frank, Jacobsen,

& Tuer, 1990; Rosenberg, 1993). However, a publication by Barry (1988) includes an appraisal of the anthropological literature that has sought to correlate frequency of alcoholic intoxication in various cultures with their socialization practices. He summarizes several pertinent studies and highlights a significant trend for frequency of drunkenness in a culture to be positively correlated with the degree to which that culture's socialization interferes with the satisfaction of dependency needs.[12]

Overall, the post-1977 literature concerned with the interaction between orality and the inclination to use oral modes of gratification is disappointing. Quite simply, few pertinent studies have been mounted. However, the scattered findings available are probably more supportive than contradictory of theoretical expectations.[13]

MISCELLANEOUS EXTRAPOLATIONS

A few investigations of orality have gone off on unusual trajectories. They are interesting because they represent explorations of new regions.

A report by Juni (1982) concerns a possible link between orality and preference for oral humor. Using a revised version of the Masling (1986) measure of orality derived from Rorschach responses, he related degree of orality (in college males and females) to expressed preferences for jokes varying in the degree to which the punch lines focused on oral, anal, or sadistic themes. The jokes classified as oral concerned food or depicted dependency. In the female sample, the data indicated that Rorschach orality was significantly positively correlated only with relative preference for oral jokes. The finding did not hold true in the male sample.

Juni (1981a) has also explored a potential link between the Masling (1986) Rorschach orality index and career choice. Male and female college students indicated their career choices by ranking 22 occupational titles (e.g., actor, artist, dentist, chef) from most to least desirable. Two of the titles (dentist, chef) referred to occupations that literally involve the mouth or mouth-related activities. As predicted,

---

[12] There continues to be evidence that alcoholics are more field dependent, as defined by the Witkin et al. (1954) typology, than are normal nonalcoholics (Spero, 1987). As earlier mentioned, field dependence has at times (but not consistently) correlated positively with indexes of orality (Bornstein, 1993).

[13] Data suggest that the inclination to use oral modes of gratification is not a generalized phenomenon, but rather is selectively differentiated in individuals. Beckworth (1986) noted in a large sample of Australian women that measures of extreme eating and smoking were not correlated and likewise measures of extreme eating and drinking were not linked. Only the correlation between drinking and smoking was positive and significant.

there was a significant positive correlation in the female sample be-tween Rorschach orality and the average degree of preference for the two oral occupations, but not in the male sample. Juni concluded: "This study suggests that the mere involvement of the mouth in a vo-cation typifies the psychosexual determinants of some careers . . ."(p. 81). Keep in mind that the data matched the hypothesis only in the female sample.[14]

Contrary to Juni's findings, Masling (personal communication to S. Fisher, 1994) reported that he was unable to establish a correlation between Rorschach orality scores and scores from a conventional test of vocational interests. Also, Kline and Storey (1980) reported that their self-report measures of oral optimism and oral sadism were not significantly linked with the choice of dentistry as a vocation or with the choice to be a wind instrument player. Obviously, such observa-tions are incongruent with Juni's data.

Bornstein, O'Neill, Galley, Leone, and Castrianno (1988) have looked at a possible connection between orality, as measured by Masling's (1986) Rorschach orality index, and disturbances in body image. Male and female college students were studied. Body image disturbance was evaluated by means of the self-report Body Image Aberration Questionnaire (Chapman, Chapman, & Raulin, 1978). In two samples (one normal and one psychiatric), the investigators ob-served that degree of orality was positively and significantly corre-lated with body image disturbance in males, but not females. Bornstein et al. speculated that the findings might reflect defective mothering experiences on the part of high-oral individuals that result in the "development of a weak unstable body ego" (p. 320). However, they really could not satisfactorily explain the sex differences in their data.

In a highly speculative extension of the oral character paradigm, Kline and Storey (1980) undertook a study (already referred to in sev-eral other contexts in this chapter) in which they examined correlations between self-report measures of oral optimism and oral pessimism with such variables as vegetarian versus nonvegetarian status, pen-chewing, and being a member of a "Dracula Society." The orality mea-sures were unrelated to vegetarian status or presumed special concern

---

[14] Juni has interpreted his orality score derived from inkblot responses as an index of degree of fixation on the oral areas of the body. He has found (as predicted) that such an index of fixation is negatively correlated with self-reported oral disgust. He rea-soned that as psychosexual zones are "abandoned" to attain higher levels of maturity, early desires with reference to such zones are defensively "turned into revulsion" (p. 694). Using the same "fixation" logic, he attempted to show that orality scores are negatively correlated with measures of the amount of sexual satisfaction derived from oral parts of the body. However, his data did not support this proposition.

about orality as defined by an unusual interest in Dracula. Kline and Storey did report that high pen-top chewers had significantly higher oral pessimism scores than did nonchewers. One does not know what to make of such a composite of observations.

The several exploratory forays just reviewed may simply be regarded as preliminary attempts to extend the oral character paradigm.

PARENTAL INFLUENCES

As described earlier, it was possible to assemble some evidence from the pre-1977 literature indicating that oral infancy experiences (e.g., length of breast feeding) may contribute to oral traits and attitudes in adulthood. However, the pertinent data were inconsistent, especially with reference to whether too much or too little oral gratification is most influential.

The post-1977 literature contains little that is directly relevant to the role of early feeding experiences on later oral attributes. However, a few studies have looked at the relationship between degree of oral orientation in adults and their images of their parents. Bornstein, Galley, and Leone (1986) obtained Rorschach orality measures (Masling, 1986) from male college students and also asked them to write descriptions of their parents. The parental descriptions were quantitatively scored in terms of criteria set forth by Blatt et al. (1979). It was found, at significant levels, that "the Rorschach orality score was correlated (positively) with descriptions of the mother as malevolent, cold, nonnurturant, punitive, weak, unsuccessful in her goals, not constructively involved with the family, and not providing a positive ideal" (p. 86). The Rorschach orality score was also significantly positively correlated with how striving and "judgmental" father was perceived to be. There were no significant correlations between orality and the conceptual levels (e.g., how articulated) of the parental descriptions. Although orality was unrelated to the amount of ambivalence shown in the description of the mother, it was positively related at a borderline level with ambivalence toward the father.

In another study, Duberstein and Talbot (1992) likewise related Rorschach orality scores (secured from male and female college students) to scores derived from the students' written descriptions of their parents (Blatt et al., 1979). Their analysis of the descriptions focused on the degree to which the students idealized their parents. Idealization was judged in terms of the use of positive superlatives and terms suggesting positive uniqueness as well as the absence of critical comments. It was assumed on the basis of earlier studies that idealization represents a form of "defensive compartmentalization" to conceal the individual's negative views and experiences of his or her parents. Analysis of the data revealed that in males (but not females) who do not produce any Rorschach oral responses, there is increased likelihood of such defensive portrayal of the parents. The less idealized, more complex parental depictions by the high-orals were interpreted as reflecting their enhanced need for expertise in interpersonal interactions to ensure their dependent needs.

Using a methodology similar to that in the two studies just cited, Duberstein (1990) found that Rorschach orality scores were positively and significantly correlated with "the ability to represent one's mother (but not father) with a high degree of complexity as an emotional being separate from oneself" (p. 65). The content of the parental representations was not scored and so there was no basis for making comparisons with the earlier cited Bornstein, Galley, and Leone (1986) observation that high-orals are particularly likely to perceive mother in negative terms.

What do these studies tell us? They suggest, first of all, that there is a connection between the individual's degree of orality and the images of his or her parents (particularly mother). Second, there are hints that with increased orality, there is a more negative, nonnurturant view of mother, but also a more complex articulated perception of her. Insofar as the findings portray the mothers of high-orals as nonnurturant they support the original formulation that the oral character mode represents a reaction to early deprivation. However, we are looking at relatively little data and must recognize that we are only speculating. The problem of interpreting such data with any degree of specificity is further complicated because many psychiatrically disturbed persons, who may or may not be orally oriented, tend to perceive their parents as nonnurturant (Bornstein & O'Neill, 1992).[15] The truth is that our original conclusion (Fisher & Greenberg, 1985) based on the pre-1977 literature still applies: "There is little information about how specific maternal (not to mention paternal) behaviors lay the foundation for later oral character traits" (p. 114).

This relatively negative view concerning our understanding of the etiology of oral character attributes can be softened if we focus on a specific central aspect of the oral character cluster: dependence. As already documented, there is good evidence that a prime aim of the

---

[15] In addition, Bornstein (1993) concluded after a review of the pertinent literature that dependency tends to be "associated with perceptions of the mother as cold, punitive, and overcontrolling" (p. 108).

Humphrey (1986) reported trends for women with eating disorders to perceive mother negatively, nonnurturantly.

Brook, Whiteman, and Gordon (1981) described the mothers of smokers to be "less traditional and affectionate" (p. 185).

oral character is to ensure dependent gratification. Bornstein (1993) has critiqued in detail what is known about the socialization experiences that influence the development of dependent behavior. He cites an impressive array of studies that particularly implicate two socialization variables: overprotectiveness and authoritarianism. He notes that significant positive correlations have been obtained in three different cultures (American, English, Indian) between dependence in individuals and the degree of overprotectiveness and authoritarianism typifying the child-rearing practices of their parents. Bornstein asserts: "The cross-cultural and cross-methodological consistency of results regarding the dependency-parenting style relationship attests to the robustness and generalizability of these findings" (p. 40).

Bornstein theorized:

> Parental overprotectiveness and authoritarianism serve simultaneously to (1) reinforce dependent behaviors in children of both sexes and (2) prevent the child from developing independent, autonomous behaviors (since the parents do not permit the child to engage in the kinds of trial-and-error learning that are involved in developing a sense of independence and mastery during childhood). . . . (p. 41)

He noted, in addition, that other socialization variables have shown up, although less prominently, in the empirical literature as promoters of dependent behavior: parental permissiveness, parental conformity, parental rejection and neglect.[16] He suggests that such parental behaviors reinforce passive behaviors in the child and discourage autonomous function. He cautions that some of this variance may come from the child, because passive behavior in children has been shown to encourage both overprotectiveness and authoritarianism in parents. This, says Bornstein, even raises the possibility that temperamental differences in passivity based on genetic factors might play some role in the etiology of dependence.

He comments that relatively consistent and significant relationships have been demonstrated between dependence in individuals and general orientations (e.g., overprotectiveness and authoritarianism) of their parents, but that little has held up with respect to dependence and specific parental feeding and weaning practices. He speculates that the general attitudes of parents should affect their early feeding

---

[16] The difficulties and complexities of defining the parental mediators of dependence are well illustrated by the observations of Rosenfarb, Becker, Khan, and Mintz (1994). They found that dependence in women was related in different, even contradictory, ways to perception of father, as a function of whether the attitudinal data were obtained with verbal or nonverbal measures.

practices and proposes more focused studies of the relationships between such attitudes and styles of early feeding and weaning. This might open the way to teasing out which aspects of early parental feeding behavior have the greatest potential for predicting dependence in offspring.

OVERVIEW OF THE ORAL PARADIGM

A number of the major facets of the original oral character paradigm have been further validated by the post-1977 data we analyzed:

1. There are additional studies affirming the existence of a cluster of characteristics that match the oral character concept.

2. A new array of research has demonstrated that oral characters are unusually invested in guaranteeing relationships in which they can securely find dependence, nurturing support, and denial of aloneness.

3. Also, pessimism and depression occur with unusual frequency in those individuals who are orally oriented.

4. Small positive increments of data have been cited in support of the proposition that the orally oriented are particularly likely to seek oral forms of gratification (e.g., overeating, smoking).

5. Tentative encouragement was provided that the oral character paradigm might be profitably extended to understanding other phenomena such as humor preferences and body image disturbance.

On the negative side, we have not uncovered consistent or meaningful findings in the post-1977 literature to clarify further the original suppositions that oral characters are unusually ambivalent[17] in their relationships or that they display heightened openness to novel experiences and ideas.

The post-1977 literature has also added little to our pre-1977 knowledge concerning the socialization conditions that mediate the development of oral character attributes. However, the literature concerned with the determinants of persons' levels of dependence

---

[17] There are scattered and contradictory findings regarding ambivalence. For example, Bornstein, Galley, and Leone (1986) noted that Rorschach orality scores were positively correlated with amount of ambivalence toward mother (in written descriptions of mother); but Bornstein et al. (1988) found a negative correlation between Rorschach orality scores and amount of ambivalence in self-representations.

highlights the possibility that parental overprotectiveness and authoritarianism are importantly involved.

The major aspects of the oral character formulation relating to
being dependent and making sure that one is adequately supported by
the power figures in one's world seem to be reasonably affirmed by
the considerable array of pertinent empirical studies. There is an oral
character style of behavior that is reliably recognizable. There is also
probably a connection between heightened preoccupation with, and
devotion to, oral body sectors and the cultivation of certain patterns of
relationships with others.[18] Bornstein (1993) has questioned how well
documented this connection actually is, and there is room for more
empirical exploration of the matter. But the level of uncertainty intensifies when we begin to explore a number of the basic oral character
concepts that have to do with etiology and maturational hierarchies.
Dependable data are sparse as to whether an oral orientation is rooted
in extremes of oral experiences during early socialization. The association of dependence with the perception of one's parents as overprotective and/or authoritarian suggests that certain parental attitudes
about giving and taking play a role in the development of oral attitudes. However, as earlier noted, we cannot go much beyond this non-
specific level of description.

A major problem arises when an integration is attempted between the available empirical data and the concept that the oral character represents an individual who is fixated at an early stage of
development and grossly below the maturity level of those who have
presumably attained higher levels (e.g., as exemplified by the genital
character). It is true that oral characters are likely to be vulnerable to

---

[18] The various psychoanalytically defined character types (and associated psychosexual stages) are each considered to be linked with a concentration of cathexis on a specific organ or part of the body. Thus, the oral character is presumably focused on the
mouth and the anal character on the anal region of the body. Fisher (1986) has shown
in a series of studies that the degree to which persons direct their attention to specific
body areas compared with others is correlated with certain personality and psychodynamic variables. For example, there is reasonable evidence that the greater the
amount of attention a right-handed man focuses on the right compared with the left
side of his body, the more inhibited he is about heterosexual relationships. Fisher has
theorized that focusing on a body area that has acquired certain meanings provides a
mechanism for maintaining awareness of particular feelings and impulses implicit in
the meanings ascribed to that area. This awareness may, in turn, be utilized to maintain inhibitory control over such impulses. Fisher's observations offer a possible empirically based prototype for the apparent association of the traits considered to
typify each of the psychoanalytically highlighted body parts (mouth, anus, genitals).
The focus on the body area presumably associated with each psychosexual stage could
be regarded as a means for controlling wishes or impulses especially prominent at
that stage.

certain forms of maladaptive reactions (e.g., depression, negative concept of self, smoking, increased susceptibility to physical disorders); and in that sense, they could be regarded as psychologically lacking (Bornstein, 1993). However, it is simultaneously true that oral characters enjoy such positive assets as superior sensitivity to, and understanding of the behaviors of others, a special adaptive readiness to seek medical consultation when signs of body illness appear, and considerable facility in relating to authority figures (Bornstein, 1993). Given the social context of most behavior, the superior social sensitivity of the oral character would appear to be a skill of potentially extraordinary value. We are left with the impression that the oral character's ratio of assets to deficiencies might not be significantly different from the ratios typifying any of the other character types.

The presumed immaturity (psychosexually fixated state) of the oral character is viewed within the psychoanalytic frame of reference as meaning that there is a deficiency in relating heterosexually. According to theory, oral characters should manifest significant difficulties in their sexual behaviors. Actually, there is no evidence that such is true. Fisher (1973) administered a battery of measures of oral attitudes (e.g., inkblot responses, perception of tachistoscopically exposed oral stimuli, associations to oral versus nonoral words) and correlated these measures (in several samples of women) with a variety of indexes of sexual behavior (e.g., orgasm consistency, frequency of intercourse, subjective satisfaction during intercourse). There proved to be no consistent relationships between these indexes and any of the orality measures. No hint emerged that high-orals were selectively deficient in their sexual functioning. No signs of sexual immaturity emerged in the high-orals.

Although the original theoretical speculations about the oral character focused on negative attributes, positive qualities were also suggested, such as being adventurous, open to new experiences, and interested in "understanding nature." However, Freud's placement of the oral character in a psychosexually inferior category probably required that the negative maladaptive aspects of this character type should be emphasized by psychoanalytic theorists. In fact, though, it is difficult at this point in time to muster objective evidence of the inferiority of the oral position.[19] The whole issue of the validity of Freud's theories concerning the maturational superiority-inferiority of the various character types will be pursued further in Chapter 5.

[19] Note Bornstein's (1993) comment with respect to this matter: "However, if there is one theme I have tried to stress throughout . . . , it is that the traditional 'deficit' view of dependency . . . is overly narrow and unnecessarily pessimistic. Dependency has proven to be associated with positive as well as negative qualities" (p. 180).

We have possibly been simplistic in our analysis of the literature about the attributes of the oral character insofar as we have not consistently confronted the possibility of there being two different oral character clusters, depending on whether the focus is on the oral optimist or the oral pessimist. Previous research (e.g., Kline & Storey, 1977) differentiated (in line with Abraham's original theoretical formulation) between an early stage of oral fixation (oral optimist) and a later one (oral pessimist). Presumably, as described by Kline and Storey, the oral optimist is typified by being dependent, talkative, cheerful, confident, and enjoying admiration; whereas the oral pessimist is more darkly portrayed as verbally aggressive, anxious, pessimistic, and inclined to use projection. These two obviously divergent concepts could conceivably complicate the process of empirically validating the oral character paradigm. For example, a researcher testing a hypothesis about orality in two different samples might obtain quite different results simply as a function of the proportions of each sample that were oral optimists versus oral pessimists. In this respect, the numerous sex differences in results that characterize the orality literature might reflect contrasts in male and female modal inclinations to be oral optimists or pessimists. In any case, it is logical to urge that future studies of the oral paradigm employ measures that tap into both dimensions.

Finally, where does the oral character configuration fit into the larger body of personality work? It is actually unique in tying various personality traits to modes of adaptation to the sensations and drives associated with a specific body sector. We are not aware of any other personality formulations that link styles of behavior to intensity of "cathexis" of focal body sectors. However, the core constituent of the oral character paradigm, the need to ensure and maintain dependent symbiotic relationships, has been represented in quite a number of formulations pertinent to personality. It has been prominent within such explanatory schemata as field dependence-independence (Witkin et al., 1954), ego or body boundary articulation (Fisher, 1986; Landis, 1970), primitive-mature developmental differentiation (Werner, 1957), locus of control (Lefcourt, 1982), and the achieving personality (McClelland, 1961).[20] The dependency component obviously overlaps the boundaries between the oral character concept and salient aspects of the schemata just cited. Of course, keep in mind that the overlap may to varying degrees represent Freud's influence on the thinking of those who developed the schemata.

---

[20] There may be some overlap between the oral character formulation and the Agreeableness dimension of the Big Five (McCrae & Costa, 1988) model, but a detailed comparison of the two variables reveals a good deal of difference and disparity.

Chapter 5

The Anal Paradigm

The concept of an anal personality structure is strongly represented in Freud's writings. As noted earlier, most of his thinking about personality types emerged in his theorizing about the anal character (Baudry, 1983). He reasoned quite simply that a personality superstructure specialized for self-control evolved from attempts to restrain anal impulses and wishes. He (1908) portrayed the anal character as follows:

> The people I am about to describe are noteworthy for a regular combination of the three following characters. They are especially *orderly, parsimonious,* and *obstinate.* Each of these words actually covers a small group or series of interrelated character-traits. "Orderly" covers the notion of bodily cleanliness, as well as of conscientiousness in carrying out small duties and trustworthiness. Its opposite would be "untidy" and "neglectful." Parsimony may appear in the exaggerated form of avarice; and obstinacy can go over into defiance, to which rage and revengefulness are easily joined. (p. 169)

Presumably these "character-traits" represent a constellation of effects and residues evoked by anal sensitivities and unconscious anal imagery threatening to break through into awareness. In referring to persons with unusually intense anal conflicts Freud (1908) noted:

> We infer that such people are born with a sexual constitution in which the erotogenicity of the anal zone is exceptionally strong. But since none of these weaknesses and idiosyncracies are to be found in them once their childhood has been passed, we must conclude that the anal zone had lost its erotogenic significance in the course of development; and it is to be suspected that the regularity with which this triad of properties is present in their character may be brought into relation with the disappearance of their anal erotism. (p. 170)

To paraphrase, Freud theorized that some individuals are born with an exceptional anal sensitivity that results in a highlighting of

99

anal experiences. As they become socialized, however, their anal focus becomes unacceptable and they must invest energy in repressing their anal wishes. Freud asserted that the process of repression results in such wishes becoming disgusting and shameful. The disgust was said to serve as a "dam" against anal impulses that aim for unregulated, uninhibited defecation and the expression of besmirching intentions. The anal character defense is depicted as immuring such impulses and channeling them into defensive and derivative modes: orderliness, parsimony, and obstinacy.

Orderliness presumably offers proof and self-assurance that one has not succumbed to the dirty, contaminating aspects of anal impulses.

Parsimony is linked by Freud with a primitive equation between feces and money. He indicates (1908):

> In reality, whenever archaic modes of thought have predominated . . . money is brought into the most intimate relationships with dirt. We know that the gold which the devil gives his paramours turns into excrement after his departure, and the devil is certainly nothing else than the personification of the repressed instinctual life . . . .
>
> It is possible that the contrast between the most precious substance known to men and the most worthless . . . has led to this specific identification of gold with faeces. (p. 174)

Basically, he regarded parsimony, with its target of saving and hoarding money, as representing in the anal character a substitutive mechanism for keeping in touch with a substance possessing secret fecal or anal connotations.

Obstinacy, the third element of the triad defining the anal character, was portrayed by Freud as an attitude that evolved as the result of the frustrating experiences accompanying socialization of bowel control. He commented too that the buttocks are often a site for the administration of punishment intended to render the child more submissive (less obstinate). Presumably anal characters, with their special sensitivity to issues of anal expression, would be particularly frustrated by the disciplining of their anal functions and react with a set to resist. Their fantasies of noncompliance are apparently mobilized by having to submit to a major form of body control.

In our original testing of Freud's anal character formulation, we (Fisher & Greenberg, 1985) asked the following questions:

1. Can one demonstrate the existence of a grouping of traits and attitudes that parallel the cluster Freud linked with the anal character?

2. Are persons classified as anal characters defensively inclined toward a neat, orderly style of life?

3. Do anal characters manifest a tendency to be parsimonious through behaviors such as hoarding, saving things, and holding onto money?

4. Are anal characters unusually obstinate (stubborn, oppositional, defiant in various camouflaged ways)? Do they have unusual difficulties with respect to managing or expressing hostile impulses?

5. Do anal modes of psychological defense predispose the anal character to develop obsessive-compulsive symptomatology (e.g., obsessive thinking, compulsive acts and rituals)?

FINDINGS PREVIOUS TO 1977

By and large, the research literature up to 1977 answered these questions in an affirmative tone:

1. Nineteen studies were found that, in the main, supported the proposition that there are traits reminiscent of Freud's concept of the anal character. The most frequently observed of such traits related to being orderly or parsimonious. Obstinacy was relatively infrequently mentioned.

2. With regard to whether orderliness typifies the anal character, a number of pertinent experimental reports described mixed results but were more supportive in female than male samples. Although we originally felt that the overall data favored Freud, they were not sufficiently strong to permit assured interpretation. We did note encouraging leads that involve apparent relationships between anality and such variables as self-investment in orderly kinds of occupations, a need to perceive things symmetrically, and efficiency in processing information that suggest a special knack for organized, orderly cognition.

3. Up to 1977, the question concerning parsimony had been explored in only a handful of projects, but the findings tended to be congruent with Freud's view. For example, Noblin (1962) demonstrated that "anals" were unusually receptive to a conditioning procedure if rewarded by money (whereas "orals" were most motivated by a food reward).

4. We originally cited a range of studies that favored a positive answer to the inquiry concerning whether obstinacy typifies the anal character (Fisher & Greenberg, 1985). We offered the following summary of this work:

> It can be said . . . that the evidence generally favors Freud's proposition that the anal character is obstinate and set to resist. We have reviewed a range of studies indicating that the anal character is quick to say "no," slow to change his opinion when persuasion is tried on him, difficult to influence in a verbal conditioning context that relies on approval as a reward. . . . (p. 158)

5. As of 1977, we could not assemble any consistent information that would clarify whether anal characters who develop psychopathology are selectively likely to manifest obsessive-compulsive symptomatology.

When we pulled together all the research information available in 1977 concerning the viability of Freud's anal character formulation, we ended up with the following:

> We would declare with simple directness that the scientific evidence gathered up to this point favors a good part of what Freud said about the anal character. There does seem to be an aggregation of traits and attitudes corresponding to the anal character image. An impressive tally of studies carried out by investigators with different theoretical perspectives has affirmed that the three major qualities (orderliness, obstinacy, parsimony) that Freud ascribed to the anally oriented do hang together understandably.[1] (p. 163)

When we originally examined the literature concerned with the origins or etiology of the anal character constellation, little of significance emerged. Contrary to Freud, there was no convincing evidence that modes or severity of toilet training, as such, played a role.[2] However, a promising trend was detected for anal characters to have been reared by mothers who manifested anal traits (e.g., as defined by variables like orderliness or stubbornness).

RECENT OBSERVATIONS

The Anal Character Cluster

As already described, numerous earlier studies affirmed a consistent trend for an anal character factor to emerge when arrays of personality measures derived from questionnaires were factor analyzed. Typically, anal clusters were identified that embraced such variables as orderliness, stinginess, stubbornness, concern about money, punctuality,

---

[1] Kline (1981) arrived at an essentially similar conclusion on the basis of his analysis of the pertinent literature.

[2] Reviews by both Kline (1981) and Pollak (1979) concur with this conclusion.

interest in collecting things, rigidity, retentiveness, anxiety over loss of control, obsessional inclinations, conservation, hoarding, and attention to detail. With only a few exceptions, the attributes in the anal clusters were apparently congruent with Freud's conceptualization of the anal character.

We have located a number of post-1977 studies (and two prior to 1977 that were originally overlooked) pertinent to the anal cluster issue. Generally, they have straightforwardly extracted familiar sounding anal factors from factor analyses of multiple questionnaire personality measures (Bromley & Lewis, 1976; Kline, 1978; Kline & Barrett, 1983; Kline & Storey, 1978a; O'Dell,[3] 1980; Stone & Gottheil,[4] 1975; Torgersen, 1980; Trijsburg & Duivenvoorden, 1987; Van den Berg & Helstone, 1975).[5]

The study by Torgersen (1980), mentioned earlier, deserves special citation because not only did he find the same basic factor structure (which included a clear-cut obsessive or anal cluster) that Lazare, Klerman, and Armor (1966, 1970) reported in their analysis of a questionnaire constructed to measure psychoanalytic character types, but he did so in Norway, a culture different from the original U.S. samples recruited by Lazare et al. Incidentally, Torgersen used both "neurotic" and "normal" twins as the subjects in his investigation and was interested in exploring whether genetic factors played a part in the various character types. He could not detect such genetic influence in relation to the obsessive (anal) factor.

Overall, the more recent findings seem to support the existence of the anal factor, that we originally described in the numerous studies previous to 1977. In 1976, Hill launched a critical attack on the soundness of the major factor analytic studies pertinent to this issue that had been published up to that point. He raised a number of criticisms about the validity of the tests used, their factorial purity, and the manner in which statistical data had been interpreted.

Kline (1978) attempted to counter Hill's critique by pointing out the consistent positive results that had been obtained by a variety of

---

[3] The O'Dell study actually represents a refactoring of a previous study by Finney (1964). O'Dell asserts that the original analysis was faulty; his refactoring of the data revealed anal factors that he thought matched Freud's anal character formulation particularly well.

[4] Although Stone and Gottheil found a factor that "resembled" aspects of the anal character, it was not a "strong" factor and not correlated with a measure of "bowel behavior."

[5] Masling and Schwartz concluded as follows from their 1979 survey of the studies concerned with anality: "Factor analytic studies with one exception were able to locate one or more anal factors, suggesting that a constellation of attitudes centering around the ideas of parsimony, obstinacy, and orderliness does occur in the test responses of Ss . . ."(p. 294).

researchers. He provided data from a new study that also isolated an anal factor from several major personality questionnaires that had been administered to a sample of college students. Kline also argued that because a test is not factor pure does not mean that the factor does not exist; and he noted that the technical flaws pointed out by Hill would introduce error that would work against rather than for significant hypothesis-supporting findings.

Hill (1979), in turn, responded and agreed that the new empirical study presented by Kline bolstered Kline's case, but he still had reservations, particularly with regard to the validity of the tests involved and the possible distorting effect of a response-bias such as social desirability. Although Hill raised some excellent methodological points, the sheer consistency of the numerous findings over the years represents a line of evidence difficult to dismiss.

OTHER EXPLORATIONS OF THE ANAL CHARACTER PARADIGM

In 1979, Pollak reviewed all the available empirical research bearing on the anal (obsessive-compulsive) character and stated: "Empirically based findings to date . . . are congruent with clinical observation, description, and prediction regarding the salient behavioral characteristics and character styles of obsessive-compulsive individuals" (p. 225). He thought the research evidence justified the following conclusions:

1. There is a cluster of traits conforming to the obsessive-compulsive formulation.
2. Obsessive-compulsive traits are normally distributed.
3. The obsessive-compulsive personality classification is not positively related to measures of neuroticism, whereas obsessional symptoms are.
4. Introversion-extroversion is probably not linked with obsessive-compulsive status.
5. There is little evidence favoring the classical psychoanalytic theory concerning the etiology of obsessive-compulsive personality, although some data suggest that "obsessive-compulsive individuals often are the progeny of obsessive-compulsive parents" (p. 238).

In addition, Pollak urged further research to explore the relationship of obsessive-compulsive (anal character) personality attributes to a wider range of phenomena not usually considered in

psychoanalytically oriented studies. For example, he proposed probing how such attributes are linked with the field independence-de-
pendence typology construct (Witkin, Lewis, Hertzman, Machover,
Meissner, & Wapner, 1954), vocational choice, attitudes toward death,
and aesthetic sensitivity. He took the position that the concept of the
anal character was on a firm footing and that it was time to expand its
applicability to new sectors of behavior.

The post-1977 empirical studies dealing with anality show impressive diversity, and as Pollak suggested, they look in new directions.

A number of studies have attempted to integrate the anal character (obsessive-compulsive) concept with the Type A behavior pattern,
which has been shown to be an independent risk factor for coronary
heart disease. Most definitions of the Type A pattern refer to a cluster
of personal attributes typified by an unusually intense need to maintain control and to struggle chronically to obtain an unlimited number
of poorly defined things in the shortest possible time, in competition
with others. Several studies (Garamoni & Schwartz, 1986; O'Neill,
1984; Schick, Arnold, & Tomedi, 1984) have demonstrated significant
positive correlations between anal character measures (e.g., Kline's,
1969, Ai3 Scale; Lazare-Klerman-Armor Trait Scales, Lazare et al.,
1966, 1970) and a measure of the Type A pattern (viz., Jenkins Activity
Survey; Glass, 1977).

Garamoni and Schwartz (1986) have quite elaborately examined
the overlap between the anal character and Type A constructs. Their
analysis focuses on a number of the major characteristics that have
emerged as typifying the anal personality.

They note, first of all, that parsimony, one of the most frequently
cited anal character attributes, has been spotted in the behavior of
Type A's. As is true of the anal character, Type A's overvalue money.
Garamoni and Schwartz cite empirical reports that Type A's are "ab-
sorbed" in money and have a tendency to use numbers or quantity as a
"measure of personal prowess" (p. 316). They indicate that, for Type
A's, the "monetary value of possessions and collections . . . functions as
a gauge of self-worth" (p. 316). Lyness (1993) notes that Type A's show
enhanced physiological reactivity in situations where they are competing for incentives like money. But further with respect to parsimony,
Garamoni and Schwartz summarize several studies indicating that
Type A's overestimate time durations and are preoccupied with saving
time, doing things in a hurry, overvaluing the importance of time. As
we have noted elsewhere (Fisher & Greenberg, 1985), anal characters
are similarly parsimonious (saving and retaining) of time.

Being obstinate has also been identified as one of the qualities
basic to the anal character; and Type A's appear to exhibit a similar resistive stance. Garamoni and Schwartz enumerate a variety of empirical

findings documenting the resistive and irritable behavior of Type A's. They point out that Type A's "strive to compete with or to challenge others" (p. 317); "exhibit excessive annoyance, irritability, anger, hostility, and aggression"; are "more likely to perceive threat in a coercive communication and to change opinions in opposition to advocacy" (p. 318). They indicate too that they found in one of their studies that Type A's scored significantly higher than Type B's on the obstinacy dimension of the Lazare et al. (1966) Trait Scales.

The triad identified by Freud as framing the anal character concept included parsimony, obstinacy, and also orderliness. Orderliness loads significantly on the obsessive (anal) factor in a number of factor analytic studies. Garamoni and Schwartz report that in an exploratory study Type A's scored significantly higher than Type B's on the orderliness dimension of the Lazare et al. (1966) Trait Scales.

They also cite promising investigations highlighting similarities between anal characters (obsessives) and Type A's with reference to being unusually "rigid" and "persevering" and manifesting a "severe superego."[6]

Overall, their recitation of the multiple ways in which the anal character and Type A categories overlap is quite convincing. They see this overlap as providing the potential for each category to illuminate the other. Despite strenuous efforts to do so, however, they were actually not able to come up with much such mutual illumination. They see the major element shared by the two categories to be an anxious determination to maintain control over events or affects that are stressful. Such concern with maintaining control was central to Freud's concept of the anal character's dilemma.[7] Garamoni and Schwartz also see overlap because there have been reports that both anal characters and Type A's experienced parents who were unusually demanding, punitive, and perfectionistic. The empirical documentation of this point is rather thin, however, and two studies

[6] Garamoni and Schwartz (1986) were not able to establish that anal characters and Type A's resemble each other with reference to "devotion to work," "indecisiveness," and "emotional constriction."

[7] If the anal character and Type A concepts share a good deal of commonality, this would suggest an interesting possibility concerning the potential physiological consequences of an anal orientation. Freud (1908) speculated that anal characters would experience an unusual number of somatic difficulties (e.g., constipation, colitis) related to anal functioning. Actually, studies have failed to demonstrate any consistent correlations between measure of anality and frequency of anal symptomatology (Fisher & Greenberg, 1985; Stone & Gottheil, 1975). But if one considers that Type A's are individuals who tend to develop coronary heart disease, the possibility arises that anal characters analogously "channel" tension to the heart. It is apropos that research by Fisher (1986) has shown that males who focus attention on their hearts are inclined to be concerned about being controlled and to experience elevated levels of guilt.

(Benjaminsen, Jorgensen, Kragh-Hansen, & Pederson, 1984; Von der Lippe & Torgersen, 1984) actually present contradictory data.

The post-1977 exploratory studies have examined, with sometimes far-fetched turns and twists, whether presumed anal-based attitudes have detectable selective effects on various levels of response.

Two studies have considered whether an anal orientation predicts selective preferences for anal humor. The Juni (1982) investigation mentioned earlier calculated "anal fixation" scores, for male and female college students, by counting the numbers of anal references in their Rorschach protocols. Incidentally, it is not clear why the Rorschach-derived scores are designated as "fixation" scores. It may be simpler and less confusing to regard them as indicators of degree of preoccupation with anal themes. In addition, the subjects rank-ordered (from most funny to least funny) a series of jokes whose content was either oral, anal, or sadistic. It was predicted that the greater the person's "anal fixation" the greater would be his or her relative preference for anal jokes. The results significantly supported this hypothesis in the female but not in the male samples.

In another study (O'Neill, Greenberg, & Fisher, 1992), women responded to a battery of measures of anal characteristics and also to a measure of degree of enjoyment of oral, anal, and phallic-Oedipal jokes. The measures of anality ranged widely: questionnaires and word completion tasks tapping modes of expressing hostility; questions concerning amount of effort customarily devoted to dealing with and combating dirt; counts of the frequency of dirt references in spontaneous reports of one's stream of thought; questionnaire inquiries concerning attitudes toward frugality and cleanliness. The data indicated significant trends for amount of enjoyment of anal humor (but not any other category of humor) to be positively correlated with degree of obstinacy, cleanliness, and parsimony.

Relatedly, Maiman (1977) administered a self-report measure (Kline Ai 3 scale) of anality (obsessionality) to male and female college students who also responded to a humor appreciation test that, among other things, evaluated selective enjoyment of three categories of humor (time, dirt, money) that should, according to the anal character formulation, represent themes of special concern for the anally oriented. The humor appreciation test also included several control categories of jokes without anal implications. The data indicated (at significant levels) that the anality scores were selectively positively correlated with amount of enjoyment of the jokes with anal connotations. Maiman noted that a "modicum of intrapsychic tension is facilitative of the enjoyment of humor" (p. xvi).

In a project noted earlier, Juni and Frenz (1981) sought, in terms of Rorschach "anal fixation" scores (based on number of anal references) to predict responses to anal words presented tachistoscopically. Juni and Frenz expected that the higher the Rorschach anal scores, the lower would be the thresholds for correctly identifying the anal words. The subjects were male and female college students. The results indicated only a chance relationship between numbers of anal references and thresholds for correctly identifying the anal words. According to the authors, however, the higher the Rorschach anal content, the greater was the overall ability to perceive accurately a variety of classes of words (oral, sadistic, anal) presented tachistoscopically. They predicted this last finding on the basis of the idea that anal characters are particularly methodical and efficient in their information-processing skills and have an enhanced "cathexis for words."

Vinck (1979) followed up data published by Fisher (1986) indicating that men with heightened awareness of the back of their bodies display anal character traits. Vinck measured amount of back awareness in a Dutch sample of males and females; and also determined the degree to which there was selectivity in recall of a list of anal and nonanal words that had been learned. In the case of the females a significant trend was found for those with greater back awareness to selectively forget (repress) anal words. However, this result was not duplicated for the males. This discrepancy in the results for males and females is but one of several such sex differences (e.g., Juni, 1982) that have shown up in the anal character literature. Actually, Kagan and Moss (1962) demonstrated significant sex differences in patterns of compulsivity that occur developmentally.

Selective perception as a function of anal traits was explored too, in the earlier cited paper by Von der Lippe and Torgersen (1984). These researchers were interested in how character traits mediate the strategies used by individuals to defend against the threatening content of two pictures presented tachistoscopically (starting at a subliminal level). The types of errors and distortions typifying subjects' reports concerning the pictures provide the basis for ascertaining the defenses employed. The subjects were pregnant women. Their degree of obsessive (anal) orientation was measured by means of a questionnaire originally derived from the Lazare et al. (1966) Traits Scales. It had been anticipated that an "isolating" form of defense would particularly correlate with possessing obsessive character traits; and the data significantly supported this hypothesis. The isolating defense was considered to be present when the figures, in each of the original tachistoscopic pictures (e.g., a hero and a peripheral threatening person), are perceived as "separated" or "isolated from each other" or one of them is not seen at all. The results were viewed as supporting Freud's original formulation that the anal/obsessive character rigidly uses isolation and reaction formation to cope with threatening images or fantasies.

Fisher (1978) probed a complex idea proposed by Kubie (1965) concerning the role of anal fantasies in racial prejudice. Kubie speculated that children are socialized to reject and hate important sectors of their bodies, especially the anal area, which is associated with dirt and filth. Kubie considered that the sense of having such bad, dirty body parts was so disturbing that it was necessary to project it onto others. He hypothesized that Negroes (Kubie's term), with their black skins, represent a prominent target on which to project negative body feelings. Black is obviously a color frequently equated in our culture with dirt and the unacceptable. Fisher attempted to test Kubie's idea by measuring, in several samples of male and female college students, degree of negative bias against blacks and relating it to a series of indexes of anal concerns and traits reflecting the degree to which the subjects perceived their body as dirty, amount of self-focus upon the back of the body, and degree to which they endorsed questionnaire items concerned with the triad (cleanliness or orderliness, obstinacy, frugality). Across multiple samples, the findings were supportive of Kubie's perspective. Those persons with higher levels of anality scores or anality traits tended significantly to be more negative toward blacks. The support was not dramatic but quite consistent.

Juni and Semel (1982) predicted that persons with an anal orientation would have a special need to stress the difference between self and authority figures. They assumed, as suggested by Freud, that the anal character is inclined to use projection as a defense mode and, therefore, to adopt an orientation that might be paraphrased: "It is he who feels this way, while I feel just the opposite" (p. 101). They add that the need to maintain a sense of difference is reinforced by the "oppositionalism and antiauthority orientation within anality" (p. 101). This formulation was tested by obtaining "anal fixation" scores from the Rorschach protocols of male and female college students and relating these scores to the differences between how individuals rated self and a group leader with respect to a number of attitudes and opinions. The data significantly supported the hypothesis in the male but not the female sample.[8]

The diverse explorations just reviewed represent a series of attempts to push the anal character concept into new territories. In some

---

[8] Clearly negative results have emerged from attempts to explore the possible intersections of anal traits with variables such as death anxiety (Pollak, 1978) and hypnotic susceptibility (Hill, 1978) that are quite distantly derivative of Freud's original anal character formulation.

instances, for example with respect to humor preferences or prejudice against blacks, the findings look promising. In other instances, for example selective response to anal versus nonanal words or perception of authority figures, the results are fragile in the sense that they apply to one sex but not the other. The anal character paradigm appears to have a potential that can be stretched profitably.

STUDIES PERTINENT TO FREUD'S CORE ASSUMPTIONS

Several projects have directly or indirectly launched attempts to check the soundness of some of Freud's core assumptions about the anal character. A number of these efforts were undertaken by Juni and his collaborators. They have often employed Kline's (1978) Ai 3 Scale as a measure of degree of anal orientation. In one study (Fischer & Juni, 1982), they examined the relationships of the Kline Scale to four variables: negativism, superego severity, self-esteem, and self-disclosure. A complex procedure was used to tap these variables. The subjects were college students. Negativism was measured by determining how long it took the subjects to agree to participate in the study when the experimenter telephoned to recruit them. Another index of negativism was based on whether subjects agreed or refused to participate; and still another on whether they did or did not show up for scheduled appointments. The data indicated at a significant level that the greater the anality, as measured by the Kline scale, the more likely subjects were to refuse to participate in the experiment; but anality had only chance correlations with the other two presumed indexes of negativism.[9]

Superego severity was derived from subjects' written statements in response to a request "to write about your own sexual attitudes and experiences" (p. 53). The statements were scored by counting the presence of the words "should," "should not," "right," "wrong," and any concepts referring to external authority, commands, guilt, or shame. As predicted, the results indicated, that the greater subjects' anality scores, the greater was the number of superego references in their protocols.

The relationships of anality to self-disclosure and self-esteem were also explored. The findings have less direct relevance to Freud's basic formulations about the anal character, but we will briefly touch on them. Degree of self-revealing behavior was judged (by means of

[9] Weiss (1969) reported a trend for individuals with an anal orientation to resist participation in an experiment that was offered as an opportunity to satisfy a course requirement.

objective criteria) from the written self-disclosure protocols of the subjects; and as predicted, the greater subjects' anality scores the less self-
revealing they were. This prediction was based on the perspective that
anal characters are "frugal, withholding, defiant, obstinate, negativistic, passive-aggressive, controlling, concerned with autonomy and ego
boundaries and eager to construe interpersonal encounters as personal
assertions of dominance . . ." (p. 51). Thus, the findings suggest a positive link between anality and a type of negativistic behavior.

It had also been anticipated that because anal traits are syntonic
with the values of Western society and likely to lead to successful coping, the anal characters should have relatively high self-esteem. A well-
standardized questionnaire was used to measure self-esteem, but
anality and self-esteem proved to be unrelated.

Juni and Fischer (1986) examined the tie between anality and
the "anal-compulsive need for regularity and repetitiveness" (p. 287).
A good case can be made that Freud conceptualized the anal character's defense against potential loss of control as anchored in regularity, ritual, and repetitiveness. Juni and Fischer tested this view by
obtaining two anality measures, the Kline Ai 3 Scale, and the previously described Juni and Frenz (1981) Rorschach-based index of anal
content, from male and female college students. Further, they determined amount of investment in regularity by asking subjects to indicate how regularly they attend church. The data indicated that the
more subjects were anally oriented, as defined by the Kline measure,
the more regularly they attended church. This was significantly
shown in both male and female samples. However, although the
Rorschach anal content scores were significantly positively correlated
with regularity of church attendance in the males, this was not true
for the females.

When Juni and Rubenstein (1982) related the Kline Ai3 Scale to
college students' degree of annoyance with a tedious repetitive task,
there was a significant negative correlation. The greater the anal orientation, the less discomforting it was to engage in a routinized process.
Interestingly, when a condition was introduced into the experiment
such that the routine task was repeatedly interrupted by a confederate
of the experimenter, it was found that the greater the anality, the more
was the annoyance with this individual who was interfering with the
fixed routine.

Rogers and Wright (1975) explored whether anal characters
(obsessive-compulsives) are unusually fixed and rigid in their behavior. They evaluated obsessive-compulsiveness, in male and female
college students, using the Psychasthenia scale of the MMPI. They
evaluated rigidity with the Schaie (1955) Test of Behavioral Rigidity;
and found (at a significant level) that the greater the presumed

obsessive-compulsiveness of subjects the more rigid they were.[10] Incidentally, there was also a significant positive correlation between obsessive-compulsiveness and authoritarianism.[11]

Trijsburg and Duivenvoorden (1987) administered the Sandler and Hazari (1960) questionnaire, a measure of anal and obsessional traits, to a sample of medical students. They also used a standardized questionnaire to ascertain concern about ability to maintain control. The data indicated, at a significant level, that the greater the anal orientation, the more concern there was about the difficulty of keeping things under control.

The studies just cited dealing with the general issue of whether anal characters are particularly invested in control, regularity, and rigidity hang together pretty well. We have seen positive correlations between anality measures and such parameters as regularity of church attendance, willingness to engage in a repetitive task, behavioral rigidity and concern about ability to maintain control. It is also pertinent that anality was found to be positively correlated with "superego severity." Almost no new research has been carried out to check directly Freud's formulations concerning the link between anality and the triad (orderliness, obstinacy, frugality). Fischer and Juni (1982), however, have made direct and indirect efforts to look at the relationship between anality and variables tapping into negativism and obstinacy. They found that two of four variables with negativistic connotations correlated positively with anality. Juni and Semel (1982) reported a significant trend for anal characters to highlight, in a somewhat oppositional stance, the difference (or contrast) between self and authority figures.

[10] Volans (1976) demonstrated that psychiatric patients with clinical obsessive-compulsive symptoms require more evidence to make a decision during a probabalistic inference task than do phobic patients or normal controls. However, obsessional personalities and clinically disturbed obsessive-compulsives differ considerably in attitudes and behavior (Trijsburg & Duivenvoorden, 1987). There is dispute about the level of psychological disturbance in obsessional personalities (anal characters) (e.g., Kline, 1979; Perry & Cooper, 1989; Pollak, 1978), but a trend can be detected for anal attributes to be negatively correlated with indexes of psychological disturbance.

[11] The need to maintain control and to avoid dirty, messy situations was highlighted in a study by Juni (1984) in which he found that the Kline Ai3 Scale scores of college students correlated positively and significantly with the degree to which disgust was experienced in reaction to a variety of deviant and unconventional behaviors. Juni and LoCascio (1985) observed a borderline trend for anally oriented males (but not females) to prefer a form of psychotherapy (cognitive-behavioral) that is particularly orderly, logical, and systematic.

OVERVIEW OF THE ANALITY PARADIGM

Our judgment in 1977 was that substantial aspects of Freud's anal character formulation had received empirical support. Others (e.g., Kline, 1972, 1981; Pollak, 1978) who also reviewed the pertinent research literature largely concurred with our perspective. As we examine the accumulated findings since 1977 we are impressed with the following points:

1. Additional data have emerged that convincingly document the clustering of those traits and attitudes that compose the anal character concept.[12]

2. Although little new work has been done to test directly the anal character triad, some further support has emerged for associating negativism and obstinacy with an anal orientation (Fischer & Juni, 1982; Juni & Semel, 1982).

3. Meaningful extensions of the anal character paradigm have been made suggesting that anal attitudes may mediate such diverse variables as Type A behavior (Garamoni & Schwartz, 1986), humor preferences (Juni, 1982; O'Neill et al., 1992), selective perceptual and memory responses to stimuli with anal connotations (e.g., Vinck, 1979), defense mechanisms (e.g., Von der Lippe & Torgersen, 1984), attitudes toward authority (Juni & Semel, 1982), and racial bias (Fisher, 1978). Most of these studies are exploratory and require further support before they can be confidently assimilated.

In our earlier discussion of the nexus between the anal character and Type A concepts, we witnessed the relevance of Freud's formulation to a more current empirically based construct. It would be meaningful to explore how the anal character concept fits into the mosaic of modern personality research. As mentioned earlier, one of the more stable findings that has emerged from contemporary personality research relates to the so-called five-factor model (Digman, 1990; McCrae & John, 1992). We noted that repeated factor analytic studies

---

[12] As we noted in 1977, a mild degree of bedlam prevails in terms of the hodgepodge of techniques used to measure anality. We have described studies that have variously employed inkblots, anality questionnaires, measures of degree of awareness of the back of the body, the Psychasthenia scale of the MMPI, amount of concern with dirt themes in one's stream of spontaneous thought, and measures of each of the anal triad (orderliness, parsimony, obstinacy). Little or nothing has been done to ascertain how these techniques are correlated with each other. It is, indeed, surprising that despite such diversity and confusion, the research findings show a certain consistency and logic.

of multiple personality measures have come up with similar five-factor solutions. These five factors are frequently labeled as follows: (a) Extroversion; (b) Agreeableness; (c) Conscientiousness; (d) Emotional Stability; (e) Intellect or Openness (Johnson & Ostendorf, 1993). Digman (1990), after reviewing the pertinent literature in this area concluded: "At a minimum, research on the five-factor model has given us a useful set of broad dimensions that characterize individual differences. These dimensions can be measured with high reliability and impressive validity. Taken together, they provide a good answer to the question of personality *structure*" (p. 436). Although such enthusiasm for the five-factor model is widespread, there are some (e.g., Carson, 1989; Waller & Ben-Porath, 1987) who are less persuaded that it will provide a sufficiently rich paradigm for understanding the full complexity of personality phenomena.

In any case, we would like to focus on the resemblance of the anal character paradigm to the "big five" factor usually labeled as conscientiousness. A particularly well-documented description of this dimension is as follows (Johnson & Ostendorf, 1993):

> Factor III was defined by the following pure items: careful, fussy/tidy, hardworking, neat, punctual, scrupulous, thrifty, and well-organized. . . . The other terms describe an abstemious, exacting, orderly, prudent, restrained, temperate person, a person who avoids excesses and pays close attention to detail. (p. 573)

Many of these descriptive terms fit well with Freud's anal triad (orderliness, parsimony, obstinacy). Words like careful, tidy, neat, and well-organized certainly match the essence of what Freud meant by orderly. Further, terms like abstemious, prudent, and thrifty conform to the underlying sense of parsimony. There is a less satisfactory match with reference to obstinacy. Only a few other terms that have been cited (Johnson & Ostendorf, 1993), such as businesslike, deliberate, fussy, and persevering, hint of the resistive or stubborn qualities associated with the obstinacy dimension. Overall, the anal character and conscientiousness categories seem to overlap to a significant extent. They exhibit obvious cognate attributes.

In view of the considerable research that has focused on the conscientiousness factor, such overlap would appear to present an opportunity to expand what we know about the anal character. In scanning the literature pertaining to conscientiousness, the reader is immediately struck with observations that genetic influences make a 50% contribution to Conscientiousness scores (Digman, 1990). This is interesting in view of Freud's repeated assertions that anal dispositions have a genetic component. For example, he (Freud, 1908) refers to people being born "with a sexual constitution in which the erotogenicity of the anal zone is exceptionally strong" (p. 170). He may have speculatively anticipated the growing stream of new empirical data indicating that temperamental and personality parameters may be mediated to a surprising degree by genetic factors.

Another interesting theme that has emerged from the literature concerned with conscientiousness relates to the positive qualities associated with this dimension. There are studies that variously document positive correlations between conscientiousness and such variables as positive affects (Watson & Clark, 1992), absence of dysphoric symptoms (Costa, Fagan, Piedmont, Ponticas, & Wise, 1992), positive body image (Costa et al., 1992), low probability of developing sexual paraphilias (Fagan, Wise, Schmidt, Ponticas, Marshall, & Costa, 1991), ability to adjust well to school (Graziano & Ward, 1992), and willingness to invest energy in the psychotherapeutic process (Miller, 1991). There seem to be a number of adaptive advantages in being a conscientious person. Because the anal character is presumably high in conscientiousness, anal character traits may bestow protective adaptive qualities. As earlier noted, measures of anal character attributes generally tend to be negatively correlated with indexes of psychological disturbance (e.g., Perry & Cooper, 1989; Pollak, 1979).[13]

As Fischer and Juni (1982) note, the complex of attitudes and traits that Freud assigned to the anal character consists of qualities held in high regard by Western societies. The investment in being self-controlled, industrious, and persevering fits well with what it takes to be successful in such societies. It is a bit of a paradox that a character type Freud depicted as fixated at an immature level should emerge as an example of what it takes to be successful. A possible interpretation of this point is that the "normal" requirements of Western cultures are so irrational or extreme they favor individuals who have developed exaggerated (similarly irrational) compensatory systems for containing their "fixations" and immaturities. Another possibility is that Freud simply misinterpreted the maladaptive significance of being "fixated" at levels short of the presumed genital ideal. Perhaps so-called genital maturity is a fiction rarely achieved by anyone; and the majority of

---

[13] The major contradiction to this statement has come from a study by Kline (1979). He reasoned, "Since Freud likened fixation at psychosexual levels to the abandonment of troops at stages of a journey and since the possession of psychosexual personality traits reflects such fixation, it follows that, if the theory is correct, these personality traits should be related (though fixation) to neuroticism" (p. 393). In line with this perspective, he anticipated that persons who obtained elevated scores on various measures of anality and orality would also be high on neuroticism. He was able to demonstrate that pooled anal and oral measures were positively correlated with neuroticism; but individual measures of anality or orality were not.

persons are orals or anals. In terms of Freud's paradigm, anality may actually represent the highest level of maturity attained by the modal individual.

A similar issue arose in our discussions of the oral character. We observed that a number of positive qualities are associated with an oral orientation, and we documented that the deficiencies in sexual adaptation presumed on theoretical grounds to be linked with "oral fixation" were not empirically supported. The data pertinent to both the oral and anal character types do not fit well with Freud's hierarchial model of psychosexual maturity. The very concept of what is mature or immature is vague and often defined more in terms of cultural political values than scientific criteria. Fisher and Fisher (1993) have analyzed in some detail whether the basic repertoire of defense mechanisms and modes of adaptation can be reliably classified into superior and inferior. They concluded:

> We are not in a position to declare that one defense mechanism is, in any general sense, "better" than another. To begin with, modesty about generalizations is demanded by the current inadequacies in our technology for measuring defense strategies. Second, the existing data can be read as contradictory and inconsistent. Finally, because the power of any particular defense mechanism depends on so many situational variables (e.g., age, type of stressor, socioeconomic status), it is unrealistic to speak in terms of any inherent or general effectiveness. (p. 120)

The parallels existing between the anal character and conscientiousness categories stand in dramatic contrast to the conceptualizations underlying these categories. The constellation of attributes associated with the anal character is depicted in a language of conflict about anal impulses and wishes, defensive repression of such impulses, and subliminating reconstructions that simultaneously deny and permit concealed satisfaction of them. The explanatory framework for conscientiousness[14] is really not tied to a well-defined or validated etiologic model, and certainly there is no mention of anal

---

[14] We have not been able to find any solid or consistent reports in the "big five" research reports that would clarify the early socialization conditions that encourage or inhibit the development of conscientiousness.

Also, in view of the Garamoni and Schwartz (1986) description of the similarities between the anal character and Type A paradigms, we have examined the literature concerning early socialization practices that apparently encourage Type A personality traits. Presumably, one might find hints in the Type A literature that would generalize to the anal character. However, in scanning such work (e.g., MacEvoy, Lambert, Karlberg, Karlberg, Klackenberg-Larsson, & Klackenberg, 1988; Mathews, 1977; Steinberg, 1985), we have not detected any convincing consistencies.

impulses or specific classes of conflicts. Genetic factors, in fact, are given impressive weight.

Beyond Freud's theoretical formulations concerning the origins of anal traits, little is solidly known empirically about etiology. No studies have consistently pinpointed particular socialization patterns as causing an anal orientation. Freud's anal character formulation is attractive because it provides a theory of broad scope that permits apparently logical statements about the nature of personality, the role of personality in symptom formation, and the impact of early experiences on later development. In contrast, McAdams (1992) has noted that constructs from the five-factor model do not easily lend themselves to addressing such issues as core personality functioning beyond the level of traits. Also, they do not consider the contextual and conditional nature of experience; nor do they probe the process of organizing and integrating personality. Freud's anal character model lends itself, perhaps only too well, to such more fluid contemplations. The fundamental contrast between the anal character and conscientiousness categories is that one employs a language of body-based unconscious psychological tensions and conflicts, whereas the other avoids paradigms involving psychodynamic or unconscious influences.

Chapter 6

Oedipal Concatenations

THE BASIC THEORETICAL IDEAS

Freud's Oedipal theory is widely perceived as the skeleton of the psychoanalytic model. It has been examined, probed, praised, and criticized in a cascade of papers and books. As pointed out by Modell and Sacks (1985), however, the complexity of Freud's Oedipal formulations makes them difficult to evaluate. They note:

> Anyone who shoots at the Oedipus complex is shooting at a moving target since what it subsumes, explicitly and implicitly, has steadily changed over the last 70 or 80 years. To make matters more confusing, some of these changes have been responses to rebellions and critiques of the Oedipus complex. Originally Oedipus 'simplex' consisted of the little boy's wishes for incest and murder, wishes that must be repressed, transformed, or in Freud's image, undergo dissolution. As the theory developed, it included castration anxiety, guilt, formation of the superego, aspects of primal-scene fantasies, and many symptomatic and characterological consequences of the failure of the Oedipus complex to dissolve. (p. 203)

The Oedipal triangle represented, for Freud, a crucial configuration packed with consequences for every aspect of the child's development. He theorized that in all families tensions evolve around issues of love and competition. The essence of the Oedipal theme is that the child becomes sexually attracted to the parent of the opposite sex and antagonistically jealous of the parent of the same sex. Around the age of 4 or 5, the child presumably enters into the Oedipal phase when he or she desires sexual contact with the opposite-sex parent and perceives the same-sex parent as a competitor or opponent. Freud actually proposed quite different versions of his theory to describe how males and females cope with the Oedipal crisis.

The Male Oedipal Phase

According to Freud's outline, the little boy initially attaches most closely to his mother and directs most of his affection toward her. She is the one most nurturantly intimate with him, and in the course of caring for his body, she stimulates his erogenous zones. By the age of 4 or 5 (phallic stage), his fantasies about her contain sexual themes, and he conjures up images of using his penis to have intercourse with her. He is gripped by his desire to possess her. Indeed, says Freud, he yearns for an exclusive monopoly, which calls for ejecting or destroying father. This creates a potential for intense rivalrous encounters. In most instances, however, serious disruptions are avoided as certain countervailing forces come into play. One of the major balancing forces presumably derives from the male child's concern that the rivalry for mother will galvanize father into castrating him. Other factors also are said to contribute to the boy's castration anxiety:

1. The discovery that girls lack a penis and the consequent conclusion that if they can lose their penis, the same thing could happen to him.
2. The experience of receiving direct or indirect castration messages from his parents when they find him masturbating.
3. The perception that father is angry about his son's rivalry and probably wants revenge.
4. Having other types of experiences that dramatize the possibility of losing parts of one's body.

Illustratively, the loss of the breast when weaning occurs may, because of the child's state of fusion with mother, be perceived as a loss involving his own body. The expulsion of feces may also be interpreted as a phenomenon involving loss of body substance. Freud's Oedipal formulation portrayed the boy's buildup of castration anxiety as a prime motivator for giving up sexual aims toward mother. This anxiety presumably results in reorienting the boy so that he identifies with (rather than opposes) father and rechannels his sexual energies toward other nonmother feminine figures.

In this reorienting process, said Freud, the boy fashions the foundation for his superego (conscience). As the boy repudiates his "bad" impulses toward mother and identifies with his father's prohibitions, he introjects father's rules and values. The Oedipal struggle is thus apparently resolved, and the boy then enters into a latency period during which sexual fantasies and action are tightly repressed. Only at puberty do sexual impulses regain prominence and eventuate in adult heterosexual relationships. The nature of these relationships is depicted by Freud as dependent on how the original Oedipal conflict was resolved. Defects in the mode of resolution can presumably result in the individual being chronically motivated to find female partners closely resembling his mother or starkly different from her. He could also emerge with the anxious sense that he ought not to have sexual transactions with any woman. The effectiveness of the Oedipal resolution was viewed as playing a key role in the likelihood of the individual later developing significant psychopathology.

The Female Oedipal Phase

In Freud's account of the Oedipal paradigm as it applies to the female, she too is depicted as initially adopting mother as her major love object. When she discovers that males have a penis, she concludes that she lost hers, that she was somehow castrated, and that her body now wears a badge of inferiority. She is invaded by feelings of deficiency and blames her lack of a penis on her mother. This disappointment in mother is said to be reinforced by other earlier frustrations (e.g., mother diverting too much of her attention to others or being punitive about masturbation) the child experienced in her relationship with her. The disappointment is said to motivate her to pull away from mother and to shift her love to father. Presumably, up to this point, her clitoris was her primary source (through masturbation) of sexual pleasure; but when she discovers she has an "inferior organ" she shifts her interest away from the phallic clitoris and focuses instead on the more passive receptive vagina. At the same time, she evolves fantasies that her new love object, father, will impregnate her via the vagina and she will be able to produce a child for him. Freud theorized that the production of a child in this context had a reparative significance, the acquisition of a penis equivalent. This is the so-called penis-baby equation. For the girl to have a child by father is to regain a representation of her lost penis. A passive feminine orientation is said to evolve that places enhanced value on the vagina. The girl is portrayed as having renounced mother and turned, in fantasy, to father for a sexual partnership that will eventuate in a compensatory baby.

Freud was less articulate in the case of the female than the male in describing how the Oedipal rivalry would get resolved. He took the position that she settles her Oedipal difficulties in a more gradual and less decisive fashion than does the male. Because she introjects parental prohibitions against her Oedipal fantasies less sharply, she is pictured as developing a less definite, less stringent superego. An underlying assumption is that because she already feels castrated, she lacks the urgent motivation for resolving the Oedipal dilemma that typifies the male, who assumes he will be immediately castrated if he does not alter his ways. Freud (1924) suggested that the "setting up of a superego" and the "breaking off of the infantile genital organization" in the girl is more the "result of upbringing and of intimidation from outside which threatens her with loss of love" (p. 178). The essence of the female's Oedipal solution is equating self with mother's sexual potential and perceiving men as providing her with a means of compensation for her lack of a penis by impregnating her and enabling her to fashion a baby that is symbolically equivalent to a penis.

Freud indicated that following the Oedipal period, the girl, like the boy, moves into a latency phase where there is a generalized repression of sexual intentions. He noted that at puberty a revival of sexual aims occurs, but the expression of these aims is influenced by the original character of the Oedipal experiences. He underscored the persistent effects of disappointment about penis loss on the female's sexuality; and elaborated how "penis envy" may enter into multiple levels of female behavior.[1]

PRE-1977 FINDINGS—THE DISTINCTION BETWEEN SAME- AND OPPOSITE-SEX PARENTS

In our (Fisher & Greenberg, 1985) original scrutiny of the pre-1977 empirical literature pertinent to Freud's Oedipal concepts, we explored the soundness of 12 different hypotheses derived from these concepts. The hypotheses concerned a range of issues, some of central and others of more peripheral importance. A centrally significant issue related to the core question whether persons adopt differential attitudes toward same- and opposite-sex parents that fit with the formulations of Oedipal love and rivalry. For example, does the modal individual feel relatively positive toward the opposite-sex parent and negative toward the same-sex parent? A number of clever studies had been published that were affirmative. Let us, by way of illustration, briefly scan several.

Friedman (1952) asked children (ranging in age from 5 to 16) to complete two "Oedipal fables" that involved engaging in a pleasurable activity alone with a parent and then meeting the other parent. He also asked each child to compose stories about two pictures, one depicting a child and a "father-surrogate" and the other a child and a "mother-surrogate." He predicted, and the data affirmed, that children would

---

[1] Freud made it clear that the usual basic description of the Oedipal process is an oversimplification: "For one gets the impression that the simple Oedipus complex is by no means its commonest form, but rather represents a simplification or schematization . . . that is to say, a boy has not merely an ambivalent attitude toward his father and an affectionate object-choice toward his mother, but at the same time he also behaves like a girl and displays an affectionate feminine attitude to his father, and a corresponding jealousy and hostility toward his mother" (p. 33).

give more negative endings to the "Oedipal fables" in which they were initially alone with the opposite-sex parent but subsequently met the same-sex parent. He also successfully predicted that boys would produce a significantly greater proportion of conflict themes than girls when the stimulus was a father-figure and girls would produce a greater proportion of conflict themes than boys when the stimulus was a mother-figure. Results of other measures administered by Friedman, intended to tap into more conscious levels of response, did not conform to theoretical expectations. Overall, he considered his findings demonstrated the existence of a core Oedipal pattern—more positive feelings toward the opposite-sex parent than toward the same-sex parent (in both boys and girls).

Imber (1969) too targeted predicted consequences of the Oedipally derived differentiation of attitudes toward same-sex versus opposite-sex parents. He measured intensity of Oedipal conflict in male college students by evaluating their responses to specific pictures of the Blacky Test (Blum, 1949). For example, one picture portrayed a dog named Blacky in rivalry with his father for mother. During one phase of the study, subjects high and low in Oedipal anxiety learned to distinguish "benevolent" from "threatening" words by being mildly shocked each time they failed to correctly classify words shown to them. Control words were also introduced. When an adequate discriminatory level had been attained, the subjects were exposed to the word "mother" or "father" and asked to indicate whether it was threatening or benevolent. As predicted, men with high Oedipal anxiety had more difficulty in responding to the word father than did those with low anxiety. However, there was no detectable difference for the word mother. In another aspect of this study, the high and low Oedipal anxiety subjects learned the same discrimination procedure (with respect to the words mother and father), except that they were given verbal rather than shock feedback. Further, their heart rates were recorded while they responded. High Oedipal anxiety individuals were observed to exceed the lows significantly for heart-rate variability when reacting to the word mother, but not with reference to father. There were no differences between the highs and lows in their reactions to control words. Overall, the findings were roughly congruent with the Oedipal paradigm.

A third example is a study by Schill (1966), who exposed male and female college students to a picture, from Blum's (1949) Blacky Test, that depicts a dog with a knife posed over its tail as if it is about to be cut off. The subjects were asked to imagine which members of the dog's family were responsible for this threat. As expected on the basis of Oedipal theory, males were significantly likely to designate father as the "castrating" agent, whereas the females blamed mother. Also in agreement with Oedipal theory, a considerable literature has accumulated documenting the prominence of castration anxiety in males (Blum, 1949; Gottschalk, Gleser, & Springer, 1963; Lewis, 1969; Schneider, 1960).

The three studies just described represent among the best of the pre-1977 confirmatory evidence for the selective attitudes toward same- and opposite-sex parents posited by Freud's Oedipal formulation. There were also several other more peripherally supportive studies (Hall, 1963; Miller, 1969; Rabin, 1958). We concluded in 1977 that such findings added to the credibility of a major aspect of the Oedipal formulation.

POST-1977 FINDINGS—THE DISTINCTION BETWEEN SAME- AND OPPOSITE-SEX PARENTS

Since 1977, researchers have resorted to multiple strategies in the process of testing various predicted consequences of the presumed differential Oedipally inspired attitudes toward same- versus opposite-sex parents. Watson and Getz (1990) rather boldly set out to measure the frequency of certain behaviors with Oedipal implications displayed by children toward their parents. They recruited male and female children from four age levels (ages 3, 4, 5, 6 years); and asked each of the children's parents to record systematically, over a 7-day period, all instances in which their children acted "aggressively" or "affectionately" toward them. The recorded incidents were classified as Oedipal if they involved the child showing affection to the opposite-sex parent or aggression toward the same-sex parent. Ratios of Oedipal to non-Oedipal behaviors were computed in relation to each mother and father.

Oedipal attitudes were further appraised by asking each child (in a laboratory setting) to use a "doll family" to complete a series of stories with Oedipal connotations (e.g., preference for being with one parent versus another). The child's story completions were scored as Oedipal whenever they indicated a positive preference for the opposite-sex parent or aggression toward the same-sex parent. There proved to be significant positive correlations (across age levels) between the Oedipal intensities of the story completion scores and the frequencies of Oedipally oriented behaviors of the children as observed by their parents.

Analysis of the observed behaviors of the children toward their parents indicated a clear predominance of the Oedipal over non-Oedipal categories. It had been specifically predicted, on the basis of Freud's Oedipal formulation, that the predominance of Oedipal behaviors would peak at age 4 and show a decline at age 6. The data did significantly indicate a peak at age 4 (as did the story completion scores), but the decline began at age 5 rather than 6. The peak at age 4 does interestingly parallel Freud's assumptions; but on the other hand, his timing of Oedipal conflict changes over the 4 to 6 age sequence was not precise enough to attach real significance to the decline in Oedipal predominance at age 5 rather than 6. What is of special pertinence from our perspective is the Watson and Getz conclusion:

> For the parent scores, it should be noted that the mothers rated their sons somewhat higher in affection and lower in aggression than they did their daughters (especially at age 4), and the fathers rated their daughters higher in affection and lower in aggression than they did their sons (especially at age 4). Thus, the reported Oedipal behaviors coincide with the common view of Oedipal relations between mothers and sons and fathers and daughters. . . . (p. 502)

Watson and Getz set as one of the objectives of their study to determine whether "social-cognitive" changes in children parallel their shifts in Oedipal attitudes that might provide a "non-Freudian" alternative explanation of such shifts. They theorized Oedipal behaviors may "arise primarily from children's confused understanding of role relations. The child may lack the role concepts necessary to disengage the roles of father, husband, and male and, likewise, the roles of mother, wife, and female" (p. 488). Presumably, such confusion could instigate the role confusions (e.g., Is the child's parent also a potential sex partner?) typifying Oedipal conflicts. To get at such a possibility, various measures were administered that tapped into cognitive capabilities in understanding social roles, especially as a function of age and power status. Watson and Getz concluded that the data "suggest that social-cognitive development may contribute to the waxing and waning of Oedipal behaviors" (p. 503). They acknowledged, however, that Freud's frame of reference could just as well explain the pattern of their findings.

The Watson and Getz findings supported Freud's notion of an early developmental phase in which Oedipal issues and conflicts peak. Two other studies appear to document such developmental specificity. Feiner (1988) appraised male and female children in the age range of roughly 2 to 6 years. One aspect of his procedure involved rating their overt levels of anxiety while they responded to a neutral task and also when responding to questions that raised issues about their feelings of body vulnerability. Scores were computed that compared amount of anxiety in the body-threatening versus neutral contexts. Feiner summarized the results that emerged as follows:

> When the results were broken down by age in years, the findings were strikingly consistent with Freudian psychosexual theory. According to this theory, the phase of development referred to as the phallic stage, is

entered around the 3rd year, and extends to around the 5th year. During this period, anxiety that one's body will be hurt or damaged is at its height. Analysis of the data indicated that, as predicted, children experienced more anxiety about body damage between the ages of 3 and 5 than at other ages. (p. 78)

In a similar vein, Berg and Berg (1983) compared male adults who had as children experienced surgery for hypospadias (genital defects) during the Oedipal phase (between ages 3 and 6) with control males who had been appendectomized as children at the same hospital for similar durations. The experimental and control subjects did not differ with respect to socioeconomic status, somatic and mental health of their parents, sibling conditions, and a number of other variables. It was hypothesized that the experience of genital surgery during the vulnerable Oedipal period would be so traumatic that it would seriously interfere with normal resolution of Oedipal conflicts with father and would therefore in the long run result in "higher anxiety level (in particular castration anxiety), more depression, and lower self-esteem than a normal male. He would also be expected to be more passive and submissive, and to have a higher level of unexpressed hostility" (p. 144). Rorschach protocols were obtained from the subjects and analyzed by means of quantitative scores for the variables (e.g., castration anxiety, self-esteem) targeted in the hypothesis. The data proved to be largely congruent with this hypothesis.

The two studies just cited (Berg & Berg, 1983; Feiner, 1988) add weight to the notion of a developmentally critical Oedipal phase. Most of the weight actually comes from the Feiner data, which are derived from a more convincing design than are the Berg and Berg results. The Berg and Berg design, after all, involves some shaky assumptions, such as, that the disturbance in the males who had received surgery for a genital defect was primarily due to the impact of that surgery within a given time frame rather than to the long-term effects of being aware that their genitals were somehow deviant.[2]

---

[2] Apropos of castration anxiety and fantasies about body mutilation, it is interesting that Graber (1981) discovered some interesting trends in his cross-cultural investigation of factors that determine whether specific cultures impose genital mutilation. Actually, Freud speculated that circumcision was a symbolic substitute for castration and represented a form of submission to "father's will." Graber hypothesized, on the basis of various theories voiced in the literature, that circumcision represents a defense mechanism whereby a man "projects his unconscious hostility toward his own father onto his son, and thereby symbolically castrates (mutilates the genitals of) his son in self-defense" (p. 420). In other words, mutilating customs are, at one level, a form of defense against the anxieties linked to Oedipal conflict. Graber analyzed the occurrence of genital mutilation in 250 cultures and concluded that two variables significantly distinguished the mutilating from nonmutilating instances. The mutilating

The mediating effects of presumably Oedipally inspired differential attitudes toward same- and opposite-sex parents were also central to an investigation by Gill (1986). It was anticipated that individuals who had experienced the loss of a parent would, in terms of the Oedipal paradigm, feel heightened guilt about the death of the same-sex parent (rival) but be inclined to idealize the death of opposite-sex parent (and also subsequent lovers or spouses), while showing aversion to the living same-sex one. To test this idea, questionnaires were administered to male and female patients just applying to an outpatient psychotherapy clinic. The questionnaires inquired concerning problems and difficulties, early childhood experiences, and current married life. Only those patients were included in the study who were between 24 and 35 years old, had lost a parent aged 55 or less, and were between 5 and 18 when the parent died. Their questionnaire responses were blindly analyzed by two judges who sorted them into those in which the reaction to the parental death conformed to the differential pattern expected as a function of whether the same-sex or opposite-sex parents were involved and those in which the reaction did not conform.

The judges' sortings significantly supported the predictions. Those who lost a same-sex parent were noted to be especially negatively affected, with a "loss of capacity to function adequately at work, and in their sex-linked roles" (p. 25). This study has certain methodological problems related to the ambiguity of how the judges were able to utilize the complex questionnaire information, but in combination with the Watson and Getz (1990) findings, it presents us with evidence that Freud's distinction concerning the child's relationship to same- versus opposite-sex parent has demonstrable power.[3]

---

cultures were more likely to be characterized by patrilocality (normal residence near the male patrilineal kinsmen of the husband) and the existence of a rather high level of political integration. Graber interpreted such data to mean that genital mutilation is more probable in cultures where males are in close proximity (and therefore in greater conflict) with each other. He notes: "Patrilocality appears to exacerbate hostile feelings of adult sons toward their fathers. One outlet for such hostility, group fission (breaking away or distancing oneself) is available to members of societies which have not developed politically . . . with the development of the state, however, environmental constraints probably significantly restrict such freedom of movement" (p. 425).

[3] Juni, Rahamin, and Brannon (1984) reported an effort to clarify the relationships between "Oedipal fixation" and the sex role attributes of both self and one's parents. Oedipal fixation was measured by asking male and female college students to respond to the Rorschach blots. These responses were then scored (by means of an objective system) for the presence of phallic images. It was assumed that the greater the number of such phallic images the greater was the "magnitude of repressed Oedipal conflict" (p. 93). Sex role was measured by means of the Bem (1981) Sex Role Inventory. Subjects

A few post-1977 studies have used the concept of castration anxiety[4] as a wedge for exploring the consequences of differential Oedipal attitudes toward parental figures. As earlier described, Freud attributed to castration anxiety a major role in the male child's resolution of his Oedipal dilemma by moving from opposition to father to identifying with him. Presumably, castration anxiety was a major source of the energy for this resolution process. Predictions about conditions that will intensify or minimize castration anxiety have been used to probe the Oedipal model.

Two studies have examined the presumed impact on levels of castration anxiety in males reared in father-absent versus father-present families. Shill (1981b) hypothesized that males who grew up without a father present during the early (Oedipal) years would be unable to resolve the Oedipal dilemma satisfactorily and, therefore, would be typified by elevated castration anxiety. Male college students were studied who had either lost father before the ages of 2 to 6 years or who had not. Degree of castration anxiety was measured by scoring the contents of stories elicited by Thematic Apperception Test pictures. The father-absent males were found to have significantly higher castration scores than the father-present males. Shill concluded: "The significantly greater castration anxiety of the father-absent subjects on the TAT suggests the importance of the father in enabling his son to master such anxiety and clearly illustrates one of the central phenomena described by psychoanalysis relating to the Oedipus Complex" (p. 143). No relationship was found in the father-present group

---

filled out the inventory items in terms of their own attributes and also as they perceived these items to apply to each of their parents. Degree of Oedipal fixation in the male sample was found to be positively and significantly correlated with the perceived femininity of mother, but not with the perceived masculinity of father. In the female sample, the Oedipal fixation score was positively and significantly correlated with the masculinity of father and the perceived femininity of mother. Since Juni et al. had originally hypothesized that "Oedipal fixation" derived from "internalization of characteristics of the same-sex parent coupled with an effort to contrast oneself from the opposite-sex parent" (p. 89), the data could be viewed as partially confirmatory in the case of the male sample and fully confirmatory with respect to the female sample.

However, we find the study uninterpretable because it is not at all clear what the term "Oedipal fixation" means and it is even less clear how the number of "phallic" responses elicited by inkblots can be translated into the concept of "Oedipal fixation." There is simply no empirical basis for asserting an association between such phallic imagery and the state of one's Oedipal attitudes.

[4] Freud's thoughts about castration anxiety were outlined in two major sources: *Three Essays on the Theory of Sexuality* (Freud, 1905) and *Inhibitions, Symptoms, and Anxiety* (Freud, 1926).

between castration scores and the subjects' ratings of how satisfactory they recalled their interactions with father to have been.[5]

Trachtman (1978) examined the same issue by comparing early-latency-aged boys whose fathers had been absent from the home during the "Oedipal phase of development" with a sample of father-present boys. A semistructured interview was conducted with the boys and their mothers. Among other variables, castration anxiety and psychological pathology were rated. Contrary to theoretical expectations, the father-present boys were judged to have significantly more castration anxiety than the father-absent boys. No differences were detected in overall psychological pathology. The findings were considered to oppose the idea that father absence during the Oedipal developmental phase has negative consequences for the boy. Obviously, this contradicts the results of the Shill (1981b) study just described. The complete reversal of the effects in the two studies is not encouraging with respect to the impact of father absence on Oedipally triggered anxiety.

The influence of presumed Oedipally derived attitudes toward one's parents has also been looked at in terms of courtship behavior and choice of mate. Winch demonstrated in early papers (e.g., 1946, 1950, 1951) that the greater the male's love attachment to his mother, the less motivated he was to engage in active courtship of women. He did not, however, show an analogous pattern with respect to a woman's intensity of liking for her father and her degree of heterosexual activity.

Special research interest has focused on the Oedipally derived proposition that a man is likely to marry someone like his mother and that a woman is inclined to marry someone resembling her father. Pre-1977 papers (Commins, 1932; Kirkpatrick, 1937; Mangus, 1936; Schiller, 1932; Strauss, 1946) that tackled this issue did not come up with consistent findings. There were, for example, several inconclusive attempts to examine the question whether first (older) male siblings (when mother would be relatively young) would choose younger wives than would subsequent siblings.

---

[5] Shill (1981a) used the Blacky Test (Blum, 1949) to explore in this same sample the idea that father-absent males would have had unusually negative relations with their mothers and, therefore, were unconsciously inclined to perceive them, even more than fathers, as castration threats. He speculated: "In the absence of a father in the house, the son would experience more of these frustrations in relation to the mother; he would experience her as the castrator more frequently than father-present sons" (p. 264). The data significantly supported Shill's hypothesis. However, the data in the other Shill's (1981b) paper based on the TAT, cause confusion in the effort to conceptualize and integrate the two sets of findings.

Post-1977, Jedlicka (1980, 1984) explored the matter of spouse-parent similarity in two rather novel designs. In his 1980 paper, he described a project that tested the hypothesis that men with inter-ethnically mixed parents are more inclined to marry into their mothers' ethnic groups, whereas women are more likely to marry into their fathers' ethnic groups. Marriage records were scanned of persons in Hawaii who were of ethnically mixed parentage. Their choices with respect to the ethnicity of their spouses were tabulated and the results significantly supported the hypothesis: "Males marry into mothers' and females into fathers' ethnic groups" (p. 298). Jedlicka concluded: "The pattern is unambiguous and it appears congruent with the psychoanalytic theory of mate selection" (p. 298). Only individuals who had been married twice were included in this sample (to test the consistency of the effect), and therefore, it is possible that the results derive in some way from biased sampling.

However, in a second sample of Hawaiian individuals whose parents were of mixed nativity and who had married only for the first time, it was once again shown (Jedlicka, 1984) at a significant level that "mate selection of sons is more influenced by mothers than is mate selection of daughters, and mate selection of daughters is more influenced by fathers than is mate selection of sons" (p. 68). That is, each sex was particularly likely to choose a spouse of the same ethnic category as their parent of the opposite sex.

Aron (1974) took a different approach to the mate selection issue. Couples were approached who were waiting in line at a marriage license bureau (Toronto) and asked to fill out individual questionnaires concerning several dimensions (e.g., dominance, trust) of their relationship with their future spouse and also how these same dimensions applied to their parents. It was hypothesized that the men would depict their relationship with the future spouse as similar to their style of relating to mother and that the women would see their mode of relating to father as the prototype for their style of interaction with the future spouse. The results supported the hypothesis at a borderline level for the men, but the data for the women were consistently (significantly) opposite to prediction. Actually, what the results indicated was that both the men and women perceived their relationships with their future spouses as most similar to their recall of how they related to mother. It was concluded, "Psychoanalytic theory does not easily explain the present results . . ." (p. 23).

Georgaklis (1987) was impressed with an earlier investigation by Terman (1938) that found that the greater the reported early attachment of women to their fathers the greater was their sexual passion (frequency of intercourse) with their husbands. Georgaklis obtained information pertinent to such matters (by means of questionnaires) from a sample of college women who were "romantically involved." Father's rated physical attractiveness correlated positively and significantly with the "passion" and "commitment" of the current romantic involvement. Also, father's rated power before the women were 10 years old correlated positively and significantly with current passion scores. However, there were also significant positive correlations between several ratings of mother and ratings of current romantic involvements. Georgaklis decided: "It is possible that there is a differential influence of mothers and fathers on daughters' ability to love and the fathers' influence has a subconsciously romantic nature reflected by passion and commitment scores" (p. 78).

The findings concerning choice of spouse or romantic partner are obviously not completely supportive of Oedipal theory. However, the trend is in a positive direction. A review of earlier research efforts in this area indicates that balancing the multiple complex variables has presented unusually difficult challenges. Jedlicka (1980, 1984) showed considerable ingenuity in using the ethnicity of one's chosen spouse as a measure of spouse similarity to one's ethnically variable parents. His approach is objective and yet involves a variable of ego-involving significance in making a choice of spouse. We are inclined to give special weight to his observations.

PRE-1977 FINDINGS—SEXUAL CONSEQUENCES

A second major axis running through the Oedipal constructs relates to sexuality. Freud was convinced that the intensity of Oedipal conflicts and the ways in which they are resolved determine, in the main, whether individuals can attain sexually mature modes. He attributed most sexual difficulties and deviations to Oedipal problems.

In our review of the pre-1977 literature dealing with the link between Oedipal difficulties and disturbances in sexual functioning, we concluded that the available information was fragmentary and tangential. Consider the following. An interesting study by Grayson (1967) indicated that loss of father by girls during the early Oedipal phase (which would presumably aggravate Oedipal conflicts) was particularly likely to be associated with heightened "psychosexual conflict" (as defined by projective test scores). Winch (1950) demonstrated that the greater a male's "love" attachment to his mother, the less active he is in his heterosexual behavior. Stephens (1962) found that indexes (derived from ratings of multiple cultures) indicative of the son's unusual closeness to mother (which would presumably create Oedipal tensions) were predictive of intensified sexual anxiety and of cultural customs reflecting special concerns about possible incestuous sexual encounters.

More negatively, a number of studies using well-standardized measures failed to detect higher levels of psychopathology in women or men with sexual difficulties than in normal controls. Fisher (1973) provides detailed documentation of this point, which contradicts what we would expect within the context of Freud's Oedipal formulation. This theory conceptualizes sexual difficulties as arising from serious Oedipal problems and therefore as indicating immaturity and psychological disturbance. If sexual disturbance mirrors Oedipally inspired psychopathology, individuals who have major (nonorganic) sexual problems (e.g., inability to attain orgasm) should evidence higher levels of psychopathology.

In short, the pre-1977 data pool did not offer much in the way of either affirming or negating the theoretically expected tie between Oedipal conflict and psychologically based sexual dysfunction.

POST-1977 FINDINGS—SEXUAL CONSEQUENCES

Since 1977, we have become aware of new and previously overlooked sources of information bearing on the issue at hand.

First, a considerable literature consistently documents troubling tension between parents and children with respect to sexuality. Fisher (1989) has summarized this literature in detail. The parent-child tension about sexuality is evident even in early childhood. Parents are reluctant to give their children sexual information; deprive them of an adequate vocabulary for talking about sexual events or labeling sexual body parts; typically take a negative inhibitory stance toward the child masturbating or being in any way sexually expressive and conceal their own sexual interests and interactions. Such irrational sexual tensions between the two generations would be anticipated from Oedipal theory. If it were true, as enunciated by Freud, that children unconsciously entertain guilt-provoking sexual fantasies about their parents and the parents, in turn, have such fantasies about their parents, it then follows that sexual themes, in a family context, would provoke anxiety and discomfort on all sides. Such observations are only in a general sense supportive of Oedipal theory. Other non-Oedipal ways of explaining intrafamily sexual disturbance are fairly easy to conjure up. For example, it could result from the antisexual attitudes of the major religious powers. However, it is certainly noteworthy that the surprisingly intense sexual discomforts typifying parent-child relationships flow logically from the Oedipal schema.

A distinctive aspect of Oedipal theory is that it traces many of the adult's sexual conflicts and difficulties back to events that occurred in early childhood. In other words, it asserts that adult sexual maladjustment is rooted in past family interactions, particularly those occurring during the Oedipal phase (around the age of 4). We have located several longitudinal studies that seem to support the importance of childhood experiences as an anlage for adult sexual disturbance. The three major investigations that we will discuss were carried out respectively by Kagan and Moss (1962), Block (1971), and Vaillant (1977).

The Kagan and Moss (1962) enterprise involved following 44 boys (living in Ohio) from birth through age 14. Thirty-six were evaluated further when they were approximately 24 years of age. Many aspects of their behavior and personality were measured by means of ratings, questionnaires, projective tests, and physiological recordings. Of special pertinence to our inquiry is that the researchers evaluated several parameters of sexual behavior including the subjects' reluctance to initiate heterosexual relationships during late adolescence and early adulthood and degree of inhibition shown in erotic behavior (e.g., coitus, petting). Measures of "sex anxiety" and "repression of sexual ideas" were also obtained. Analysis of the complex set of data indicated that early childhood signs of passivity and fear of body damage were significantly predictive of later sexual difficulties. Also, certain attitudes on mother's part (e.g., being overprotective) predicted her son's later inhibition in heterosexual involvement. Kagan and Moss concluded:

> The boys who showed evidence of intense physical harm anxiety during the preschool years were, as adults, anxious about sexuality, uninvolved in traditional masculine activities. . . . Anxiety over bodily harm in the 5-year-old boy is prognostic both of future withdrawal from competitive activities with other males and with inhibition of heterosexual behavior; it is associated with failure to adopt the traditional masculine ego ideal in adolescence and adulthood. (pp. 191–192)

The Block (1971) longitudinal effort appraised 87 men (living in California) who had been tested, observed, and followed since childhood. A good deal of information was gathered describing sexually relevant behaviors (e.g., interest in the opposite sex, investment in sex-typed activities, dating behavior, age of marriage). Such information permitted construction of a picture of how comfortably the area of sexuality had been managed for each subject. Certain clusters (defined by Q-factor analysis) of the men were found to be sexually maladjusted and other clusters were typified by good sexual adjustment. The maturity of sexual behavior proved to be linked with measures of the nature of early relationships between the children and their parents. Sexually inhibited men were likely to have had mothers who were authoritarian and limited their sons from doing things independently. Block depicts one type of sexually inhibiting mother as follows: "tense, rigid,

gloomy, neurotically fatigued, sexually inhibited" (p. 167). The sexually inhibiting fathers were depicted as "energyless, diffident, withdrawn" (p. 167).

Those males who grew up to be sexually comfortable and active
were described as having had parents who, early on, were portrayed in
such terms as "a strong, outgoing, accomplished father teamed with a
loving mother who enjoyed mothering and was not personally neurotic
or conflict-creating in her child" (p. 149).

Finally, Vaillant (1977) analyzed a huge corpus of interview, test,
and questionnaire data that had accumulated over a 30-year period
concerning 95 men who were first evaluated when they were undergraduates at Harvard. The sexual behavior of the men had been probed
in terms of early contacts with girls and later interactions with wives,
self-reports about satisfaction secured from sexual action, and interview statements about sexual difficulties. A particularly pertinent
finding was that men whose mothers had, early on, been domineering
had the greatest difficulties in maintaining satisfying heterosexual relationships. A number of other correlates between parents' attitudes
and the sexual behaviors of their offspring were also reported.[6]

All three of the longitudinal studies just cited confirm that individuals' early experiences with their parents are predictive of important aspects of their sexual behavior as adults. Some of the observed
patterns could easily accommodate to the Oedipal paradigm. For example, reports of correlations between mother's dominance and son's
sexual difficulties might mirror the fact that an overpowering mother
could, both because of her power role and her overcloseness, interfere
with her son identifying with father (who presumably would appear to
be relatively ineffectual) and thereby block the resolution of the Oedipal dilemma as Freud pictured it. On the more negative side with respect to the Oedipus-sexual-adaptation issue, the majority of studies in
the literature concerned with the determinants of orgasm consistency
in women are not congruent with Freud's notion of how women can
most adaptively resolve their Oedipal conflicts. Freud, in essence, theorized that the average normal woman copes optimally with her Oedipal problems by adopting a passive role associated with the stereotype
of conventional femininity. Presumably, the resolution process involves
giving up the active clitoral (phallic) site as a preferred area for sexual
stimulation and accepting the passivity implicit in the vagina becoming the major sexual organ indicative of a readiness to be penetrated.
However, the major tenor of the empirical research concerned with

---

[6] Arndt and Ladd (1981) reported that an index of Oedipal conflict (based on sibling
incest aversion) was positively correlated in both sexes with generalized feelings of
sexual guilt.

orgasm consistency in women contradicts this theoretical position (Fisher, 1973, 1989; Kay-Reczek, 1977; Newcomb, 1984; Paxton, 1978). In fact, the data demonstrate that orgasm consistency is positively correlated with the degree to which a woman is active, assertive, goal-oriented, persistent, and unwilling to be a passive recipient. There is also evidence (Fisher, 1989) that sexual difficulties in men are associated with passive personality traits.

Freud's idea that a shift from clitoral to vaginal erotogenicity is necessary for a woman if she is to attain a mature level of sexuality has not held up well to empirical testing. Even previous to 1977, Fisher (1973) had shown not only that women who prefer clitoral stimulation are not more maladjusted than those preferring vaginal stimulation, but that, in fact, the vaginally oriented tended to exhibit higher levels of anxiety and to adopt defense modes emphasizing the muting and shutting out of stimuli. A majority of women indicate that they require a considerable amount of direct clitoral stimulation to attain orgasm. A predominance of vaginal sensitivity does not, contrary to Freud, characterize the average woman. The shutting-out style of the vaginally oriented was originally demonstrated by Fisher (1973) in a sample of white women. This work, however, has since been repeated with a black sample (Fisher, 1980) and equivalent results emerged. In summarizing the existing data pertinent to the clitoral-vaginal distinction, Fisher (1989) stated:

> One must underscore again that Freud's original idea that vaginal preference betokens greater maturity or superior personality development remains completely unsubstantiated. If anything, the vaginally oriented seem to operate under a heavier negative load. (p. 74)

THE OEDIPUS AND HOMOSEXUALITY

Continuing our analysis of Freud's ideas about the link between Oedipal variables and sexual behavior, we will appraise his assertion that Oedipal conflicts are central to the etiology of homosexuality. However, he also attributed considerable significance to "constitutional" factors. He presumed that each sex has anatomic characteristics of the other (e.g., the clitoris represents a miniature penis) and that bisexual tendencies are reflected in males and females at a psychological level. He repeatedly referred to the strength of "bisexual dispositions," presumably of innate origin, as mediating whether persons turn to homosexuality. Surprisingly, despite his psychodynamic formulations concerning homosexuality, he would have been sympathetic to those who now espouse biological explanations of homosexual phenomena and who, incidentally, usually see themselves as opposed to Freud's views.

Male Homosexuality

At the psychodynamic level, Freud assumed that male homosexuals were individuals who could not cope with the Oedipal intricacies. He (Freud, 1910, 1923, 1924) proposed that their difficulties stemmed from the formation of an overly strong "erotic attachment" to mother, which was "favored by too much love from the mother herself" and reinforced by the "retirement or absence of the father during the childhood period." This meant they had to cope with intensified "feminine influence." Presumably the boy's Oedipal conflict with father would be heightened by this state of affairs; and, in turn, this would magnify his castration anxiety. Such anxiety would then interfere with taking any woman as a love object. The individual would unconsciously equate sexual intimacy with any woman as equivalent to his father-forbidden relationship with his mother; and consequently find that his heterosexual contacts generated guilt and anxiety of such intensity as to be intolerable.

Freud theorized further that when the male who is to become homosexual finds he cannot safely love mother he takes refuge in a special defense mode. He "identifies himself with her" and directs his love toward others as he assumes she would. That is, he takes on her role instead of relating to her as a love object. However, he also targets himself as a model of whom mother would prefer and therefore seeks males who resemble himself. In his homosexual mode, the sex object he prefers is himself, but within a "mother loves me" context. The sex object he seeks, says Freud, must possess a penis whose presence will soothe castration anxieties. In these terms, one might say that the homosexual wants a "girl with a penis" as his love object.

Pre-1977 Findings

Two major hypotheses that we originally extracted from Freud's formulations concerning homosexuality were that male homosexuals have had a particularly hostile negative relationship with father and an unusually close and intimate one with mother.

We found 22 studies in the literature that were roughly supportive of either or both of these two hypotheses and 6 that were not. After reviewing them, we (Fisher & Greenberg, 1985) concluded:

> What kind of a summary statement can be made concerning the material just reviewed? First, the reports concerning the male homosexual's view of his father are overwhelmingly supportive of Freud's hypothesis. With only a few exceptions, the male homosexual declares that father

has been a negative influence in his life. He refers to him with such adjectives as cold, unfriendly, punishing, brutal, distant, detached. There
is not a single even moderately well controlled study that we have been
able to locate in which male homosexuals refer to father positively or affectionately. On the contrary, they consistently regard him as an antag-
onist. He easily fills the unusually intense, competitive Oedipal role
Freud ascribed to him. (p. 242)

However, the data were somewhat less supportive of the hypothesis about mother. About half of the published studies concerned with
homosexual sons' views of their mothers supported the idea that
mother is unusually "close" or intimate. The other half either depicted
her as not different from mothers of heterosexual men or applied terms
not relevant to the intimacy dimension. We tentatively concluded that
the data gave a small supportive edge to Freud's hypothesis concerning
mothers of homosexuals.

At a more general level, Silverman, Kwawer, Wolitzky, and Coron
(1973) and also Silverman, Bronstein, and Mendelsohn (1976) demonstrated, in male homosexual samples, that the tachistoscopic subliminal input of an incest message ("Fuck Mommy") increased the sexual
attractiveness of male pictures (compared with female pictures). No
significant effects were detected for control stimuli or in heterosexual
males. The results could be interpreted to mean that the arousal of
Oedipal anxiety increased the need for a defensive "I love men (not
women)" set. They were congruent with the basic Oedipal framework
within which Freud explained homosexual interests.

Post-1977 Findings

In 1989, Fisher identified 58 empirical studies in the total literature
concerned with parents of homosexuals. We have not located any additional relevant findings that have appeared since 1989. Fisher analyzed
the 58 studies and reported that a large majority supported the notion
that homosexual sons perceive their fathers as negative, distant, unfriendly figures. However, Fisher stated that only a minority of the
studies supported the concept that homosexual men perceive their
mothers as unusually close and seductive.

Fisher emphasized that this entire literature is based on a strategy of asking adult homosexual subjects (and the adult heterosexual
controls) to remember how their parents treated them during childhood. The questionnaires made such inquiries as, "Was your mother
overly close to you?" "Was she intrusive?" "Was your father cold?"
"Was he weak?" "Was he distant?" Fisher was skeptical that Freud
would have accepted the idea that the homosexual male's original
childhood experiences with his parents would have been "recorded"

with any accuracy at a conscious level; and even if they had, how available would the original perceptions be to the individual answering a questionnaire many years later? Fisher remarked:

> From this perspective, there would be so much chance noise in the recall of adults about parent closeness-distance issues that it would apparently require a miracle for any possibly existing relationships between being homosexual and the styles of one's parents to show up. This would seem to be especially true within the context of the importance psychoanalytic paradigms place on unconscious feelings. One would a priori assume that a fair test of Freud's formulations requires some means of measuring the homosexual male's unconscious views of each of his parents. (p. 167)

However, Fisher then noted: "It is therefore astounding how many of the studies utilizing straight-forward questioning of homosexual men (either by questionnaire or interview) have shown significant trends" . . . (pp. 167–168) for such men to depict their fathers in negative terms. Others (e.g., Ruse, 1981) have also commented on the apparent solidity of the findings in the literature concerned with this matter.

As already mentioned, the apparent pre-1977 trend for the mothers of male homosexuals to be described as close and seductive did not hold up in the larger set of post-1977 data.

Fisher further qualified the findings concerning the negative images of father by pointing out that many of the studies in this area suffered from potentially serious defects, which he specified as follows:

1. Some of the studies were based on highly selective samples (e.g., homosexuals in treatment or institutionalized for some reason).
2. The definitions of "homosexual" were in some instances so vague that one cannot distinguish whether subjects were possibly bisexual or had simply experimented on a limited basis with homosexual acts.
3. Bias was introduced into responses because some subjects were in psychoanalytic therapy and therefore had already been indoctrinated with Freud's theory of homosexuality.
4. Few attempts were made to differentiate subjects with reference to mediating variables such as degree of integration into the homosexual community, age at which consistent homosexual behavior began, or degree of masculinity-femininity.

Fisher concluded that despite such defects, the overall trend of the findings was significant. In addition, he pointed out that these were individual studies (e.g., Pledger, 1977) of unusually high quality in which a number of the confounding variables just mentioned were well controlled, and the results still supported the "negative father" hypothesis.

Cross-cultural studies specifically concerned with homosexuality have added some support for this hypothesis. Carroll (1978a) analyzed coded data available from anthropological observations of 186 societies (Standard Cross-Cultural Sample) described by Murdock and White (1969) and found significant affirmation for the psychoanalytically derived hypothesis that the frequency of homosexuality in a culture would be inversely related to the closeness of contact between fathers and sons. This matches the previously described findings that homosexual men tend to perceive their fathers as negative, distant figures.

In the same vein, Broude (1981) reported, on the basis of cross-cultural data, that homosexuality is less frequent in those cultures "where fathers are the regular companions of their children" (p. 654). But this trend did not attain statistical significance. More tangentially, Dizinno (1983) detected a significant tendency, in anthropological measures secured from multiple societies, for the prevalence of homosexuality to be positively correlated with the amount of competition and hostility existing among the male members of the various cultures. Such a link between homosexuality and negativity of male relationships is analogous to Freud's concept that sons who have negative (hostile) fathers are more likely to become homosexual.

A note of contradiction was raised by Herdt (1981, 1984), who intensively studied various tribes in New Guinea. He discovered that the men, in a number of instances, go through a unique socialization requiring them to be exclusively homosexual from boyhood until they marry and then to become exclusively heterosexual. The homosexual phase seems to provide the adolescent boy with the opportunity to relate intimately with men and thereby to build up a solid sense of masculinity as a step toward becoming a mature heterosexual male. Herdt (1984) pointed to such data as indicating that cultural contexts may dramatically modify and mediate homosexual behavior. He felt that the Freudian model of homosexuality attributed "too much emphasis to parental figures; and to place homosexuality in an inappropriate and invalid Western framework" (p. 360).

Malinowski (1927, 1929) analogously doubted that various aspects of Freud's Oedipal theory could be applied universally across cultures and attempted to document his doubts with his observations in the Trobriand Islands. Debate about cultural relativism in this respect has flourished. Spiro (1982) launched a voluminous and spirited rebuttal of Malinowski's skeptical position, which, by the way, had been widely accepted and considered to be a serious blow to Freud's concept of the universalism of the Oedipal pattern. Readers of both the Malinowsky and Spiro essays are struck with how subjective such qualitative anthropological observations are and how easily they can be interpreted to fit different theoretical expectations.

The post-1977 material we have reviewed concerning male homosexuality has narrowed the apparent support for Freud's formulation in this area. Previously, we regarded the empirical data to be congruent with Freud's theory that male homosexuality derives from too much closeness to mother and a distant negative relationship with father. As noted, the increased pool of data available reinforces the concept of the negative father but fails to support the idea of the overly close, seductive mother. The concept of the negative father is strengthened not only by additional studies based on questionnaire responses and subliminal inputs but also cross-cultural quantitative indexes.

So, we are left with only one of the major elements in Freud's original formula concerning the parental vectors that are involved in moving a male child toward homosexuality. This reduction in confirmed points on the graph makes it all too easy to conjure up alternative theories of homosexuality that could incorporate the "negative father" data. For example, investigators could speculate that the negative father simply does not provide his son with the opportunity to identify with a model of how to be a male with heterosexual aims. There would be no need to appeal to the Oedipal image of a son competing with his father for mother's love.

Female Homosexuality

As was true of his account of the origins of the male homosexual, Freud assumed that constitutional bisexuality to some unknown degree influences women to become homosexual. His psychodynamic formulation concerning women is really a mirroring of his view concerning the male homosexual. He specified that during the Oedipal phase the girl becomes disappointed in her mother, to whom she has been closely linked for years. Presumably, a major source of her disappointment is her discovery that she lacks a penis. She is said to blame mother for her lack and to be beset by feelings that she is inferior to the phallic male. At this point, says Freud, she turns to her father with the belief that if she can get close to him he will impregnate her and the child she bears will become a penis equivalent permitting her to regain her lost phallus. In this context, Freud theorized that the homosexual girl experiences an unusually high degree of disappointment when seeking father as a love object. In her disappointment, she is said to defensively identify with him and in so doing to turn (regressively) to adopting mother (and other feminine figures) as love objects. This means, in a sense, returning to a previous relationship, her attachment to her mother. Freud suggested, too, that adopting mother as a love object could serve defensively as a compensation for intense hostility toward her—to placate her that her daughter intended no competition for the available males. The presumed identification of the female homosexual with her father, consequent on her frustration with his reception of her, parallels the identification with mother that Freud attributed to the male homosexual. Another way that Freud conceptualized the matter was to describe the girl's homosexuality as deriving from a persistent "masculinity complex" based on a "profound envy of the penis."

Pre-1977 Findings

We had difficulty in 1977 in generating testable hypotheses from Freud's formulations about the female homosexual. One hypothesis that seemed justified was that she had had an unusually frustrating or disturbing relationship with her father. This would seem logical if Freud were correct in assuming her retreat from active heterosexuality and her defensive identification with father were rooted in frustrating interactions with him.

We did not consider it possible to derive a clear hypothesis concerning how the female homosexual would regard her mother.

The pre-1977 data (Fisher & Greenberg, 1985) based on questionnaire responses collected in six studies did, as hypothesized, support the view that the "female homosexual thinks of her father as an unfriendly, unpleasant person who had little to offer by way of a relationship" (p. 251).

Nothing of significance was found that would in any way clarify the nature of the homosexual girl's relationship with her mother.

Post-1977

Since 1977, Fisher (1989) has pulled together a total of 18 studies that have used questionnaire or interview techniques to assess quantitatively whether homosexual and heterosexual women differ in their views of their parents. We have not found any additional pertinent studies published since 1989. Fisher indicated that no significant trends emerged with respect to differences in attitudes toward mother. However, 11 of the 18 studies pictured the homosexual woman as feeling that father was negative or distant or frustrating; 6 studies did not; and 1 study presented data too vague to be meaningful. One of the best studies (Bell, Weinberg, & Hammersmith, 1981) that also included one of the largest diverse samples supported the "negative father" concept. The authors concluded: "Broadly speaking, then, the path model indicates that the women who felt their fathers were detached or hostile toward them were somewhat likely to become homosexual" (pp. 129–130). Although Bell et al. deemphasized the overall importance of this "father" factor in the development of female homosexuality, significant effects were apparent in their data.

Generally, the findings tend to be in agreement with Freud's idea of a "negative father." It is noteworthy that the same result emerged for males. Both female and male homosexuals apparently felt highly estranged from their fathers. As already mentioned, while the "negative father" findings fit with one aspect of Freud's theory of homosexuality, there are various other aspects that have either not been tested or have failed to be confirmed. The idea of the overly close and seductive mother[7] who magnifies Oedipal tensions for her son and thereby moves him toward homosexuality has not held up empirically. Also, we do not have any serious empirical data concerning other levels of the theory having to do, for example, with such variables as the homosexual female's presumed intensive disillusionment with her mother or her supposed defensive identification with her father.

The fact that both male and female homosexuals entertain a negative father image could easily fit other paradigms besides Freud's. Thus, Fisher (1989) suggested that since a considerable literature (e.g., Biller, 1976) indicates father typically carries a disproportionate amount of the responsibility for enforcing and encouraging conventional sex typing in the family, it is possible that a distant negative father would be relatively ineffectual in his efforts to influence sex typing and thereby encourage deviant sex role attitudes such as might be associated with becoming homosexual. This account would not correspond to Freud's Oedipal construction of the homosexual "choice."

Before closing this discussion, it should be acknowledged that there are increasing declarations in the literature that homosexuality derives to a significant degree from genetic or so-called biological factors (e.g., Allen & Gorski, 1992; Bailey & Pillard, 1991; Gartrell, 1982; Hoult, 1984; LeVay, 1993). However, the data underlying such assertions have not yet received consistent cross-validation, and the entire matter remains in a state of uncertainty (Byrne & Parsons, 1993; Friedman & Downey, 1993). It would be premature to conclude in any large sense that a biological etiology for homosexuality has been dependably demonstrated.

---

[7] A few empirical studies (e.g., Peskin, 1973; Stephens, 1962) document the negative Oedipal impact on the male child of an overly close mother.

THE EFFECTS OF OEDIPAL FANTASY INPUTS

We turn now to investigations that have looked at whether Oedipal fantasy inputs have predictable effects (usually negative) on behavior.

Some of the earliest efforts in this direction were carried out by Reyher and various associates (e.g., Karnilow, 1973; Reyher, 1958; Sommerschield & Reyher, 1973). They employed a methodology that measured the impact of an input (at an unconscious level) of an Oedipal theme on psychopathology. To implant an Oedipal theme, they hypnotized the subjects (normal college students) and created the false memory of having had a sexual experience with an "older woman." Further, the subjects were instructed that on awakening from the hypnosis they would have no memory of the experience, but that whenever certain key words were mentioned sexual feelings toward the woman would be aroused again. Subsequently, the subjects were visually presented with a series of words, some of which were associated with the paramnesia. Inquiries were made after the presentation of each word to measure the amount of psychological disturbance elicited. Significantly more disturbance was shown after the critical than the control words. An additional control was introduced in several of the studies (e.g., Sommerschield & Reyher, 1973) by using "simulators," who were put through the identical procedure as the hypnotic subjects and pretended to be hypnotized. These simulators manifested significantly fewer symptoms in response to the critical words than did those who had been actually hypnotized. In the Karnilow (1973) study, the specific power of the Oedipal components of the paramnesia was assessed by using two groups of hypnotic subjects. One group received the Oedipal message, whereas the other received a message identical in every way except that the woman in the story was depicted as being about the same age as the subjects rather than a considerably older equivalent of an Oedipal mother figure. The data indicated that the story from which the Oedipal theme had been removed produced significantly less disturbance than the one containing the theme.

Silverman and his associates (Silverman, Ross, Adler, & Lustig, 1978) are responsible for a particularly ambitious effort to demonstrate that an Oedipal input can affect behavior in a fashion predictable from Freud's Oedipal paradigm. In essence, they initiated and inspired a number of subsequent efforts to determine whether subliminal messages with Oedipal content have specified effects. They utilized the subliminal psychodynamic activation technique developed by Silverman et al. (1982), which involves 4-msec tachistoscopic exposures of conflict-related and control verbal and pictorial stimuli designed to arouse specific unconscious conflicts. They sought to demonstrate that male subjects (college students) exposed to subliminal messages that either sanctioned or condemned the idea of defeating father (the presumed Oedipal rival) would show, respectively, either improvement or deterioration in a subsequent dart-throwing competitive task. It was assumed that all men harbor residues of their Oedipal conflicts with father and that activating or deactivating their conflicts can alter their ability to engage in competitive behavior. The Oedipal message took the form of either "Beating Dad Is OK" or "Beating Dad Is Wrong." A control message stated: "People Are Walking." Pictorial representations of such verbal statements accompanied their presentations. Other messages were also included in the design. The tachistoscopic inputs were implemented double-blind. The subjects were "primed" to be sensitive to the Oedipal inputs by first having them answer questions about their parents and asking them to respond to projective test materials with parental connotations. It was found that the two Oedipal stimuli had significant effects in the expected directions. The Beating Dad Is OK input resulted in better dart-throwing performance than the control input. The Beating Dad Is Wrong had the opposite effect. There were other complexities in the findings, but for our purposes the central aspect was that the Oedipal messages about father had predicted positive or negative effects on competitive behavior.

These findings evoked considerable controversy; and a series of studies appeared that either claimed to affirm or contradict them. One investigation by Palumbo and Gillman (1984) is especially noteworthy because it duplicated the essential features of the Silverman et al. design, but it also included two additional control messages ("Beating Him Is OK" and "Beating Him Is Wrong"). They were introduced to influence competitive motives, but outside the Oedipal context that is linked to using terms such as "Dad" (e.g., Beating Dad Is OK). The Beating Dad Is OK message led to significantly greater dart-throwing accuracy than did each of the other message conditions. Lonski and Palumbo (cited in Silverman, 1983) also duplicated the Silverman design but included two special control messages ("Beating Mom Is OK" and "Beating Mom Is Wrong") to ascertain the specificity required of the Oedipal message to produce an effect on male subjects. The data indicated that the mother messages (in contrast to the Dad inputs) had no effect on dart-throwing accuracy.

Several studies have either failed (e.g., Haspel & Harris, 1982; Vitiello, Carlin, Becker, Barris, & Dutton, 1989) to replicate the Silverman et al. (1978) results or only weakly replicated them (Weinberger & Silverman, 1990). Disputes about the significance of the tachistoscopic studies have spilled over into published attacks and rejoinders (e.g., Heilbrun, 1982; Silverman, 1982). Silverman (1983) reported that, overall, five studies had clearly supported his original findings; five had partially replicated them; and five had not been able to replicate.

Silverman speculated about the multiple factors (e.g., experimenter personality) that might produce such variability. In any case, after reviewing the evidence, our judgment, is that although the impact of the Oedipal inputs may be fragile, they have been detected with sufficient frequency (in the context of meaningful controls) to be taken seriously.[8]

Another investigation involving subliminal input of an Oedipally relevant theme is described by Sturman (1980). He exposed different samples of male and female college students to the following tachistoscopically (subliminal) presented messages: "Father Castrates," "Father Argues," "People Walking." Before and after each message several dependent measures were administered (e.g., inkblots, questionnaire tapping state anxiety). The inkblots were scored for level of perceptual development. It had been hypothesized that the castration theme would (in accordance with Freud's emphasis on the special role of castration anxiety in the male compared with the female) have a greater negative impact on the male than female subjects. The other themes were introduced for control purposes.

The results indicated that both the castration and aggression themes produced significant regression in levels of perceptual responding as defined by inkblot criteria. Contrary to the hypothesis, no difference could be detected in the amount of regression evoked by the castration theme in males compared with females. Also, no differences were apparent in terms of the other dependent measures administered. Sturman concluded, among other things, that Freud may have underestimated the importance of unconscious castration dynamics in the female. He noted, for example, that the development of the female breast during the adolescent/pubertal stage might have phallic significance and induce investment in a prized organ whose potential loss could stir castration anxiety quite analogous to that of the male who fears loss of the penis.[9] The subliminal input did not result in the differential effects on males and females that had been predicted.

[8] It is of possible pertinence to the Oedipal paradigm that Jackson (1983) reported that the subliminal inputs of the messages "Mommy And I Are One" and "Daddy And I Are One" have different effects on male compared with female "differentiated schizophrenics." In the past, the oneness messages have been shown to decrease pathology in schizophrenic individuals. Jackson found that the male schizophrenics responded with decreased pathology after Mommy And I Are One but not after Daddy and I Are One; whereas for the females the results were reversed. The potential soothing or stabilizing effects occurred only when the message involved the opposite-sex parent, who, according to the Oedipal theory, is the one perceived most positively.

[9] Cherry (1977) similarly reported that males and females did not differ in their responses to a subliminal castration input ("I Have No Penis"). Both sexes evidenced an increased defensive tendency "to avoid success" (as measured by TAT-like tasks) in reaction to the castration theme.

Schumacher (1988) utilized an Oedipal input to test the presumed association in male Oedipal fantasies between incestuous wishes toward mother and parricidal intent. The male child's desire for exclusive sexual possession of mother is said to generate wishes to destroy father. Schumacher's research strategy was based on exposing males to an input (film) with strong mother-incest meaning to ascertain whether this would affect responses to subsequently encountered depictions of parricide. The responses of these subjects were compared with those of a control group who viewed a sexually arousing film (but without an incest theme) before viewing the film with the parricide theme. Measures of reactions to the films were based on subjects' Osgood (Osgood, Suci, & Tannenbaum, 1957) Semantic Differential ratings of various terms and images at different points in the procedure. Analysis of the data did not, contrary to prediction, detect any differences between the experimental and control subjects with respect to how they responded to the film depicting the death of a father figure. The incest film did not prime for a stronger response to the parricide theme than did the nonincest film. However, a serious defect in the design of the study is that both the experimental and control groups were required to view a neutral film (4 minutes in duration) of an ocean scene for an interval between the incest or sexual film and the presentation of the parricide film. The rationale offered for doing this was "to provide a neutral and/or somewhat positive interlude," "to clear the conscious psychological palate by diminishing excitement" (p. 54). Our view is that this merely attenuated the impact of the incest film and therefore decreased the probability of obtaining the predicted experimental effect.

In the context of Oedipal inputs, Hoyt (1979a, 1979b, 1979c) published some novel explorations of primal-scene phenomena. Freud considered that witnessing parents having sexual intercourse has a traumatic impact on children, often interpreted in Oedipal terms (e.g., "Father is hurting mother and I will stop him"). Primal scene experiences were regarded as complicating and intensifying Oedipal interactions. They have been depicted as producing intense sexual excitement that cannot be adequately discharged; encouraging sadomasochistic misunderstandings of the sexual act; and stirring overly intense identifications with one or both of the sexual participants. In one study, Hoyt (1979b) actually found suggestive empirical evidence that males "in competition with and females enamored of their fathers" (p. 234) were significantly less likely to be aware of the sexual aspects of their parents' relationship. He referred to this as an "Oedipal-type dynamic" (p. 234).

In any case, he sought to trigger a response to the primal scene theme by creating a provocative internal stimulus. The stimulus arose from his instruction to the subjects to imagine "Your parents having sexual relations together" and then to describe "the feelings and reactions that scene evokes in you" (p. 97) by rating a series of descriptive terms (e.g., alone, angry, sexual, shocked). Six other scenes (e.g., "Having a sexual experience with a sibling" or "Losing someone close to you") were likewise imagined and rated by each subject. An elaborate profile analysis of the multiple ratings of the various scenes indicated that the primal-scene image was most likely to elicit themes related to being alone and "incestuous sexuality." The subjects rated their responses to the imagined primal scenes as falling within a mild to moderate level of anxiety. When Hoyt (1979b, 1979c) interviewed college students about their having witnessed primal scenes, the majority said they were originally quite distressed. However, no evidence was found that primal-scene witnesses (looking back as adults) differed from nonwitnesses in their ratings of their degree of happiness or the importance of sex in their own lives.

The outcomes of the heterogeneous efforts, just reviewed, to predict the effects of various types of Oedipal inputs do not allow a manageable generalization. This could be anticipated in terms of the diversity of intents and designs. There does seem to be encouraging evidence, as defined by the work of Reyher and also Silverman, that implanting in males (at an unconscious level) Oedipal imagery involving incestuous contacts with mother selectively produces disruption in psychological functioning. Oedipal images introduced at a conscious level (as was done by Schumacher and also Hoyt) apparently did not have much impact, although the Schumacher study may be so flawed that the results need not be given any import.

RESOLVING THE OEDIPAL DILEMMA

Freud focused in some detail on how the major Oedipal tensions are typically resolved. As outlined earlier, he theorized that males resolve their Oedipal competition with father out of fear of being castrated by him. This fear presumably motivates them to identify with him and give up their Oedipal wishes for mother. Freud also devised the elaborate penis-baby equation paradigm to explain how females resolve their Oedipal struggles with mother. In essence, he proposed that when the girl rejects mother because, among other things, she blames mother for depriving her of a penis (symbol of power and superiority), she turns to father with the unconscious intent to be impregnated by him and thereby to produce a baby that will serve as a penis substitute.

The Penis-Baby Equation

Freud's formulation about the baby-penis equation is particularly remarkable because of its complexity and daring counterintuitive content. In essence, he proposed that a woman cannot achieve normal femininity unless she succeeds in assuring herself that she has acquired an illusory penis. He indicated that all women are confronted with a problem of penis-envy and typically have three possible ways of coping with it. The first is simply to turn one's back on sexuality. This mode is said to characterize women who feel so inferior about their lack of a phallus that they give up all phallic aspirations and thereby sexuality in general. A second is to hold on firmly to one's phallic aspirations and to persist in seeking a penis by emulating male activities (even including taking a homosexual object choice). According to Freud, only the third choice, anchored in the idea of bearing father (or father substitute) a child, can lead to normal (healthy) femininity.

The pre-1977 empirical literature concerned with penis-envy includes only a few scattered investigations. These studies (Bombard, 1969; Ellman, 1970; Levin, 1966), in concordance with Freud, found a trend for women who are unusually invested in what are conventionally considered to be male occupations and who are particularly hostile to men to project images suggestive of penis-envy[10] in their responses to the Rorschach blots. Illustratively, Levin (1966) studied a group of women who because of their occupational and marriage history seem to have devoted themselves to a "masculine social role" with phallic investments. These were career women (unmarried and employed in so-called masculine occupations); and they were contrasted with a control group of women who were "homemakers" (married, mothers, not employed outside of the home). A scoring system that quantified Rorschach responses (e.g., confusion about sexual identity) presumably indicative of concern about penis loss indicated significantly greater anxiety about such loss in the group apparently seized by penis envy than the conventionally feminine group. A later study by Ellman (1970) was roughly corroborative, whereas the one by Bombard (1969) was not.

We (Greenberg & Fisher, 1980, 1983) were originally drawn to an appraisal of the penis-baby equation theory because of its exotic character. Somewhat skeptically, we decided to test it empirically. Our approach derived directly from Freud's equation of baby with penis in the fantasies of women when they are impregnated. We reasoned that if pregnancy is somehow a penis equivalent for women, they should have increased unconscious phallic sensations or feelings at that time. One of our first tasks was to develop a quantitative measure of phallic imagery. We utilized responses to the Holtzman Inkblot Test (Holtzman, Thorpe, Swartz, & Herron, 1961) to this end. The phallic scoring

---

[10] Touhey (1977) demonstrated that women who are high on "penis-envy" (as defined by responses to Blum's, 1949, Blacky Test) are particularly likely to favor castration-like punishment for males who are perceived as sexually aggressive.

system is based on a count of all responses involving projections, protrusions, and elongations that can be interpreted as having phallic connotations. It derives from Freud's (1900) statement that all "elongated objects" can represent the phallus. He enumerated such objects as sticks, umbrellas, snakes, and airplanes as potential phallic symbols. The detailed scoring system we devised could be applied with high reliability (97% agreement between two independent scorers). Note that other investigators have had occasion to devise specialized measures of sexual symbolism in studying such phenomena as sex differences and sexual identity (e.g., Franck & Rosen, 1949; Nathan, 1978; Winter & Prescott, 1957).

In an initial study, we tested the hypothesis that women who are pregnant should have elevated phallic scores. We compared their phallic scores during pregnancy with their scores in a nonpregnant state; and we also compared their scores with those of a control group of nonpregnant women. The expectant women had been pregnant on the average for 24 weeks when we initially tested them with Form B of the Holtzman Inkblot Test. They wrote their own responses. One month after delivery, each of the woman responded to Form A of the Holtzman Blots. The nonpregnant control groups (who were equated for age and education) responded to Form B of the blots.

The findings were nicely congruent with the hypothesis. Women produced significantly more phallic imagery (scored blindly) when in a pregnant than nonpregnant state. Also, the phallic scores during pregnancy were significantly higher than those of the nonpregnant control women. However, the scores of these control subjects did not differ significantly from those of the experimental subjects when tested in the nonpregnant state. As Freud had predicted, the pregnant women seemed to be particularly preoccupied with phallic fantasies (presumably because of the phallic significance ascribed to the fetus).

In a second study, we moved on to a more complex design in which we examined the impact of a subliminal pregnancy message on the production of phallic imagery. We assumed that if we could successfully communicate (at an unconscious level) a message about becoming pregnant, this should (in Freud's terms) initiate increased phallic imagery. An experimental sample of women first responded to Form B of the Holtzman Blots (by writing their responses) and then to Form A while exposed to a continuous auditory, subliminal pregnancy message such as, "I should become pregnant. Entering my uterus. Entering my womb. I could become pregnant. To be fertilized. Becoming pregnant." Control subjects went through the same procedure except that the subliminal message (e.g., "I feel opened up. Things are getting through. It gets into me") did not refer to pregnancy but rather the theme of being penetrated. The results indicated, as predicted, that the women who received the subliminal pregnancy input increased significantly in the number of phallic images produced; but there was no such increase in the case of the control women who were exposed to the subliminal penetration (nonpregnancy) theme.

The overall findings of the two studies just reviewed were certainly supportive of Freud's penis-baby equation. The meaningfulness of the data depends on whether phallic images projected onto inkblot stimuli truly represent the sort of phallic fantasies that Freud had in mind. Because the phallic scoring system applied to the blots was based on Freud's own criteria, we are inclined to regard the phallic scores as sensibly paralleling his construct.

Encouraged by such results, we embarked on several other tests of the penis-baby formulation. First, we undertook a study that started with the premise that if being pregnant affects phallic imagery, then a clear sign of not being pregnant, such as onset of menstruation, should also have phallic effects. We proposed that the impact would be dependent on how invested a woman is in attaining a traditional feminine identity by having a baby. Presumably, the greater the value an individual woman ascribes to producing a baby, the more negatively she would experience menstruation because of its signal that pregnancy will not occur. Our study was specifically directed at determining the relationship between phallic imagery during menstruation and desire to become pregnant.

Research has demonstrated that a woman's concept of her sex role affects her attitudes toward menstruation. Those who are more traditionally feminine seem to attribute more importance and self-defining meaning to menstruation (Miller & Smith, 1975; Rossi & Rossi, 1977). Erikson (1977) reported that women who feel positively during the ovulation phase are inclined to experience negative affects during menstruation; those who react negatively at the time of ovulation respond positively to menstruation. That is, women who feel more positively during a phase of high fertility are more disturbed during nonfertile periods. One would expect the conventionally feminine woman to be typified by a similar pattern. Generalizing from such data, one would anticipate that women who resolved their Oedipal dilemma in the fashion proposed by Freud (seeking pregnancy) would be particularly sensitive to the significance of menstruating or not menstruating. Presumably, menstruation constitutes a contradiction to the Oedipal solution delineated by Freud and would be disturbing to women desiring a baby, since it would denote that the wish for pregnancy had failed.

If phallic imagery is conceptualized as a symbolization of power and prowess, one might expect that because those most motivated to become pregnant regard menstruation as a failure, they would be less likely to produce phallic imagery while menstruating. This formulation was converted into the following functional hypothesis: The less phallic imagery a woman displays during menstruation, the less time she will delay in becoming pregnant following marriage. That is, the more negatively (as demonstrated by low phallic scores) menstruation seems to affect a woman, the greater would be her motivation to become pregnant and therefore the earlier she would have become pregnant subsequent to having arrived at a conventional opportunity (getting married) to do so.

The hypothesis was evaluated in two different samples of married women. Phallic scores were obtained from Holtzman Inkblots administered within 1 to 3 days after the onset of menstrual flow and also during a nonmenstrual phase. In both samples, it was found, at a significant level, that the lower a woman's phallic score during menstruation, the shorter was her delay in becoming pregnant (as ascertained from questionnaire) following marriage. There were no correlations of significance between phallic scores obtained during a nonmenstrual phase and the amount of delay in becoming pregnant. These findings were clearly congruent with what had been predicted.

Another related study was derived from the literature (e.g., Douvan & Adelson, 1966; Kehoe, 1977; Olds & Schaver, 1980) suggesting a positive relationship between menstrual irregularity and having a traditional feminine sex role orientation. We were especially impressed with Kehoe's (1977) observation that not only is menstrual irregularity positively linked with traditional femininity, but also desire for pregnancy. Indeed, irregular women were described as less likely than regulars to use effective birth control techniques. In the past, various clinicians (e.g., Deutsch, 1944–1945; Gill, 1943) have speculated about a connection between irregularity and a wish to become pregnant. If so, one might expect the functionally irregular woman to feel selectively negative during menstruation because it confirms that pregnancy has not occurred. It was specifically predicted that women with irregular menstrual periods will increase their phallic scores from menstrual to nonmenstrual phases to a greater degree than will women who are regular. Phallic scores were computed from Holtzman Inkblot responses obtained during menstrual and nonmenstrual phases. The data indicated significantly that the irregular women shifted, as predicted, to higher phallic scores when not menstruating. Women with regular menstrual periods did not manifest a shift in phallic imagery from menstrual to nonmenstrual phases.[11]

---

[11] A third study was also carried out that looked at the relationship between phallic scores and frequency of masturbation. It was based on the assumption that the more a woman has moved in the direction of solving the Oedipal dilemma via the penis-baby

We were impressed with how well the various hypotheses derived from the penis-baby model fared. It proved to have surprising
predictive utility at a number of different levels pertaining to the reproductive process. We were also impressed that the relatively crude
measure of phallic imagery employed could sustain the load imposed
by such complex formulations. Before appraising in more detail the implications of the penis-baby findings, we will present additional pertinent work carried out elsewhere.

There has been an interesting elaboration by Jones (1989, 1991,
1994) of the work with phallic imagery just described. She set out to
test an idea widely accepted in psychoanalytic circles and derived
from Freud's Oedipal and penis-baby equation formulations. Jones
(1989) explored the validity of the notion that "menstrually-related
symptoms stem from cyclic reactivation of penis envy and the con-
comitant reemergence of the female's sense of body mutilation and
body inferiority." She referred to the notion that the "premenstruum is
a time of heightened phallic concern: a woman's conscious or unconscious knowledge of the imminence of her menstrual flow is thought
to reactivate her conflicts concerning penis loss and pregnancy . . ."
(p. 4). Essentially, Jones investigated whether the imminence of the
onset of menstruation (with its connotations of bleeding and potential
genital injury) activates Oedipal themes, especially the fantasy that
producing a baby can compensate for the presumed sense of deficiency
associated with not possessing a penis.

Jones speculated that if during the premenstruum women are
concerned with their lack of a penis, they should become more preoccupied with phallic imagery. She particularly wondered whether the
"premenstruum would be a time of heightened phallic concern for
women most desirous of a baby since, up until the advent of the menstrual flow, their fantasies of pregnancy are still viable" (p. 28). With
the Greenberg and Fisher (1980, 1983) work described earlier as a partial background, she hypothesized that women could report more

---

equation, the less she will engage in the phallic form of satisfaction represented by
masturbation (which is largely clitorally directed). Preference for the penis-baby solution was measured in terms of phallic scores during pregnancy and during menstruation. It was predicted that phallic scores during pregnancy would be negatively
correlated with frequency of masturbation, whereas phallic scores during menstruation would be positively correlated. The results for the phallic scores during pregnancy were in the predicted direction but not significant. The results for the phallic
scores during menstruation were significantly in the predicted direction. Basically,
producing higher numbers of phallic responses during pregnancy (indicative of a
penis-baby orientation) was negatively correlated with masturbation frequency,
whereas the production of such responses during menstruation correlated in the opposite direction with the masturbation index.

phallic image responses to inkblots when they are premenstrual (presumably because the imminence of bleeding activates penis-envy fantasies) versus when they are between menstruations. She administered the Holtzman Inkblot Test to unmarried college women during the week before onset of menses and a parallel form of the inkblots during an intermenstrual phase. The responses of the subjects were scored (using the Greenberg-Fisher criteria) for phallic content. The results significantly supported the hypothesis that women would produce more phallic images premenstrually than intermenstrually.

Several questionnaires measuring masculinity-femininity were also administered. It had been predicted that women with nontraditional feminine sex-role attitudes would report higher levels of phallic imagery than the traditionally feminine. But the masculinity-femininity scores proved to be unrelated to levels of phallic imagery.

Jones concluded that the findings concerning elevated phallic scores during the premenstruum support the view that the "imminence of menstruation intensifies . . . awareness of a (woman's) penisless condition, and thereby reactivates her conflicts concerning penis loss and pregnancy . . ." (p. 41). She noted that "Freud implicated a reintensification of woman's 'penis envy' in all her reproductive crises" (p. 41). She devoted considerable discussion to whether penis envy is literally a wish to possess the male organ or a symbolic expression of a desire for the power and social privilege associated with masculinity. In support of the symbolic metamorphic interpretation, she cites work by Nathan (1981) who found (in a survey of 20 cultures) that the higher a woman's status in a culture the less phallic content in her reported dreams. If she feels she has acceptable status, she has less reason to focus on phallic themes with their power connotations. Such a cultural interpretation would not have been acceptable to Freud, who defined penis envy strictly in body terms.

Jones' findings are indirectly supportive of our (Greenberg & Fisher, 1980, 1983) original observations concerning variations in phallic scores as a function of factors with reproductive implications. However, we were somewhat surprised that she found phallic scores to be *generally* elevated during the premenstruum. Our own data had suggested that some women increase and others decrease their phallic scores during menstruation depending on whether they are oriented toward the penis-baby equation route for coping with their Oedipal conflicts or some other less conventionally feminine mode. Because, in these terms, phallic scores could be either enhanced or minimized in relation to the onset of menstruation, presumably it would be difficult to find a generalized increase of phallic scores in a diverse sample of women. It is possible that Jones' sample of young college women was made up of an unusually high percentage of individuals who were not motivated to adopt the conventional penis-baby equation mode and who therefore felt more positively (more in a position of power?) when they perceived they were not going to be pregnant. This is a credible possibility in view of Jones's report that questionnaire scores measuring acceptance of feminist values were unusually high in her sample.

In a subsequent investigation, Jones (1991, 1994) undertook an ambitious series of studies primarily designed to test the Greenberg and Fisher (1980, 1983) study demonstrating that women exposed to a subliminal pregnancy message manifest a higher preoccupation with phallic imagery than do women exposed to a subliminal control message involving themes of being penetrated. The heightened phallic scores during the subliminal pregnancy input were predicted on the basis of Freud's penis-baby equation theory that pregnancy provides an opportunity to acquire, in fantasy, a substitute phallus. Jones studied female college students who were randomly assigned to either receiving an auditory subliminal message about becoming pregnant or being penetrated. The penetration message was actively delivered in two different versions. One was the same as the original Greenberg and Fisher message and a second was filled with explicit sexual imagery. The second was intended to control for what Jones considered to be differences in the number of sexual references contained in the original Greenberg-Fisher versions of the pregnancy versus penetration tape messages. Holtzman Inkblots were administered previous to exposure to the subliminal messages and a parallel inkblot series was administered during exposure. All blot protocols were blindly scored for phallic content (using the Greenberg-Fisher criteria). The data indicated, as predicted, that the pregnancy message produced a significant increase in phallic content, whereas the control penetration messages did not.

As an additional analysis, Jones compared the impact of delivering the pregnancy and penetration messages liminally instead of subliminally. At the liminal level there were no differences in phallic imagery change scores induced by the pregnancy compared with the penetration tape conditions. This finding is congruent with Bornstein's (1990) meta-analysis indicating that subliminal presentations of "drive-related stimuli" have larger effects on behavior than do supraliminal presentation of the same stimuli.

A clever addition to the Jones study involved the inclusion of male samples who were exposed to the same pregnancy and control messages as were the females. The results indicated that the males did not manifest the same increase in phallic scores during exposure to the pregnancy tape as had typified the females. The use of male subjects was intended to test Freud's idea that the penis-baby equation dynamic is one that applies uniquely to females.

Another twist to the Jones design aimed to clarify whether the phallic score changes resulting from reproductive events (e.g., pregnancy, menstruation) are due to activating a woman's literal envy for a penis or are the result of intensifying a woman's concerns and struggles with power and achievement fantasies (symbolized in phallic terms). Jones labeled the first alternative as "Freudian traditionalist" and the second as "culturalist." She attempted to evaluate these two alternatives by devising a scoring system for quantifying the amount of achievement/power imagery in the inkblot responses of the subjects. She reasoned that if the pregnancy tape increased phallic scores but failed to do so with reference to achievement/power scores, this would mean that the pregnancy theme was not having an effect because it altered achievement/power (cultural) fantasies but rather because it affected images anchored in the body.

This was exactly the pattern of findings reported by Jones, and she concluded that the "current findings are at odds with a large body of work which disputes a strictly literal, anatomically-based explanation of womens' phallic concerns" (p. 122). After reviewing these findings in the context of other observations (e.g., Nathan, 1981), indicating a cultural element in phallic imagery, she concluded: "Women's phallic concerns potentially implicate both primitive, anatomically-based longings, as well as more symbolic strivings" (p. 130).

We have provided a rather full account of the various findings pertinent to the penis-baby equation theory because they are almost startling in their clarity and consistency. We have seen that one of Freud's most extreme and counterintuitive Oedipal formulations (also widely viewed skeptically) has stood up well to a number of different empirical probes. Far-fetched predictions, such as an increase in phallic imagery during pregnancy, have been affirmed in contexts of careful experimental control. One of the most impressive results is the demonstration by both Greenberg and Fisher (1980) and Jones (1991) that a subliminal (auditory) pregnancy message produces an increase in phallic images in women, whereas control messages do not. It was also noteworthy in the Jones study that the pregnancy message had a predicted significant effect on the phallic fantasies of female subjects but none at all in the case of males.

This work illustrates the possibility of testing Freud's ideas in their full complexity but with objective experimental methodologies. The successful outcomes of these penis-baby equation studies may derive from the targeting of unconscious levels of functioning, which are, after all, central to most of Freud's models. In our summation and analysis of the total research findings concerning the Oedipal paradigm, we attach special importance to such studies.

THE SHAPING OF THE SUPEREGO

Males

Freud regarded Oedipal factors as potent in the shaping of those attitudes and standards collectively subsumed by the label "superego." He conceived the superego[12] of the male as taken over in the course of identifying with father to resolve the intense competitive crisis said to typify the height of the Oedipal phase. In short, the male child is portrayed as adopting his father's superego values as part of a process energized by fear (castration anxiety).

We originally found little corroboration (in the pre-1977 literature) of Freud's idea that the male child resolves his Oedipal difficulties when, out of fear of being hurt by his threatening, "castrating" father he is forced to join with and identify with him. Presumably, the child identifies with him to cope with his fear of him. However, an analysis of the pertinent research indicated quite straightforwardly that a boy's alliance with his father is more likely to be facilitated by a nurturant than a fear-inspiring stance on the part of father. It is the father's warmth rather than his fear-arousing qualities that primarily encourage his son to identify with him. This finding was very robust. Only a few studies of additional consequence bearing on the matter have shown up in the post-1977 literature; and they are of the same tenor (e.g., Hetherington, Cox, & Cox, 1978).

---

[12] In another context (Fisher & Greenberg, 1985), we noted with reference to the term "superego":

> An immediate question that needs to be faced in looking at any issue involving the superego is whether it can be treated as a unified entity. Freud typically conceptualizes the superego as if it were an internally consistent system. . . . However, those who have examined the moral decisions and behavior of persons in a variety of situations find only a low order of consistency. . . . Numerous studies have found only limited interrelationships among measures of moral behavior in the same person. . . . It is important to keep in mind, then, that the term superego as used by Freud was oversimplified in its connotations of unity. (p. 208)

Note also that multiple dimensions (e.g., antisocial and prosocial elements) have been implicated in the structure of conscience (e.g., Kochanska, 1993).

Pre-1977

Our original sifting of the pre-1977 literature concerned with the variables mediating the development of the superego revealed little support for Freud's position. Quite a number of studies turned up that had examined the nature of the link between the severity of the male's superego standards and how punitively or harshly his father had behaved. Because of Freud's Oedipal theory, considerable research had targeted this issue. Analysis of the pertinent studies (e.g., Bandura & Walters, 1959; Minkowich, 1959; Sears, Maccoby, & Levin, 1957) indicated clearly that fathers of males with strong moral qualities are not characterized by strictness. At that time, we concluded: "It is difficult to find a single well-designed and convincing study in which the strictness of the male's conscience has been shown to be positively and significantly correlated with how punishing or tough father has been" (p. 209). We added:

> One would have to conclude from the available scientific evidence that a punitive paternal stance does not facilitate the development of strict superego standards. In actuality, there are solid hints that a nurturant and friendly father is likely to encourage a strong moral structure in his son. This does not fit well with the picture of superego formation Freud gave us in his Oedipal theory. (p. 201)[13]

Post-1977

An increasing mass of data has accumulated indicating that the internalization of superego (conscience) values is more likely to occur when parents behave in friendly, nurturant ways than when they employ fear-arousing power strategies. A considerable attribution research literature demonstrates (Lewis, 1987) that applying controls beyond those minimally necessary to obtain compliance with a rule interferes with the internalization of the norm or injunction involved. It is, in fact, difficult to find any empirical studies in the post-1977 literature congruent with Freud's notion that the male superego is transferred primarily through fear and intimidation. Kochanska (1993) states quite firmly: "The existing evidence suggests that power-oriented socialization is almost universally detrimental for moral socialization in populations unselected for children's temperament . . ." (p. 331). Multiple

---

[13] Another defect in Freud's formulation relates to the fact that he grossly underestimated the influence of mother on her son's superego values. Multiple studies had appeared prior to 1977 that demonstrated significant correlates between mothers' attributes and their sons' superego characteristics. Still, it is interesting that Carroll (1978a) found in a survey of 51 societies that superego strength tended to be positively related with amount of contact with father.

publications that have appeared since 1977 concur with this view (e.g., Eisenberg, 1988; Maccoby & Martin, 1983; Radke-Yarrow, Zahn-Waxler, & Chapman, 1983; Staub, 1979). In addition, Edwards (1981) cites studies carried out in non-Western cultures that also link moral development with the extent to which parents interact in affectionate and positive ways with their children.

More recent research (e.g., Kochanska, 1991, 1993) has not only highlighted the role of parental (both father and mother) nurturant and nonpower practices in facilitating the internalization of the elements of conscience, but also the complexity of the phenomena involved. For example, the impact of the degree to which parents employ power tactics is complexly mediated by the child's temperament. Kochanska (1993) showed that children who are relatively anxious are particularly likely to internalize the elements of conscience when parents employ "low-power discipline." They seem to have a lower threshold for experiencing the internal discomfort aroused by wrongdoing and even quite minimal judgmental parental cues. There may be other temperamental factors in children that interact with the amount of power parents use in their enforcements. Kochanska suggests that children who are easily aroused to anger may be especially resentful when parents impose rules forcefully and therefore are likely to reject such rules.

Freud did not sufficiently recognize the importance of positive motivations in the construction of the child's superego values. He did not realize the extent to which conscience arises out of a reciprocal trusting parent-child relationship that renders the child receptive to parental expectations (Londerville & Martin, 1981). He also did not grasp the sheer complexity of the multiple variables that influence the crystallization of superego constituents.

Females

Freud was, to say the least, rather imprecise in his account of how females evolve a superego. He suggested that they derive their superego values from father and to a lesser extent from mother. He felt that the special status of the father in the patriarchal family highlighted the importance of paternal standards. This formulation differs in its logic from his statement about the male superego, which presumably represents one aspect of coming to terms with the parent who is, in Oedipal terms, the major opponent or threat. One might have expected that because mother is depicted as the major frustrator of the female child, she would also be the major influence in that child's superego formation. Freud, however, assigned father this prime role.

One of the clearest ideas to emerge from his description of female superego formation was the notion that the female acquires a less strict or severe superego than the male. Presumably, this is because the female ends her Oedipal confrontation out of fear of loss of love, whereas the male does so because of fear of castration. The fear of castration was considered to be more threatening and more demanding of a decisive resolution.[14] Therefore, the female would be under less pressure to introject a definitive superego structure.

Pre-1977

Our pre-1977 investigation of the literature relevant to whether males have more strict and decisive superego standards than females concluded that about an equal number of studies supported either the alternative of greater male strictness or greater female strictness. There was a slight trend favoring Freud's view, but it was of such small magnitude that it hardly matched his rather dramatic distinction between the sexes.

Post-1977

A good deal of solid energy has gone into post-1977 empirical tests of whether sex differences in morality can be detected. Major reviews and analyses of this work have appeared (Baumeister, Stillwell, & Heatherton, 1994; Cohn, 1991; Colby & Kohlberg, 1987; Gilligan, 1982; Lei, 1994; Lifton, 1985; Rest, 1979; Thoma, 1986; Walker, 1984). Literally hundreds of studies have directly or indirectly dealt with sex differences in such variables as moral principles, guilt, altruism, and conscience. Techniques for measuring superego-pertinent dimensions have diversely involved interviews, questionnaires, story completions, and laboratory situations testing one's ability to resist doing the forbidden. Also, the populations studied have embraced the entire developmental range from young children to adults.

In contemplating the maze of results from the various studies, one is first of all impressed that in a majority of instances no sex differences could be detected and the differences that were demonstrated were usually of small magnitude. Also, contrary to Freud's formulation, whenever significant differences were observed, they tended to depict females as having stricter superego standards than males.

Let us consider in a bit more detail several of the major publications bearing on the issue of sex differences. Lifton (1985) pointed out that Freud was one of the first major theorists to posit sex differences in superego "in favor of men." However, both Piaget (1965) and Kohlberg (1984) were also inclined to see men as more morally mature than women. Gilligan (1982) conceptualized the difference between the sexes

---

[14] Actually, a number of studies have shown that fear of loss of love is among the strongest of motivating forces (e.g., Kohlberg, 1966).

in qualitative rather than quantitative terms. She took the position that men prefer a moral position based on justice criteria, whereas women prefer a more nurturant "caring" definition. Lifton searched and found, in 1983, 45 studies that specifically discerned either the presence or absence of sex differences in moral development. Less than half (40%) reported significant differences; and about two-thirds in this category depicted women as more moral than men in their orientation.

Baumeister et al. (1994) examined the literature concerned with sex differences in guilt and concluded: "The sex difference of higher guilt in women is not large but is significant" (p. 255).

Walker (1984) reviewed the evidence for sex differences in moral reasoning in 79 studies in which Kohlberg's Moral Judgment Interview was utilized. No overall sex differences emerged. There were sex differences in only 6 of 41 samples of children and adolescents and in 6 of 46 samples of high school and university students. Among 21 samples of adults, there were only 4 significant differences (all favoring the men).

Thoma (1986) analyzed 54 studies in which Rest's (1979) paper-and-pencil measure of moral judgment (based on identifying issues that need to be considered in resolving a series of moral dilemmas) had been administered. There was an overall significant trend for the females (including high school, college, and adult subjects) to obtain higher moral reasoning scores.

Lei (1994) and Miller (1994), after reviewing cross-cultural data (derived respectively from Indian and Chinese samples) bearing on moral standards in males versus females, were inclined to be skeptical of any gross quantitative sex differences in degree of morality. Lei considered that there might be sex differences in style of morality.

The brief review just provided illustrates the two basic findings relevant to sex differences in morality:

1. A majority of studies do not indicate a quantitative difference between males and females in the strictness of their moral standards.
2. Within the minority that reveal a sex difference, females tend to a small degree to be more strict.

These results clash with Freud's insistence on the idea that males have a more structured and severe superego than females.

A final word is in order concerning a study by Boldizar, Wilson, and Deemer (1989). They followed the "moral judgment development" [measured by means of Rest's (1979) questionnaire calling for solutions to hypothetical moral dilemmas] of male and female samples over a 10-year span, from high school to young adulthood. The moral

judgment scores of the adult males and females were found not to differ significantly. A novel feature of this study, however, was that path
analysis was utilized to estimate the effects over time of educational
experiences, occupational variables, and marriage on the subjects'
moral judgment development. Such analyses revealed that males and
females differed in the "processes that determined moral judgment
development in adulthood" (p. 236). Illustratively, career success was a
powerful predictor of positive moral development in the male but not
in the female. Interestingly, too, marriage "detracted" from women's
moral judgment development, but had little or no effect on men's
development.

Adequate explanations for such findings were not really provided. However, the findings underscore that there may be fundamental contrasts in how the two sexes travel the path to an adult superego
value system. Although they may not differ in their gross levels of
superego strictness, the similarity may actually conceal more complex
underlying developmental differences. Lifton (1985) found that moral
judgments were linked with different personality characteristics in
young men and women. In males, they were correlated with variables
indicative of the development of a "sense of self-identity," whereas in
females the correlation was with the development of a "sense of social-
identity" (p. 326). It would be interesting, as more data become available concerning this matter, to ascertain whether the male versus
female patterns are possibly tied to factors Freud labeled as Oedipal.
For example, it is intriguing that Boldinzar et al. reported that getting
married negatively affects the level of moral judgment in women but
not in men. By hypothesizing that getting married reactivates basic
Oedipal tensions vis-à-vis one's parents, we could loosely speculate
that females are more affected than males because (as Freud suggested) they originally attained a less definite (stable) resolution of the
Oedipal crisis than did males. Other simpler explanations might also
be conjured up. The Boldinzar et al. data underscore not only that
superego development is considerably affected by multiple life events
extending well beyond the Oedipal period but also that the range and
complexity of the contributing events are greater than Freud envisioned. Such wider influences have been documented too at a cross-
cultural level (Edwards, 1981).

OVERVIEW

The crowded elements packed into Freud's Oedipal concepts and the
wide-ranging studies they have inspired do not lend themselves to
neat unidimensional appraisals. As earlier noted, his Oedipal theory is

actually a string of theories about a wide sweep of developmental issues. It deals not only with how power and sexual relationships are managed within the family, but also the vicissitudes of identification with one's parents, the transmission of values about good and evil, the process of becoming a sexually and reproductively active individual, and the achieving of a balance for intensely angry and dependent intentions.

We will now undertake an overall review of the material in this chapter. We will consider the findings pertinent to each of a series of issues and finally arrive at a judgment of how well the major components of the theory have held up to empirical probing.

The Liked and Disliked Parent Distinction

One of the fundamental features of the Oedipal paradigm is the prediction that the child will come to love the parent of the opposite sex and perceive the parent of the same sex as a negative, competing figure. This pattern of differentiating between one's parents is central to the entire Oedipal story. Data were already available from our original (pre-1977) evaluation that affirmed such differential attitudes toward one's parents. Additional post-1977 studies have been described that further bolster this distinction.

We are especially impressed with the Watson and Getz (1990) study that straightforwardly obtained observations of how often children behave aggressively or affectionately toward same-sex versus opposite-sex parents; and found that the relative frequencies matched the theoretical Oedipal paradigm. The commonsense simplicity of its approach to a fundamental issue is appealing. It was also impressive that when the frequencies of the Oedipal type pattern were plotted over four age levels, they peaked at age 4 which Freud defined as the height of the Oedipal confrontation. Feiner (1988) and Berg and Berg (1983) also found evidence for a predicted selective sensitivity to certain kinds of body threat during the presumed childhood Oedipal phase. Of related relevance to the issue of perceiving one's mother and father differentially is that Gill (1986) detected a differential response, congruent with the Oedipal theory, to the deaths of same-sex versus opposite-sex parents. Thus, guilt was experienced with reference to the loss of the same-sex parent, whereas the death of the opposite-sex parent was idealized.

We feel justified in concluding that, from several perspectives, the overall evidence supports Freud's Oedipal picture of the positive attraction between opposite-sex parent and child and the negative tension between the same-sex pair. Were this pattern not to be verified, it would undermine the crux of Freud's portrayal of the Oedipal love-hate drama.

Sexual Parameters

Another basic tenet of Freud's Oedipal theory is that sexual dysfunction is rooted in the inability to resolve major Oedipal problems and conflicts. The pre-1977 empirical literature had little to say about this matter that was consistent or dependable. However, there were negative reports (Fisher, 1989) indicating that, contrary to expectation, sexual difficulties, in either men or women, were not correlated with measures of psychopathology. This conflicted with Freud's underlying assumption that sexual dysfunction is one aspect of a more general species of psychopathology stemming from Oedipal difficulties.

Post-1977 publications dealing with sexuality are somewhat discouraging and confusing with respect to Freud's speculations about sexual problems in the context of Oedipal theory. This is true despite general evidence, in accordance with Freud, that parents and children experience a good deal of negative tension when their communications touch on sexual issues and also that some aspects of adult sexual behavior are tied to the character of early parent-child interactions. However, there are data that raise questions about Freud's Oedipally derived sexual formulations at several levels. First, it has become apparent (e.g., Fisher, 1989; Paxton & Turner, 1978) that orgasm consistency in women is positively correlated with how active, assertive, and goal-oriented women are. This does not fit with Freud's view that for a woman to become a normally sexually functioning person she must resolve her Oedipal struggles by adopting a passive role associated with the stereotype of conventional femininity. Second, empirical findings do not match Freud's view that part of the process for a woman to emerge into mature sexuality is to shift from clitoral to vaginal erotogenicity. Empirical observations (Fisher, 1973, 1980) have, in fact, shown that women who prefer vaginal to clitoral stimulation are not more "mature" than those who are clitorally oriented; and, if anything, are more susceptible to becoming anxious and upset when stressed.

Continuing our critique of Oedipally pertinent sexual issues, let us turn to the research dealing with homosexuality. Freud conceptualized the development of homosexuality in the male as resulting from flawed Oedipal relationships, namely, too much closeness to mother and too much distance from father. The actual empirical data have supported the notion of a negative, distant father, but not of the overly close mother. As earlier noted, this represents validation for one important element of Freud's theory of homosexuality but also lack of verification for another major component. Some support also emerged for the negative father concept as it applies to female homosexuals. There are other aspects of the theory, with reference to males (e.g., close identification with mother, seeking narcissistic representations of self in the same-sex love object) that simply have not been methodi-cally appraised. It is somewhat impressive that Freud's theory success-fully predicts the negative father image in both male and female homosexuals. However, the lack of verification for the close mother concept in the case of the males, the difficulty in generating testable hypotheses about the females, and the still sizable areas of Freud's thinking about homosexuality that have not even been looked at em-pirically give the impression of a structure floating in uncertainty.

Surprisingly few of Freud's predictions about sexuality in the context of Oedipal theory have recruited empirical backing. No consis-tent support has emerged for his linking of sexual dysfunction to psychopathology or his view that the ability of women to be sexually responsive is related to adopting a passive feminine orientation or his concept that a preference for experiencing vaginal rather than clitoral stimulation (as evidence of a shift to greater psychosexual maturity) represents a "healthier," more satisfying sexual mode. Additionally, his ideas about the etiology of homosexuality remain, as judged by em-pirical criteria, in either a borderline or untested status. Because the Oedipal history of individuals was portrayed by Freud as a large influ-ence in sexual development and functioning, we would have to say that the points just cited add up to a significant rebuff to his formulations in this area.

Resolution of the Oedipal Dilemmas

Some of Freud's richest and most complex thinking about Oedipal phe-nomena was directed at explaining how individuals resolve their Oedi-pal tensions and thereby move on to greater psychosexual maturity and the construction of new coping mechanisms. As already described, he conjured up a particularly labyrinthine account of how females re-solve their resentment about lacking a penis and their conflict with mother whom they presumably blame for their deficiency. This ac-count is packaged in the penis-baby equation story, which revolves around the idea that when the female moves away from what she per-ceives as a depriving mother, she turns to father with the unconscious intent to be impregnated by him (or a substitute) and thereby to create a baby that will function as a penis substitute. Freud was actually proposing that a woman cannot achieve normal femininity and sexual-ity unless she acquires an illusory penis.

There is a potential note of absurdity in the idea that a woman has to come into possession of a pretend penis to become a "real woman." However, as has been recounted, a formidable collection of research findings fits with Freud's model. We have reviewed our own studies (Greenberg & Fisher, 1980, 1983) and those of Jones (1989, 1991, 1994) that have diversely shown, in agreement with the penis-baby model, that pregnant women are unusually preoccupied with phallic images, that subliminal pregnancy messages produce increased phallic imagery in nonpregnant women (but not in men), and that there are variations in phallic scores during menstruation as a function of intensity of motivation to become pregnant. It is particularly striking that Jones found that the increase in phallic imagery following exposure to the subliminal pregnancy message was not a reflection of a generalized increase in achievement/power fantasies but rather seemed to be anchored in body (phallic) feelings. This signified to her that the observed increase in phallic imagery could be better conceptualized within the "Freudian traditionalist" than the "culturalist" paradigm. That is, Freud's notion was affirmed that pregnancy induces fantasies relevant to gaining a new phallic body part.

We are strongly swayed by this array of observations. As earlier indicated, it is impressive that Freud's theory, with all of its symbolically esoteric and counterintuitive qualities, should fare so well in a succession of stringent experimental designs. As we analyzed the findings, we were struck that the various experiments were to an unusual degree phrased in a Freudian patois. That is, they focused on symbolism, on unconsciously created meanings, and on measurement techniques applied to spontaneous material elicited by stimulation at unconscious levels. There was little or no use of response material based on conscious reasoning, questionnaires, and other easily censored channels. It is apropos to recall the numerous studies employing subliminal stimulation techniques (Bornstein & Pittman, 1992; Silverman et al., 1982) that have apparently supported various Freudian hypotheses (e.g., concerning homosexuality, Oedipal competition, oral impulses). Many complaints in the past have issued from the conventional psychoanalytic establishment concerning the naive simplicity of numerous research attempts to test psychoanalytic hypotheses. The success of the more sophisticated and complex designs applied to the penis-baby issue suggest that such complaints may, in part, be justified.[15]

---

[15] Even within psychoanalytic circles, there has been growing opposition to Freud's ideas about how women came to be sexually mature and "feminine." Objections have been voiced to the idea that a girl's wish to have a baby is basically a reaction to not possessing a penis and, indeed, that her entry into the Oedipal fray was originally energized by awareness of lacking a masculine attribute (Parens, 1990). It has been urged that her sexual development be defined more in terms of unique feminine needs and body experiences rather than as compensations for not being sufficiently somatically masculine. This position has been reinforced by more contemporary psychoanalytic observers (Parens, Polleck, Stern, & Kramer, 1976), who have followed the development of a number of children over an extended time period. They employed rather impressionistic methods for gathering and interpreting their data. Parens (1990), in summarizing their observations, stated: "The wish to have a baby . . . is not necessarily, in origin, a substitute for a penis. In the girls who formed the data based

If the research findings concerning the penis-baby equation continue to be sustained, this would almost mandate acceptance of a significant segment of Oedipal theory as it applies to females. It would mean that Freud had successfully detected the bizarre role the female child is forced to adopt to achieve what is called normal femininity in a Western culture. Presumably, the female child is inculcated with the belief that her body makes sense only insofar at it matches the male body. The antifeminine values prevailing would appear to dictate to females the need to construct an illusory maleness, which then becomes the anlage for what is considered to be an acceptable form of identity. It is as if only after the infusion of self with certain phallic attributes is a woman secure enough to embark on other, larger aspects of the unfolding of herself as an adult agent with social and reproductive responsibilities. Bem (1993) has documented at some length the degree to which women are required to define themselves in terms of male body standards.

Identification and Superego Formation as a Function of Fear

No adequate scientific support can be mustered for Freud's theory that the male child is motivated by his Oedipal fears vis-à-vis father to identify with him and thereby to resolve a frightening confrontation. That is, fear was presumed to be the major variable in this identification process. Freud basically assumed that the male child's degree of identification with father in the Oedipal period would be a positive function of the intensity of threat associated with father. But, as described, multiple studies have shown that the male child's identification with father is fostered more by friendly, nurturant parental attitudes than by negative anxiety-arousing ones.

We have seen too that Freud's theories concerning the forces that mold the superego are not empirically sound. Contrary to his idea that the superego evolves in the male during the course of identifying with father, out of Oedipally inspired fear (castration anxiety), the research literature unambiguously demonstrates that superego values are most likely to be internalized in the context of

---

for this study, the wish to have a penis and the distress reactions associated with it (castration complex) were not invariable antecedents of the wish to have a baby. . . . Where the wish to have a baby is experienced by the girl as a substitute for a penis, it is generally so secondarily . . ." (p. 757).

Other psychoanalysts, as reviewed by Chehrazi (1986), have also pointed to observations that prior to the Oedipal phase there is already vaginal awareness in the female child that carries with it a sense of "femaleness." It is disputed that the female child initially sees herself as a "little boy"; and it is asserted, "The wish for a baby can be seen prior to the penis envy reaction and is often as expression of identification with the mother, as well as an inborn gender characteristic" (p. 148).

friendly, nurturant transactions between children and their parents. Freud exaggerated the role of fear in motivating children to "take in" their parents' concepts of good and evil.

Further, Freud incorrectly assumed that females have a less strict and decisive superego than males. As noted, most studies find few or no quantitative differences between the sexes in this respect. The empirical data may even suggest slightly more strict superego standards in females than males.

CONCLUSION

Is there a pattern in the material just reviewed that can rationalize the Oedipal findings in some overall fashion? What distinguishes the blocs of results that are or are not affirming of Freud's major Oedipal ideas? His formulations have fared most negatively in their depictions of superego phenomena and in their accounts of the Oedipal factors mediating sexual responsiveness in females. On the more positive side, the results have, first of all, documented the existence of basic differential (loving and hating) attitudes toward mother and father. The Oedipal triangle looks like a solid notion. A second group of positive results seems to involve primarily the role of body-oriented fantasy in Oedipal psychodynamics. Freud assigned considerable importance in the Oedipal process to such variables as becoming aware that males and females have unlike genitals and compensating for presumed deficiencies in one's sexual parts. Thus, he hypothesized that females embark on their Oedipal rivalry as the result of discovering they "lack" a penis and that they come to terms with their dilemma by acquiring a phantom penis symbolized by becoming pregnant and producing a baby. In the case of males, he presumed that fear of losing one's penis (because of father's angry retaliatory potential) initiated the tapering off of the Oedipal confrontation with father by motivating an identification with him. He exaggerated the role of fear in this process.

From what has been validated, Oedipal theory supports a picture of the family as the early site of a rivalry between parent and child of the same sex, probably for the favor (love) of, or an intimate alliance with, the parent of the opposite sex. Themes relating to intergenerational power, gender roles, and the structuring of heterosexual interactions seem to predominate in this family context. But further, if one considers the relative elevation of castration anxiety in the male and the compensatory preoccupation with the penis-baby equation in the female, one wonders whether the real underlying Oedipal agenda is to frame the world in phallic terms. That is, the Oedipal phase seems to be a time of heightened awareness of sex differences and of the advantages of possessing a penis. The male child is portrayed by Freud as desperately concerned that the power disparity between father and himself will result in the loss of his phallic badge; and the female child is said to be forced into the exotic acquisition of a phantom penis to reassure herself that she has at least some minimal (penis-defined) significance in the family group. It is as if one first had to be able to anchor oneself in a phallic paradigm to feel sufficiently oriented or adequate to undertake other life roles and tasks. The phallic paradigm seems to serve in this context as a map for locating oneself in a male social space. It dramatizes the monopoly of a phallocentric orientation.[16] The power of the male perspective is translated into body image equivalents.

The use of body imagery to express culturally expected patterns of conduct or role taking is a well-documented phenomenon (Fisher, 1986). Thus, individuals may focus an unusual amount of attention on a body area as a persistent self-reminder to approach or avoid certain classes of objects. It has been shown (Fisher, 1986) that intensified focus on the back of one's body (anal sector) may serve as a cue to carefully contain one's aggressive and besmirching impulses. That is, the focus on the back is a representation of a cultural taboo about expressing certain anally tinged feelings. Or focusing on the outer muscular sheath (boundary) of the body may be a persistent message to self to behave in an expected vigorous, achievement-oriented fashion (Fisher, 1986). Douglas (1970) offers a variety of examples suggesting how individual preoccupation with particular parts of one's body (e.g., body openings) may mirror parallel social concerns (e.g., about being invaded or contaminated by others).

Fundamentally, the Oedipal experience seems to be typified by an exaggerated intensive immersion in the meanings of one's body (especially with respect to gender) vis-à-vis the bodies of the other family members. It is a time for complex symbolic manipulations of such body meanings with the intent of specifying not only how to get intimately close to the body of the opposite-sex parent but also how to maintain a protective distance from the parent of the same sex.

Some of the best validated aspects of the Oedipal theory pertain to feelings and fantasies about one's body. Terms like "castration anxiety" and "penis-baby equation" radiate obvious body image connotations.

---

[16] It is a provocative coincidence that Carroll (1978b), in the process of analyzing the Oedipus myth by means of the Levi-Strauss structural approach, identified the major theme as having to do with the "devaluation/affirmation of patrilineal kin" (p. 813). This theme presumably relates to the strengthening or weakening of the masculine line. It bears an obvious parallel to our view that a basic aspect of the Oedipal experience (as defined by the best validated empirical data) revolves about anchoring oneself in a phallic paradigm.

The overall content of Freud's formulations includes major segments that are phrased in a body image vocabulary. He often conceptualized psychological phenomena in terms of body fantasies. Note Fisher's (1970) comments concerning this matter:

> Many of Freud's formulations stressed the importance of the body as a psychological object in the development of an ego structure and also in the etiology of psychopathology. Body image concepts were prominent in his theory of the developmental process, which was depicted as leaning heavily on "libido localization." They were explicit in his statements concerning the part played by fixation of interest upon a limited body zone in the derivation of character types (e.g., "anal character"); and were also apparent as he spelled out the role of body symbolism in conversion hysteria. However, psychoanalytic theory subsequently became increasingly "social" in its orientation; and concepts concerned with libido localization, castration anxiety, and body symbolism were attenuated and appraised as having little importance. The neo-Freudian theories almost entirely ignored the "gut" aspects of Freudian theory. (p. 601)

On the basis of our review, a case can be made for the position that Freud's ideas (at least in the Oedipal context) have an increased chance of being validated when they deal with events at the level of body experiences and attitudes. This may reflect, in part, that most of the raw data originally available to Freud were his patients' introspective reports of feelings, sensations, and self-observations. Because of their self-observing quality, these reports might be expected to be rich with information about a spectrum of body-related experiences; and therefore, to provide a particularly dependable base for theorizing at this level.

Let us make one last pass at Freud's Oedipal schemata. His formulations in this area are of anfractuous intricacy, and the findings pertaining to their validity are equally complex. Although the data support the basic notion of the Oedipal triangle and the existence of certain mechanisms to cope with the tensions created by Oedipal confrontations, they fail to corroborate other major features. The evidence is clearly negative with respect to linking maladjustment and sexual difficulties to Oedipally derived variables; and it, therefore, disputes the widespread inclination of psychoanalytic clinicians routinely to trace their patients' symptoms and difficulties to defects in Oedipal relationships. The evidence is also negative with reference to Freud's rather constricted theory about the process underlying identifying with one's parents and taking over their superego standards. His narrow fear-centered explanatory models are considerably off the mark. There is a good deal of inaccuracy in his ideas about how parent-child relationships evolve and what motivates their twistings and turnings. He deserves credit for spotting the Oedipal elements (love and hate) in parent-child interactions and for detecting the cultural pressures on both male and female children to yield to translating themselves (via body images) into phallocentric modes.

Freud's attempt to construct a grand theory that would explain within one framework many of the multiple developmental events involved in achieving sexual and moral identities does not hold up well to empirical inspection. It is doubtful that any theory will ever be devised capable of convincingly pulling together such diverse components.

Chapter 7

The Dream Theory

Camouflage and Venting

In *The Interpretation of Dreams*, Freud (1900) presented what appeared to be a rather straightforward model of the dreaming process. He depicted the dream as a camouflaged creation that hides beneath its outer form a latent meaning which is actually a "wish" for something forbidden. He specified that the dream provides an outlet for an unconscious wish in a guise that prevents the dreamer's awareness of harboring such impulses or desires. As he outlined the process, persons' defenses against repressed unconscious wishes become less effective during the sleep state. Therefore, pressures from the unconscious intensify and that which has been repressed takes advantage of the diminished control to seek outlet in the visual images of dreaming. These dream images are said to be heavily camouflaged "manifest" representations of "latent" wishes. Freud explicitly attributed a sleep-preserving function to the camouflaging process. He theorized that it provided a pathway for unconscious impulses to seep through in a fashion that was minimally alarming and therefore relatively nondisruptive of the sleep of the individual involved.

We will briefly review the dream theory as conceptualized in Freud's own vocabulary. He (Freud, 1900) indicated that the "motive power for producing dreams is furnished by the Ucs (unconscious)" (p. 541). Further, he proposed that in the sleep state there is a "lowering of the resistance which guards the frontier between the unconscious and preconscious . . ." (p. 542). The dream provides a method "of bringing back under the control of the preconscious the excitation in the unconscious which has been left free . . ." (p. 579).

The dream is presumably a compromise way of bypassing repressive censorship. Freud assumed that penetrating the censorship requires that the unconscious wish adhere to a nonthreatening "residue" from past experiences inhabiting the preconscious. He stated: "An unconscious idea is as such quite incapable of entering the preconscious and that it can only exercise any effect there by establishing a connection with an idea which already belongs to the preconscious, by transferring its intensity on to it and by getting itself 'covered' by it" (pp. 562–563). The unconscious wish adhering to the "day residue" strives for an outlet, but it cannot obtain direct expression because motoric exits are in a state of paralysis related to the sleep state. Therefore, said Freud, the wish (impulse) travels a "regressive" route to the sensory end of the psychic apparatus, where it initiates the wish-fulfilling (but disguised) visual images characteristic of the dream.

In one of his overview statements concerning dream formation, Freud (1900) noted:

> Dreaming has taken on the task of bringing back under control of the preconscious, the excitation in the unconscious which has been left free; in doing so, it discharges the unconscious excitation, serves it as a safety valve and at the same time preserves the sleep of the preconscious in return for a small expenditure of waking activity. (p. 570)

There are two major features of Freud's dream formulation (wish fulfillment and sleep preservation). At another level, a pervasive paradigm in Freud's thinking about the dream has to do with the distinction between the manifest and latent content. Presumably, the manifest content is a meaningless shell, whereas the latent content (said to be decodable only by means of the individual's free associations) conveys the true meaning of the dream.

In our 1977 analysis of the dream theory, we raised questions about how meaningful it is to interpret literally Freud's concept that each dream is a vehicle for a specific repressed wish. We pointed out, first of all, that among the many dreams decoded in *The Interpretation of Dreams,* we rarely found instances in which the contents were reduced to a single simple wish (especially an "infantile" one). The dreams described by Freud involve complex feelings and sentiments that go beyond bare, wishful themes. We noted: "Whatever Freud may have said *formally* about the adult's dream wish *always* being reducible to an infantile aim, the fact remains that in his published clinical examples he rarely adhered to such a formulation. The concept 'wish,' as he applied it in his published writings, had broad connotations" (p. 24).

Further, Freud was hard-pressed to defend a simple wish fulfillment concept because many reported dreams are filled with disturbing images. Why would dreams constructed for wishful reasons be containers·of threat? Freud was confronted too with explaining why persons who have experienced a severe trauma may for long periods (and with much attached pain) repeat it in their dreams. He offered various possible explanations for such phenomena (e.g., masochistic inclinations, "repetition compulsion"), but the very fact that they defined exceptions to the simple wish concept significantly diluted the theory.

It is true that in sifting through Freud's writings about dreams, investigators can find here and there references to the possibility that dreams may have a problem-solving function. In one of his essays, he explicitly referred to a class of dreams with no wish fulfillment intent (Freud, 1992):

> Actual experiences of the day are sometimes simply repeated in sleep; reproductions of traumatic scenes in "dreams" have led us only lately to revise the theory of dreams. There are dreams which are to be distinguished from the usual type by certain special qualities, which are, properly speaking, nothing but night-phantasies, not having undergone additions or alterations of any kind and being in all other ways similar to the familiar daydream. It would be awkward, no doubt, to exclude these structures from the domain of "dreams." But still they all come from within, are products of our mental life. (p. 26)

What particularly impressed us was that Freud himself was not comfortable with the simple notion of dream as wish fulfillment. He dodged and twisted and ended up with the view that dreams are wish fulfillments because all things that arise in the unconscious convey wishes. Note his (Freud, 1900) comments on this point:

> But there are reasons for continuing a little with our consideration of wishes as the sole psychical force for the construction of dreams. We have accepted the idea that the reasons why dreams are invariably wish-fulfillments is that they are the products of the system Unconscious, whose activity knows no other aim than the fulfillment of wishes and which has at its command no other forces than wishful impulses. (p. 568)

He elaborates the point by remarking that *all* psychoneurotic symptoms "are to be regarded as fulfillments of unconscious wishes" (p. 569). Further diluting the specificity of the wish concept, he states:

> Thought is after all nothing but a substitute for a hallucinatory wish; and it is self-evident that dreams must be wish-fulfillments, since nothing but a wish can set our mental apparatus at work. Dreams, which

fulfill their wishes along the short path of regression, have merely pre-
served for us in that respect a sample of the psychical apparatus'
method of working. (p. 567)

Thus, we end up with the concept that the dream is wish-fulfilling
in the same sense that thought is. On the basis of such excerpts from
Freud's work we concluded, in 1977:

> When Freud said that dreams are wish fulfilling he simply meant that
> they portray impulses that come from the unconscious. They may be re-
> garded as no more *specifically* or uniquely wish fulfilling than a neurotic
> symptom or a slip of the tongue or any of the other myriad "uncon-
> scious manifestations" he scrutinized. What Freud referred to as
> wishes in many of his dream analyses could just as meaningfully be la-
> beled feelings, attitudes, and conflicts. It is our view that if one exam-
> ines Freud's *total* writings and operations vis-à-vis dreams, it is
> reasonable to conclude that he regarded the dream as a vehicle for the
> *expression* of a variety of unconscious phenomena, such as wishes, at-
> tempts to master anxiety-producing stimuli, and registration of vague
> or subliminal impressions. . . .
>   One should note that although Freud typically ends his analysis of
> each of the dreams he cites in *The Interpretation of Dreams* with a state-
> ment concerning its central wish, he also precedes each with a careful
> inventory of the various disguised feelings and attitudes it seems to
> contain. The final wish formulation represents a generalization from a
> crisscross of themes that have been teased out in this way. The themes
> that appear in Freud's dream analyses variously concern feelings about
> other people, warnings to oneself about dangers, beliefs, criticisms of
> others, and so forth. Freud is *operationally* explicit in his assumption that
> such themes exist in the latent content of the dream. If so, one may rea-
> sonably ask: Do they not have as much reality as the final formulation to
> which he reduces them? Indeed, one could argue that the wish aspect of
> the dream is actually more of an abstraction and less real than the raw
> manifest themes from which Freud considered he had derived them.
> (p. 27)

We further concluded in 1985:

> We see this as one more reason for approaching Freud's dream theory as
> a statement about multiple experiences emanating from the uncon-
> scious sector of the "psychic apparatus" rather than as a single narrow
> category called "wishes." It is a theory about unconscious impulses and
> tensions being vented in a special form of imagery. (pp. 27–28)

This is the version of Freud's dream theory we chose to address in
1977 and we will continue to do so in the present context.

HOW MEANINGFUL IS THE MANIFEST CONTENT?

When we originally set out to test how well Freud's dream theory would stand up to scientific scrutiny, our approach was shaped by the specific version of the wish fulfillment concept we just outlined. But before we could evaluate the scientific literature applicable to this version, we were confronted with the issue of what categories of data were pertinent. This referred essentially to the question whether one could only use studies in which the latent dream content had been examined or whether it was also meaningful to examine data derived from manifest content. In our original efforts to cope with this issue, we analyzed more than a dozen studies that had examined the nature of the relationships existing between manifest and latent dream content. These studies focused on whether there were correlations between the contents of manifest and latent dream categories and also between the contents of manifest dream imagery and imagery elicited by projective stimuli that might be considered comparable to the unconscious latent dream level. In addition, there were a number of interesting explorations of the degree to which significant life experiences and personality attributes of the dreamer registered in the manifest dream structure.

After analyzing this body of literature we concluded that the manifest content is, indeed, sensitive to significant environmental conditions. Further, we judged that it correlates with personality variables; significantly parallels dimensions tapped by projective tests; and changes over the course of the night in logically consistent ways. Basically, we ascertained that ratings of dreams based on manifest content correlate significantly with ratings anchored in the latent content or presumed equivalents. Therefore, we felt there was justification for including studies founded on manifest content in any test of Freud's "wish fulfillment" hypothesis.

We have sifted through the post-1977 dream literature to ascertain what additional information has become available concerning the relationships between manifest and latent content. One of the best studies we located was carried out by Luborsky and Crits-Cristoph (1990). It used transcriptions of multiple psychotherapy sessions with each of three patients (two women and a man). A number of dreams were extracted from each of the therapy transcripts, and they were quantitatively analyzed with the Core Conflictual Relationship Theme (CCRT) technique devised by Luborsky and Crits-Cristoph. The CCRT is a measure that evolved out of the observation that persons in psychotherapy are individually typified by a preoccupation with a specific life theme or conflict. Such themes may concern issues such as closeness-distance, dependence-independence, and confronting or avoiding conflict. It has been shown that CCRT themes persist, in shifting guises, throughout any sequence of therapy sessions and represent major conflictual foci in the individual's life. CCRT ratings can be made with adequate reliability from therapy transcriptions. The major purpose of this study was to determine if the CCRT themes identified from relationship events portrayed in the therapy sessions would match themes derived from dream reports during therapy. What is of particular importance from our perspective is that the CCRT judgments involving the dreams were made under three different conditions:

1. On the basis of the dreams alone.
2. Using the dreams plus the patient's dream associations.
3. In terms of the dreams plus the patient's dream associations plus whatever else occurred during the sessions that included the relationship episodes.

This provides us with the opportunity to determine how the CCRT ratings based simply on the manifest dream content compare with those derived from manifest plus latent content (as defined by associations to the dream material). Luborsky and Crits-Cristoph, after analyzing their findings, arrived at the following conclusions:

> (1) The CCRT could be reliably applied to dreams; (2) the dream-based CCRT's were not significantly altered by the addition of associations to the dreams; and (3) the dream-based and narrative-based CCRT's have significant agreement, which is a basic finding and implies that the CCRT reflects a general central relationship pattern. (p. 172)

With reference to manifest versus latent content, they added:

> Considering the importance accorded to the use of associations to arrive at any understanding of conflictual issues revealed in dreams, more differences might have been expected. (p. 169)

In other words, the addition of the free associations did not significantly alter the character of the CCRT as it had been derived from the manifest content alone. This is a noteworthy finding because, although the CCRT theme is conceptualized as a core (unconscious) personality component, it can apparently be quite adequately reconstructed from the manifest dream content. It is impressive that the CCRT formulation based on the manifest content matched well also with that extracted from the full range of the material in the therapy transcriptions. Overall, this study was unusually well designed and deserves considerable weight.

Another study should be cited that compared certain aspects of manifest and latent dream content. Smith (1986) was interested in the frequency of occurrence of themes of death and separation in dreams compared with the frequency as determined from the associations to such dreams. The subjects in the study were patients on an inpatient cardiology service. After they described a dream to the experimenter, they were then asked to free associate to it. The contents of the dream imagery and of the associations were objectively scored for the presence of death and separation themes. The data indicated that the addition of the dream associations significantly increased the numbers of such theme references. However, Smith concluded that this finding in no way demonstrates that the use of associations provides a more meaningful interpretation of the dream. He noted that although using the dream content alone might exclude some important references that would be provided by dream associations, the use of associative content also might introduce "spurious references to a dream variable" (p. 995).

A few other studies have simply examined certain aspects of the associations individuals give when responding to the manifest content of their dreams. Robbins and Tanck (1978) asked subjects to think of incidents that the contents of their dreams called to mind and subsequently to rate each incident with respect to whether there were associated hopes or wishes that fell into various categories (e.g., sexual, achieving). Scores derived from such ratings were shown to correlate significantly with independent measures of the variables involved. For example, persons with elevated achievement scores on a standard measure of achievement drive, but whose grade point averages were unusually low, turned out to be those who displayed an unusual degree of concern with achievement themes in their associations to the incidents they recalled as linked to their dreams.

A study by Cavallero (1987) merely established that when associations to a dream are obtained shortly after the dream occurs and again two months later, there are significant discrepancies in the material elicited. He concluded that for the more distant (in time) associations, "new affective-cognitive connections are established which are no longer comparable with those existing at the specific moment when the dream was produced" (p. 82). These two studies just cited indicate, on the one hand, that the latent dream content (as defined by associations to the manifest dream) can supply meaningful data, but that there may be limitations on how dream associations can be validly obtained.

In any case, the Luborsky and Crits-Cristoph (1990) study stands out as one of the best (both pre- and post-1977) to be concerned with a direct comparison of manifest and latent dream content. It establishes that the manifest content can, quite independently of the latent level, provide meaningful information about a major psychodynamic variable. This, of course, is not congruent with Freud's dream schema.

Another more indirect approach to the nature of the manifest content has involved examining the relationships between manifest content indexes and measures derived from projective tests. There is reasonable evidence that projective tests (e.g., Rorschach Inkblot Test, Thematic Apperception Test) can tap attitudes and concerns that exist in what Freud regarded as the unconscious sector. Multiple studies (e.g., Goldfried, Stricker, & Weiner, 1971; Witkin, Dyk, Faterson, Goodenough, & Karp, 1962) have demonstrated significant connections between projective measures and others derived from procedures (e.g., exposing individuals to tachistoscopically presented stimuli) that bypass surface defenses. Because Freud regarded the manifest dream as a superficial facade, measures of manifest attributes presumably would not be correlated with projective measures that depict unconscious levels. In our pre-1977 review of this area, however, we detected what we considered to be a trend for certain manifest dream and projective measures to be significantly related. More than a dozen pertinent studies were available, most of which involved the Thematic Apperception Test (Fisher & Greenberg, 1985). The findings were not entirely consistent but were still sufficiently strong to permit reasonable interpretation. We concluded at that time:

> The weight of the studies . . . is in the direction of indicating that the manifest content mirrors attitudes and feelings similar to those that are picked up by projective techniques like the Rorschach inkblots and the Thematic Apperception pictures. If one accepts the assumption that projective tests do not tap superficial defenses but, rather, basic personality vectors, it would seem logical to conclude that the manifest dream content can tap similar vectors. (p. 36)

Since 1977, there has been little evidence in the literature of interest in pursuing the matter. We found only two studies that directly investigated the degree of relationship between measures of manifest content and projective test dimensions. One (Blume, 1979) reported significant positive correlations between the two classes of measures and another (Zepelin, 1980–1981) failed to do so. A certain amount of such inconsistency was, as mentioned, also apparent in the string of pre-1977 studies. We have not been able to tease out any variables that would possibly explain why some studies detect significant correlations and others have not. However, there is much variation in the designs of the studies, such that different Thematic Apperception pictures were used, subjects of markedly different ages participated, and quite different measures were applied to both the dream and projective test contents. Still, we concluded that there are clear instances in which manifest dream content is linked with measures presumably descriptive of unconscious phenomena.

A further approach to exploring the nature of the manifest content derives from observations of the effects of life conditions and experimental manipulations on dreams. By analyzing such effects, the researcher can arrive at a more definitive idea of what manifest imagery represents. In our pre-1977 analyses of the pertinent literature, we concluded that the manifest dream content does, indeed, reflect important life conditions and changes and also basic ego states such as represented by personality parameters. We reviewed published papers that documented correlations between manifest content and such diverse parameters as community conditions (e.g., level of community violence), the state of one's body (e.g., being pregnant, suffering a body defect, menstrual status), sex role, age, and socioeconomic level. Also, there was good evidence that presleep stimuli (e.g., movies, pictures, word associations) presented in a laboratory setting can be objectively detected in subsequent manifest dream content. Finally, we found that differences in manifest dream content are logically related to such personality traits as introversion, orderliness, authoritarianism, and field independence. These data persuaded us (Fisher & Greenberg, 1985) that manifest content is a "reliable source of significant data about the states of dreamers, their personalities, and how they cope, with certain life issues" (p. 46).

Since 1977, additional studies have touched on the various parameters just considered. They have moderately affirmed that the manifest content reflects important life events and conditions. Consider some examples: Smith (1987) has shown that the number of explicit references to death and separation in dreams is positively correlated with the severity of the individual's somatic symptoms (cardiac dysfunction). Kilner (1988) documented that the manifest content of dreams produced by women in the United States differs from that of Gussi women (living in Kenya). The differences were logically related to the contrasting life conditions of the two samples. Blake and Reimann (1993) described the high frequency of pregnancy dream themes in pregnant women. Melstrom and Cartwright (1983) demonstrated that psychotherapy experiences influenced certain manifest content categories. Wood, Bootzin, Rosenhan, Nolen-Hoeksema, and Jourden (1992) observed that experiencing an earthquake increases the frequency of nightmares. Trenholme, Cartwright, and Greenberg (1984) reported that being involved in a divorce significantly affects dream themes.

Davies (1978) found that particular manifest content indicators (e.g., explicit sexual references, hostile images) significantly predict levels of anxiety and psychological disturbance.

Other studies depict the significant impact of presleep experiences on the manifest contents of dreams. Thus, Cipolli, Fagioli, Maccolini, and Salzarulo (1983) showed that exposure to presleep stimuli composed of statements in sentence form could result in the incorporation of such stimuli into the subsequent manifest dream content. Relatedly, de Jong and Visser (1983) and Lauer, Riemann, Lund, and Berger (1987) reported that presleep exposure to films influenced the manifest mood and anxiety level of subsequent dreams. Interestingly, Hoelscher, Klinger, and Barta (1981) were able to modify manifest dream content by presenting stimuli to subjects while they were asleep.

These illustrative citations reaffirm the pre-1977 findings that the manifest content mirrors a spectrum of life experiences and personality variables.

DREAMS AS VENTING OUTLETS

Pre-1977 Findings

As already noted, we originally concluded that the core of Freud's dream theory relates to the idea that dreams are primarily a vehicle for venting tensions, conflicts, and wishes from the unconscious. Our review of the pre-1977 literature pertinent to this issue considered three lines of research. First, we examined the available studies dealing with the effects of REM sleep deprivation[1] (which presumably robs the individual of a substantial amount of dream time). If dreaming is a significant outlet for unconscious tensions, interference with dreaming should have serious negative psychological effects. We found that although early researchers (e.g., Dement, 1960; Dement & Fisher, 1963) had exaggerated such effects (e.g., even suggesting that psychosis could be triggered), there did appear to be a definite trend, across a considerable number of studies, for dream deprivation to produce at least some degree of psychological upset or adaptation. We (Fisher & Greenberg, 1985) concluded: "At least indirectly, the observations support Freud's hypothesis that the dream helps to maintain psychological equilibrium by providing a partial means for discharging unconscious impulses" (p. 53).

---

[1] REM (Rapid Eye Movements) refers to a phase of sleep characterized by such eye movements and associated with frequent reports of dreaming by individuals when awakened.

Next, we appraised a spectrum of publications concerned with the effects on dreams of inputs that are deeply personally involving or specifically directed at mobilizing unconscious responses. Presumably, such inputs would build up pressures in the unconscious that would require venting and therefore register in various forms of corresponding dream imagery. We considered that the majority of the past studies in this area affirmed the expectation. For example, Breger, Hunter, and Lane (1971) demonstrated that normal individuals exposed to highly involving group therapy sessions that probed intimate issues evidenced alterations in their dreams (obtained pre- and post-therapy in a sleep laboratory), such that they displayed more anxiety, cognitive disturbance, and intensity of personal involvement. Breger et al. were also able to show similar dream alterations in persons exposed to the massive threat of surgery. Other analogous vectors that had been studied involved viewing emotionally charged films, experiencing disturbing failure, and coping with the arousal of feelings of personal inadequacy.

Third, we looked at the pre-1977 literature pertinent to determining whether psychological maladjustment, which in the context of Freudian theory presumably signals that unacceptable tensions have mounted and are seeking outlet, registers in dream venting imagery. Presumably, those who are psychologically upset would require either an unusual amount of dream time or dream experiences of unusual intensity (for extra venting). We (Fisher & Greenberg, 1985) thought in general that there were fairly impressive indications in the literature "that the more disturbed individual will have a greater need to vent material in his dreams" (p. 60).

Overall, the accumulated pre-1977 research findings seemed to be congruent with the notion that dreams can serve a basic venting function. Despite this congruence, however, we did not feel the data specifically documented the centrality of a venting model. Dreams appeared to serve venting functions, but how often they actually did so was not definable, nor could investigators specify how large a part venting played modally in the dream process. We also noted that even if dreams did provide venting outlets, there was no assurance that Freud was correct in declaring that only unconscious tensions get expressed. Indeed, previous studies (e.g., Breger, Hunter, & Lane, 1971) indicated that tensions may exist at a conscious level and still be targeted preoccupations in dreams.

A particularly important conclusion we reached on the basis of the literature was that although dreams occur in a unique sleep state, dream imagery does not represent a unique class, but rather is part of the larger category of fantasy. Is there any reason to assume that because daydreaming occurs in the awake state that daydream fantasy is distinct from dream fantasy? We could find little basis for assuming such a lack of continuity. Apropos of this point we (Fisher & Greenberg, 1985) noted: "There is little rationale for assuming that continuity does not prevail between processes that occur at different stages of consciousness" (p. 65). We pointed out that Fiss, Klein, and Bokert (1966) demonstrated that fantasy typifying an individual's REM state carries over into fantasy material secured immediately on awakening from that state. They indicated that stories obtained from subjects after interrupted REM sleep contained more visual, bizarre, and emotional imagery than did stories during control waking periods, and they concluded: "The results strongly suggest that the distinguishing properties of a sleep stage are not 'switched off' following awakening, but may persist into the waking stage" (p. 65). We have already referred to a literature indicating significant correlations between the contents of persons' dreams and the contents of the fantasies they produce when responding in the awake state to various projective tests. On the basis of such observations, it seemed logical to regard dreaming as having many of the same functions as other forms of fantasy and thought: to process information, to organize ideas, and to arrive at creative constructions.

Post-1977 Findings

The post-1977 dream literature abounds with many new hypotheses and leads concerning the nature of dreaming. There are even assertions by some (e.g., Hobson & McCarley, 1977) that dreams are basically meaningless attempts to integrate random excitatory inputs from the brain stem into the cortex or that they are simply a form of "neural dumping" (Crick & Mitchison, 1986) that removes from semantic memory superfluous and interfering information left over from the previous day. However, considerable research pointing up the continuity of dream sequences and the problem-solving capabilities of dream imagery (e.g., Domhoff, 1993; Koulack, 1993; Vogel, Vogel, McAbee, Barker, & Thurmond, 1980; Winson, 1992) convincingly challenges theories that portray dreaming as simply a physiological epiphenomenon.

What now is apparent in the research literature is that dreaming may serve many functions. This is in line with our own previously described position that dreaming can fulfill the same variety of purposes typifying any of the general waking forms of fantasy and thought. Foulkes (1993), after surveying the pertinent research, offered a compact summary of such a perspective:

> The immediate function (effect) of dreaming is comparable to the immediate function of waking consciousness: making plausible sense of currently impinging or accessible information. All that is different about

dreaming is the nature of this information. In the extreme case, the difference is between dreaming's diffusely active and unrelated mnemonic sources and waking's attentively focused and naturally patterned perceptual sources. But our best evidence now is that the cognitive interpretive system . . . operating on information is, dreaming or waking, one and the same. This suggests that the search for "special" functions for dream consciousness may be misguided. To the degree that dream experience is different from waking experience, that difference only reflects the more dissociated sources of dreaming. (p. 14)

In appraising the multiple functions currently ascribed to dreaming, we were impressed that they generally involved notions about how the dream process facilitates coping with stress and unpleasantness. A number of researchers have hit on the idea that dreams, in contexts of frustration and problem-solving, serve to integrate important realms of information. These researchers emphasize that dreaming facilitates integrating present experiences with past related memories. Greenberg and Pearlman (1993), who are prime advocates[2] of this concept, portray dreams "as providing the opportunity to store recent memories by matching them with memories from the past, thus providing a sense of integration and continuity" (p. 369). They see this integrative process as facilitating "schemata for the performance of certain complicated activities of which the most important . . . is the management of emotional life and its interaction with the environment" (p. 377). This "information processing" view of dreaming was derived from experiments that variously demonstrated that the brain is highly activated during REM dreaming and that tasks requiring creative thinking are impaired by prior REM deprivation (Greenberg & Pearlman, 1993).

Relatedly, Domhoff (1993) proposed that dreams are "an attempt at resolving emotional preoccupations" (p. 295). They are, he said, a form of preoccupation with unresolved problems. He notes that many previous theorists (e.g., Breger, 1967; French & Fromm, 1964; Hartmann, 1984; Kramer, 1982) adopted a similar view. In his analysis of the contents of traumatic dreams, recurrent dreams, lifelong nightmares, and long dream series, he is impressed with how they represent persistent defensive efforts to cope with disturbing problems. Thus, he cites some evidence that recurrent dreams tend to disappear when the underlying issue or conflict represented repetitively in the dreams is resolved.

Koulack (1993) has examined in detail the concept of the dream as having adaptive value. He points out that with the flood of papers demonstrating that dreams are affected by such diverse inputs as

---

[2] See also Palombo (1978).

illness, experiencing group therapy, threatening films, social isolation, stressful intellectual demands, and menstruation, it was logical to speculate about possible adaptive functions. It was considered that adaptation could take such multiple forms as incorporating threatening material into the dream to integrate it with other memories or themes, desensitizing threat by incorporating it into the dream without any accompanying emotions, and instilling into the dream themes that compensatorily represent the opposite of the threat.

Koulack cites studies showing that the impact of presleep negative experiences on subsequent morning mood after awakening is mediated by the manner and degree to which the negativity has been incorporated into the intervening dream process. He indicates that the repertoire of strategies for mastering stressful issues found in dream constructions is analogous to that seen in waking defensive efforts. As conditions require, the dream content may focus on the threat, deny the threat, or alternately focus on and deny, and so forth. The presumed flexibility of such defensive modes is highlighted in Koulack's statement that although clearly recalled incorporation of a stressful event into a dream may represent an attempt at mastery, not remembering a dream at all might serve as an effective form of defensive denial. The experimental literature cited by Koulack in support of his statements is far from conclusive but is clearly suggestive.

Rotenberg (1993) conceptualizes dreaming as playing a significant role in what he refers to as "search activity," which he defines as "activity designed to change the situation or the subject's attitude to it in the absence of a definite forecast of the results of such activity . . . but with constant monitoring of the results at all stages of activity" (p. 262). "Search activity" represents active attempts at mastery and problem solving; and stands in contrast to passivity, surrender, and giving up in the face of adversity. A good deal of evidence exists that renunciation of search often results in negative biological and psychological consequences. Rotenberg carried out a number of experiments that support the idea that REM sleep and the accompanying dreams play a role in "permitting compensation for the biologically, psychologically, and socially harmful state of renunciation of search" (p. 272). Illustratively, it has been shown that top-class athletes who suffer serious athletic defeat that might cause a reaction of surrender begin to manifest longer periods of REM. Another study demonstrated that students who experienced signs of "unproductive emotional tension" as a consequence of taking examinations had greater REM on the postexamination night than did students not exhibiting such signs.

Numerous other interpreters of the research literature have come up with analogous perspectives. Winson (1992), after analyzing a number of studies concerned with REM, concluded:

In keeping with evaluation and evidence derived from dream reports, I suggest that dreams reflect each individual's strategy for survival. The ideas are broad ranging, including self-image, insecurities as well as secure areas and grandiose ideas, sexual orientation and desires, and jealousy and love. (pp. 353–354)

Ellman (1992) who has undertaken a program of research (involving animals and humans) concerned with the motivational systems underlying the dream process stated: "Dreams in later childhood and adulthood contain wishes and frequently represent conflict. However, the original impetus for a dream is to represent drive behaviors so that they may be facilitated in waking life" (p. 371). Although Ellman is more impressed than most contemporary observers with the wish element in dreams, he focuses on the dream as a means of facilitating adaptation to danger, conflict, and reaching "consummatory" goals.

Other scattered ideas concerning the functions of dreams exist that do not focus specifically on issues of adaptation and problem solving.[3] However, the major theme in most of the current analyses of dream functions relates to facilitating adaptation to difficulty and stress. The accumulating literature in this area does not favor a venting or drive-reduction concept of dreaming. The trend has been to move away from formulations that focus on some narrow function of dreaming and instead to favor theories highlighting the general defensive or self-protective role of the dream process.

Overall, the pre-1977 findings concerning the presumed venting role of dreams are diffuse and imprecise. The lack of precision applies particularly to testing the proposition that dreams are outlets for tensions that accumulate specifically in the unconscious. Many of the studies cited in favor of the venting model really take off from the assumption that individuals who are exposed to stressful or traumatic stimuli necessarily experience strong unconscious tensions that require venting. The fact is that we have little validated knowledge of how stressful events register at unconscious levels. There is solid work indicating that defined inputs below conscious awareness can trigger predicted defensive and "release" phenomena (e.g., Bornstein & Pittman, 1992; Silverman, 1983), thereby suggesting that they have a targeted impact on a psychological region equivalent to Freud's concept of the unconscious. It is, however, a bit of a leap to assume that such a targeted unconscious effect will result from stimuli that are not specifically designed to gain access to unconscious levels.

---

[3] For example, Fiss (1993) presents data indicating the power of dreams for detecting significant sensations and feelings within oneself. He recounts a study that found a statistically significant positive correlation between severity of cardiac illness and the frequency of references to death and separation in one's dreams.

What in the post-1977 literature is pertinent to the effects of REM deprivation on the venting process? A good deal has been learned about REM deprivation research that points up the limitations of this approach. It is now documented (e.g., Foulkes, 1985; Hunt, 1989; McGrath & Cohen, 1978) that REM deprivation may only partially interfere with dreaming because it can also occur during NREM periods. Further, it is apparent that the repeated awakenings of subjects at the outset of REM to block dreaming produce fatigue and other negative feelings that are difficult to disentangle from the presumed effects of dream deprivation as such. The defects in the usual REM deprivation design are quite serious and encourage skepticism about studies based on that paradigm. Perhaps because of such growing skepticism and the emergence of data concerning the general problem-solving functions of dreaming, there has been a marked decline in the number of studies using REM deprivation to evaluate Freud's venting hypothesis. We have located only a few even remotely pertinent efforts in the post-1977 literature (e.g., Glaubman, Orbach, Aviram, Frieder, Frieman, Pelled, & Glaubman, 1978; Greenberg, 1981; Greenberg, Pearlman, Schwartz, & Grossman, 1983; McGrath & Cohen, 1980; Pearlman, 1982).

These studies largely deal with the cognitive effects (e.g., memory, divergent thinking) of REM deprivation and have little bearing on Freud's concept of venting. Also, our previous assumption that studies showing changes in dreams as a function of exposure to stress or the occurrence of psychopathology were relevant to the venting hypothesis now appears to have been ill considered. The assumption simply lacks meaningful specificity. The studies in question can be more economically interpreted within the framework of adaptation or defense than within the venting concept.

Levin (1990), after extensively reviewing the research concerned with the validity of Freud's dream venting hypothesis, decided that the findings were too vague and contradictory to permit a reasonable conclusion. He states: "Despite the findings of a biological need for REM, the inability to obtain consistent results regarding drive outlet mitigates against the Freudian model of economic discharge, which emphasizes the need for reduction of pent-up excitation" (p. 30).

SLEEP PRESERVATION

As earlier mentioned, Freud theorized that dreams have a sleep-preserving function. He suggested that unconscious impulses seeking outlet at night might alarm the sleeper and result in awakening and disruption of sleep. He proposed that dreaming could provide partial release for the impulses, but in a sufficiently disguised (by the manifest content) fashion to prevent the buildup of anxiety to an intensity that might disrupt sleep. In our pre-1977 evaluation of Freud's formulation, we asserted that there was no support for it in the scientific literature. We (Fisher & Greenberg, 1985) referred to findings that indicated:

> Dreaming occurs in a regular cyclical fashion . . . closer to a fixed bio-logical rhythm than to a pattern indicating adaptation to threatening stimuli from moment to moment. . . . It is not initiated at scattered or ir-regular times, such as one might expect if it were a response to stimuli, dangerous to sleep, that appear unpredictably. In other words, dream-ing follows a rather rigid schedule relatively independent of the events confronting an individual while asleep. (p. 62)

Others (e.g., Dement, 1964) were equally negative regarding the sleep preservation notion.

Since 1977, however, there are stirrings in the literature indicative of a possible shift in perspective. Hunt (1989) speculates that REM sleep may be "compensatory for and protective of the lengthy deep sleep necessary for large-brained creatures: Without the periodic corti-cal arousal of the REM state, the restitution either would be endan-gered or would itself endanger cortical homeostasis" (p. 33). Actually, this comment is only tangentially pertinent to Freud's specific concept of sleep preservation.

Kramer (1993) offers several more specific points that he feels favor Freud's formulation. He states:

> Freud . . . has proposed that dreaming serves to protect the continuity of sleep. Taking our lead from this proposal, the physiological study of REM sleep . . . has contributed two observations that buttress this sug-gestion. First, if the dream is related to maintaining sleep and if the longer one sleeps the more likely one is to wake up, after the initial set-tling down process, then the distribution of REM sleep across the usual sleep period is appropriate: it is positively accelerated, more of it occur-ring later in the night. . . . The second observation about the dream's role in the continuity of sleep relates to the frequent finding that a pe-riod of dreaming sleep, REM sleep, often ends in a brief arousal. . . . The rise and fall in the intensity of affect and content across the dream pe-riod is consonant with the possibility that during REM sleep there is a surge of emotion. We speculate that a function of dreaming is to contain or attempt to contain this surge. (pp. 143, 145)

Kramer conjectures that if a dream is successful in containing the "emotional surge" characterizing each REM period, the brief arousal that occurs is not remembered. However, if the dreamer is emotionally upset[4] and therefore hyperresponsive, the surge may not be "contained" and the probability of a frightening awakening is presumably increased. Kramer reviews the literature indicating the essential need for a sufficient amount of "core sleep" and proposes that every effort has to be made to safeguard such sleep by maximizing dream fantasy that is reassuring and denying of underlying feelings of threat. These are interesting ideas, but they obviously require more specific empirical support before one can regard them as scientifically anchored.

OVERVIEW

Essentially, two major points have emerged from our analysis of the dream literature. First, we have been able to reaffirm that the manifest content of the dream is full of meaning relatively easy to access. It is not simply, as Freud theorized, a cover or camouflage for the real meaning of the dream that is contained in the latent core. The concept of "latent content" remains vague, and the process (free associating) recommended by Freud for decoding the latent core remains operationally unreliable.

Second, the expanding dream research literature renders Freud's venting model of the dream less tenable as a major form of explanation. Perhaps dreams do sometimes provide outlets for releasing tensions, but the accumulating research portrays the dream process in more general adaptive terms. Apparently, dreams can provide multiple levels of defense and self-protection. They may highlight issues or deny them; conjure up potential solutions; or alternatively shift from one defense mode to another. Specific forms of dreaming have diversely been shown to facilitate complex learning, to neutralize stress, to provide sensitive signal detection powers, and to invent creative images. Some researchers (Purcell, Moffitt, & Hoffman, 1993) urge that the fantasy modes (e.g., primary process), said by Freud to underlie dream construction, may be just as differentiated, complex, and clever as secondary process.

The flawed character of Freud's original dream theory should have been evident in his own confusion about manifest versus latent content. As Grunbaum (1984) and others (e.g., Erikson, 1954) have shown, Freud frequently used elements in the so-called manifest content to develop

---

[4] Kramer (1993) cites research data indicating that persons who experience disturbed ("noncontained") dreaming are more likely to show signs of maladjustment (as measured by standard psychological tests) than do those individuals who do not report such dream upset.

his dream interpretations. Operationally, he repeatedly ignored the theoretical distinction between the "manifest" and "latent." Of course, we now know that the manifest dream story explicitly mirrors powerful feelings, attitudes, and experiences of the individual involved. It is patently not a meaningless deceptive facade. Incidentally, in our (Fisher & Greenberg, 1985) original discussion of the manifest-latent distinction, we noted the relativity involved. We pointed out, for example, that the meanings to be extracted by observers from the manifest dream story could vary widely as a function of how much they knew about symbols, their ability to understand metaphor, and so forth.

Once the assumed camouflaging function of the manifest content came into question, this rendered implausible Freud's concept of the dream as a special vehicle for expressing repressed wishes. If the explicit dream is full of transparent meaning, it cannot sensibly be pictured as a device designed for concealment. It does not, then, lend itself to a repression paradigm, let alone the assertion that the dream is specifically designed to give partial (but concealed) outlets for secret wishes.

In the general sense that he perceived underlying adaptive intent in dream construction and attempted to conceptualize this process within an apparent empirical framework, Freud was a genuine pathfinder. As earlier noted, there were times when he seemed to grasp the general adaptive and defensive properties of dreaming. However, he could not really give up the originality and uniqueness of his wish-fulfillment formulation and basically stuck with it. Also, he was so infatuated with the concept of the dream as a channel to and from the unconscious that he did not recognize the role of the dream in contemplating or scanning just everyday frustrations and difficulties. He did not grasp the general nature of the dream as a cognitive processor.[5] Relatedly, he did not recognize that the cognitive events of the dream state, despite their context of a less articulated level of consciousness, could be as complex and oriented to problem solving as those ascribed by him to secondary process. Curiously, it has turned out that the original differences among Freud, Jung, and Adler concerning the functions of dreaming (ranging across a drive-venting, compensatory, and self-protective spectrum) were not as contradictory as they appeared and, in their very range, anticipated the eclectic picture of function prevalent in the contemporary dream research scene.

---

[5] See Foulkes (1985) for a detailed application of a cognitive-psychological frame to dream phenomena.

Questions concerning the functions[6] of dreaming are even further complicated by the possible roles of cultural and individual relativities. Anthropological studies have shown that cultures differ considerably in how open and comfortable they are with experiences that depart from the well-articulated waking level. McManus, Laughlin, and Shearer (1993) offer a classification of cultures with respect to this dimension. At one extreme are "monophasic" cultures that

> tend to value experiences occurring only in "normal" waking state. These are cultures that effectively give credence to only those phases of consciousness that lie at the external adaptation pole in the circadian cycle. Exploration of dream and other alternative phases is typically proscribed, disparaged, or simply not socially facilitated in development. (p. 35)

At the other extreme are the "transcendental polyphasic" cultures that

> believe that exploration of dreaming and other alternative phases is a route to the realization of an ultimate Transcendental Experience (e.g., union with a godhead, experience of the essence of mind, void consciousness, enlightenment. (p. 37)

Individuals living in cultures at either of these extremes might well differ in the degree to which they rely on dream imagery to inform themselves concerning their internal feelings or to communicate dream events to others as a way of influencing them. Data indicate that individuals can, if suitably motivated, learn to manipulate the vividness of their dream experiences and even to alter their contents (Hunt, 1989; Purcell, Moffitt, & Hoffmann, 1993). If a culture encouraged the cultivation of such skills, individuals might very well devise new ways of utilizing their dreams for purposes of problem solving, creativity, and detection of emotional issues that would otherwise go unrecognized. Thus, they would be able to fashion new functions for their basic dream capability.

It is likely that persons who differ in personality or defense modes might approach their dreams differentially and learn to utilize them in specialized ways suited to their idiosyncratic needs (e.g., Hunt, 1989). Those who are sensitizers might approach their dreams looking for additional imagery and signs to reinforce their view that the world is a dangerous, threatening place. Repressors might cultivate a quite different dream pattern. A dream style might be fashioned that

---

[6] Antrobus (1993) discusses the possibility that dreams may have no functions.

would serve to reinforce a particular worldview or self-concept. Some individuals might find that dream imagery could fill many highly useful functions for them, whereas others would limit such functions to a minimal level. Implicit in this view is the idea that dreaming involves multiple levels of response and multiple kinds of skills and each individual may be in a position to create a unique profile of functions for self.[7] If so, it becomes less and less creditable to pigeonhole dreaming into a few narrow functional categories.

[7] In discussing the potential for influencing one's dreams, Purcell, Moffitt, and Hoffman (1993) state: "This freedom to choose, influence, or control dream structure and events, including the conscious decision not to exercise such control, is spontaneous but can be enhanced by learning, expands with practice, and includes the acquisition of many dream skills" (p. 214).

PART TWO

The Therapy

Chapter 8

Evaluating Psychoanalytic Therapy

Once More into the Abyss

There are several significant obstacles to evaluating the efficacy of Freud's approach to psychological treatment. Perhaps most significant is that the term psychoanalysis or psychoanalytic treatment has not been applied with precision. In fact, when we reviewed the evidence pertaining to Freud's brand of treatment several years ago, we concluded that a unified and consistent approach to treatment called "psychoanalysis" does not exist (Fisher & Greenberg, 1985).[1] We described study after study documenting considerable disagreement among analytic practitioners regarding such things as treatment techniques, case conceptualization, the goals for treatment outcome, and the types of cases best suited for psychoanalysis.

Historically, dissension within the analytic establishment is reflected in the findings of a committee set up by the American Psychoanalytic Association in 1947. The committee concluded that the Association's members showed strong resistance even to studying the question of what constitutes psychoanalysis or psychoanalytic psychotherapy (Rangell, 1954). Up to the present day, there has been a pervasive tendency to obliterate any distinction between treatments labeled psychoanalysis and those labeled "psychodynamic" psychotherapy among mental health practitioners and the general public.

---

[1] *The Scientific Credibility of Freud's Theories and Therapy* was originally published in 1977 by Basic Books. It was subsequently reissued in 1985 by Columbia University Press. We are using the 1985 citation throughout this volume.

Some of the ambiguity about the process of psychoanalysis can be traced directly to Freud, who was quite hesitant to describe details of the technique of psychoanalysis. Freud (1913), presenting an analogy between chess and psychotherapy, concluded that only some of the opening and closing moves could be known, with the rest being left to intuitively applied guidelines. Strachey (1958) felt there were a number of reasons for Freud's reluctance to publish material on his technique. Among them were Freud's hesitation to allow his patients to know too many details of his approach, his feeling that hard-and-fast rules should not be given to analysts, and his belief that clinical experiences and the analyst's analysis were superior to reading books for acquiring mastery of psychoanalysis.

Freud's unwillingness to describe in detail how to implement his therapy is antithetical to the modern psychotherapy researcher's push to produce elaborate, manualized accounts of specific approaches to conducting psychotherapy. These treatment guidebooks (e.g., Beck, Rush, Shaw, & Emery, 1979; Klerman, Weismann, Rounsaville, & Chevron, 1984; Luborsky, 1984; Strupp & Binder, 1984) may serve multiple purposes. They specify the techniques to be used in a particular approach, provide a blueprint for training practitioners, and furnish possible guidelines for empirically assessing a therapist's adherence to a particular approach possibly through a process analysis of recorded sessions (Stiles, Shapiro, & Elliot, 1986). Freud was much looser in stipulating his requirements for therapeutic ingredients than modern-day researchers would find desirable. His somewhat sketchy, global picture of his approach to treatment is illustrated by one of his statements defining psychoanalytic therapy:

> It may thus be said that the theory of psychoanalysis is an attempt to account for two striking and unexpected facts of observation which emerge whenever an attempt is made to trace the symptoms of a neurotic back to their sources in his past life: the facts of transference and resistance. Any line of investigation (therapy) which recognizes these two facts and takes them as the starting-point of its work has a right to call itself psychoanalysis even though it arrives at results other than my own. But anyone who takes up other sides of the problem while avoiding these two hypotheses will hardly escape a charge of misappropriation of property by attempted impersonation, if he persists in calling himself a psychoanalyst. (Freud, 1914, p. 16)

Freud's apparent disdain for detailing psychoanalytic technique presents an obstacle to evaluating treatment outcome because it makes it extremely difficult (if not impossible) to demonstrate that the treatment being evaluated is actually taking place. The ambiguity in Freud's statements has undoubtedly played a role in the demonstrated unreliability that "analysts" bring to clinical tasks (Fisher & Greenberg, 1985).[2] One result of this evidence of lack of precision is that examinations of the efficacy of psychoanalytic treatment are less tests of Freud's approach than they are observations about how a multitude of clinicians present their versions of what they believe Freud might have meant.

Another impediment to an objective, empirical evaluation of psychoanalysis as a treatment method has been the hesitation of analytic practitioners to move beyond describing single cases to viewing aggregated data derived from pools of patients. Emotional and vehement opinion has surged around whether it is more meaningful to evaluate psychoanalysis through the reporting of personal observations and testimonials about individual cases or through the presentation of impersonal, research data that can be more easily subjected to statistical analysis.[3] As with other issues, Freud's statements can be seen as endorsing each of these opposing viewpoints at different times. For example, in an essay written about Leonardo da Vinci, Freud (1910) stepped away from supporting personal testimonial, in stating approvingly of Leonardo: "He dared to utter the bold assertion which contains within itself the justification for all independent research . . . (that) 'he who appeals to authority when there is a difference of opinion works with his memory rather than with his reason'" (p. 122).

At other times, Freud took a clearly antiempirical stance, as in his remarks (1933) on the Berlin Psychoanalytic Institute's report on 10 years of treatment outcome data:

> Its therapeutic successes give grounds neither for boasting nor for being ashamed. But statistics of that kind are in general uninstructive; the material worked upon is so heterogeneous that only very large numbers would show anything. It is wiser to examine one's individual experiences. (p. 152)

Also hindering assessments of Freud's treatment was his apparent withdrawal from concerns about outcome. In our previous review

---

[2] In the past, we have discussed that psychoanalytic concepts can be reliably judged when the variables are operationally defined in a consistent manner among judges, as they are in many research studies (Fisher & Greenberg, 1985, p. 296). Caston (1993) and Caston and Martin (1993) have reviewed and cleverly demonstrated the potential for reliable analyst judgments in research contexts.

[3] We are aware that meaningful empirical research can be conducted with single-case research designs (see, e.g., the special section devoted to single-case psychotherapy research edited by E. E. Jones in the *Journal of Consulting and Clinical Psychology*, 1993, *61*, 371–420). Our concerns are aimed at the purely anecdotal case report as evidence of efficacy.

(Fisher & Greenberg, 1985), we detailed Freud's shift away from an initial interest in symptom alleviation to an emphasis on finding substantiation within therapy sessions for his developing theories of personality. He initially believed that the revelation to the patient of the underlying dynamics of conflicts would automatically alleviate symptoms. Understanding of the theoretical causes of discomforts (insight) was assumed to translate directly into therapeutic success. This unproven hypothesis gradually led Freud to slide away almost entirely from the question of whether his treatment was beneficial to his patients. In fact, when we reviewed the cases he had written about, we discovered that very few were presented in any detail, that the presentations were selective, and that his patient sample was biased in terms of social class, age, and gender (Fisher & Greenberg, 1985). Surprisingly, we were forced to conclude that no evidence was ever presented by Freud, in either case study or statistical form, to show that his treatment was benefiting a significant number of his own patients.

Freud's desire to deflect focus away from treatment outcome is codified in his warnings against "furor therapeuticus." Greenacre documented that these warnings appear in numerous places in Freud's writings (Oberndorf, Greenacre, & Kubie, 1949). There is a seeming paradox in Freud's ambitious goal of fundamental personality change and his espousing goallessness as the proper technical analytic stance. This inconsistency has been noted and discussed by Wallerstein (1965). The paradox reflects Freud's preoccupation with proving that he was not influencing the verbal productions of his patients. Obtaining nondistorted patient accounts of their innermost feelings, unsullied by suggestion, was necessary for providing evidence to support his theoretical hypotheses about the development of personality and psychopathology.

Elsewhere (Fisher & Greenberg, 1985) we have taken the position that findings from social psychological studies demonstrate the impossibility of entering an interaction with the object of observation without influencing the material produced (e.g., Rosenthal, 1966). We have cited compelling evidence for the idea that having a predetermined theoretical bias leads clinicians to distorted perceptions and the discovery of relationships in data even when the relationships are absent in the presented material (e.g., Chapman & Chapman, 1967). Detailed philosophical critiques have also highlighted the evidential weaknesses in trying simultaneously to demonstrate therapeutic efficacy and personality theory validity from case study reports (Grunbaum, 1984, 1993).

Nonetheless, Freud, undeterred by the possibility that suggestion was tainting his patients' productions, pressed on with creating the illusion of undistorted data. He even seemed willing to ignore the question of patient benefit in his quest to create an enduring explanatory scheme for personality development and symptom creation. Freud's shift from treatment outcome concerns to accentuating psychoanalysis as a theoretical explanatory model is reflected in statements he made near the end of his career. For example, he wrote, "Analysis in claiming to cure neuroses by ensuring control over instinct, is always right in theory but not always right in practice" (Freud, 1937, p. 229). Similarly, he stated:

> I have told you that psychoanalysis began as a method of treatment, but I do not want to commend it to your interest as a method of treatment but on account of the truths it contains, on account of the information it gives us about what concerns human beings most of all—their own nature—and on account of the connections it discloses between the most different of their activities. (Freud, 1933, pp. 156–157).

Freud's shift from outcome concerns to an emphasis on theory substantiation, in concert with his reliance on case study material, is an implicit endorsement of analyst retreat from subjecting work to an empirical test of efficacy. It is therefore not difficult to understand why the apparent theoretical coherence of a patient's in-therapy narrative may be reassuring to the clinician, even when the patient's extratherapy behavior has not changed. A model placing little emphasis on outcome is very much in line with the ultimate thrust of Freud's writings.

Our initial task in this chapter is to briefly review what is known about the outcome of treatments labeled psychoanalytic psychotherapy. As we are suggesting, however, this task is to some degree contaminated by the impurities that unreliable psychotherapists introduce into the process. Later, we will review the evidence regarding the importance of the variables that Freud regarded as significant therapeutic ingredients.

TESTING PSYCHOANALYTIC THERAPY OUTCOME

In our comprehensive review of the evidence through 1976 on psychoanalytic psychotherapy outcome, we grouped studies into three general categories: surveys; comparisons with no treatment groups; and comparisons with groups treated by alternative psychotherapies (Fisher & Greenberg, 1985). Although we discussed the results obtained from eight large-scale surveys of the results of psychoanalysis (Alexander, 1954; Feldman, 1968; Fenichel, 1930; Hamburg et al., 1967; Hyman, 1936; Jones, 1926–1936; Kessel & Hyman, 1933; Knight, 1941), we concluded that such findings had little meaning because of a lack of control groups and comparative data. Therefore—even setting aside the problem of subjectivity in the outcome ratings—it was impossible to reasonably demonstrate that comparable success rates would not have been achieved without treatment or with the use of alternative approaches. The major difficulties inherent in trying to interpret survey data are well described by Meltzoff and Kornreich (1970):

> More often than not, surveys have been retrospective in nature. They consist of tabulation of judgments of success and failure, either dichotomized or scaled to reflect the degree of improvement, and are summarized in a percentage of improvement. In most surveys, there is no way of knowing what such terms as "recovered," "much improved," and "slightly improved" mean. There is little constancy in the meaning of these terms from survey to survey. The original data is poor because it usually relies exclusively on the subjective judgment of the therapist or that of the researcher, who depends on case records written by the therapist. The errors are compounded by a reviewer . . . who takes the improvement percentages (which may be grossly inaccurate to start with) from diverse sources and averages them to arrive at a total estimate of outcome regarded as authoritative because it is based upon so many thousands of cases. The size of the N in such an amalgamation is bound to be impressive but contributes not at all to the validity of the information. (pp. 64–65)

Concluding that survey research showed limited usefulness, we turned our attention to studies that might demonstrate the superiority of psychoanalytic therapy to no-treatment or to alternative treatment approaches. Our search for studies permitting a contrast between psychoanalysis and no-treatment uncovered six investigations. All indicated that psychoanalysis produces positive change when compared with no-treatment. However, all the reports presented obvious methodological deficiencies. Three of the publications were based on the case ratings of individual therapists (Cappon, 1964; Orgel, 1958; Schjelderup, 1955). The results are therefore questionable as confirmations of psychoanalytic efficacy because outcome might be as easily attributed to specific therapist characteristics as to the employment of a psychoanalytic treatment method. Furthermore, the researchers assumed, in these studies, that improvement would not have occurred without treatment because the treated patients had experienced many years of unremitting symptoms before undergoing psychoanalytic care. Of the remaining three studies, two indicated that patients treated with a psychoanalytic approach showed greater improvement in somatic symptoms than no-treatment control groups (Duhrssen & Jorswieck, 1965; O'Conner et al., 1964). Yet, neither report presented much detail on the specifics of the therapy or therapists employed, and one did not report the outcome in statistical terms or use a no-treatment control group that had an initial level of psychological health equivalent to the treatment group (O'Connor et al., 1964). The remaining study, offering a comparison of psychoanalysis with no-treatment, used inexperienced therapists and did not assign patients to the treatment and wait-list conditions in a random fashion (Barendregt, Bastiaans, & Vermeul-van Mullen, 1961). Eight measures of outcome were obtained (some of dubious sensitivity to therapeutic effects), and only one showed a difference favoring the treatment group. In this study, those treated by psychoanalysis became less defensive and more flexible.

In sum, the six investigations produced relatively consistent but flawed evidence that psychoanalytic treatment produces results that are superior to no-treatment for patients with chronic problems.

Our past attempt to compare the results of psychoanalysis to alternative treatments resulted in a review of 10 studies (Barendregt et al., 1961; Cartwright, 1966; Cremerius, 1962; Dudek, 1970; Ellis, 1957; Heilbrunn, 1963, 1966; Heine, 1953; Kernberg et al., 1972; O'Conner et al., 1964; Weber, Elinson, & Moss, 1966, 1967). In some ways, interpretations of these comparisons were hampered even more than the contrasts with no-treatment because of the vagueness in defining the various treatments and the typical failure to demonstrate a priori that the alternative treatments were distinct from each other on important dimensions. The problem is particularly amplified in studies attempting to show differential outcomes between treatments labeled "psychoanalysis" and those labeled "psychoanalytically oriented." Here the distinction appears to rest primarily on the supposition that psychoanalysis is a more intensive therapy with a less active therapist that lasts for a longer period of time and places a greater emphasis on the transference aspects of the relationship. Adding to the confusion is that approaches branded as "psychoanalytic" frequently turn out to be an amalgam of diverse approaches.

As our original review noted, the studies in this group present striking deficiencies in methodology. Perhaps the major deficiency for most is a lack of random assignment of patients to treatments. Often there is an underlying assumption that psychoanalysis is the superior treatment, and therefore assigning alternative approaches to prognostically desirable patients (those who have greater emotional and intellectual assets) would be doing them a disservice. Because of the failure to initially assign treatments randomly, any differences in outcomes cannot with certainty be attributed to the treatments rather than to the patient qualities or other factors.

Surprisingly, despite the lack of randomness in patient assignment and other methodological weaknesses we previously described (Fisher & Greenberg, 1985), the few studies comparing psychoanalysis either to psychoanalytically oriented treatments or to approaches based on different theoretical foundations, failed to reveal any consistent differences in outcome. After reviewing the findings in painstaking detail, we came to the general conclusion "that there is very little evidence in the experimental literature even suggesting that the results of therapies called 'psychoanalysis' are in any way different from the results obtained by treatments given other labels" (Fisher & Greenberg, 1985, p. 324). This finding offered a stark contrast to indications that psychoanalysis achieved results superior to no-treatment. Another interesting conclusion, derived from our appraisal of studies comparing orthodox psychoanalysis and the less intensive psychoanalytically oriented psychotherapies, was that these two treatment approaches ultimately achieved similar levels of success, but the rate of change was significantly slower with the orthodox approach (Fisher & Greenberg, 1985).

Since the initial publication of our review of psychoanalytic outcome studies, two other reviews of this literature have appeared (Bachrach, Galatzer-Levy, Skolnikoff, & Waldron, 1991; Luborsky & Spence, 1978). These reviews significantly parallel our original offering in terms of material reviewed, tone, study critiques, and conclusions. For example, Luborsky and Spence (1978) state:

> Simple, unspecified outcome studies of psychoanalysis have not been useful, even toward their main aim of showing the efficacy of the treatment. . . . Controlled comparisons with other forms of treatment are almost nonexistent. . . . The implication of this conclusion is obvious, it is impossible to say that one type of psychotherapy is better than another. . . . For those comparisons for which a sufficient number of studies exist, there is usually a non-significant difference in percentage of patients improving with each treatment (with only a couple of nonimpressive exceptions). (pp. 337, 338)

The most recent review of the efficacy of psychoanalysis focuses on the results obtained from six clinical quantitative studies involving more than 500 patients treated at four different psychoanalytic training centers (Bachrach et al., 1991). Although the reviewers conclude that improvement rates for suitable patients are typically in the 60% to 90% range, they go on to document that the studies all contain significant methodological weaknesses, including the possibility of bias affecting the ratings of outcome. All the data are based on large single-sample studies, and none present comparisons with either placebo or wait-list control groups. As the authors point out, none of the material gathered permits meaningful comparisons of the effectiveness of psychoanalysis with that of other forms of treatment. Our

concern about the unreliability of psychoanalytic practitioners is reinforced by this most recent inspection of the evidence. For example,
after their journey through the existing citations on efficacy and a declaration that the reports do not meet the standards for modern research methods, Bachrach and his colleagues (1991) state:

> Matters of definition and conceptualization, however, limit the studies
> insofar as there was no clear consensus about the meanings of terms, or
> the method of measurement of clinical concepts even if operational def-
> initions were employed. Whether it is a working definition of psycho-
> analysis, or the meaning of terms such as "improvement," "therapeutic
> benefit," "analytic process," or even "circumstances of termination," all
> such terms exist within varied conceptual and institutional frame-
> works, and were measured differently in the studies. (p. 910)

Several observations emerge from a reading of the reviews and individual studies focused on the outcome of psychoanalysis. Of particular significance is the lack of methodological rigor in virtually all the
investigations that have been reported. In fact, there is no study of psychoanalysis as a treatment that cannot be dismissed because of seriously
contaminated or compromised data. All the various studies are flawed
in one or more of the following ways: total reliance on cases treated by a
single practitioner; the failure to demonstrate that a standard, reliable
treatment (psychoanalysis) is actually taking place; the lack of a no-
treatment or alternate treatment control group; the use of inexperienced
psychotherapists; the failure to assign patients randomly to different
types of treatments in the few comparative studies; the frequent dependence on potentially unreliable therapist outcome ratings or ratings of
therapist case notes as the sole measure of treatment efficacy.

A provocative possibility that emerges from the literature is that
orthodox psychoanalysis is simply an inefficient form of the briefer
psychodynamic psychotherapies. The strength of such a conclusion
must be tempered by the fact that typical outcome measures may not
be those most suitable for assessing change with psychoanalysis. For
example, outcome is most often measured in terms of symptom improvement rather than character change or insights attained. In addition, the distinction between long-lasting change and short-term
benefits is typically left unaddressed. It could turn out that clearer research focus on these issues will show that orthodox psychoanalysis
possesses some unique advantages.

Nevertheless, the onus of demonstrating that orthodox psychoanalysis (with its years of treatment and multisessions per week regi-
men) results in some of the speculated unique benefits rests with
those who espouse such claims. To this point, the empirical evidence

to support these assertions is lacking. In fact, the existing findings afford little comfort to those who would suggest that psychoanalysis will turn out to be a more beneficial treatment than psychodynamic psychotherapy. For example, in addition to the studies we reviewed indicating equivalent outcomes for psychoanalysis and psychoanalytically oriented psychotherapy (Fisher & Greenberg, 1985), we are impressed by statements from analysts who were unable to find any evidence of differential outcome in cases treated with varying levels of adherence to a strict psychoanalytic model. Although the cases in these reports were not randomly assigned to the treatments (which should produce an advantage for psychoanalysis with its more prognostically desirable cases), the outcomes were not distinguishable. Heilbrunn (1963, 1966), in two surveys of his psychoanalytic practice, compared the improvement rates for patients he had seen using four different levels of treatment duration and intensity. To his surprise, he could document no significant outcome differences among the various methods.

More recently, Wallerstein (1986a) published an extensive overview of the cases studied over an 18-year period in the Menninger Clinic's Psychotherapy Research Project. Half of the 42 cases had been treated with psychoanalysis and half with psychoanalytically oriented psychotherapy. Again, patients were not randomly assigned to treatments and again, counter to Wallerstein's expectations, the two types of therapies appeared to blur together both in terms of active ingredients and results for the patients. He was finally led to "question strongly the continued usefulness of this effort to link the *kind* of change achieved ('real' change, 'better' change) with the intervention modes by which it is brought about" (pp. 720–721). Moreover, in comparing the patients treated by the two types of therapies, he judged, "We must accept the fact that the interpretive, uncovering mode does not have an exclusive corner on inducing structural change" (p. 721). He later states, ". . . the good results in one modality were not overall less stable, less enduring, or less proof against subsequent environmental vicissitude than the good results in the other" (p. 726).

After a microscopically detailed study of the treatment outcomes produced by psychoanalysis and psychodynamic psychotherapy, Wallerstein (1986a) reached the following conclusions:

1. The treatment results, with patients selected either as suitable for trials at psychoanalysis or as appropriate for varying mixes of expressive-supportive psychotherapeutic approaches, tended with this population sample to converge rather than to diverge in outcome.
2. Across the whole spectrum of treatment courses in the 42 patients—ranging from the most analytic-expressive through the inextricably blended to the most single-mindedly supportive—in almost

every instance (the psychoanalyses included), the treatment carried more supportive elements than originally intended, and these supportive elements accounted for more of the changes achieved than had been originally anticipated.

3. The nature of supportive therapy—or, better, the supportive aspects of all psychotherapy, as conceptualized within a psychoanalytic theoretical framework—deserves far more respectful specification in all its forms and variants than has usually been accorded in the psychodynamic literature. . . .

4. The kinds of changes reached by this cohort of patients—those reached primarily on an uncovering, insight-aiming basis, and those reached primarily on the basis of the opposed covering-up varieties of supporting techniques—often seemed quite indistinguishable from each other in terms of being so-called "real" or "structural" changes in personality functioning, at least by the usually deployed indications. (p. 730)

Wallerstein's conclusions are presaged by the sentiments of other analysts as well. Several decades ago, Glover (1954) noted:

No accurate records or after-histories of psychoanalytical treatments exist: such rough figures as can be obtained do not suggest that psychoanalysis is notably more successful than other forms of therapy and in any case none of the figures is corrected for spontaneous remission or resolution of symptoms. (p. 393)

Similarly, Rangell (1981), reflecting on more than 25 years of experience, judged that the results of psycho-analysis and psychodynamic psychotherapy are more comparable then many assume them to be. He wrote:

Structural change of time-enduring quality, also thought previously to characterize mainly psychoanalysis, can be achieved in analytic therapy carefully chosen and performed. . . . I have been able to reach convincing elements of patients' infantile neuroses in consistent analytic psychotherapy, with results comparable to what I have come to expect in psychoanalysis. (pp. 679–680)

It may surprise some to learn that Freud, too, had his doubts about the unique benefits of psychoanalysis. As he moved toward greater emphasis on the merits of psychoanalysis as a theory of personality, his writings repeatedly indicated his misgivings about the therapeutic potential of his techniques. These statements seem to anticipate the outcome limitations reflected in the analyst impressions and research reports we have cited. For instance, in the *New Introductory Lectures on*

Psycho-Analysis, he remarked, "Psycho-analysis is really a method of treatment like others. It has its triumphs and its defeats, its difficulties, its limitations, its indications. . . . Its therapeutic successes give grounds neither for boasting nor for being ashamed" (Freud, 1933, p. 152). He went on to state, "I do not think our cures can compete with those of Lourdes. There are so many more people who believe in the miracles of the Blessed Virgin than in the existence of the unconscious" (p. 152). Near the end of his career, doubts about the results of his therapy clearly surfaced in his essay "Analysis Terminable and Interminable" (Freud, 1937). In probably his most complete statement about his conclusions regarding the treatment benefits of psychoanalysis, he wrote:

> One has the impression that one ought not to be surprised if it should turn out in the end that the difference between a person who has not been analyzed and the behavior of a person after he has been analyzed is not so thorough-going as we aim at making it and as we expect and maintain it to be. . . . I really cannot commit myself to a decision at this point, nor do I know whether a decision is possible at the present time. (p. 228)

Now, many decades since Freud expressed his concerns about the outcome of psychoanalysis, the available evidence offers added weight to his suspicions. Psychoanalytic psychotherapy outcome, to the extent it has been tested, has not turned out to be superior (or inferior) to that of alternative approaches. There is also no evidence, so far, that its benefits are more enduring.

Because the difference in treatment duration has been a major factor distinguishing formal psychoanalysis from psychodynamic therapy, it is of interest that variations in treatment length have not always translated directly into added benefits for patients. A number of psychotherapy meta-analyses failed to establish a simple, direct relationship between treatment duration and effectiveness (e.g., Miller & Berman, 1983; Robinson, Berman, & Neimeyer, 1990; Shapiro & Shapiro, 1982; Smith, Glass, & Miller, 1980). When we last reviewed the psychoanalytic and psychodynamic treatment evidence on this issue, we concluded that there were some observable relationships between outcome and length of treatment, but that the rate of change appeared to be slower with orthodox psychoanalysis (Fisher & Greenberg, 1985). Data indicated that the percentage of psychoanalyzed patients rated as showing significant change increased dramatically when treatment lengthened into years. In contrast, on average, psychodynamically treated patients reached an optimal level of benefit in less than 12 months.

Differences in rates of improvement were attributed, at least in part, to therapist expectations about how long therapy should last to be beneficial. For many psychoanalysts, there seemed to be an expectation that "longer" treatments offer more meaningful outcomes and that there is no urgency in pushing for faster changes (recall Freud's admonitions about "furor therapeuticus"). The probability that analyst attitudes slow down progress is suggested by the research showing that patient perceptions of their rates of improvement are influenced by therapist expectations about treatment duration (Frank, 1973, pp. 158–159; Goldstein, 1962, pp. 76–84).

Reviews of the research on brief psychotherapy treatments bolster the idea that psychotherapists tend to believe more extended treatments offer better outcomes. These reviews indicate that the relationship between treatment outcome and duration is more likely to be found when therapists provide the outcome ratings then when patients do (Gelso & Johnson, 1983; Johnson & Gelso, 1980; Steenbarger, 1994). This finding implies that psychotherapists' expectations may color their assessment of outcome. Such reviews also parallel our conclusions by showing that the association between treatment outcome and duration is frequently not simple or direct. Steenbarger (1994), for example, in an extensive analysis of the research literature, highlights that conclusions about the relationship between duration and outcome may be significantly shaped by how outcomes are measured, as well as when they are assessed and by whom. Of particular pertinence to psychodynamic treatments is that change seems to occur in waves, with symptom relief coming before changes on interpersonal or trait-like dimensions (Barth et al., 1988; Crits-Cristoph, 1992; Husby, 1985; Johnson & Gelso, 1980; Steenbarger, 1992). Steenbarger (1994) concludes that the evidence supports the notion of different types of changes occurring within different time frames, with symptom relief and alleviation of distress being the quickest and easiest benefit to attain. These results could be interpreted to mean that the lengthened treatment durations of the typical orthodox psychoanalysis might yet prove to produce superior outcomes on non-symptom related measures of outcome. However, the research evidence on duration and outcome has focused almost entirely on relatively brief treatments usually lasting no more than about 25 to 30 sessions.

In addition, there is some evidence showing that the percentage of patients who display measurable benefits with psychotherapy treatments does not increase linearly—in terms of symptom improvement—as treatment duration lengthens. Howard, Kopta, Krause, and Orlinsky (1986) documented that the percentage of patients displaying measurable improvements between Sessions 1 and 8 increased from 15% to approximately 50%. By the 26th session, the proportion of improved patients increased to 75% and improvement was shown by 83% of the patients by the end of one year. These authors therefore concluded that the symptom improvement benefits of psychotherapy for most patients occur relatively early in treatment. Similarly, Steenbarger (1994) points to the work of Gelso and Johnson (1983), in suggesting that relapse rates were significantly reduced for those receiving 16 psychotherapy sessions rather than 8 but very little additional advantage was measured beyond that point. Again, however, measurement did not extend even to the 50 or more sessions typical of psychoanalytic treatment.

Hints about the possible value of lengthier treatments are provided by McNeilly and Howard (1991). Using the data collected by Howard et al. (1986) and comparing it with figures obtained for spontaneous remission,[4] McNeilly and Howard documented a clear superiority in outcome for psychotherapy treated versus nontreated patients. The differences in outcome relating to treatment "dosage" were striking. For example, improvement rates for the treated group were 41% in 4 weeks, 83% in 1 year, and 90% of the patients in 2 years. The corresponding rates for untreated patients were 1%, 46%, and 70%. Other indications of the value of somewhat longer treatments are provided by Kopta, Howard, Lowry, and Beutler (1994), who demonstrated that the treatment durations (or dosages) required to reach recovery were considerably longer than the durations necessary to just show improvements (as in Howard et al., 1986). Furthermore, the treatment dosages needed to attain substantial improvements varied depending on the types of symptoms measured. Acute distress symptoms responded more rapidly than chronic distress symptoms, and characterological symptoms showed the slowest response rates. In general, as in previous research, all classes of symptoms exhibited proportionally greater improvements during earlier treatment sessions. Seventy-five percent of patients attained recovery from acute or chronic distress symptoms within 58 sessions, a bit more than a year of once-a-week therapy. Because characterological symptoms did not respond well to the approximately one year of treatment possible in this study, it was concluded that a longer time frame would be needed for this class of discomforts, which included symptoms typically associated with psychoticism and the more severe personality disorders.

---

[4] Our previous review of the evidence on "spontaneous remission"—the idea that patients will improve simply with the passage of time—highlighted the oversimplification often created by this concept. Variations among studies on several important dimensions led to the conclusion that no one figure could be logically used as the nontreatment standard of comparison for all psychotherapy outcome studies (Fisher & Greenberg, 1985, pp. 309–312).

It is an open matter at this point whether research findings on brief psychotherapy or alternative psychotherapy approaches to treatment can be generalized to include psychoanalysis. However, the difficulties in demonstrating differences in outcomes between various treatment approaches suggest the possible relevance of findings in the general psychotherapy literature for the understanding of psychodynamic process and outcome. If outcomes are similar, perhaps the mechanisms mediating the outcomes are also similar. Furthermore, if psychoanalysis proves to be roughly equivalent in outcome to the more efficient widely applied and studied psychodynamic psychotherapy (as our review suggests), it might be of value to look at how psychodynamic approaches have fared when compared with other types of psychotherapy treatment.

REVISITING THE DODO BIRD'S DOMAIN

The verdict of the Dodo bird in *Alice's Adventures in Wonderland* (Carroll, 1865/1962)—"*Everybody* has won, and all must have prizes"— has been used as the subtitle for some classical papers on psychotherapy outcome by Rosenzweig (1936) and Luborsky, Singer, and Luborsky (1975). As used by these authors, the quote implies that all psychotherapies produce benefits and that the distinctions between brands of psychotherapy have not been shown to lead to significant outcome differences. Reading and rereading the evidence on the outcome of psychoanalysis reawakens thoughts of the Dodo's joyful pronouncement. Our thoughts are stirred by the evidence, limited as it is, that orthodox psychoanalysis ultimately appears to be about as effective as psychodynamic psychotherapy. Perhaps of greater interest, however, is the question of how psychodynamic psychotherapy—the more widely utilized derivative of Freud's treatment—compares in effectiveness to other forms of psychological treatment. Psychodynamic psychotherapy has received more adequate empirical attention than psychoanalysis, and therefore, findings about its comparative effectiveness rest on somewhat firmer footing. We caution, however, that conclusions based on this evidence must be moderated by the fact that the term "psychodynamic psychotherapy" does not signify a single treatment approach but represents several variants of psychotherapy derived from Freud's ideas.

Three reviews of the evidence highlight the issues and findings that have appeared when psychodynamic psychotherapy outcomes have been compared with the outcomes attained with alternative treatment approaches (Crits-Christoph, 1992; Luborsky et al., 1993; Svartberg & Stiles, 1991). The first of these reviews (in chronological terms) concluded that short-term psychodynamic psychotherapies are generally less effective than alternative psychotherapies, although they are superior to no-treatment control groups (Svartberg & Stiles, 1991). The two subsequent reviews are at variance with this conclusion in demonstrating no difference in effectiveness between brief psychodynamic treatments and other types of therapy, with all being successful (Crits-Christoph, 1992; Luborsky et al., 1993). To demonstrate the complexity involved in trying to make comparative judgments about competing brands of psychotherapy, a short description of each of these reviews follows.

Svartberg and Stiles (1991) conducted a meta-analysis of the comparative effects of treatments they judged to fit the label short-term psychodynamic psychotherapy. They identified 19 studies published between 1978 and 1988 that met the following inclusion criteria for their review: (a) Study designs had to include either a no-treatment or alternative therapy group (or both) in addition to a short-term psychodynamic psychotherapy treatment condition; (b) the psychodynamic psychotherapy groups were identified by adherence to an underlying psychoanalytic or psychodynamic theory, a stated goal of insight acquisition or personality change, and an emphasis on the techniques of interpretation and work on the transference. Any two out of the three stipulations included in (b) were considered sufficient to label a treatment as brief psychodynamic psychotherapy. Other criteria required that the treatment be of planned brief duration (i.e., no more than 40 sessions), be conducted individually, and involve nonpsychotic patients.

The treatment durations of the identified studies averaged only 14 or 15 sessions (with a range of 6 to 28 sessions). Therapists varied widely in experience (from 1.5 to 23 years) and in the number of years of specific training in the treatment modality they were using (ranging from 0 to 20 years). The problems being treated also ranged widely and included studies focused variously on such conditions as anxiety, depression, personality disorders, drug addiction, psychosomatic disorders, and eating disorders. Multiple outcome measures were used in all but two of the studies, but only one effect size (consisting of the average effect size across all outcome measures) was utilized for each study. Effect sizes were weighted by an index of methodological quality.

Overall, Svartberg and Stiles (1991) concluded that brief dynamic psychotherapy patients did somewhat better in treatment than patients left on waiting lists. However, those treated with alternative psychotherapies did slightly better than those in psychodynamic treatment. The authors observed that the psychodynamic treatment effect increased as duration lengthened beyond 12 sessions. Svartberg and Stiles also noted that many of their findings had to be regarded as tentative because of the small number of studies involved, the small sample sizes, and the consequent lack of power in testing for statistical differences. In reading their report, it is difficult not to feel uneasy about the questionable robustness of the findings because of the reliance on a limited assortment of studies with mixed methodologies and diverse outcome measures. The authors acknowledge the uncertainty about the solidity of the results.

Crits-Christoph (1992) published a meta-analysis based on more well-controlled studies of the efficacy of brief dynamic psychotherapy. The review included both published studies and those reported at conferences. Inclusion criteria required that each study had to use a group receiving a specific form of brief psychotherapy as represented in a treatment manual or manual-like guide. The comparison groups were made up of individuals on waiting lists or those receiving nonpsychiatric treatments, alternative psychotherapies, pharmacotherapy, or some other form of dynamic psychotherapy. Experienced therapists who had specific training in brief dynamic therapy (using the treatment manuals) were required for inclusion of a study in the review. To be included, treatments had to last at least 12 sessions. Finally, rather then relying on heterogeneous measures of outcome, only three specific areas of outcome were assessed using common measures across studies: target symptoms, general psychiatric symptoms, and social functioning. In short, in contrast to the Svartberg and Stiles (1991) meta-analysis, this review relied on longer treatments performed by more experienced therapists with specific training in clearly documented treatments and more focused measures of outcome. Eleven studies met these criteria.

Results showed large positive differences in outcome for those treated with dynamic psychotherapy rather than being left on a waiting list. When effect sizes were translated into percentages, the average patient receiving brief dynamic therapy was better off than 86% of the waiting list patients on measures of target symptoms. Similarly, the average treated patient surpassed 79% of the untreated on measures of general symptoms and social adjustment. The advantages of dynamic psychotherapy turned out to be quite variable, depending on the study, when comparisons were made with alternative nonpsychiatric treatments (such as self-help groups or low-contact treatments). Although even these comparisons revealed a small advantage for dynamic treatments on target symptoms, variations in study conditions and dropout rates, combined with the small number (5) of studies made it difficult to draw "meaningful" conclusions about the comparisons with nonpsychiatric treatments. Finally, the psychodynamic treatments were compared (in 9 of the studies) with other types of psychological and psychiatric treatments (such as medications and assorted cognitive and behavioral therapies). In these comparisons, no clear advantage emerged for any of the approaches on any of the measures.

In discussing the results of his study, Crits-Cristoph was clearly struck by the failure to document outcome differences across recognized treatment approaches, although all treatments appeared far superior to doing nothing. The rigorous control of treatment delivery in these studies was seen as an advantage in ensuring high-quality service, but a possible disadvantage in limiting the flexibility of practitioners. Generalizability to everyday practice was also limited by the small number of studies and omission of some types of psychodynamic treatment, patient groups, and outcome measures. Several studies possibly lowered the estimate of treatment effectiveness by focusing on particularly difficult-to-treat patient groups (opiate addicts, cocaine abusers, and personality-disordered patients).

Building on the studies collected in other reviews of the general psychotherapy literature, Luborsky et al. (1993) present a review of studies comparing other forms of psychotherapy with psychodynamic treatments. Unlike Svartberg and Stiles (1991) and Crits-Cristoph (1992), they did not review comparisons with no-treatment controls. Included studies had to use adult (usually nonpsychotic) patients. Treatments had to be "real" with role-playing studies excluded, and they had to be delivered in an individual format rather than as group, family, or marital therapy. Treatments of "habit disturbances" (e.g., smoking, overeating) were also eliminated. Two main types of outcome measures were analyzed: general adjustment measures and specific symptom outcome measures. Studies were weighted according to how well they matched the following criteria for adequacy of design:

1. Random assignments of patients (or stratified assignment on prognostic variables) were made to each group.

2. Real patients were used, not actors or student volunteers.

3. Therapists for each group were equally competent.

4. Therapists were experienced and knowledgeable about the form of therapy they were to do.

5. Treatments were equally valued by the patients and therapists in each group.

6. The outcome measures reflected the target goals of the treatment.

7. Treatment outcome was evaluated by independent measures.

8. Information was obtained about the patients' concurrent use of treatments other than that intended, both formal and informal.

9. Samples of each of the compared treatments were independently evaluated for extent to which the therapists adhered to the manual-designated form of the treatment.

10. Each of the compared treatments was given in an equal amount in terms of length or frequency.

11. Each treatment was given in an amount that was reasonable and appropriate to the form of treatment.

12. Sample size was adequate.

The review by Luborsky and his associates comprised 13 studies meeting the preceding general criteria. Only seven of the studies overlapped with Svartberg and Stiles (1991). This was partly because the Luborsky group did not include studies comparing psychodynamic therapy with no-treatment controls, but also because they judged a number of the studies to have been inappropriately included by Svartberg and Stiles. The two reviews also differed in methods of statistical analysis and the way outcome measures were handled.

Seventeen outcome comparisons were derived for the 13 studies. Fourteen of the comparisons showed no significant differences between dynamic therapies and other treatments, one comparison revealed an advantage for dynamic therapy, and two showed it to be inferior to other psychotherapies. In general, using either a box-score method or a meta-analysis, Luborsky and his colleagues concluded that even after studies are corrected for quality, there is no difference in efficacy between psychodynamic therapies and alternative approaches at either termination or follow-up.[5] The finding of outcome equivalence between brands of therapy echoes Luborsky, Singer, and Luborsky's (1975) earlier review of 100 general psychotherapy studies and Smith, Glass, and Miller's (1980) meta-analysis of 475 studies. It is also consistent with Stubbs and Bozarth's (1994) overview of more then four decades of psychotherapy outcome research.

WRESTLING WITH THE DODO BIRD

Even though repeated empirical sweeps through the psychotherapy outcome literature consistently demonstrate the beneficial impact of treatment, the failure to find clear differences in comparative worth among competing brands of psychotherapy has proven to be disquieting

---

[5] In addition to findings of outcome equivalence between dynamic therapy versus other therapies, Luborsky et al. (1993) also reported no difference effects between group versus individual therapy, time-limited versus time-unlimited psychotherapy, client-centered versus other therapies, and behavior therapy versus other therapies.

to many researchers and clinicians. There is an uneasy feeling that the Dodo bird verdict of treatment equivalence must either be disproven or shown to be the consequence of some perfectly understandable previously hidden factors. The notion that distinctions in treatment results will eventually emerge, given enough research sophistication and studies, permeates even the reports demonstrating relatively identical clinical outcomes. Several authors have tried their hand at positing explanations for the equivalence finding or pointing toward paths that will eventually lead to the documentation of clearly distinguishable treatment outcomes (e.g., Beutler, 1991; Luborsky, Singer, & Luborsky, 1975; Luborsky et al., 1993; Ryle, 1984; Shadish & Sweeney, 1991; Stiles, Shapiro, & Elliot, 1986).

The idea that common, therapeutic factors cut across different approaches to psychotherapy is probably the most prominent explanation given for similar outcomes (e.g., Luborsky et al., 1993; Stiles, Shapiro, & Elliot, 1986; Stubbs & Bozarth, 1994). Such factors are thought to be powerful enough to dwarf components specific to any individual approach. Among the central ingredients is the nature of the therapist-patient relationship. Spurred on by Fiedler's (1950a, 1950b, 1951) early work showing that therapists and clients of different theoretical orientations share a view of the ideal therapy relationship, research has gone on to document the significant impact of support in helping relationships. The chance to vent thoughts and feelings in a caring relationship with a strong therapist figure who serves a mediating role between the patient and society is a potent factor common to most psychotherapies as well as influence processes in general (e.g., Frank & Frank, 1991; Strupp & Hadley, 1979).

In addition to the need for close involvement with an understanding figure, many studies of psychotherapy process point to the importance of helping patients develop new ways of looking at themselves and their problems (see general overviews by Luborsky et al., 1993; Stiles, Shapiro, & Elliot, 1986). Early on, Rosenzweig (1936) raised the idea that all psychotherapies should include a reasonable explanatory scheme for the patient's problems. It now appears that providing a coherent rational framework for conceptualizing problems may be of more importance then what the particular framework happens to be. Consistent with this idea Luborsky (1984) found that the degree of adherence to a treatment manual (the degree of treatment "purity") predicted outcome with different treatments regardless of which treatment model was used.[6]

---

[6] A review of 10 methodologically diverse studies seeking to associate treatment adherence with outcome found significant relationships in 4 of the studies (Luborsky & Barber, 1993). In concluding that research offers support for the idea of a relationship

The success of psychotherapeutic treatments is also a factor in blurring distinctions in outcome. Oddly enough, the relatively high level of effectiveness shown by reviews of outcome studies of different psychotherapies (e.g., Lambert, Shapiro, & Bergin, 1986; Meltzoff & Kornreich, 1970; Smith, Glass, & Miller, 1980) makes it difficult to demonstrate an advantage for any one approach. Thus, when Meltzoff and Kornreich (1970) conclude that approximately 80% of patients in various psychotherapies show treatment benefits or Bachrach and colleagues (1991) estimate improvements with psychoanalysis in up to 90% of the patients, there is relatively little room left for an alternative treatment to show more effectiveness. The problem of finding differences is compounded because most comparative studies sample sizes are not particularly large. Therefore, there may not be enough statistical power to demonstrate the significance of small differences in effectiveness (Kazdin & Bass, 1989; Luborsky et al., 1993).

The lack of specificity in treatments and measures of outcome is also thought to potentially obscure any differences in outcome that might exist. Thus, treatments applied without adherence to any particular manual or focused theory may be too diffuse in practice to differentiate from other forms of treatment, even though they are given labels suggesting that they are clearly different approaches. Similarly, outcome measures are often unfocused and not geared to the specific goals of a particular treatment. For example, psychoanalytic practitioners might complain that global ratings of change in studies of psychodynamic therapy may disregard changes in insight or the distinction between initial symptom improvement and enduring changes in personality style. Stiles and his colleagues (1986) note that "projecting multiple dimensions onto a single dimension of 'improvement' or 'change' by using averaged scales or effect sizes makes therapies comparable but at a cost of masking their diversity and potency of effect" (p. 171). The speculation that greater specificity of treatments and measures is more likely to reveal differences in outcomes is clearly embodied in Gordon Paul's (1967) well-known statement: "The question towards which all outcome research should ultimately be directed is the following: *What* treatment by *whom*, is most effective for

---

between adherence and outcome, the reviewers speculated that sometimes the relationship may be obscured when the range of adherence scores is small or when adherence is scored without reference to the competence with which the techniques are being employed. Other reviewers, using meta-analytic statistical techniques, have not found a relationship between adherence to treatment manuals and improved efficacy (Robinson, Berman, & Neimeyer, 1990). Moreover, Henry, Schacht, Strupp, Butler, and Binder (1993) reported negative treatment effects when therapists rigidly conformed to a training manual for time-limited psychodynamic therapy (see Chapter 9 for a discussion of these results).

this individual with *that* specific problem, and under *which* set of circumstances" (p. 111). Unfortunately, to this point, attempts to demonstrate the validity of specific psychotherapy "prescriptions," as envisioned by Paul's pronouncement, have yielded sparse and inconsistent results (e.g., Goldstein & Stein, 1976; Lambert, Shapiro, & Bergin, 1986; Shapiro, 1985).

A review of the evolution of psychotherapy efficacy research from the 1950s through the 1990s reached similar pessimistic conclusions about the possibility of achieving pinpoint treatment recipes (Stubbs & Bozarth, 1994). Aside from the failure of research to document reliable, generalizable specific treatment prescriptions, some authors also point out the methodological nightmare that would be created by trying to design studies that involved multiple kinds of treatments, therapists, patients, problems, and settings. Based on these considerations, the goal of validated differential treatment specificity—appealing as it is—has been declared by some to be impractical, unrealistic, and scientifically unattainable (Kisch & Kroll, 1980; Stiles et al., 1986; Stubbs & Bozarth, 1994). Beutler (1991) highlights the magnitude of the problem by showing that even a short list of presumably relevant variables related to therapy, therapist, phase of treatment, and patient types, results in approximately 1.5 million possible combinations that would need to be studied to rule out pertinent differences among treatment types.[7]

Luborsky and his colleagues (1993) point to a variety of "extratherapeutic conditions" that may make it difficult to equate treatment groups in comparative studies. These conditions create another barrier to finding unique outcomes. For instance, there may be important and uncontrolled differences in such factors as symptom severity, the ability of patients (or therapists) to form treatment alliances, therapist competence, adherence to a specific treatment model and patient ability to internalize treatment gains. According to the Luborsky argument, contrasting studies may randomly favor one type of treatment or another on these and other prognostic factors, with the result that a set of studies can cancel out each other's results.

Finally, the objectivity of comparative psychotherapy research can be compromised by the theoretical orientation of the researcher. Possible bias obviously clouds the search for clear outcome distinctions among treatments. Corroboration of bias has come from the fact that the outcomes of comparative treatment studies have been shown to be

---

[7] Beutler (1991) goes on to reason that careful melding of existing theoretical and empirical research could significantly reduce the number of variables and meaningful dimensions so that perhaps fewer than a thousand permutations would need to be checked out!

influenced by the investigator's theoretical allegiance (Berman, 1989; Luborsky et al., 1975; Luborsky et al., 1993). There is evidence that researchers tend to find stronger effects in treatments that they favor (Smith, Glass, & Miller, 1980). Furthermore, as Berman, Miller, and Massman (1985) demonstrated in comparisons of behavioral and cognitive approaches, the apparent advantage of one type of intervention over another vanishes when the researcher's theoretical predilection is factored into the result.

SHOULD THE DODO BIRD BE KILLED OR NURTURED?

Despite the frequent finding of equivalent outcomes among competing therapy systems, psychodynamic advocates still tend to feel that the Dodo bird judgment will not endure. They have faith that additional studies with better methodology will eventually reveal the special merit of psychodynamic therapies. For example, Luborsky et al. (1993), in suggesting that the "special virtues" of dynamic treatments will be substantiated in the future, state:

> The studies have not yet dealt with possible long-term benefits. Nor have they dealt well enough with the distinction between changes in symptoms and changes in general adjustment. The benefits of treatment tend to reflect the focus of treatment; dynamic treatment tends to be focused less on the symptom improvement and more on the general adjustment changes, which are harder to accomplish. And, of course, the concept of insight has not yet been adequately operationalized and therefore has not been used as an outcome measure in any form of psychotherapy. (pp. 511–512)

Related to the hopeful promises that future research will support the differential effectiveness of psychodynamic treatment are the proclamations of those labeled "pluralists" by Omer and London (1988). Such individuals seek to preserve the need for separate schools of treatment and react against the idea of consolidating and integrating the various psychotherapy systems. They feel that it is necessary and useful for practice and theory to have a variety of ways for viewing the world. Omer and London (1988) stress that pluralists believe:

> There are many ways of being mentally healthy, while all psychopathology involves rigidity, lack of options, and relative lack of variation. Different therapies promote different ideals of health. Therapists should tell clients which health goals their therapy promotes. Research should address the diversity of outcomes from different therapies. (p. 176)

In contrast to the pluralist contention that distinct schools of psychotherapy are meaningful entities worth preserving is the idea that the age of various systems of psychotherapy may be coming to an end. In reviewing the evidence for this proposition, Omer and London (1988, 1989) highlight three events that are undermining the viability of discrete therapy camps. In addition to the repeated failure of research to show outcome differences, they point to the growth of a multitude of useful therapy techniques that have attracted adherents from a variety of schools, and the criticism by major theorists of central assumptions of their own systems. Within psychoanalytic circles, criticism has focused on such disparate issues as the irrelevance of Freud's meta-psychology for treatment, doubts about the historical truth of analytically obtained memories, and questioning of the need for accurate interpretations in securing positive treatment outcomes (e.g., Holt, 1975; Klein, 1973; Loch, 1977; Omer & London, 1988; Schafer, 1976; Spence, 1982a, 1982b; Viderman, 1979). Also promoting the waning of traditional psychotherapy systems are calls for greater treatment integration based on empirical findings and demonstrations of what works (e.g., Beutler & Clarkin, 1990; Castonguay & Goldfried, 1994; Goldfried, 1980; Goldfried & Padawer, 1982; Omer & London, 1988; Wachtel, 1977).

CONCLUSION

As the quantity and quality of psychotherapy research have expanded, it has become increasingly clear that no single system has demonstrated a monopoly on effectiveness. The common factors that pervade most treatment methods appear to be more central to the process of change than many have thought. Because of the evidence supporting the Dodo's recurring message that all systems are prizeworthy, there is growing acknowledgment that common factors should be regarded more as "signal" than "noise" when searching for effective treatment ingredients (e.g., Omer & London, 1988, 1989). At the same time, research seems to be shifting away from a focus on comparative outcome studies of specific "types of treatment" (e.g., psychoanalysis, behavior therapy, cognitive therapy) as the most meaningful way to get at what makes psychotherapy work (Omer & Dar, 1992). Treatment brands may simply be too grossly defined to be of help in furthering knowledge about how to improve treatment outcome.[8] Ultimately, it may prove

[8] In addition to the problem of vagueness surrounding meaningful distinctions among schools of psychotherapy, reviews of the evidence suggest that reliance on traditional diagnostic categories may also hamper the search for effective problem-specific

more useful to examine the process factors or procedures thought to uniquely underlie each approach to see whether they actually play a part in mediating or moderating outcome (e.g., Omer & London, 1988, 1989; Parloff, 1986; Shadish & Sweeney, 1991). For psychodynamic treatment, this means empirically evaluating the significance of such concepts as interpretation, transference, and insight—a task we will undertake in Chapter 9.

---

treatments (e.g., Beutler & Clarkin, 1990; Kirk & Kutchins, 1992). This is because the traditional diagnostic systems such as that provided by the *Diagnostic and Statistical Manual of Mental Disorders*, American Psychiatric Association, 1980, 1987, 1994 (DSM-III, DSM-III-R, DSM-IV) have suspect validity and reliability, are colored by political concerns, are atheoretical, and are blind to issues of etiology. Moreover, the systems largely neglect such potentially relevant dimensions as problem complexity and the interpersonal context in which the patient's problems occur.

Chapter 9

Psychodynamic Treatment Ingredients

The Pursuit of Insight

At the core of Freud's proclamations about psychotherapy rests the notion that making the patient aware of underlying motivations for behavior, repressed impulses, and stifled memories of traumatic events is the central task of psychoanalytic therapy. At first, Freud assumed that symptom alleviation would flow naturally from the insights gained and the subjugation of resistance to "making the unconscious conscious" (e.g., Freud, 1914c, 1919b). However, the technique for facilitating insight changed as Freud extended his experience and refined his thoughts. After initial emphasis on having hypnotized patients affectively recollect traumatic experiences believed to underlie their neuroses, Freud's therapy was altered to accentuate helping patients recall, while they were awake, important memories that had been defensively purged from awareness. The aim was to accurately reconstruct the past through the interpretation of patients' free associations, dreams, and slips of the tongue. The therapy also gradually shifted from emphasizing merely the recovery of memories to a demonstration of how the past led to unnecessary distortions and repetitive handicapping patterns in current relationships with others and with the analyst (transference). Verbal interpretations were portrayed as the key element in helping patients overcome their internal resistances to greater awareness and in revealing the ties between past and present. Most basic to the approach was the idea that the patients' growing awareness and understanding of their "deepest" motivations and thoughts would be beneficial. Furthermore, Freud, in promoting his theories of personality development and psychopathology, needed to

218

stress that change was not to come about through analyst persuasion or suggestion, but through the patients' attainment of a truthful picture of themselves and their feelings. He felt that cures would be impermanent if only the patients' symptoms, rather than underlying "true" causes, were treated. Thus, if the original symptoms were relieved without understanding, untreated, unresolved, underlying conflicts could lead to the development of new symptoms (see Fisher & Greenberg, 1985; Gordon & Zax, 1981, for reviews of the evidence on symptom substitution).

Central to Freud's writing about psychoanalysis as a treatment is the proposition that a therapy promoting insight about the causes of behavior will be superior to symptom-focused treatments in outcome and stability. Freud, particularly in his early work, suggested that the probability of lasting cure would be directly linked to how far into the past the patient could delve for the historical roots of current problems (e.g., Freud, 1905b, 1905c). By implication, the "deeper" the analysis, the more durable the outcome. Although self-education and self-knowledge can themselves be seen as treatment goals, Freud's early assumptions held out the promise that reaching these goals would automatically and directly translate into other beneficial changes in symptoms and personality structure. The linkage of change to the attainment of insight became the cornerstone of dynamic treatments, despite Freud's expressions of doubt, late in his career, about the unique therapeutic potential of psychoanalytic therapy (Freud, 1937a).

The conviction, engendered by Freud's statements, that change is a by-product of insight seems to have persuaded many therapists that significant change can occur only when preceded by insight. This has led to some analysts advancing the circular argument that insight without change is not "real" insight and that change without insight is either not real or only apparently short on insight (e.g., Abroms, 1968; Brady, 1967; London, 1964). Analysts have posited a distinction between "emotional" insight (which is change-inducing) and "intellectual" insight (which consists of rationalizations that do not induce change), in an attempt to account for the observation that insight does not always lead to change (see Crits-Christoph, Barber, Miller, & Beebe, 1993; Strachey, 1934). The distinction between emotional and intellectual insight, although accepted by many clinicians, has thus far evaded empirical validation. Another attempt to explain the possibility of change without apparent insight appears in a modern glossary of psychoanalytic terms sanctioned by the American Psychoanalytic Association. In this book, Moore and Fine (1990) indicate that during the psychic reorganization process cognitive awareness of insight is frequently re-repressed. They believe this need not hinder continued new emotional freedom. In highlighting the difficulties this view poses for research, Crits-Christoph, Barber, Miller, and Beebe (1993) wonder how an investigator would be able to identify with certainty the presence of "valid" insight, if the patient expresses no awareness of this knowledge. Analyst attempts to embellish the hypothesis of a link between insight and change have often added to the difficulty of applying objective research methods to study the issue.

Freud, too, ultimately moved away from the idea of a simple association between gaining self-knowledge and automatic symptom remission. His later writing on therapy placed more emphasis on overcoming patient resistance to the analyst's interpretations than on the discovery of repressed memories. The introduction of several factors that tended to increase the duration of psychoanalytic treatment (such as the overdetermination of symptoms and the need for transference interpretations) also helped to create distance from the simple idea that insight alone could produce change. Freud, in his discussion of "wild" psychoanalysis, carefully addressed the limitations of insight and the potential dangers involved in prematurely and indiscriminately compelling patients to face information that they might not wish to accept. He wrote:

> It is a long superseded idea, and one derived from superficial appearances, that the patient suffers from a sort of ignorance, and that if one removes his ignorance by giving him information . . . he is bound to recover. The pathological factor is not his ignorance in itself, but the root of his ignorance in his *inner resistances*. . . . The task of the treatment is in combating these resistances. Informing the patient of what he does not know because he has repressed it is only one of the necessary preliminaries to the treatment . . . for informing the patient of his unconscious regularly results in an intensification of the conflict in him and an exacerbation of his troubles. . . . Since, however, psychoanalysis cannot dispense with giving this information, it lays down that this shall not be done before two conditions have been fulfilled. First the patient must, through preparation, himself have reached the neighborhood of what he has repressed, and secondly, he must have formed a sufficient attachment (transference) to the physician for his emotional relationship to him to make a fresh flight impossible. (Freud, 1910d, pp. 225–226)

Freud further diminished the part that insight plays in producing change with his introduction of the concept of "working through." The concept stressed the need for time in which the patient would be repeatedly faced with how feelings and perceptions from the past were unnecessarily coloring current reality and the relationship with the analyst. Through the persistent tying of present distortions to past experiences, the patient's resistance to the new, presumably more objective, view of the world was to be overcome and "worked through." The "working through" concept, so critical to Freud's theory of change, is largely ignored by researchers in their study of treatments labeled insight-oriented. Most often, researchers, like many clinicians, follow Freud's early, less complex, writings suggesting that change derives simply and directly from insight. However, as Freud (1914c) plainly stated in his later writing:

> One must allow the patient time to become more conversant with this resistance with which he has now become acquainted, to *work through* it, to overcome it, by continuing, in defiance of it, the analytic work according to the fundamental rule of analysis. . . . This working-through of the resistances may in practice turn out to be an arduous task for the subject of the analysis and a trial of patience for the analyst. Nevertheless, it is a part of the work which effects the greatest changes in the patient and which distinguishes analytic treatment from any kind of treatment by suggestion. (pp. 155–156)

PAST REVIEW OF THE INSIGHT RESEARCH LITERATURE

In our previous work, we presented a review and analysis of the empirical evidence, up through the late 1970s, on the insight concept (Fisher & Greenberg, 1985). The review highlighted several issues and problems common to the work that had been done. For example, a number of studies provided comparative data on the outcomes of insight versus non-insight-oriented psychotherapies. Typically, these studies lacked an independent measure of insight that could reflect change with treatment. Instead the studies assumed that providing interpretations was synonymous with patients attaining insights about their past and current difficulties. Without an objective assessment of insight (separate from merely the furnishing of interpretations), there is no way to generate evidence about whether interpretations lead to insight or whether insight leads to change. Indeed, as we have suggested in the past, without insight measurement, therapies emphasizing interpretations might be more accurately labeled as "interpretive" rather than "insight-oriented."

Other problems with the research literature we previously reviewed also limit its usefulness as tests of Freud's ideas. For instance, the idea that insights by themselves lead simply and directly to change has been translated by researchers to mean that only a very small number of psychotherapy sessions should be needed to achieve significant gains. This, of course, is not consistent with our reading of Freud's later refinements of his theory of therapy. His discussion of the risks involved in prematurely forcing interpretations on patients and the need for the concept of working through (Freud, 1910d, 1914c) argue against the possibility of testing his treatment ideas in very brief therapy formats. Similarly, most of the studies included in our previous review had questionable bearing on Freud's insight model because they relied on treatments that were so different in appearance from what he had described. The level of therapist training, the types of patients, the therapy formats (group instead of individual treatment) and the basic therapy conditions (treatment frequency and therapy techniques) were often not consistent with the approach laid out by Freud. Our past review showed that most researchers addressed the insight issue through studies that used either recruited college students or schizophrenic patients as subjects. Both groups seem inappropriate for generating reasonable tests of Freud's ideas because he did not recommend psychoanalytic psychotherapy for either schizophrenic patients or the treatment of acute limited disorders in real patients, let alone pseudo-patients. Obviously, the use of inexperienced therapists with limited training in the techniques they are applying, which is so common to the research literature, is of questionable value in assessing the usefulness of a therapy approach.

In the past, we suggested that deficiencies in experimental methodology and the lack of a single, coherent measure of the "insight" concept are perhaps the biggest obstacles to an empirical assessment of the linkage between insight and change (Fisher & Greenberg, 1985). If changes in insight have not been *independently* demonstrated, no conclusions can be rendered about whether various measures of treatment outcome are associated with insights gained. Roback (1974) summarized this issue well in his review of the insight literature. He, too, highlighted that most studies do not define what they are labeling insight; do not attempt to measure the quantity or type of insight produced; do not confirm specific therapist operations; and, of greatest importance, do not test whether patients receiving "insight" treatments achieve greater levels of insight than those who do not.

Even the few studies that have tried to operationalize measures of insight have typically not come up with insight definitions that bear much resemblance to Freud's statements. As our past work suggested, insight, for Freud, seems to demand a growing awareness of the connection between current neurotic problems and early conflicts deriving from past relationships. The essence of the insight concept lies in the explanation of current feelings and behavior on the basis of past interactions. The work we reviewed up through the 1970s operationalized insight in contrasting, but non-Freudian ways (Fisher & Greenberg, 1985; Roback, 1974). Insight in those studies was variously defined as the ability to respond to a series of test questions as another person would (empathic insight), the similarity between an individual's descriptions of self and the view that others have of the individual, the capacity to understand the motivations of others, and the degree to which individuals (typically diagnosed as schizophrenic) are cognizant of their own intellectual or emotional impairment. A more recent exploration of insight research echoes our concerns about insight measurement and raises questions about the validity and relevance to psychoanalytic understanding of most of the measures that have been used (Crits-Christoph, Barber, Miller, & Beebe, 1993).

INSIGHT AND PSYCHOTHERAPY OUTCOME

In our original attempt to determine whether psychotherapy outcome is related to insight, we examined two groups of research reports—16 comparative studies of insight therapy not measuring insight change, and 4 therapy studies that attempted to relate measured changes in insight to adjustment (Fisher & Greenberg, 1985).

The comparative studies, which most often contrasted an interpretive treatment with a behavioral approach, revealed virtually no evidence for the superiority of interpretive treatments. Indeed, the behavioral approaches tended to be either equivalent in outcome or superior in those instances where the treatment focus was on circumscribed problems that were neither severely disabling nor long-standing. However, the studies were typically conducted by behaviorally oriented clinicians (with an apparent vested interest in finding the behavioral treatments superior), and the interpretive treatments were, as a group, loosely and vaguely defined. Overall, the comparisons had a "straw man" quality, with no measurements to demonstrate that any of the treatments resulted in the attainment of insight. We concluded that the amorphous interpretive therapies misleadingly permitted almost any meetings between individuals respectively designated as patients and therapists to be called "insight-oriented."

The four studies we uncovered that attempted an independent assessment of insight and therapeutic change were woefully inadequate as tests of psychodynamic ideas. Insight, as diversely measured in these reports, had virtually nothing to do with the understanding of the relationship between past and present. Furthermore, the "patient" samples for all the studies comprised either recruited college students or hospitalized psychotic patients. Treatment, which was carried out in group formats, lasted for no more than 3 to 6 weeks. We concluded that the researchers had created caricatures to represent "insight therapy" and that the unrealistic brevity and superficiality of treatments ignored the working-through concept. Not surprisingly, there appeared to be little evidence of differential change favoring the insight treatments brought about by a few hours' worth of interpretations hurled at recruited college students or chronic psychotic patients.

Subsequent to our past review, seven additional reports attempting to relate insight to psychotherapy outcome have appeared in the literature (Crits-Christoph & Luborsky, 1990; Eisenstein, Levy, & Marmor, 1994; Hoglend, Engelstad, Sorbye, & Heyerdahl, in press; Morgan, Luborsky, Crits-Christoph, Curtis, & Solomon, 1982; O'Conner, Edelstein, Berry, & Weiss, 1994; O'Malley, Chong, & Strupp, 1983; Wallerstein, 1986). As in the earlier studies, the findings from these reports revealed relatively little evidence of a significant relationship between insight and outcome. Morgan et al. (1982) reported an investigation trying to predict the outcome of psychodynamic psychotherapy (with a median duration of approximately one year) by means of an insight rating scale, as well as from scales designed to rate the helping alliance, therapist facilitative behaviors, and the degree of patient resistance. Transcript segments of two early psychotherapy sessions and two late psychotherapy sessions were rated by two experienced psychoanalysts, trained in using the various rating scales to a reliable degree. The following insight items, each rated on a 10-point Likert-type scale, were based on the definition of emotional insight provided by Reid and Finesinger (1952):

1. Patient recognizes specific phenomena (ideation, affect, behavior) relevant to the problems being discussed.

2. Patient recognizes habitual patterns of behavior.

3. Patient recognizes that he or she plays an active rather than a passive role in producing his or her symptoms and experiences. He or she becomes increasingly conscious of provoking behaviors that are related to production of symptoms and experiences.

4. Patient recognizes particular behaviors as indications of defensiveness or resistance.

5. Patient connects two problems that were previously unconnected, or sees their immediate relevance.

6. Patient becomes increasingly aware of previously unconscious (repressed) thoughts, feelings, or impulses.

7. Patient is able to relate present events to past events.

8. Patient is able to relate present experiences to childhood experiences.

9. Patient's awareness of psychological experience appears to be cumulative.

The patient sample consisted of the 10 most and the 10 least improved patients (as assessed by two composite outcome measures) treated in the Penn Psychotherapy Research Project (Luborsky, Crits-Christoph, Mintz, & Auerbach, 1988). Although the study found that the helping alliance measures (ratings of whether the therapist was helping the patient and whether they were working together) predicted outcome, the ratings of insight did not. Comparing the 10 most improved and the 10 least improved patients revealed no significant differences on the insight scale. That is, the most improved and the least improved patients did not differ in ratings of insight either early in treatment or late in treatment. Importantly, there was no interaction effect between outcome and treatment phase. Thus, the more improved patients did not show greater gains in insight from an early- to a late-treatment phase.

Another study having some relevance to the issue of whether insight is related to outcome has been reported by O'Malley, Chong, and Strupp (1983). They attempted to predict the outcome of brief dynamic psychotherapy from the Vanderbilt Psychotherapy Process Scales. One dimension that emerged from these scales was labeled Exploratory Processes and was a composite consisting of 29 items relating to the patient's level of self-exploration and attempts to understand the underlying reasons for problems, the therapist's attempts to examine the patient's psychodynamics and help the patient understand the reason behind his or her reactions, and the patient's level of psychic distress. Although, the Exploratory Processes dimension contained items relevant to the issue of insight, these were mixed with items pertaining to self-examination and symptom severity.

Two psychologists rated the Exploratory Processes dimension (along with two other process dimensions) from three 5-minute tape segments taken from each of the first three sessions of psychotherapy. These measures were used to try to predict overall outcome and change in target symptoms. The Exploratory process measure (obtained at Session 3) predicted overall outcome and improvement in target complaints, but only when these outcome measures were based on the therapists' ratings. Outcome ratings produced by the patient and by an independent clinician who interviewed each patient at intake and termination proved to be unrelated to the Exploratory Process measure. In contrast, a Patient Involvement Dimension (which tapped the level of patient participation and cooperation) was shown to be significantly related to outcome from all three vantage points (patient, therapist, and independent clinician).

Overall, the study does not clearly indicate that the patients' level of insight predicts outcome. However, this conclusion is clouded because no pure measure of insight was used. Also, as others have pointed out, this study may be of limited value in testing questions about insight because there is no attempt to measure gain in insight, the emphasis being simply on attempts to engage in or facilitate patient self-examination (Crits-Christoph, Barber, Miller, & Beebe, 1993). We might add that the findings we have summarized suggest the provocative possibility that *therapists* are more likely to perceive positive outcomes when they spend more time exploring and pointing out patient psychodynamics. However, at least in this study, neither the patients nor an independent observer seemed to detect the same relationship between outcome and psychodynamic exploration.

An interesting investigation trying to relate patients' level of self-understanding to psychotherapy outcome evolved from work on the Core Conflictual Relationship Theme (CCRT). The CCRT is a systematic methodology designed to obtain reliable dynamic formulations of the principal conflicts in patients' relationship themes (Luborsky, 1977). Patient in-therapy narratives about their interpersonal interactions are abstracted to reveal characteristic patterns of relating to others. Crits-Christoph and Luborsky (1990) reported that the level of self-understanding assessed by the CCRT ratings in early psychotherapy sessions (averaged over psychotherapy Sessions 3 and 5) was significantly related to a few different measures of outcome. However, they felt their measure of self-understanding was largely a reflection of the patients' general level of psychological mindedness and, therefore, of possibly limited usefulness in determining the connection between insight and outcome. In particular, their data did not permit them to examine the more theoretically relevant question of whether good outcome is associated with gains in self-understanding over the course of therapy. No significant results were found in examining the relationship between outcome and gains in self-understanding between Sessions 3 and 5. Yet, as the authors of this study acknowledged, changes in insight over a much longer period of time would be needed to draw meaningful conclusions about the ties between outcome and insight.

The paucity of evidence to support the idea that insight plays a central role in outcome for most psychotherapy patients is reinforced by Wallerstein's (1986a, 1989) reports on the Psychotherapy Research Project of the Menninger Foundation. Although this work was based on a "naturalistic," rather than a tightly controlled study of 42 patients seen in either orthodox psychoanalysis or other variants of supportive-expressive psychodynamic treatment, the results are thought-provoking and generally in keeping with the trends indicated by the other research we have cited. Wallerstein's conclusions are based on a detailed examination of the case histories and life histories of the 42 patients. Aside from concluding that the outcome results achieved with psychoanalysis were more limited than had been expected, Wallerstein's dissection of the various treatments attempted to gauge the degree to which structural changes in patient personality could be associated with the development of insight. Surprisingly, only 24% of the patients achieved a level of insight that seemed commensurate with the degree of change they reached, and 45% of the patients were reported to achieve changes that "substantially outstripped" the insights they had developed in treatment. Of the remaining patients, 7% were viewed as exhibiting change that fell far short of the insights attained and 24% showed little indication of either change or the acquisition of insight. Thus, for most patients, insight and change did not seem appreciably correlated.

Some of the conclusions drawn from this microscopic analysis of treatment were that the spectrum of psychodynamic treatments (including orthodox psychoanalysis) included more supportive relationship elements then had been anticipated and that these factors were more responsible for change than had been expected. Conversely, the insight-interpretive aspects of therapy were seen as less likely to account for change then had been assumed. Overall, outcomes derived from treatments emphasizing insight attainment proved to be indistinguishable from treatments relying on more supportive techniques.

Three experienced analysts, Eisenstein, Levy, and Marmor (1994), offer a similar challenge to the proposition that therapeutic benefit in psychoanalytic therapy is mainly a result of insights gained from verbal interpretations. They based their conclusions on a series of systematic observations independently gathered while viewing every session of a case of long-term psychoanalytic therapy. Results were derived from standardized worksheets developed to permit the organized and uniform recording of impressions and observations. The method allowed for the comparison of observers' ratings with those of the therapist. The project, originally organized by the well-known psychoanalyst Franz Alexander, remained unpublished for many years because of his untimely death.

The analyst team was particularly struck by the perception that cognitive interpretations, and the insights they were presumably creating for the patient, were not as central to the creation of change as analysts typically believe. Instead, their observations led them to conclude that the therapist's personality, value system, and style are much more important to the process than most analysts assume. They came to acknowledge that therapist suggestion and persuasion were significant elements in inducing change. The analyst's nonverbal cues were seen as especially impactful. Their conclusions also highlighted the importance of other change-inducing ingredients such as catharsis (whereby there is a release of emotional tension as patients unburden themselves of troubling problems), identification (as patients learn to imitate a therapist model), and the "corrective emotional experience."

This last factor refers to therapists behaving in a more constructive and supportive manner toward patients than the significant authority figures did in the patients' past. In general, the interesting investigation produced by the team of psychoanalysts emphasizes the complex verbal and nonverbal interaction that occurs in the therapy dyad and takes issue with the idea that analysts are merely neutral, distant transmitters of interpretations.

Two "pilot studies" reported by O'Conner, Edelstein, Berry, and Weiss (1994) offer a set of germane preliminary findings. They demonstrated that patients' frequency of insight statements (defined in terms of compatibility with an independently made dynamic case formulation) followed a characteristic form during brief psychodynamic psychotherapy. Each of the five patients studied showed a parabolic pattern wherein the number of insight-statements decreased as therapy progressed only to rise again toward termination (at 16 sessions of treatment) and to increase even more during the 6 months following treatment. Although patients' average frequency of insight statements over the course of therapy was related to outcome, the few patients studied were not making more insightful statements at the end of treatment then they were at the beginning. The authors suggested that the quality of insights attained might be more important than the quantity in terms of impact on outcome. Better outcome seemed to be associated with insight statements made with greater patient assurance and conviction. A potential problem for this research is the built-in assumption that frequency of insightful statements is a good index of level of insight. This may turn out to be an incorrect assumption.

Another relevant set of observations comes from the work of Hoglend and his associates (Hoglend, Engelstad, Sorbye, & Heyerdahl, in press; Hoglend, Sorbye, Sorlie, Fossum, & Engelstad, 1992; Hoglend, Sorlie, Heyerdahl, Sorbye, & Amlo, 1993). They focused on trying to detect whether a variety of factors affect the outcome of brief dynamic psychotherapy. Insight was one of the factors of interest. Unlike the other investigators we have cited, they emphasized that the influence of insight would be most apparent in the period following treatment termination. For example, after acknowledging that the relatively quick improvements in symptomatology brought about by psychotherapy might be significantly attributed to the experience of a good therapy relationship and the cognitive learning of coping abilities, they suggested that it might take several years beyond the therapy experience for the patient to translate acquired self-understanding or insight into long-term stable "dynamic change" in such areas as interpersonal functioning, self-esteem, and problem-solving ability (Hoglend et al., 1993, in press). To address this issue, their papers describe a long-term follow-up study of patients using theory-related measures of dynamic change.

The project involved appraisals of the brief psychodynamic treatment of 43 outpatients by a group of seven psychiatrists. Treatment duration ranged from 9 to 53 weekly sessions (mean 27.5 sessions; median 31 sessions). Therapy followed a technical manual modeled after a number of well-known brief therapy approaches. At the outset, each patient was rated by the group of clinicians on a series of suitability criteria. Target complaints were listed, and a consensus dynamic formulation and diagnosis were reached. In addition, the level of pretreatment insight was rated.

Outcome was measured at Points 2 and 4, years after treatment was terminated. At those follow-up times, the patients were reinterviewed by the clinical group, the reports of the pretreatment evaluations were read by each of the clinicians, and independent ratings of outcome were made on seven outcome scales. Two of the scales focused on symptomatic change (target complaints and global assessment), and the remaining scales were measures of dynamic change (interpersonal relations, self-esteem, new cognitive learning, problem-solving capacity, and self-understanding or insight).

Results indicated that pretreatment level of insight predicted the likelihood of staying in treatment and seeking additional treatment in the follow-up period. Pretreatment insight was not directly associated with long-term symptomatic or dynamic change. However, pretreatment insight, in combination with treatment length, was associated with all aspects of outcome. More treatment sessions were required for successful outcome with initially less insightful patients, whereas more insightful patients did equally well with brief or longer treatments. More insightful patients also tended to receive more psychotherapy sessions than the less insightful. Among other things, these results suggest that those patients rated as more insightful at the beginning of treatment are probably more comfortable with the therapy process and inclined to stay in treatment longer, even if they do not need the additional sessions. It is also possible that therapists are inclined to work longer with patients whom they perceive to be insightful. Hoglend and colleagues concluded that initial level of insight is probably not one of the more important variables mediating outcome. Conclusions from their study about the value of pretreatment level of insight are weakened because initial judgments of insight (they used an average rating in their data analysis) proved to be of relatively low reliability across raters.

Of possibly greater interest for the purposes of this chapter is whether gains in insight were associated with better outcome. In this project, gains in insight rated at the 2-year follow-up proved to be the strongest predictor of dynamic change 4 years after therapy termination. Insight gains at the 2-year follow-up mark did not predict symptom improvement. The authors conclude that insights gained during and after therapy promote stable dynamic change (although not symptom change).

This is the only published study thus far to examine the relationship between long-term outcome and gains in insight. However, several methodological problems hamper the report. For instance, as noted, most of the insight ratings proved to be of low reliability. Also, conclusions were based on correlational data, leaving open the possibility that there was no cause-and-effect relationship between the measures of insight and the other measures of change. Furthermore, the clinicians' ratings were open to bias because they were assessing both insight and other measures of change concurrently and they were not blind to the pretreatment evaluations.

In sum, there have been relatively few empirical attempts to directly link psychotherapy outcome with a measure of insight. Those studies that have looked at this issue have generally not found much support for an insight-change association. However, any conclusions must be very tentative at this point, not only because of the lack of studies, but also because the measurement of insight is at such a primitive level. There is a glaring need for the development of widely accepted insight measures with demonstrated reliability and validity. As others have also noted (Crits-Christoph, Barber, Miller, & Beebe, 1993), such measures could be profitably used to answer a wide variety of outstanding research questions: How and when does insight evolve? Is insight accompanied by emotional arousal more beneficial to patients than simply intellectual insight? Are insight-promoting techniques more effective with certain types of patients? Are certain types of problems more likely to be ameliorated with insight attainment?

Because insight within the psychodynamic model is most often thought to derive from the psychotherapist's employment of interpretive techniques, we will next review the research literature on interpretations. Although the use of interpretations does not guarantee the attainment of insights, the finding of an association between interpretations and outcome would at least be consistent with the potential importance of insight and support the value of interpretive techniques as a central ingredient facilitating change in psychodynamic treatments.

APPRAISING THE RESEARCH ON INTERPRETATIONS

The idea that the therapist's accurate interpretations of the patient's motivations, resistances, and transference feelings promote positive treatment outcomes is at the heart of psychodynamic psychotherapy. The clinical literature on psychoanalysis has described interpretation as the "supreme agent in the hierarchy of therapeutic principles"

(Bibring, 1954, p. 763) and the "ultimate operative factor in the therapeutic action" (Strachey, 1934, p. 152). Yet, up until the 1980s, relatively
little empirical research had appeared that might test these declarations. Now, however, a growing network of findings is emerging to
clarify the value of interpretive techniques. Orlinsky, Grawe, and Parks
(1994), in a wide-ranging thorough review linking psychotherapy process and outcome research, concluded that interpretations, as used
across many different types of psychotherapy, have "emerged as a
rather effective mode of intervention" (p. 307). Their review showed
that interpretation was associated with positive therapy outcome in
63% of 38 findings that had accumulated in the literature. This conclusion is reinforced by Beutler, Machado, and Allstetter Neufeldt (1994)
in their review of therapist variables that predict psychotherapy outcome. They found a number of studies, using therapists with different
theoretical orientations and mixed samples of clinical patients, that
demonstrated an association between the frequency of interpretations
and benefits accruing to patients (Elliott, Barker, Caskey, & Pistrang,
1982; Gomez, 1982; Jacobs & Warner, 1981).

Two reviews, published in the 1990s, focused specifically on the
research pertinent to the use of interpretations in psychodynamic
treatment approaches (Crits-Christoph, Barber, Baranackie, & Cooper,
1993; Henry, Strupp, Schacht, & Gaston, 1994). These reviews provide a
good base for highlighting the major issues and findings that have
come out of the empirical literature concerned with psychodynamic interpretations. The use of transference interpretations and interpretation accuracy are areas that have received special attention.

Researchers operating from a psychodynamic perspective have
shown a particular interest in assessing the value of transference interpretations. In general, these interpretations are designed to reveal
to patients that some of their impulses and feelings for the therapist
are derived from emotions and thoughts regarding significant others
in the past, which are then projected onto the therapist. In discussing
the importance of the transference concept, Gill (1982) cites Freud's
general definition of transference as "new editions of the old conflicts" (p. 49). Within the psychoanalytic literature, interpretations of
the patient-therapist relationship and its parallels to past relationships have often been portrayed as having particular potency compared with other types of interpretations. They have been seen as
playing a unique and critical role in facilitating change (e.g., Gill,
1982; Strachey, 1934). The clinical lore regarding the special merits of
transference interpretations initially received some support from attempts to empirically check out the validity of the anecdotal claims
(Malan, 1976; Marziali & Sullivan, 1980). However, further studies,
with more refined methodologies, have consistently failed to support

an association between higher frequencies of transference interpreta-
tions and better therapy outcomes (Henry, Schacht, Strupp, Butler, &
Binder, 1993; Henry, Strupp, Butler, Schacht, & Binder, 1993;
McCullough et al., 1991; Piper, Azim, Joyce, & McCallum, 1991; Piper,
Debbane, Bienvenu, Carufel, & Garant, 1986).

Early support for the special utility of transference interpretations was suggested by Malan (1976) in a naturalistic study of brief dynamic psychotherapy. This work reported that the proportion of
interpretations linking the patients' transference feelings with feelings toward parents was positively and uniquely associated with positive treatment outcome. However, the study suffered from numerous
methodological weaknesses. The data for the study were drawn from
case-notes written from memory rather than from transcripts or audiotapes of the sessions. Additionally, the raters of the interpretations
were not blind to outcome, the definition for "interpretations" was not
well specified, and only one outcome measure was used. Furthermore,
the strongest study finding was only marginally significant and that
with the use of a one-tailed test.

To rectify some of the research design flaws, Marziali and Sullivan (1980) had Malan's case material re-rated by researchers who were
blind to the outcome results. This resulted in a replication of Malan's
findings. Yet, aside from the lack of blindness, all the methodological
problems of the original study remained. Marziali (1984) then presented an even more careful attempt to test the stability of Malan's
findings by using blind raters of interpretations, audiotapes of psychotherapy sessions instead of case notes, and five measures of psychodynamic outcome rather than one. The results of this study were
much less supportive of Malan's conclusions than the earlier work had
been. Only two out of five outcome subscores proved to be correlated
with the frequency of transference/parent link interpretations. Moreover, other types of interpretations proved to be equally related to outcome, undermining the idea of the transference/parent interpretations
having some unique impact. It has also been suggested that because
this study relied on measures of frequency of interpretations, rather
than proportions of different types of interpretation, the results may
simply reflect the level of therapist activity instead of the efficacy of a
particular type of interpretation (Piper et al., 1986).

As noted, later more methodologically sophisticated studies
inspired by Malan's early work have consistently not supported any
special beneficial association between treatment outcome and interpretations focusing on the linkage between transference feelings and feelings about parents. Piper et al. (1986) explored the relationships between
outcome and the object (person) focus of therapist interpretations in 21

patients seen in short-term psychotherapy. Ratings of the audiotapes of 168 psychotherapy sessions produced very few significant correlations (no more than would be expected by chance) between 17 measures of outcome and 10 types of therapist interventions (including 4 categories of interpretation). No evidence was uncovered to support a relationship between proportion of transference interpretations and outcome.

Attempts to explain the failure to find evidence for a relationship between the object of interpretations and outcome have focused on several potentially important variables left unaddressed by Piper et al. (1986). These include interpretation timing and accuracy and the possibility that other therapy elements (e.g., therapist and relationship characteristics) may be more important than the focus of interpretations in determining outcome (Crits-Christoph, Barber, Barnackie, & Cooper, 1993; Piper et al., 1986). Of particular significance is the idea that various types of interpretations may have differential impacts depending on the personality characteristics of the patient who is receiving them.

As a follow-up to earlier work, Piper and his colleagues published an expanded study looking at the effects of transference interpretations on 64 patients who received approximately 20 sessions of short-term dynamically oriented psychotherapy (Piper, Azim, Joyce, & McCallum, 1991). In addition to interest in whether transference interpretations were associated with outcome, the investigators also explored the possible impact of transference interpretations on the therapeutic alliance (the working relationship between the patient and the therapist) and whether the patient's level of object relations (a measure of the patient's historic ability to relate to others, ranging from "mature" to "primitive") mediated the impact of interpretations. The proportion of transference interpretations observed in the 22,500 interventions rated was used to avoid confounding the therapist's activity level with the use of transference interpretations.

The results of this study are quite provocative in that they showed an *inverse* relationship between the proportion of transference interpretations and measures of both therapy outcome and therapeutic alliance. Greater reliance on transference interpretations was associated with more negative treatment outcomes and a more negative impact on the therapist-patient relationship. The effects were particularly striking at high concentrations of transference interpretations and among the patients who had displayed a characteristic previous pattern of higher level relationships. The authors were especially concerned that brief, time-limited psychotherapies might pressure psychotherapists into providing transference interpretations more frequently and more quickly than is advisable; this practice could, according to their data, lead to negative treatment effects and possibly even patient deterioration. They issued the following warning:

> While our findings must be regarded as tentative, we believe that the evidence is sufficiently strong to warrant alerting clinicians to the possibilities of negative effects and the seeming ineffectiveness of trying to improve alliance or resolve resistance by providing high levels of transference interpretations during short-term psychotherapy. (p. 952)

In discussing their results, Piper and his colleagues highlighted that, at high levels of usage, transference interpretations may lead patients to withdraw because of feeling criticized. Another possibility, also consistent with this study's data, is that therapists may increase the level of transference interpretations when they are experiencing difficulties with a particular patient (e.g., resistance, negative transference, weak alliance) in a misguided attempt to overcome a therapeutic impasse. We should note that, even before the appearance of the Piper group's empirical results, a number of psychoanalysts had foreseen the danger of a heavy reliance on transference interpretations and issued words of caution. Advocates of employing transference interpretations, such as Gill (1982) and Strachey (1934), stressed both care and moderation in their use. In any event, high concentrations of transference interpretations, with little regard for proper timing or accuracy (both unaddressed factors in this research), appear to be harmful and not consistent with the theoretical and technical writings of several analysts.

The suggestion that a high concentration of transference interpretations can be antitherapeutic is not limited to the findings of Piper's group. Research performed at Vanderbilt University on the effects of training in time-limited psychotherapy also suggests that countertherapeutic processes may well follow an overemphasis on transference interpretations (Henry, Schacht, Strupp, Butler, & Binder, 1993; Henry, Strupp, Butler, Schacht, & Binder, 1993; Henry, Strupp, Schacht, & Gaston, 1994). The 5-year project involved 16 experienced therapists learning to apply a manualized focused form of time-limited dynamic psychotherapy to 80 cases. The approach stressed the importance of repeatedly exploring the patient-therapist relationship over the 25 sessions of treatment.

The study produced some unexpected findings with implications for the use of transference interpretations, although it was not originally designed to do so. The pertinent data analyses were made possible because the project included ratings, both early and late in the course of therapy, of the frequency with which therapists attended to the relationship between the patient and the therapist and tied perceptions of the therapy relationship to the patient's patterns of relating to others. As a result of training, therapists increased their activities significantly and produced more interventions that could be classified as transference interpretations. The design allowed therapists to be used as their own controls in contrasting those of their patients who received relatively high interpretation levels with those who received relatively low levels of interpretation.

Unexpectedly, after training emphasizing a higher level of attention to and interpretation of transference, there was a significant deterioration in some of the interactional and interpersonal aspects of therapy that have been associated with positive therapy process and outcome. Measures revealed that following training, the therapists were delivering more hostile and critical messages. Also, the therapists were judged as becoming more authoritarian and defensive, less approving, less supportive, and less engaged in evaluating patients' feelings. Patients viewed their therapists as more impatient. As the authors noted, adherence to the treatment manual (and therefore, to a general emphasis on transference issues) proved to be negatively related to outcome. In sharp contrast to the Vanderbilt research group's initial expectation that an increase in transference interpretations would enhance the interpersonal process, their results showed just the opposite. These findings are consistent with the warning by Piper's research group cited earlier.

Indications that high concentrations of transference interpretations can produce detrimental effects does not mean that transference interpretations are never helpful. However, even the idea that judiciously used transference interpretations will produce positive effects—because of their ability to facilitate patient affect—has not received unqualified empirical support. Research has revealed that no single pattern of response to transference interpretations characterizes all patients. In addition, research has been unable to show that transference interpretations are generally any different from nontransference interpretations in the patient responses they elicit.

Luborsky, Bachrach, Graff, Pulver, and Christoph (1979) studied the immediate response to transference interpretations in three psychoanalyses that had three distinctly different outcomes: poor, moderate and very positive. Trained psychoanalysts rated a variety of process variables (e.g., resistance, affect expression, understanding) from the 250 words uttered by patients before and after 16 transference interpretations. Each patient showed a characteristic and consistent response to such interpretations, with the poor-outcome patient displaying the most resistant and negative response. The relevant finding here is that no one type of response to interpretations typified all patients.

Another investigation demonstrating divergent reactions to inter-pretations is reported by McCullough et al. (1991). This group of in-vestigators was interested in the postinterpretation responses of 16 patients involved in one of two forms of brief dynamic psychotherapy. Patient responses to transference and nontransference interpretations (as well as clarifications) were rated as either affective or defensive and analyzed against ratings of treatment outcome. The complexity in-volved in studying therapist interventions is underscored by the re-sults. Overall, neither the type of therapist intervention nor the type of patient response was correlated with outcome when each was viewed separately. When viewed in the context of the therapy interaction, how-ever, a positive correlation with outcome was observed if transference interpretations were followed by affect; and a negative association with outcome was observed if any type of interpretation was followed by patient defensiveness. Nontransference interpretations followed by affect also showed a positive association with outcome, but this result did not reach statistical significance because of the small sample size.

In general, then, this study revealed the expected association be-tween transference interpretations, patient affective response, and positive outcome. It showed, too, that patients sometimes respond to transference interpretations with defensiveness (rather than affect) and that this bodes poorly for outcome. The data did not provide strong evidence that transference interpretations have a unique impact when compared with other types of interpretations. Porter (1987), in a study roughly comparable to the one reported by the McCullough group, also failed to find a unique patient response to transference in-terpretations. He did find indications—again like the McCullough group—that interpretations may often be met with defensive re-sponses rather than therapeutic affect. Similarly, a series of studies from a group of researchers at the Mount Zion Medical Center in San Francisco have also demonstrated that transference interpretations are no more effective than nontransference interpretations in promoting immediate within-psychotherapy-session progress (Fretter, 1984; Fret-ter, Bucci, Broitman, Silberschatz, & Curtis, 1994; Silberschatz, Fretter, & Curtis, 1986).

Overall, the interpretation findings suggest that interpretive techniques have been shown to be generally useful and often related to positive outcome across many types of psychotherapy. However, their singular contribution to positive outcome in psychodynamic psy-chotherapy has not yet been clearly established. Of special concern is the possibility that transference interpretations can be detrimental to treatment if they are delivered with high frequency. Interestingly, the negative impact of an overreliance on transference interpretations may be particularly apparent in patients who are more adept at relating to others. There have been a few attempts to try to account for this finding. It has been speculated that more interpersonally adept individuals might be exposed to higher levels of transference interpretations (which are often perceived as criticism) because of a mistaken assumption that they could tolerate a more intensive focus on the relationship than patients with a less positive interpersonal history. On the other hand, those with poorer interpersonal relationships may find the possible negative effects of high concentrations of transference interpretations mitigated by the desire for an active interpersonal connection with the therapist regardless of interpretation content. Overall, attempts to study the effects of transference interpretations have not demonstrated that they are more therapeutic than other types of interpretations or that they contribute more to outcome than other aspects of the therapy process, such as the therapist's ability to provide a comforting, accepting relationship.

The conclusions that can be drawn from the literature on interpretations must be tempered by the knowledge that they are based not only on a relatively small number of studies but also largely ignore whether the delivered interpretations are accurate or off the mark. Obviously, most therapists would not expect positive results from interpretations that were incompatible with a patient's problems or experience. Yet studies of interpretations have largely not addressed this complex issue. In the next sections, we will review what has been learned about the accuracy of interpretations.

OBSTACLES TO MEASURING INTERPRETATION ACCURACY

Research indicates that investigators have not had an easy time demonstrating that interpretations play a unique and substantial role (when compared with other therapy ingredients) in determining treatment outcome. But, for the most part, studies have not addressed the question of interpretation accuracy. Therefore, the therapeutic impact of interpretations may be undervalued in the research literature because of the usual failure to take accuracy into account. Intuitively, it seems reasonable to conclude that interpretations tailored to fit patients and their circumstances would be more beneficial than those that are not. Substantiating the validity of this claim has proven to be a tricky affair, and there have been relatively few attempts to do so. A major obstacle for this research resides in the inherent difficulty of trying to distinguish which interpretations are suitable and meet the goodness-of-fit test. Which criteria should be used in deciding that an interpretation is on the mark? Before reviewing the limited research evidence on interpretation accuracy, we will provide some background for the problem of delineating suitability by briefly describing relevant historical and empirical issues.

Early on, Freud's pronouncements created the impression that his psychoanalytic treatment was both unique and superior because of its reliance on patient insights gained through accurate interpretations by the therapist. Freud distanced himself from the possibility that his treatment's effects could derive in any significant way from the analyst's suggestions or attempts to persuade. He created the illusion that the analytic situation, with its "blank screen" therapist and "freely associating" patient, brought about a self-awareness that was untainted by analyst attempts to influence the patient. It was important for him to do this because he was arguing that the observations of the analyst were objective and required no independent verification by conventional scientific methods. He wanted his system to be accepted not only for its treatment potential, but also as a tool for generating scientific "truths" about the development of personality. Therapeutic success was equated with theoretical correctness. If a patient improved, it was assumed that the case conceptualization and the interpretations derived from it were accurate.

As Freud's therapy moved away from an emphasis on uncovering repressed memories toward overcoming the patient's resistances to the analyst's interpretations, it became hard for him not to admit that the analyst was attempting to sway and maneuver the patient's beliefs. Elsewhere, we (Fisher & Greenberg, 1985) described the seepage of persuasion into the psychoanalytic process as follows:

> Freud's emphasis on the formation of a strong patient attachment to the analyst (transference) and the necessity for "working through" patient resistances fosters a view of the analyst as a convincer and a persuader. Despite the analyst's stated objective of non-interference with the patient's productions, a positive dependent relationship is purposefully established and explicitly used to prepare the patient to accept unacceptable ideas and agree with thoughts that would initially be denied. (p. 362)

The analyst's role as persuader, as opposed to simply a neutral participant in the therapy process, is well documented by Freud's own remarks. In a number of places, statements make it apparent that patient belief in interpretations was frequently coerced and shaped along the lines Freud chose, thus rendering patient acceptance questionable as proof of interpretation accuracy. For instance, Freud detailed how difficult it was for him to extract recollections of seduction from hysterical patients who insistently denied memories of the traumatic scenes (Freud, 1896). He later wrote:

Having diagnosed a case of neurasthenic neurosis with certainty and having classified its symptoms correctly, we are in a position to translate the symptomatology into aetiology; and we may then boldly demand confirmation of our suspicions from the patient. We must not be led astray by initial denials. If we keep firmly to what we have inferred, we shall in the end conquer every resistance by emphasizing the unshakable nature of our convictions. (Freud, 1898, p. 269)

A comparable casting aside of patient response as an index of interpretation accuracy is revealed in Freud's description of the case of Dora (Freud, 1905a). Here, as well reviewed by Flowerman (1954), Freud concluded that any patient response to an interpretation (agreement, denial, or hesitation) could be used as evidence for its validity! In Freud's description of the case of Little Hans (Freud, 1909a) he also implicitly advocated influencing patient productions by stating that Hans needed to be led to conclusions that "he had shown no signs of possessing" (p. 104) and that his attention needed to be directed toward ideas that his father felt were important (Freud, 1909a).

Ultimately, Freud could not deny that suggestion played a role in his treatment, although he did not acknowledge that this undermined the use of in-therapy responses as the sole proof for his theories of personality. In discussing his thoughts on the therapist-patient relationship (transference) he wrote:

We readily admit that the results of psychoanalysis rest upon suggestion; by suggestion, however, we must understand . . . the influencing of a person by means of the transference phenomena which are possible in his case. We take care of the patient's final independence by employing suggestion in order to get him to accomplish a piece of psychical work which has as its necessary result a permanent improvement in his physical functioning. (Freud, 1912b, p. 106)

Freud's initial conviction that the "correctness" of an interpretation could be assessed from the patient's response, is not supported by the research evidence. In contradistinction to what Grunbaum (1984) labeled Freud's Tally Argument (that effective interpretations tally with what is real), a variety of lines of evidence show that patient belief in interpretations and subsequent anxiety reduction do not necessarily require accurate interpretations. For instance, research on the "Barnum effect" (Meehl, 1956) shows that bogus interpretations (those based on vague, general personality descriptions) will often be enthusiastically accepted by individuals as specifically accurate for them (e.g., Fisher & Greenberg, 1985; Snyder, Shenkel, & Lowery, 1977). Furthermore, it has been suggested and demonstrated that the Barnum effect may be used purposefully by clinicians to facilitate behavioral and cognitive changes (Halperin & Snyder, 1979; Petty & Brock, 1979; Snyder, Shenkel, & Lowery, 1977). Similarly, it has been argued, based on an array of observations, that interpretations do not have to square with the material produced by the patient to influence behavior. For instance, Gordon (1957) found that subjects experienced a sense of relief from hypnotically induced conflicts when they hit on plausible, although incorrect explanations for their feelings, and Mendell (1964) reported that intentionally inaccurate interpretations, which did not follow from the patient's productions, could still induce positive changes.

Eventually, even Freud admitted that the correctness of an interpretation could not be deciphered from the patient's response. He wrote:

> It appears, therefore, that the direct utterances of the patient after he has been offered a construction afford very little evidence upon the question whether we have been right or wrong. (Freud, 1937b, p. 263)

However, Freud was not able to totally divorce himself from the idea that insight based on accurate interpretations could be differentiated from analyst suggestion, and he went on to state that the future course of an analysis, as revealed through patient associations, could help in distinguishing insight from therapist suggestion.

In attempting to pinpoint interpretation accuracy, a related issue is whether correctness needs to be defined in terms of historical truth (Wetzler, 1985). This could be problematic because several lines of psychological research have challenged the assumption that people are usually able to produce highly accurate, detailed memories of what occurred in the past. Research suggests that memory can be molded to a significant degree by such factors as suggestion and the need to perceive consistency and continuity between current attitudes and behaviors and past experiences (e.g., Loftus, 1993; Ross & Conway, 1986). Brewin, Andrews, and Gotlib (1993), in a critical review of the evidence on the accuracy of retrospective reports, conclude that autobiographical memory is deficient. However, they also judge that claims about the degree of unreliability may be exaggerated:

> Obtaining the retrospective recall of childhood events appears, therefore, to be a flawed process that can be shaped by both internal and external factors. Social influences, childhood amnesia, and the simple fallibility of memory all impose limitations on the accuracy of recall, and fear of consequences of disclosure may further disadvantage this process. However, provided that individuals are questioned about the

occurrence of specific events or facts that they were sufficiently old and well placed to know about, the central features of their accounts are likely to be reasonably accurate. (p. 94)

On balance, the literature on the fidelity of memory for past events certainly questions whether such data can be routinely used to generate historically accurate interpretations. Although patient retrospective reports are likely to contain "kernels of truth" (a phrase embraced by Freud), they are also affected by a variety of psychological forces impelling the individual to tell a coherent and compelling story that may not in some respects reflect the way things actually were. This problem, as we have consistently suggested, precludes the use of patient concoctions to validate psychoanalytic theories of personality. But, the problem does not invalidate patient-produced material as potentially useful for generating therapeutic interventions that are accurate in the sense of being consistent with patient-produced narratives and perceptions.

The latter point is consonant with the position taken by those espousing a hermeneutic position (e.g., Bouchard & Guerette, 1991; Schafer, 1976; Spence, 1982a, 1982b). This position emphasizes that there are many realities, not one, and that the task in psychoanalysis (as well as other therapies) is to construct a coherent, plausible explanatory version of reality for the patient that fits with his or her presentation (although not necessarily with what others might deem to be historical accuracy). A distinction is made between historical and narrative truth and, in line with the constructivist position espoused by some cognitive-behavioral therapists (e.g., Guidano & Liotti, 1983; Mahoney, 1991), emphasis is placed on "the gradual construction of a more adaptive perception of self, rather than the replacement of distorted beliefs by an accurate and objective view of reality" (Castonguay & Goldfried, 1994, p. 163).

Researchers in designing studies to test whether interpretation accuracy is related to treatment effectiveness have had to come to terms with whether interpretations need to follow from historical truth to be considered accurate or whether accuracy could be simply derived from consistency with the patient narrative. The existing studies have, without exception, measured accuracy in terms of "narrative truth" rather than requiring a demonstration of "historical truth."

Freud failed to distinguish between the two kinds of "truth" and vacillated between portraying the analyst as a kind of archaeologist, faithfully uncovering true artifacts from the past, and an architect, creating a coherent structure from a variety of both historically true and false story fragments obtained from interactions with a patient (Bouchard & Guerette, 1991; Spence, 1982a, 1982b). Freud sometimes stressed the need for discovering factual truth as in the following statement:

> What we are in search of is a picture of the patients' forgotten years that shall be alike trustworthy and in all essential respects complete. (Freud, 1937b, p. 258)

On the other hand, he simultaneously held out the analyst as a person who tries to make sense out of forgotten memory traces through creative constructions. In the end, Freud acknowledged his doubts about recovering historical truths from analytic sessions and indicated that this might not even be necessary for an effective analysis. He wrote:

> The path that starts from the analyst's construction ought to end in the patient's recollection, but it does not always lead so far. Quite often we do not succeed in bringing the patient to recollect what has been repressed. Instead of that, if the analysis is carried out correctly, we produce in him an assured conviction of the truth of the construction which achieves the same therapeutic result as a recaptured memory. (Freud, 1937b, pp. 265–266)

The substitution of "this is what must have happened to you" for "this is what really happened" is an open admission that the treatment rests on a strong suggestive element. It also disqualifies the material obtained in analytic sessions as objective evidence for validating the historical accuracy of interpretations.

STUDIES OF INTERPRETATION ACCURACY

How, then, have researchers tried to determine the suitability of interpretations? Despite differences in measures and focus, three groups of investigators who have attempted to study the effects of interpretation accuracy from a psychodynamic perspective have all adopted a similar strategy. First, they derive a formulation of patient dynamics from early psychotherapy material. They then look to see if therapist interpretations at later points in the treatment are consistent with the original formulation. Finally, measures of the degree of consistency with the early case formulation are related to indexes of psychotherapy process and outcome. With this methodology, an interpretation is declared accurate if it is consistent with the original case formulation. There is no guarantee that the interpretation, even though judged to be accurate, would be wholly veridical if compared with an independent objective examination of the facts about a person's history, although it appears that this is usually assumed to be so. The methods used for case formulation in most of these studies have been tested and found to be reliable across judges.

One set of findings has emerged from a research group at the Mt. Zion Medical Center in San Francisco whose studies grow from a psychodynamic theory of therapy advanced by Weiss, Sampson, and the Mount Zion Psychotherapy Research Group (1986). The theory proposes that psychopathology originates from unconscious grim pathogenic beliefs based on childhood experiences. The beliefs are irrational and lead to feelings of anxiety and fear about the dangers of pursuing various goals or attempting to gratify impulses. According to the theory, each patient enters psychotherapy with a Plan (strategy) for testing out pathogenic assumptions in the therapist-patient relationship with the hope of disconfirming the beliefs. It is hypothesized that if therapist interpretations are compatible with the Plan, they will be beneficial because they invalidate the pathogenic beliefs standing in the way of reaching the patient's goals.

Silberschatz, Fretter, and Curtis (1986) used the Plan diagnosis methodology to evaluate the progress of three randomly selected patients who reflected treatment outcomes ranging from excellent to good to poor. Each had been treated with 16 sessions of brief dynamic psychotherapy. Initially, a Plan formulation was derived for each case by a team of clinicians working from transcripts of the intake interview and the first two psychotherapy sessions. Another set of judges independently identified all interpretations (both transference and nontransference) in the therapy transcripts. These interpretations were then isolated and presented in random order to another set of judges who rated them for compatibility with the Plan. Finally, still another set of judges rated patient progress (as measured by the Experiencing Scale developed by Klein, Mathieu, Gendlin, & Kiesler, 1970) from material produced directly before and after each interpretation.

Results showed that there was no difference on the depth of experiencing measure related to transference versus nontransference interpretations. However, the level of experiencing was significantly associated with Plan compatibility. Patient progress, as reflected by the ability to simultaneously focus on and experience feelings, was significantly enhanced when Plan-compatible interpretations were received. The authors observed that the varied outcomes of the cases were directly related to the proportion of Plan-compatible interpretations that had been made. Thus, the percentage of suitable (or consistent with the Plan) interpretations was significantly higher in the two good outcome cases compared with the poor outcome case. The study concluded that accuracy of interpretation was important for patient progress, although the category of interpretation (transference versus nontransference) was not.

Conclusions about the generalizability of both the process and the outcome findings in this study are severely limited by the small number of subjects in the sample. Furthermore, as others have pointed out, only one type of process measure was used and this also limits the robustness of the findings regarding patient progress (Crits-Christoph, Barber, Baranackie, & Cooper, 1993). The concern about the limitations of using only one process measure is addressed in a later study by Fretter, Bucci, Broitman, Silberschatz, and Curtis (1994). These authors went back to the original psychotherapy transcripts and had the material scored for two additional process measures (Insight and Referential Activity). Insight was measured both in terms of a global scale and Morgan's (1977) Patient Insight Scale, which assesses the degree of insight for each of seven types of behavior. The Referential Activity Scale is a linguistic measure that had previously been useful in predicting outcome variables and classifying treatment hours in terms of "work" as opposed to "resistance" sessions. High scores on the Referential Activity Scale dimensions indicate that the patient's language is rich in sensory detail and has a quality of immediacy suggesting that the speaker is reliving an experience in imagination.

Results of the analyses for the two new process measures (Insight and Referential Activity) were consistent with the results of the previous study. Again, the patient's immediate progress was not aided more by transference interpretations than by nontransference interpretations. However, suitability of interpretations (as measured by Plan-Compatibility) was consistently related to patient progress on the Insight and Referential Activity measures. An additional idea, raised by the findings, is that it is more beneficial to adopt a wider view of transference, encompassing patient pathogenic beliefs across a variety of significant people, than to limit the concept exclusively to the relationship with the therapist. In any event, this study, like its predecessor, suggests the importance of interpretation accuracy. But, like its predecessor, the study's reliance on only three subjects raises questions about the generalizability of the results.

Another set of studies bearing on the issue of interpretation accuracy comes from a group of researchers at the University of Pennsylvania. This work uses Luborsky's Core Conflictual Relationship Theme (CCRT) (Luborsky, 1977; Luborsky & Crits-Christoph, 1990) as the basis for determining accuracy of interpretations. The CCRT is a measure of patients' central relationship patterns as reflected on three dimensions: (a) the patient's main wishes, needs, or intentions toward others as revealed in the psychotherapy session narrative; (b) the patient's descriptions of the other person's responses; and (c) the response of the self. Interpersonal components of the core theme are represented by the patient's wish and response of others categories, whereas the response of self is viewed more as an indicator of the patient's feeling state.

Crits-Christoph, Cooper, and Luborsky (1988) used a set of judges to derive dynamic case formulations for 43 patients using the CCRT method. Patients had been seen, on average, for about a year of weekly psychodynamic psychotherapy sessions. The CCRT measure was derived from two early psychotherapy sessions. Another set of judges independently rated interpretations provided in early psychotherapy sessions for the degree of agreement with the CCRT formulations. In addition, separate measures were used to rate errors in technique and the helping alliance.

Analyses showed that accuracy of interpretations, as reflected by congruence with the interpersonal CCRT dimensions, predicted outcome. Accuracy on the response of self dimension did not. The authors felt the results demonstrated that more progress in treatment occurs when there is accurate focus on patient interpersonal material than when emphasis is placed on the patient's usual feeling states. Surprisingly, the results proved to be independent of the measures of therapy alliance and general technical skill. It was, therefore, suggested that accuracy of interpretation may be a specific skill, unrelated to more global skill indexes, and that accurate interpretations may not require a positive therapeutic alliance to produce benefits. The latter suggestion was made with some caution because of the possibility that the study contained too few therapy dyads with a clearly negative alliance to test for a meaningful interaction between interpretation accuracy and the quality of the therapy alliance.

A related study was subsequently published by Crits-Christoph, Barber, and Kurcias (1993). They were interested in whether therapist interpretation accuracy early in treatment would predict changes in the therapy alliance over the course of treatment for 33 patients. As before, accuracy of interpretations was assessed by the concordance with CCRT ratings for patients selected from the Penn Psychotherapy Project. The Helping Alliance Scale (Luborsky, Crits-Christoph, Alexander, Margolis, & Cohen, 1983) was applied to the first 30 minutes of each of two early and two late sessions for each patient. The late session measures were made at a point approximately three-quarters through the treatment (after about 40 weeks of treatment).

Results showed that although interpretation accuracy was unrelated to therapeutic alliance early in treatment, it was significantly associated with a positive alliance later on. The researchers concluded that accurate attention early on to the interpersonal aspects of patient's relationship patterns may repair a poor treatment alliance or maintain a positive one. In addition, the data suggested that early appropriate focus on the patient's feeling states (response of self) might be helpful in the initial formation of a therapeutic attachment. Despite the authors' appropriate caveats about generalizing their findings to other types of patient samples and different kinds of therapies, they underscore the importance of therapist skill in providing accurate interpretations of the patient's central interpersonal issues for facilitating a positive treatment alliance. This finding is important because consistent research evidence shows an association between a positive alliance and good treatment outcome (see reviews by Henry, Strupp, Schacht, & Gaston, 1994; Horvath & Symonds, 1991).

A few reports of research relating to interpretation accuracy in psychodynamic psychotherapy have also been presented by Canadian researchers (Joyce, 1991, 1992; Piper, 1991). These unpublished papers were presented at annual meetings of the Society for Psychotherapy Research and subsequently described in two overviews of interpretation accuracy research (Crits-Christoph, Barber, Baranackie, & Cooper, 1993; Henry, Strupp, Schacht, & Gaston, 1994). The presentations highlight the complexity involved in reaching empirically based conclusions about the effects of accurate interpretations.

The Canadian work was conducted on the sample of 64 cases studied by Piper, Azim, Joyce, and McCallum (1991) in their investigation of transference interpretations (reviewed in the previous section). In these papers, accuracy was defined in terms of correspondence between interpretations and the therapists' own initial dynamic formulations of the cases. In essence, the questions being asked pertained to whether the therapists' degree of interpretation consistency with their own case conceptualizations would affect the immediate patient response to interpretations, the treatment alliance, and outcome. Data analyses also focused on the relationship among these variables and the patients' initial level of object-relations.

Results showed that transference interpretations congruent with the case formulation were predictive of immediate patient reactions. High correspondence was associated with increased patient involvement as reflected by greater patient openness and self-disclosure and a decrease in hesitation about confirming the therapist's interpretations.

Associations between interpretation accuracy (or correspondence) and measures of alliance and outcome proved to be complicated. In fact, no relationships appeared until the sample was divided into high and low quality of object-relations groups. For the low quality of object-relations group, correspondence was associated with poorer alliance ratings and worse outcomes at 6-month follow-up. In this group, accurate interpretations appeared harmful to the treatment. The results were complex for the high quality of object-relations group. There was no relationship between correspondence and either alliance or outcome at treatment termination. However, a significant interaction appeared at follow-up between correspondence and the concentration of transference interpretations in predicting improvement of general symptomatology. Correspondence was associated with better outcomes at follow-up, but only when the concentration of transference interpretations was low. No relationships appeared between correspondence and outcome when the concentration levels of transference interpretations were high.

In general, the results of the Canadian researchers, like the findings from the other centers, indicate associations between interpretation correspondence and a few measures of therapy process and outcome. But, the data also reveal that the linkages with interpretation consistency may not always be positive and the benefits of accurate interpretations may be limited to individuals with particular characteristics, such as a history of mature interpersonal relationships. Faith in the solidity of the Canadian results is also restricted because accuracy was measured by the congruence between interpretations and the therapist's own original case conceptualizations. Thus, unlike the groups of researchers in San Francisco and Philadelphia whose case formulations were based on objective systems, proven to be consistent across judges, there is no way of gauging the suitability, or reliability, of the original case formulations in the Canadian work because each one was based on the unchecked constructions of a single therapist.

CONCLUSION

This chapter has focused on one of Freud's cardinal beliefs: that the attainment of insight is basic to producing change in psychodynamic psychotherapy. We assessed the importance of understanding for achieving psychotherapeutic benefit by placing the issue in historical context, exploring obstacles to empirical study, and reviewing three related areas of research focusing respectively on interpretations, interpretation accuracy, and attempts to link measures of insight to therapeutic change. A number of studies have been published since our last foray into this area (Fisher & Greenberg, 1985). In addition, there have been some interesting and notable innovations in methodology, such as the Luborsky group's development of the CCRT for appraising characteristic patterns of relationships and the work, stemming from Weiss and Sampson's control mastery theory, which examines patient attempts to test pathogenic beliefs within the therapy relationship.

Evidence for a direct association between insight attainment and outcome continues to be sparse. The relatively small number of applicable investigations appearing over several decades fail to reveal definite indications that growth in self-knowledge is the primary element for producing symptomatic improvement, even within psychodynamic psychotherapy. Although there is little doubt that the search for an insight-change link has been impeded by the absence of a widely used objective, reliable measure of insight, the consistency of the non-findings must be disheartening and frustrating to those who expected to discover a simple association tying insight to change. Similarly, attempts to prove that transference interpretations play a unique role in facilitating change in psychodynamic psychotherapy have not fared well. Based on the investigations to date, there is no reason to believe that transference interpretations (narrowly defined as focus on the therapist-patient relationship) are more facilitative of movement in therapy than are nontransference interpretations (or other types of intervention for that matter). The published reports hint that rigid adherence to a heavy emphasis on transference interpretations may often be counterproductive and potentially harmful to the therapy relationship.

At first glance, the lack of success in finding transference interpretations uniquely facilitative is surprising because there has been research corroborating several of Freud's observations about transference. For example, Luborsky and his research group have produced an array of studies showing that people display characteristic and consistent patterns of relating to others, that the patterns for each individual are consonant with descriptions of relationships with parental figures, and that the idiosyncratic patterns are reflected in the relationship with the therapist (Luborsky, Barber, & Crits-Christoph, 1990; Luborsky & Crits-Christoph, 1990).

Why, then, has much of the research literature not clearly supported the value of interpretive activities? Several possibilities come to mind. Foremost is the likelihood that simply producing interpretations does not ensure benefit. As we have seen, the frequency of interpretations is not a predictor of outcome. The measure is too crude and the therapy process is too complex to hinge on a single, unrefined variable. A similar point is made by Gaston, Piper, Debbane, Bienvenu, and Garant (1994) who conclude that therapist techniques or interventions per se have seldom been found to make a large contribution to outcome (e.g., Elliott, Hill, Stiles, Friedlander, Mahrer, & Margison, 1987; Hill Helms, Tichenor, Speigel, O'Grady, & Perry, 1988; Horowitz, Marmar, Weiss, DeWitt, & Rosenbaum, 1984; Orlinsky & Howard, 1986).

Stiles and Shapiro (1994), finding themselves unable to uncover significant relationships in their data between several process variables (including interpretations) and outcome, also deride the assumption of a simple association between production of any one type of therapist activity and the production of patient benefits. They disavow the drug metaphor for psychotherapy, which suggests that "if a process component is an active ingredient, then clients who receive relatively more of it should tend to improve more . . ." (p. 942). Instead, they stress the need to focus on appropriate interpersonal responsiveness and the intricate, continual adjustments in communication that are made by therapy participants based on the moment-to-moment feedback received from the other member of the dyad.

From our perspective, it appears unlikely that interpretations can be shown to affect outcome without simultaneously considering the role played by other therapy elements such as the nature of the relationship (alliance) or the accuracy of the intervention. Freud, too, came to recognize that the association between interpretations, insight, and change is not direct or easy to achieve. Aside from his statements about proper timing and the desirability of developing an appropriate analytic alliance, he incorporated the idea of working through into his system. This is a time-consuming process during which patients are faced over and over again with examples of how past perceptions and feelings lead to a pattern of repetitive distortions in current relationships (Freud, 1914c). The hard work of overcoming patient resistances to new ways of interpretating experiences became an important part of his technique.

The failure to use a wider definition for what constitutes a transference interpretation may have also prevented the attainment of significant empirical results in many studies. It now appears that defining transference interpretations solely in terms of the therapist-patient relationship reduces the probability of demonstrating a connection with outcome. Although Freud and other psychoanalytic writers (e.g., Gill, 1982; Stone, 1967; Strachey, 1969) stressed the supremacy of narrowly defined transference interpretations, research suggests that it is more important to address transference in terms of distorted beliefs about all the significant people in the patient's life, rather than placing a unique focus on the relationship with the therapist (Fretter, Bucci, Broitman, Silberschatz, & Curtis, 1994; Silberschatz, Fretter, & Curtis, 1986).

How well the interpretation fits the patient is another factor that needs to be taken into account. It is amazing that several studies have been directed at discovering the impact of interpretations without considering whether some standard of accuracy is being met. Of the groups of studies reviewed in this chapter, those dealing with interpretation accuracy hold perhaps the most promise. The finding that process and outcome are benefited by having a case formulation that is objective and consistent across judges is a potentially important breakthrough for psychotherapy research. Even here, though, it is necessary to be circumspect about the results. Speculations about the benefits of accuracy are based on relatively few cases. In addition, accuracy is defined in these studies in terms of maintaining a consistent focus on interpersonal themes derived from a case formulation. We do not yet know whether the continued focus, in and of itself, may be the potent factor in these results. It could turn out that the particular theory used to fashion a case formulation is less important than the production of a consistent stream of interventions drawn from any one of a several plausible explanatory schemes. Others have suggested that therapists who are consistent may also be the ones most confident about their case conceptualizations, raising the possibility that the communication of confidence is the agent of change (Henry, Strupp, Schacht, & Gaston, 1994).

Also deserving of study is whether interpretations must surpass a certain threshold level of consistency (accuracy) to be effective. Current reports have compared therapist interventions in terms of relative consistency with an underlying theme and ignored the absolute level of accuracy in calculating effects. This may conceal the fact that consistency of focus needs to move beyond a critical point to create benefits. It is notable that some of the studies have found that the typical therapist's level of interpretation consistency is relatively low (Henry, Strupp, Schacht, & Gaston, 1994; Luborsky & Crits-Christoph, 1990). Would training to increase therapist focus to higher levels significantly improve treatment? Do therapists judged as skillful naturally achieve high levels of consistency in their interventions? Relatedly, research has not yet addressed the issue of when interpretations should occur in the therapy process. Is timing important and are there optimal points for providing patients with an explanatory framework for their discomforts?

Finally, our review of the evidence highlights that an approach strongly emphasizing interpretations may not be best for everyone, even when the interpretations are accurate. The patient's personality characteristics seem to play a role in determining response to an interpretive approach. Variables like the patient's historic ability to relate to others (quality of object relations) appear to affect the response to interpretations, with the best response occurring when high-functioning patients are presented with a limited flow of carefully selected accurate interpretations (Joyce, 1992; Piper, Azim, Joyce, & McCallum, 1991; Piper, Joyce, McCallum, & Azim, 1993; Piper, McCallum, Azim, & Joyce, 1993). Other hints that an insight-oriented approach may be differentially effective because of patient factors appears in the work of Beutler and Mitchell (1981) and Calvert, Beutler, and Crago (1988). These investigators found that analytically oriented therapists were significantly more effective when working with patients whose coping styles were internal/intropunitive rather than external/impulsive.

In contrast, behavioral clinicians obtained their best results with patients relying on externalizing, acting-out coping mechanisms. Similarly, Horowitz, Rosenberg, and Kalehzan (1992) demonstrated that a hostile/dominant interpersonal style augurs poorly for the outcome of brief dynamic psychotherapy. Patients displaying this style seem to have difficulty clearly describing their relationships with others, and this may, among other things, make it harder for therapists to arrive at and present a lucid case formulation.

Blatt is another researcher-clinician who stresses the importance of attending to differential patient characteristics for improving outcome with psychodynamic psychotherapy. He and a colleague argue that "different kinds of folks may need different kinds of strokes" (Blatt & Felson, 1993). Their presentation of the results from three studies shows that distinguishing patients on the basis of their characteristic personality styles (rather than their diagnoses) reveals which patients are likely to be most responsive to a psychoanalytic treatment. In brief, patients who were cognitively oriented, self-critical, and concerned with issues of autonomy and self-worth proved more likely than interpersonally oriented, dependent patients to benefit from psychoanalysis. In addition to potential for improvement with psychoanalytic treatment, patients who had a greater investment in cognitive functioning also appeared more apt to benefit from cognitive behavioral therapy.

Our review of the insight-related research literature is a reminder of how complex the psychotherapy process really is. As we have seen in the past (Fisher & Greenberg, 1985), self-understanding does not automatically translate into symptom improvement and interpretive techniques viewed in isolation do not predict outcome. Notwithstanding some of Freud's comments, both his treatment approach and that of modern practitioners contain persuasion and suggestion as basic elements. Psychoanalytic insights need to be viewed in the context of a treatment that is an influence process. Furthermore, to be meaningfully addressed, outcome within psychodynamic psychotherapy, as with other approaches, appears to require the examination of the interplay of several factors including the status of the treatment relationship, the accuracy, consistency, or focus of the interpretations provided, and the personality attributes of the patient. To this point, investigators have not exposed a set of active treatment ingredients clearly separating psychodynamic psychotherapy from all other psychotherapy systems. No one orientation appears destined to emerge as superior to the others. Faced with the accumulating evidence for this conclusion, and the pressure to provide accountability for clinical actions, it seems inevitable that the many brands of practitioners will be drawn toward fundamental accommodations with each other in the search to find out what works, for whom, and under what conditions. The richness of the psychodynamic perspective combined with increasingly sophisticated research methodology should contribute significantly to this enterprise.

PART THREE

Integration

Chapter 10

A Pantoscopic View

Evaluation and Revision

We have sifted and pondered a rich blend of research pertinent to Freud's various theories and therapeutic formulations. In this chapter, we will sweep across the multiple areas we have covered and arrive at some wider perspectives. We do not intend, however, to stray far from the actual database we mobilized in our searches through the scientific literature. If there is anything unique about our enterprise, it is that we were determined to appraise Freud's work on the basis of controlled observation rather than philosophical or theoretical paradigms. All too often, the unending commentaries in the literature concerning the soundness of Freud's ideas are based on speculative preferences for this or that methodological approach. Critical deconstructions of Freud are variously based on declarations that he favored an instinct-venting paradigm, that he was not sufficiently aware of the role of the self in psychological functioning, that he posited exaggerated continuity in development, that he used hydraulic metaphors, and so forth. Such critical commentaries and also those of a more positive flavor based on clinical lore and reassuring assumptions can be interesting and even informative, but they sidestep the demanding task of matching each of Freud's formulations with the results of experiments designed to test them. As we have asserted repeatedly, the psychoanalytic literature is chaotically flooded with opinions about what is right or wrong in the Freudian corpus. We are told that certain fashionable ideas or theories clash with or support Freud, but rarely are we provided with detailed, point-by-point citations of relevant research data that would offer reasonable documentation. Freud's formulation in any specific area might well clash with some more current fashionable paradigm, but still prove to be valid in terms of data collected on the ground.

SUMMARY OF FINDINGS

Our first task in this chapter will be to summarize the major findings of our analysis of the research literature concerned with Freud's prime propositions and then to derive their more generalized implications.

The Paranoid Paradigm

Freud, in his theory of paranoia, basically, depicted paranoia as a defense against unacceptable homosexual impulses. Presumably, Oedipal conflicts render it difficult for the paranoid-inclined individual to resolve Oedipal issues with the same-sex parent and therefore result in a defensively submissive relation with that parent; but the homosexual overtones of that relation are said to be so unacceptable that they require a defensive paranoid transformation of "I love" that parent (person) to "I hate" that parent (person), and ultimately to that parent (person) "hates me." A majority of the better controlled investigations of this theory supported its validity. That this was true with reference to both males and females was particularly impressive. We did caution, though, that other factors besides repressed homosexuality (e.g., powerlessness) apparently contribute to a paranoid stance.

Depression

What did we find with respect to Freud's theory of depression? A prime element in the theory is the assumption that vulnerability to depression is increased as a function of having suffered loss experiences. By and large, it has been difficult to demonstrate a clear, consistent connection between depression and loss experiences. In the majority of depressed individuals, it was not possible to show that their depression was triggered by a loss, as such. However, there was tentative evidence that a combination of early and current loss might be a selective precipitant of depression.

Second, Freud proposed that vulnerability to depression was heightened by early socialization experiences involving parents who were nonnurturant and disapproving. It turned out that the research data roughly affirmed this proposition. But, at the same time, there was evidence that those vulnerable to depression were inclined to perceive their parents as having been overprotective. The concept that depressogenic parents are both nonnurturant and overprotective suggests that they behaved ambivalently or contradictorily vis-à-vis their children, and this supports Freud's emphasis on the idea that those susceptible to depression are unusually ambivalent in the ways they relate to persons and objects. Freud portrayed ambivalence as playing a key role in how "introjection of the lost object" initiates the depressive process. Presumably, positive feelings toward the object motivate the close identification maneuver referred to as "intro-jection," but the other side of the ambivalence (the hostility felt to-ward the object) sets the stage for attacking what has become part of oneself. Congruent with Freud's focus on the role of ambivalence in depression, studies (e.g., King & Emmons, 1990) have actually docu-mented an elevation in general measures of ambivalence in depressed individuals.

Third, Freud linked depression with the inclination to be passive and dependent (orally fixated). As noted, a large reservoir of findings favors this view. To complicate the matter, however, there is probably one form of depression tied to dependent (anaclitic) attitudes and an-other (introjective) associated with feelings of guilt and worthlessness (as proposed by Blatt et al., 1976).

Fourth, Freud associated depression with the individual's ten-dency to be self-critical and self-attacking, and a profuse collection of empirical data supports him. Overall, we concluded that the match be-tween Freud's complex portrayal of the nature of depression and the pertinent research findings in the literature was reasonably good.

Both the paranoid and the depression formulations were judged to have received fairly solid support. It is noteworthy that both of Freud's testable hypotheses in the realm of psychopathology have held up.

Oral Character Paradigm

The "oral character" was portrayed as one who was unable to master the problems of the oral stage and who, consequently, was fixated on issues more pertinent to the oral phase than to those of genital matu-rity. It was considered that the persistence of unsatisfied oral drives and wishes led to a character structure that provided indirect modes for releasing oral tensions and also repressive defenses for denying them. The oral orientation was ascribed to parents who were too frus-trating or overgratifying of the child's oral needs. The dynamics of the oral character were said to result in a heightened preoccupation with being supported, nurtured, and cared for. Other attributes assigned to the oral character were depression, ambivalence, and the need for ex-aggerated modes of oral gratification (e.g., overeating, alcohol). Analy-sis of the pertinent research literature indicated that the major traits attributed to the oral character clustered together meaningfully, as de-fined by factor analysis. Further, the findings demonstrated, as pre-dicted, that the oral orientation was accompanied by a need to seek dependent ties, a low threshold for depression, and perhaps the experi-ence of having been reared by parents who were unusually overprotec-tive or authoritarian. Basically, the research observations matched reasonably well with theoretical expectations.

Anal Paradigm

Freud thought of the anal character as one who had exceptional anal sensitivities that highlighted anal experiences, but who found them unacceptable (disgusting, shameful) and. therefore repressed them. There was presumably a chronic underlying fear of anal impulses breaking out and resulting in loss of control. The anal character's concern about such potential loss of control was said by Freud to eventuate in certain defensive trait derivatives referred to as the anal triad: orderliness, parsimony, and obstinacy. The accumulated research concerned with testing the anal character formulation demonstrated that there is an identifiable (by means of factor analysis) and consistent cluster of personality traits in accord with the anal character description. Support can be mustered for the existence of each of the traits constituting the anal triad, but the evidence is particularly strong with respect to obstinacy. The power of the anal character concept can be seen in the fact that anal attitudes have been shown to mediate such diverse variables as humor preferences, Type A behavior, selective responses to stimuli with anal connotations, defense mechanisms, and attitudes toward authority. The anal character concept seems to overlap significantly with "conscientiousness," a fundamental personality factor.

Oedipal Formulations

Multiple hypotheses can be derived from Freud's account of the Oedipal confrontation and how it is resolved. His Oedipal theory assumes as inevitable the child's sexual attraction to the parent of the opposite sex and the development of jealous antagonism toward the same-sex parent. The studies that have been reviewed affirm the underlying Oedipal notion of positive attraction between opposite-sex parent and child and of negative tension between the same-sex pair. This would seem to be the minimally necessary requirement for the validity of the Oedipal concept.

Freud's ideas concerning the role of Oedipal factors in sexual dysfunction have not stood up well to empirical testing. Orgasm consistency in women is not correlated with possessing the kinds of passive-feminine attributes that Freud considered to be indicative of satisfactory resolution of the Oedipal crisis. The scientific data indicate that preference for vaginal as contrasted with clitoral stimulation (presumably a sign of mature feminine sexuality) is not reflected in a superior level of psychological adjustment.

Flawed Oedipal relationships were considered by Freud to explain the etiology of homosexuality. In essence, the flaw, in the case of the male, related to having too much closeness to mother and too much distance from father. This presumably interfered with resolving Oedipal conflicts and, therefore, perpetuated tensions (castration anxiety) that inhibit a heterosexual orientation. The multiple studies pertinent to this issue have, as predicted, found that homosexual males perceive father as unusually distant and unfriendly, but have not consistently affirmed that mother is perceived as overly close or intrusive.

Freud's speculations about the origins of homosexuality in women were likewise phrased in Oedipal terms, but in a less clear and sometimes confusing fashion. A possible deduction from his formulation was that female homosexuals would regard father in negative terms. Some verification of this point emerged from the research literature. Overall, we judged from the available data that Freud's theory of homosexuality, while partially supported, was still largely either untested or equivocal with reference to evidence.

A complex story frames the various efforts to test Freud's views of how Oedipal conflicts and attachments are negotiated and resolved. In the case of the male, Freud theorized that the resolution of the Oedipal conflict was powered by fear of father's retaliatory potential (castration anxiety). Presumably the male child was, in this fashion, induced to give up his jealous antagonistic stance and instead to identify with father; and in the process to introject father's superego values. A considerable research literature sharply contradicts Freud's concept that the male child ultimately identifies with father and adopts his values out of fear. Instead, the data strongly indicate that identification with father's values is best facilitated when father is perceived as behaving in a friendly, nurturant fashion. There is no research evidence for Freud's idea that the nature of the Oedipal process results in males having a more severe superego than females.

One of the most fanciful of Freud's Oedipal constructions relates to how females presumably make use of the penis-baby equation to resolve their Oedipal dilemmas. He proposed that a woman could not achieve adequate femininity unless she succeeded in assuring herself that she had acquired an illusory penis (symbolically represented by becoming pregnant and delivering a child). A series of studies (Greenberg & Fisher, 1980, 1983; Jones, 1989, 1991, 1994) has surprisingly supported this formulation. As predicted from the theory, women have been shown to increase their phallic imagery during pregnancy and also in response to subliminal pregnancy messages. Other predicted changes in phallic scores as a function of phase of the menstrual cycle and intensity of motivation to become pregnant were also documented. The data were congruent with the penis-baby equation model.

Dream Theory

In essence, Freud proposed that dreams represent disguised vehicles for the expression of wishes. He assumed that the dream consists of two major components: (a) an inner or latent element representing an unconscious wish; (b) the outer, manifest dream narrative that serves to camouflage the latent element. As described, the research findings are grossly in disagreement with this portrayal. There is more and more evidence that dreaming is simply another form of thinking or cognitive processing and is not limited to the narrow functions Freud ascribed to it. Only in the general sense that Freud conceptualized dreaming as having adaptive attributes, can one say that his dream theory makes sense in the context of what dream researchers have uncovered.

Psychoanalytic Psychotherapy

Our review of the research literature relevant to psychoanalytic psychotherapy focused specifically on issues of outcome and process. We wanted to know whether treatments conducted from a psychodynamic perspective are generally successful and whether the effects of this type of treatment can be most clearly ascribed to the gaining of insight and the technique most often hypothesized to promote self-understanding, namely interpretations. Trying to pinpoint responses to these questions proved to be an arduous task because of the ambiguity in some of Freud's concepts, a variety of deficiencies in many of the studies that have been done, limitations in measures that have been developed, and the tangle of variables that come into play during any psychotherapeutic encounter. Nonetheless, our analysis of the evidence led us to several conclusions.

Although theorists and practitioners have been inclined to make sharp distinctions between psychoanalysis and psychodynamic therapy in terms of the range of permissible techniques or the loftiness of the treatment goals (e.g., refashioning personality structure versus promoting symptom reduction), the research literature has not been able to support a distinction with regard to outcome. The existing data suggest that treatments derived from Freud's psychodynamic propositions produce positive effects and that the magnitude of the effects is not more limited in treatments designated "psychodynamic therapy" than in those labeled "psychoanalysis." If anything, the evidence indicates that psychodynamic treatments (which tend to be briefer and allow for a broader scope of therapist intervention possibilities) are more efficient than orthodox psychoanalysis in helping patients to achieve desirable changes. Because the more prognostically desirable cases have tended to be placed in psychoanalysis rather than psychodynamic therapy, it is especially surprising that psychoanalysis has not been shown to be the superior treatment. Overall, our review supports the idea that patients are better off when treated from a psychodynamic perspective than they would be if left untreated. This conclusion is consistent with meta-analytic results showing that the average psychodynamically treated patient exhibits more improvement than about 75% of the untreated (Smith & Glass, 1977; Smith, Glass, & Miller, 1980). However, comparisons with other brands of therapy usually show roughly equivalent levels of helpfulness.

Our reading of the literature also leads us to conclude that relationship factors common to all psychotherapy approaches (attention, empathy, understanding, and support) are more central to the change process within psychoanalytic therapy than Freud acknowledged. His recommendation that analysts should remain "opaque" and "emotionally cold" (Freud, 1912a, 1912b) appears to be overly limiting and out of step with a good deal of evidence illustrating the benefits that accrue from the promotion of a positive treatment relationship. Similarly, his warnings not to pursue behavioral change too vigorously or directly may also be too restricting. Freud's motivation for these admonitions probably reflected his desire to advance psychoanalytic psychotherapy sessions as pristine laboratories for producing unbiased data confirming his various theories about personality development and psychopathology. The data do not support the idea that psychoanalytic therapy is an approach devoid of persuasive and suggestive elements, and even Freud eventually came to recognize this fact.

It is important to ask whether psychoanalytic or psychodynamic treatment effects are a result of ingredients beyond the relationship factors. Do interpretations and insight attainment play a role in securing a positive outcome as Freud suggested? Evidence on these propositions is scanty (but growing) and some of the findings are complex. But, on the whole, we speculate that the results achieved in psychoanalytic therapies can frequently be attributed to more than just the formation of a positive treatment alliance (although this is certainly an important factor). Our reasoning is based, in part, on a review of meta-analytic findings demonstrating that psychotherapy (across orientations) is significantly superior to various nonspecific (or placebo)[1]

---

[1] Drug researchers have found it helpful to contrast the effects of medications with the reactions arising from pharmacologically inert substances, called placebos. They want to separate the results due strictly to biochemical stimuli from those due to psychological mechanisms. Several investigators argue against the meaningfulness of the placebo concept for psychotherapy research (e.g., Critelli & Neumann, 1984; Dush, 1986; Horvath, 1988; Lambert & Bergin, 1994; Senger, 1987; Wilkins, 1984). In psychotherapy research, the effects of all the treatments, both formalized approaches and those resting purely on the relationship ("placebos"), can be attributed to psychological factors. In essence, the argument asserts that there are no psychologically inert encounters possible within psychotherapy, rendering the placebo concept meaningless in this context. Similarly, the term "nonspecific factors," which usually refers to relationship elements, is questioned. As labels are put on the various relationship ingredients (e.g., warmth, empathy), they become "specific" and potentially measurable. The term "common factors" has become the preferred phrase for referring to the elements that are not particular to any one technique.

procedures as well as no-treatment alternatives (Lambert & Bergin, 1994). Therefore, because psychoanalytically based treatments have proven to have outcomes equivalent to those achieved by other sorts of treatments, the results should exceed nonspecific effects as well. There are, however, no studies directly comparing psychoanalysis with a control approach relying solely on relationship ingredients such as attention. Thus, the definitive word on this matter awaits additional future investigations that try to separate out the relative contributions of relationship factors and various psychoanalytic techniques (a differentiation that some may regard as unachievable).

Looking at studies that have tried to directly link measures of insight and interpretations to outcome yields a mixed bag of results. All the findings are derived from studies of psychodynamic therapies, not orthodox psychoanalysis. By and large, analysts seem to have eschewed the empirical method for validating their theories about the therapeutic process. Most basically, the studies have not been very supportive of Freud's early idea that patient insights, facilitated by therapist interpretations, translate directly into decreased symptomatology and positive outcomes. Although we need better measures, particularly of the insight concept, the idea of a simple association between interpretations, insight, and outcome has not been verified. Other elements such as the suitability of the interpretations, the personality characteristics of the patients receiving them, and the interpersonal context in which they are offered need to be simultaneously taken into account. For example, the frequency of either transference or nontransference interpretations does not predict outcome. Yet, there are increasing hints that interpretations can have positive impacts if they fit with reliable conceptualizations of the patient's dynamics and characteristic patterns of relating to others. Moreover, although there is validation for several of Freud's ideas about transference, there are signs that interpretations emphasizing only the relationship with the therapist may be less potent than those more widely focused on relationships with all the significant people in the patient's life.

In addition, researchers are uncovering evidence that an interpretative treatment might work better for some types of patients than for others. For example, patients displaying the following attributes seem more predisposed to benefit from an interpretative treatment: a history of relating well to others; an internal/intropunitive coping style; an affinity for assessing things cognitively; and a concern for issues of autonomy.

Another complication that may hinder attempts to tease out active ingredients in psychoanalytic psychotherapy is that a variety of therapist behaviors that do not involve verbal interpretations may also evoke change and perhaps even induce insight. For instance, therapist neutrality or acceptance could be of help in disconfirming a patient's old pathogenic beliefs about themselves or others. There is no proof, at this point, that unlinking from misguided expectations based on past experiences requires verbal interpretations or even that patients need to become aware of their own dynamics.

Broadly speaking, Freud's early writings suggest an ease and directness in converting insights into therapeutic benefits that are not mirrored by the research literature. However, Freud's later work shows a developing awareness of the complexities of the therapy process that is more consistent with what we have found. Also consistent with our conclusions are Freud's expressed doubts, toward the end of his career, about the unique effectiveness of his treatment.

COMPARISONS BETWEEN PRE- AND POST-1977 CONCLUSIONS

How do the new findings we have summarized concerning Freud's theoretical formulations compare with what we concluded in our original pre-1977 overview (Fisher & Greenberg, 1985) of the pertinent literature? In a number of instances, the conclusions are essentially the same, but there are also some discernible shifts.

It is fair to say that agreement prevails with reference to the soundness of the oral and the anal character typologies. This is also true in the case of the theory of paranoia.

However, it is a more complex matter to describe the fit between the pre- and post-1977 conclusions with reference to Oedipal concepts. As required by Freud's basic depiction of the Oedipal triangle, there is agreement that the modal individual feels relatively positive toward the opposite-sex parent and negatively toward the same-sex parent. There is congruence too in the conclusions that, contrary to Freud, the evidence indicates that male children are more likely to identify with father if he is perceived as friendly and nurturant rather than threatening (castrating). The pre- and post-1977 conclusions likewise correspond in finding no relationship between Oedipal variables and sexual difficulties and no links between Oedipal factors and psychopathology.

Divergence has emerged in two areas. First, the post-1977 studies are less supportive of Freud's analysis of the socialization origins of homosexuality in males. Although the studies corroborate the apparent distant, negative stance of the father of the homosexual male (as is also true in the case of female homosexuals), they contradict what previously seemed to be the fact of the overcloseness of the mother. In the case of the male, the potential role of such father negativity in the etiology of homosexuality could just as well be explained in terms of a negative father figure providing a poor heterosexual identification model as it could in terms of the Oedipal paradigm. Second, the post-1977 literature, in contrast to the pre-1977 data, produced new multiple forms of support for Freud's account of how the penis-baby equation mediates the resolution of Oedipal conflicts in women.

Moving on to another area, the post-1977 data concerned with Freud's dream theory demonstrate even more clearly its inadequacies. The one aspect of the theory—the venting functions of dreams—that seemed at least partially valid on the basis of the pre-1977 findings was firmly challenged by post-1977 observations.

Conclusions drawn from our review of the psychoanalytic psychotherapy empirical literature remain largely consistent with our earlier appraisal. The observations are strengthened not only by the accumulation of additional investigations, but also by the use of improved and sophisticated methods of study. Although psychoanalytic treatments produce positive effects, accolades need to be tempered by the continuing realization that briefer less orthodox variations of psychoanalytic techniques produce equally good results. Furthermore, other nonpsychoanalytic approaches very often achieve comparable (or sometimes even better) outcomes. Important post-1977 findings are beginning to clarify the role of interpretations and insight in bringing about therapeutic gain. It appears very clear that verbal interpretations do not bring about changes simply or directly. The relationship context in which they are embedded and a variety of patient, therapist, and technique factors (patient interpersonal and coping styles, therapist skillfulness, and the accuracy and timing of interpretations) seem crucial for determining whether change will follow. The growing stockpile of evidence indicates that Freud's rendering of the psychoanalytic treatment process was overly simplified and too limited in its recognition of psychoanalysis as an influence process.

We are impressed with how relatively stable the findings concerning Freud's basic theoretical formulations have been over the years. A majority of the conclusions we reached in 1977 have been reaffirmed. Even the heightened doubt we now entertain concerning the dream formulation was actually somewhat anticipated by criticisms we voiced in our 1977 analysis. The largest shift has come in our downgrading of the validity of the theory of homosexuality. Because the data no longer support the proposition that male homosexuals perceive mother as unusually close and the ambiguous sectors of the theory have remained not testable, it would seem prudent to adopt a position of significant skepticism. As mentioned, one other particularly note-worthy shift involves the accumulation of studies favoring Freud's penis-baby equation theory. These particular studies add substance not only to Freud's general Oedipal paradigm but also to his account of a major phase of female development.

It is an interesting exercise to sort the positive and negative findings into larger categories. First, Freud's formulations bearing on pre-Oedipal phenomena have fared particularly well. Both the oral and anal character types have emerged as exceptionally affirmed by the empirical literature. Next, it is striking that both of Freud's theories concerning the origins of psychopathology (paranoia, depression) were largely congruent with the available scientific data.

In a sense, it is paradoxical that least empirical support appears to exist in those instances where Freud predicted variables that would affect specific sexual behaviors. As described, he was wrong with respect to his formulations about the determinants of orgasm consistency in women and the nature of clitoral versus vaginal stimulation preferences. Further, one has to remain skeptical with respect to his thinking about what leads to receptivity to homosexual forms of sexual arousal.

Finally, contrary to the widespread notion (including our own stated view in 1977) that Freud was more often right about male than female dynamics, we have shown that a number of his basic concepts about how males resolve the Oedipal crisis and evolve superego standards are blatantly out of step with research observations; whereas his account of how women resolve Oedipal tensions fits neatly with a series of published findings.

What does it mean that certain elements in any one of Freud's theories fit with experimental findings? For example, does the manifestation of predicted traits and conflicts by the anal character also substantiate Freud's broader underlying developmental schema or his assumptions about fixed stages or his concepts of fixation and regression? Does the selective anxiety of paranoid individuals about homosexual themes signify that Freud was correct with reference to his general model of psychopathology based on the notion of repression of unacceptable impulses? Does the experimental support for the formulation that women phallicize pregnancy validate Freud's general idea that the Oedipally upset female turns to father (seeking a baby from him) because of various disappointments with mother? Obviously, the leap to any of the broader generalizations is largely of a speculative order. Real insurance concerning the broader concepts can only come from more detailed studies. It is also true, however, that as networks of diverse findings apparently match various levels of Freud's theoretical images, the probabilities increase that his metaphors have worthwhile explanatory value.

Actually, it is still our position that Freud's statements and speculations add up to a series of minitheories rather than a grand integrated structure.[2] Our analysis of the data indicates that particular blocs of Freud's ideas may prove to be wrong without invalidating other blocs. Illustratively, the finding that dreams are not secret vehicles of wishes in no way negates that various traits hang together as would be predicted by either the oral character or anal character constructions. Or the fact that women who prefer vaginal stimulation are not more psychologically mature than those who are clitorally oriented does not impact on Freud's theory of depression. Even within a particular circumscribed area of theory, one element could be divergent without negating other major elements. In the case of the Oedipal theory, as it applies to males, the fact that the confrontation with father may be resolved more through positive identification with, rather than fear of, him need not necessarily contradict other major Oedipal themes (e.g., castration anxiety).

The psychoanalytic corpus consists of diverse elements that are entwined to some degree but also in many instances only peripherally linked. Westen (1990) cogently refers to the wide spectrum of components inside the psychoanalytic container that hazily overlap but are obviously diverse. He states:

> At present, the psychoanalytic perspective is probably best categorized prototypically rather than through any particular set of defining features. Psychoanalytic approaches are those that take as axiomatic the importance of conflicting mental processes; unconscious processes; compromises among competing psychological tendencies that may be negotiated unconsciously; defense and self-deception; the influence of the past on current functioning; the enduring effects of interpersonal patterns laid down in childhood; and the role of sexual and aggressive wishes in consciously and unconsciously influencing thought, feeling, and behavior. (p. 22)

It would be truly amazing if any general theory could convincingly embrace such a range of variables and issues.

Overall, we are impressed with how robust many of Freud's minitheories have shown themselves to be. Significant chunks of his

---

[2] Philip Holzman (in Grunbaum, 1993) takes a similar position: "I regard psychoanalysis not as a unified theory, but rather as many theories loosely tied together. The theories are heterogenous in content and in level of abstraction, and they appear scattered among Freud's papers . . . more as working, tentative formulations than as a final systematic theory" (p. xvii).

theorizing have held up well to probing. Even in the face of research agendas that have all too often not reasonably addressed the complexity and subtlety of what he had in mind. Although it is fashionable (e.g., Barron, Eagle, & Wolitzky, 1992) to declare that psychoanalytic concepts have moved on since Freud and are now more sophisticatedly up to date, our view is that, if anything, a larger proportion of Freud's original formulations have been scientifically supported than would be true of various more contemporary variations (e.g., Erikson, 1963, 1968; Fairbairn, 1952; Kohut, 1977).

Actually, our analysis of the scientific literature has not captured the full extent to which Freud's ideas have been verified. We have not even touched the formidable array of studies validating Freud's conception of the importance of unconscious processes in psychological functioning. His depiction of an unconscious realm was one of his most novel and influential contributions. Despite great resistance to this concept, convincing supportive data have accumulated. Multiple levels of research document the pervasive role of unconscious attitudes and motives (e.g., Bornstein & Pittman, 1992; Bowers & Meichenbaum, 1984; Kihlstrom, 1987; Kline, 1987; Shevrin & Dickman, 1980; Silverman, Lachman, & Milich, 1982). Although this research has uncovered complexities and qualities in unconscious processes that Freud was not cognizant of (e.g., Epstein, 1994; Kihlstrom, 1987), it still mirrors many of his basic notions.[3]

We have also not reviewed blocs of research supporting and extending a number of Freud's ideas about repression (e.g., Davis & Schwartz, 1987; Geisler, 1986; Newton & Contrada, 1992; Singer, 1990); verbal slips (e.g., Motley, 1980; Motley & Baars, 1976); and defense mechanisms (e.g., Cramer, 1987, 1988; Fisher & Fisher, 1993; Ihilevich & Gleser, 1986; Suls & Fletcher, 1985; Vaillant, 1977, 1986).

We are aware too that certain other research studies that lie outside the areas we analyzed have not been favorable to Freud. Thus, his picture of how the infant behaves and copes has been substantially contradicted (e.g., Lachmann & Beebe, 1992; Silverman, 1986; Stern, 1977, 1985). To a lesser degree, there have also been empirical negative presentations with respect to Freud's model of motivation (e.g., Shevrin, 1984) and his stage concept of development (Brim & Kagan, 1980). However, assaying the entire reservoir of pertinent research, one must acknowledge the frequency with which Freud's models and metaphors have passed empirical tests. Substantial parts of Freud's

---

[3] It is ironic that although Freud (1900) enunciated many of his notable and provocative principles concerning the unconscious in his *Interpretation of Dreams,* the dream theory itself seems not to be valid. This supports our view that the Freudian corpus involves a number of fairly separate domains.

hypotheses have recruited scientific support. In the same vein, Kline, after his 1981 review of the empirical literature directed at Freud's work, concluded: "As has been shown in this book, much of it (psycho-analytic theory) has been confirmed" (p. 447). Certainly, the research literature stands in stark opposition to those (e.g., Eysenck & Wilson, 1973; Macmillan, 1991; Torrey, 1992) who insist that Freud's concepts are without merit—a sham, a shadow of genuine science. It also does not match Grunbaum's (1984, 1993) pessimistic stance vis-à-vis the scientific probity of Freud's propositions, although he recognized that controlled research might eventually verify significant segments of Freud's work.

Our analysis mobilizes more dependable support for a number of Freud's major ideas than has been previously been available. Grun-baum (1993) documented in convincing detail how limited and fragile has been the evidence offered by clinical observations and case histories. Without the data we have harvested from a broad network of laboratory-based studies, the empirical status of Freud's theories is not convincingly defensible. Grunbaum was correct in asserting that the scientific future of psychoanalysis hinges more on the outcome of extraclinical controlled observations than on piling up still more anecdotal clinical accounts. He is directly on target with his assertions that suggestion and placebo effects pretty much rule out most raw clinical situations as a sound context for testing Freud's constructions. Whereas the typical research setting does not supply the richness of information native to clinical encounters, it more than compensates by virtue of the objectivity and protection against bias that are built in.

As we noted in our earlier book (Fisher & Greenberg, 1985), the orthodox psychoanalytic establishment seems to be phobic about making contact with the pertinent scientific literature. If it could be desensitized, new sources of reassurance and vitalization would open up. There seems to be an underlying dread that once the door to empirical data is ajar, loss of control will follow. This implies a lurking lack of basic confidence in the solidity of Freud's thinking. If genuine confidence existed, there would not be so much anxiety and defensive posturing with reference to what scientific inquiry might uncover. With respect to this matter, we have pointed out (Fisher & Greenberg, 1985):

> The chief way in which psychoanalysts have hurt themselves in not pursuing the scientific testing of their ideas is that they have not been able to rid themselves of that which is defective and to replace it from the reservoir of new data accumulated by the work of the various behavioral science disciplines. What changes have managed to occur have reflected the power status or persuasive fluency of individuals pleading their special views. (pp. 6–7)

IMPLICATIONS OF MAJOR FINDINGS

Oral and Anal Characters

It is worthwhile to think through some of the implications of the empirical findings that did or did not support Freud. First, ample and consistent verification of both of the character typologies (oral, anal) emerged. What are we thereby justified in concluding and speculating? Perhaps the best way to answer this question is to enumerate the prime constituents of the two paradigms:

1. Both of the character formulations are anchored in the idea that individuals move through a progression of developmental stages.

2. Both assume that each stage is marked by the dominance of a specific body area, which is associated with a particular drive or somatic sensitivity (selectivity).

3. Both conceptualize the possibility of remaining fixated at a specific stage or of regressing to it as the result of various frustrations and traumas.

4. Both are said to be associated with specific trait patterns that presumably evolve out of defensive denials of a drive and also as unconsciously selected channels for obtaining compensatory gratifications.

5. Both are based on an underlying premise that childhood modes of adaptation carry over into adult behavior.

The Body Connection

We are immediately struck with the uniqueness of linking character traits to the prominence of specific body areas as sources of excitation (drives) and landmarks for interpretively framing events. The depictions of the oral and anal character types are phrased in body imagery. Oral traits are traced to themes associated with the mouth and anal traits to the anal region. Freud tells us that it is in the process of coping with experiences associated with these body sectors that the oral and anal characterological compensations evolve. In the case of the oral character, we know that measures of the degree to which individuals are preoccupied with literal oral imagery (e.g., Masling, 1986) are significantly correlated with various traits (e.g., dependence) typifying the oral character orientation. As we documented, there are also low-level but definite trends for oral traits to be linked with special investments in oral modes of gratification.

A connection between anal character attributes and literal preoccupation with anal imagery is somewhat less apparent. It is true that there are some findings (e.g., Fisher, 1978; Rosenwald, 1972) suggestive of correlations between dirt and filth imagery (conveying anal connotations) and anal character attributes. Also, a few studies (e.g., Adelson & Redmond, 1958) have described correlations between responses to pictures with explicit anal meaning and indexes of anal traits. However, the most telling findings involve correlations between anal character traits and the so-called anal triad (orderliness, parsimony, and obstinacy). Freud derived the triad in the context of picturing individuals who are beset by dirty, besmirching impulses and who construct defenses against them that reflect the underlying anal meanings involved. For example, orderliness is presumed to offer proof that one has not succumbed to dirty anal impulses. Parsimony is linked by Freud with an equation between feces and money; and obstinacy was conceived as resulting from the frustrations associated with toilet training. In other words, the triad derives directly from anally phrased imagery.

Freud's anchoring of specific personality traits in body image paradigms is quite unique. We are not aware of any other personality theories that do so. Actually, a perusal of Freud's major formulations shows that they are saturated with body-oriented concepts, as apparent in the following examples:

- The libido theory was phrased in terms of shifts in cathexis at different body sites as a function of developmental and psychodynamic variables.
- Anxiety about loss of body parts (castration anxiety) was seen as a prime motivating force in male Oedipal events.
- Awareness of the anatomic differences between males and females was ascribed large importance in triggering penis envy in girls and women.
- Localized sites on the body were portrayed as capable of nonverbally expressing (via discomfort and other symptomatology) unconscious repressed impulses. This was the basic explanation for conversion hysteric symptoms.

Apropos of the same issue, Freud was forever aware of the potential contributory roles of genetic (biological) variables to the phenomena he explored.

Quite paradoxically, although there is now a considerably better understanding of the body as a biological system, there has been diminished interest in psychoanalytic circles in the body as a psychological phenomenon. This is true even though there has been a dramatic growth in research concerned with body image processes (e.g., Cash &

Pruzinsky, 1990; Fisher, 1986). The various offshoots of Freud's theories (e.g., object-relations) have moved perceptibly in the direction of explaining things in terms of social interaction and social representational concepts and are less interested in the experienced body as a setting for psychological events. Relative to this point, we (Fisher & Greenberg, 1985) noted:

> Most contemporary personality theories pay only lip service to drives and body needs as playing a role in character development. They do not give us an account of how a specific need, manifesting itself in the sensations occurring in a real live body, interacts over time with life events and thereby results in certain personality dispositions. Freud highlighted the existence of needs as personal experiences. . . . He explicitly noted that body experiences can produce diverse responses such as disgust, anger, enhanced narcissism, and sensual pleasure. . . . Many of the most frequently cited personality variables in the current scientific literature have an abstract quality that divorces them from the body realm. Variables such as achievement drive, external versus internal orientation, guilt, authoritarianism, and so forth are presented as if they were neat cognitive forces tucked away in some brain center. We are given little or no hint that they involve a massive framework of body experiences and perhaps have been crucially shaped by parent-child body transactions.[4] (p. 166)

The positive scientific support for Freud's oral and anal personality ideas should be an incentive for other personality theorists to incorporate body-oriented concepts into their thinking. Illustratively, the associations we described between anal variables and the "big five" conscientiousness or the Type A categorization should encourage researchers in these areas to include measures of body attitudes and body image when further exploring these dimensions. With rare exceptions, the published papers dealing with conscientiousness do not even hint that conscientious behavior occurs in sentient emotion—experiencing bodies with appurtenances like viscera and genitals. To a puzzling degree, many of our major personality variables (e.g., introversion-extroversion, locus of control, achievement need, self-concept) have a disembodied quality. Magnusson and Torestad (1993), in their overall critique of the personality literature, commented on how frequently personality variables have been reduced to abstractions that lack "person" quality.

---

[4] As earlier noted, it has been shown in some detail (Fisher, 1986) that indexes of orality and anality are meaningfully related, respectively, to measures of awareness of the oral and anal regions of the body.

Continuity

Another major theme implicit in the oral and anal character formulations is continuity from early childhood to adulthood. Freud assumed that early experiences pertinent to the gratification or frustration of oral or anal needs registered in such a fashion as to shape character structure in later life. This implies too that individuals will show consistencies, in personality over their life span. Considerable debate can be found in the scientific literature concerning the nature of the continuity, if any, that exists. As is so often the case, definitions of continuity vary considerably as a function of numerous variables, such as types of measures employed; whether the focus is on phenotype or genotype levels; whether personality variables are viewed as separate or as members of trait hierarchies; and the statistical definitions of consistency adopted (e.g., Baltes & Schaie, 1973; Brim & Kagan, 1980; Schaie, 1983).

It is not our intention, at this point, to review the considerable literature bearing on such issues. What we have asked ourselves is whether that literature leaves open the possibility that the type of developmental continuity envisioned by Freud could exist. Numerous researchers have presented data congruent with Freud's perspective (e.g., Asendorpf & van Aken, 1991; Caspi & Bem, 1990; Friedman et al., 1993; Leon, Gillum, Gillum, & Gouze, 1979; Levinson, 1977; Mischel, Shoda, & Peake, 1988; Rohner, 1975). However, there are also those who offer observations that apparently contradict the continuity concept (e.g., Brim & Kagan, 1980; Lefkowitz, Eron, Walder, & Huesmann, 1977; Whitbourne, Zuschlag, Elliot, & Waterman, 1992).

As noted, such differences reflect varying definitions, methodologies, and interpretations. Our own conclusion is that certain continuities comparable to those theorized by Freud have been at least tentatively demonstrated. For example, in a well-controlled study, Mischel et al. (1988) found that measures of ability to delay gratification in 4-year-old children significantly predicted a number of social attributes and competencies in these children when they reached adolescence. And Levinson (1977) in his quantitative analysis of 45 cultures detected significant correlations between early child-rearing practices and adult personality attributes. Lewis, Feiring, McGuffog, and Jaskir (1984) reported that measures of male children's attachment relationships at 1 year of age predicted their degree of psychopathology at age 6 (although such relationships did not hold true for female children).[5] Two studies (Franz, McClelland, & Weinberger, 1991;

---

[5] However, to underscore further the disagreement typifying discussions of continuity, it should be added that Kagan (1980) interprets the findings of a number of major longitudinal studies as indicative of low levels of continuity.

Koestner, Franz, & Weinberger, 1990) demonstrated that measures of parental behavior obtained during early childhood (roughly in the Oedipal phase) predicted a number of personality traits of the children during adulthood.

While contradictory data confront us, it would appear that the prime task is to tease out which developmental variables show continuity and which do not. In any case, since some continuities have been observed broadly paralleling what Freud had in mind, the fact that he links adult personality traits to early experiences (as he does in the case of both the oral and anal characters) is within reason, even if only provisionally so.

A related issue is whether Freud's model of a series of fixed psychosexual stages fits with the empirical work in this area. Actually, no direct validation of such stages has ever occurred. As detailed by Hay (1986), Slade and Aber (1992), and Demos (1992), the concept of fixed qualitatively different developmental phases is less and less supported by studies of how perceptual, cognitive, and emotional abilities evolve. More contemporary data indicate considerable overlap in so-called developmental phases. Demos (1993) notes:

> All of the developmental changes discussed . . . involve gradual continual processes of change. They do not lend themselves easily to stagelike formulations or to set progressions of skills. Instead, these changes seem to depend on continuous transactions with the environment. . . . (p. 228).

However, it is still true that stagelike phenomena have been observed in some studies. Thus, in summarizing the literature on cognitive development, Fischer and Silvern (1985) stated: "Cognitive development shows evidence of stagelike change and of consistency across dimensions" (p. 614). The specific internally generated fixed developmental paradigm conjured up by Freud seems to be rather improbable, but it is still conceivable that the oral and anal "stages" (or any of the other "psychosexual phases") could involve loosely defined time periods in which certain problems and conflicts gradually become prominent and are to varying degrees, mastered or not mastered.

Psychopathology

Our searches have uncovered support for Freud's theories of both paranoia and depression. Interestingly, the concepts underlying these two constructions are of a somewhat different order. The paranoia theory conforms to Freud's basic paradigm concerning the origin of psychopathology: the repression of unacceptable wishes that continue to exert pressures in their unconscious form and in so doing mobilize defensive strategies which are manifested in symptoms and deviances. However, the depression theory is rooted in the concept that a lost object may compensatorily be identified with and then introjected, made a part of self. It is the ambivalence toward the introjected object that is said to produce depressive disturbance. Presumably, the negative side of the ambivalence results in directing hostility and derogation toward the interiorized object. This means ultimately attacking self, becoming a target for guilt-producing accusations and recriminations—a prominent theme in the depressive stance.

In applying the paranoia formulation to men, no one has empirically shown that the anxiety about homosexual wishes that Freud considered to be basic to inciting the paranoid defense is specifically a consequence of disturbed Oedipal relationships with father. As documented, there seems to be good evidence of a selective concern with homosexual themes among paranoid individuals. However, the theory would gain more credibility if it could be shown that paranoia is associated with having been socialized by a father who made his son feel that heterosexual intent was wrong or forbidden and who expected passive submission. What are the child-rearing attitudes of fathers of paranoids? How authoritarian are such fathers as compared with those of nonparanoid sons?

The defensive maneuver of shifting from "I love him" to ultimately "He hates me" that Freud attributed to the paranoid process of coming to terms with homosexual anxiety is certainly conceivable in terms of the large literature about defense mechanisms. Numerous observers have described the use of projection for defending against various anxieties (e.g., Cramer, 1988; Ihilevich & Gleser, 1986; Kline, 1987; Suls & Fletcher, 1985; Vaillant, 1986). The concept of projection as Freud portrayed it has been well described in both the clinical and experimental literature. In particular, Ihilevich and Gleser (1986) have sketched a variety of logical relationships between measures of the use of projection as a defense mechanism and other variables. It is especially relevant that they cite several studies in which paranoid schizophrenics are significantly more likely to employ projection as a defense than are nonparanoid schizophrenics.

In Freud's theory of depression, he envisioned one of the major mechanisms involved to be the ambivalent introjection of the lost object. He considered other variables as contributory to depression (e.g., oral fixation, masochism), but the introjection process seems to have been central in his thinking. The paramount and most novel feature of his theory of depression relates to the concept of identifying with a lost object, somehow introjecting it, and then relating ambivalently to it after making it part of self. The question we wish to address is whether there are empirically based psychological structures that match Freud's concept in this respect. We have already referred to a considerable literature (e.g., Derry & Kuiper, 1981; Hewitt & Genest, 1990; Ingram, 1990) documenting the notion of internalized self-representations containing both positive and negative elements and serving as a framework for selectively processing information. The self-schema is represented as a composite structure constructed out of experiences and relationships. It is, indeed, appealing to regard Freud's depiction of the structure resulting from the assimilation of the lost object into the ego structure as simply one variant of the class "self-schema."

The research of McGuire and McGuire (1982) is particularly cogent because it conceptualizes a "self-space" that is a composite of various contents. They studied this "self-space" by asking individuals to "Tell us about yourself" and then analyzing the contents of the self-descriptions that emerged. They have reported a variety of interesting sex and age differences with reference to the prominence of images of others in the self-space. In any case, their data indicate that images and representations of significant others are basic constituents of the self-space. The qualities of these imported representations of others will influence the sense of self. It is difficult to see how the McGuire and McGuire version of a self-space, whose qualities are partially contingent on the representations of relationships with others that are part of that space, really differs much from Freud's introjected object paradigm.

Research on "object-relations" also provides empirical analogies to Freud's introjection idea (e.g., Urist, 1980). Object-relations theory, in fact, assumes that one's experiences with significant others become coded as internal representations (often at an unconscious level) that provide schemata for guiding behavior. These internal representations have been diversely sampled by means of projective tests, analysis of interviews, and the contents of psychotherapy sessions. They have turned out to be predictive of some forms of psychopathology, quality of interpersonal relations, and specific expectations of others (e.g., Krohn & Mayman, 1974; Mayman, 1967, 1968). Certain phenomena such as "splitting," which characterize some defensive versions of particular object-representations, are analogous to the split good-bad qualities Freud ascribed to the modal lost object introjection.[6]

---

[6] It is a striking coincidence that research (Kuiper, MacDonald, & Derry, 1983) concerned with the self-schemas of mildly depressed individuals has detected a positive-negative selective form of information processing not found in nondepressed normal individuals. It has been shown that when nondepressed individuals learn self-referring words with positive or negative connotations, they are selectively superior in their recall of the positive terms. However, in the mildly depressed, selective superiority for self-referring words is manifested for both positive and negative terms. This special selectivity with reference to both the positive and negative is not typical, however, of more severely depressed persons.

Oedipal Data

The data we have scrutinized bearing on the validity of what Freud had to say about the massive theoretical Oedipal edifice has uncovered an underlying fragmentation. What we have discovered is that some pieces of the theory look solid, some are clearly wrong, and some remain indeterminate. There is no need to repeat in detail the positives and the negatives. In essence, we have found support for the basic concept of the Oedipal triangle, the formulation concerning selective castration anxiety in the male, and the complex account of how females resolve (via the penis-baby equation) their Oedipal dilemma.

On the other hand, we have raised troubling questions about Freud's statements concerning the Oedipal conditions underlying homosexuality; we have pointed out deficits in his ideas about what feelings or emotions inspire males to identify with father; we have piled up evidence contradicting his ideas about the nature of conscience (superego) development and severity of conscience in males, and have generally found little that is reliable about his notions of how Oedipal factors influence sexual functioning.

These findings present quite a mixed picture. The core idea of an Oedipal struggle or confrontation seems to be sound. The sense of threat to the male child's body integrity growing out of the struggle also looks like a reliable phenomenon. Further, the depiction of the female child's need to master the negative Oedipal position she finds herself in by means of the penis-baby phallicizing process has surprising credibility. But the potential negative consequences (sexual dysfunction, homosexuality) attributed by Freud to the Oedipal confrontation seem insufficiently supported; and he is apparently grossly incorrect in his concept of what inspires males to identify with father and to adopt his values.

Note particularly Freud's misjudgments concerning the presumed crucial role of Oedipal transactions in the future development of psychopathology and sexual dysfunction. We have not been able to discern any consistent correlations between Oedipal markers and indexes of psychopathology. In addition, a large research literature has accumulated indicating that a composite of complex variables, going well beyond Oedipal matters, contributes to breakdowns in function. With regard to psychopathology, we now know that the probability of developing significant clinical levels of disturbance is influenced by such a range of factors as amount of life stress encountered, social support available, degree of marital conflict, social class, educational level, and exposure to severe trauma (e.g., Coyne, 1991). As noted earlier, several longitudinal studies have shown meaningful links between early socialization experiences and ability to enjoy sexuality in adulthood, but the nature of these links is only vaguely defined and has not been shown specifically to involve Oedipal factors. In any case, Freud's Oedipal paradigm, which pinpoints Oedipal factors as the root of so many forms of disturbance, does not fit with data indicating few consistent correlations between sexual dysfunction and measures of psychopathology or with findings concerning the factors contributing to orgasm capacity in women (Fisher, 1989).

Freud's overblown ideas about the consequences of Oedipal transactions become obvious when we examine the large role he assigned to the Oedipal relationship between father and son in the development of the son's superego values. He thought that the concept of Oedipal rivalry and fear could largely explain superego formation. The basic acquisition of superego was presumably traceable to the rivalrous Oedipal paradigm. We have discovered that Freud made erroneous assumptions about how values and standards underlying conscience (superego) are acquired. The research literature indicates that values are most likely to be taken over from one's parents (particularly father) in the context of a friendly nurturant bond rather than one rooted in fear and distrust. Also, we know that multiple other factors contribute to the shape of the child's moral structure, aside from what happens between father and self.

Freud may have exaggerated the degree to which Oedipal transactions are about rivalry, incestuous love, and hate. He may have underestimated the extent to which positive feelings shape adaptations that he attributed to the Oedipal phase. It may indeed be true that an important element of Oedipal interaction relates to comparing self competitively with the same-sex parent and looking at the opposite-sex parent as a potential sex-object. However, it is also possible that a more fundamental way of looking at Oedipal interaction is that it represents a time of becoming aware of the sexual potential of one's body, of the power and meaning of sex organs, of the rules governing heterosexuality, and of the panphallic frame of reference that prevails.

Having said the foregoing about Oedipal findings, we must admit that we are still uneasy about where we have come out with reference to Freud's theory of homosexuality. We have rather conservatively concluded, given the absence of evidence that homosexuality in males is associated with overcloseness to mother, that we cannot consider the evidence of unusual father distance and hostility in this context as sufficient support for Freud's position. However, there are some worrisome incongruent details. It is striking that father's distance has been demonstrated to be true in the case of both male and female homosexuals. We are particularly impressed that cross-cultural data (e.g., Broude, 1981) have shown that the degree of homosexuality practiced in various cultures is positively correlated with indexes of father's degree of distance or negativity during the socialization process. Also, we cannot but be impressed that Silverman et al. (1978) were able, by means of subliminal Oedipal inputs, to intensify homoerotic feelings in homosexual men. Such a result would appear to depend on a finely tuned theoretical sequence. Presumably, the Oedipal stimuli increase Oedipal fantasies that are unacceptable and therefore mobilize compensatory (defensive) homosexual feelings. If the Silverman et al. study is methodologically sound (as it appears to be), the pinpointed result implies considerable power in the theory from which it was derived. However, in balancing such findings against the total sweep of other data and also the lacunae (especially with reference to homosexuality in women) where essential data are lacking, we concluded that it was sensible to adopt a skeptical stance—but uncertainty persists.

The consistent picture of father distance and negativity associated with homosexuality in both males and females keeps pressing for explanation. It might reflect the possibility that, because father is the parent usually most concerned with enforcing sex-typing in the family (Fisher, 1989), his taking a distant position could interfere with acting as the sex-typer and therefore permit his children greater experimentation with sex-role fantasies congruent with being homosexual. As we pondered this matter of father distance, we were impressed with how often issues of closeness-distance arise when examining data pertinent to Freud's various formulations. The depression hypothesis is largely based on the notion of rescuing the lost object from its distant (lost) position and bringing it into a unique closeness to self (by interiorizing it). Or the paranoia hypothesis assumes that the male's "He hates me" defense is an attempt to deny fantasies of overcloseness to father. Further, we have shown that Freud's story concerning what motivates the male child to adopt his father's (superego) values is not the hostility between them but rather their friendly closeness.[7] These examples may be no more than metaphors, but they point up a general fascination with spatial metaphors in Freud's theories. We have commented on this matter at some length elsewhere (Fisher & Greenberg, 1993).

The Dream Theory

What are we to make of the essentially negative review of Freud's dream theory that has emerged? How do these negative findings instruct us?

---

[7] In a related but more tangential vein, certain aspects of female sexual functioning about which Freud theorized have turned out, in the course of several studies, to be linked to concepts related to perceptual closeness-distance. Thus, there are reliable data (Fisher, 1973) indicating that women with orgasm difficulties are likely to find the buildup of orgastic excitement disturbing because it makes them feel as if they are moving away from (out of contact with) objects. Also, there is evidence (Fisher, 1973) that women who prefer vaginal stimulation (compared with clitoral) are particularly oriented to avoiding closeness to strong sensory inputs.

Our analysis of the discrepancies in Freud's dream concepts leads us to conclude that he entertained a rather one-sided and narrow notion of unconscious processing and judgment. In most of his descriptions of the unconscious realm, Freud employed stereotyped terms such as "primitive," "bizarre," and "irrational." He envisioned the "unconscious" as a container of powerful sexual and aggressive currents constantly seething and pushing the individual toward irrational behaviors and symptom displays. For this reason, when he conceptualized the sleep state as one in which the usual repressive restraints on the unconscious are loosened, he almost inevitably had to portray dreaming as somehow devoted to containing and camouflaging what could potentially burst out of that primitive sector of the self. Presumably, the diminished ego control available during sleep meant that the unconscious would misbehave. So, dreaming had to be portrayed as simply a camouflaged outlet or compromise representation of the primitive bad stuff. In a sense, Freud considered all thinking and expression as potentially uncontrolled outlets for unconscious elements; and his descriptions of "slips," jokes, and other forms of spontaneous expression often focus on their simultaneous potential for revealing bad wishes and defensively safeguarding the self.

In fact, as research has mounted concerning what goes on at unconscious levels, we have learned that there is a good deal more than cauldronlike bubbling. All that occurs in unconscious spaces is not primitive and frightening. Fischer and Pipp (1984) have proposed a view of "unconscious thought" that highlights new perspectives. In essence, they have merged concepts from psychoanalysis and cognitive psychology and concluded that the unconscious is not a fixed primitive entity. They state:

> The traditional psychoanalytic equation of unconscious functioning with the developmentally primitive mind is giving way to the view that there are continuing developments in both conscious and unconscious processes throughout childhood and perhaps in adulthood as well. (p. 89)

They cite observations indicating that unconscious functioning increases in complexity as individuals attain greater cognitive maturity. They note:

> From the position we are presenting, the unconscious is a type of process—a way of *constructing* perceptions, memories, and other kinds of cognition that change systematically with development. It is not a portion of the mind. Indeed, instead of the unconscious, it is more appropriately referred to as "unconscious thought," since it is not a unitary entity but a way of processing information. (p. 91)

Presumably, as children's intellectual prowess increases and differentiates, this is equivalently reflected in how they cope with unconscious material. Fischer and Pipp illustrate in some detail that the basic characteristics of primary process (condensation, displacement, magical thinking) may be quite different with respect to how they are manifested in young children compared with adults.

There is a good deal of dispute about how intellectually complex or sophisticated the research data portray unconscious functioning to be. All shades of opinion are represented in a series of papers devoted to this topic in a 1992 issue of the *American Psychologist*. The participants (Bruner, 1992; Erdelyi, 1992; Greenwald, 1992; Jacoby, Lindsay, & Toth, 1992; Kihlstrom, Barnhardt, & Tataryn, 1992; Lewicki, Hill, & Czyzewska, 1992; Loftus & Klinger, 1992; Merikle, 1992) disagree considerably. However, they all agree that the unconscious not only processes material involving strong affect but also deals with a wide variety of other kinds of information. The most extreme position with regard to the sophistication of unconscious processing is taken by Lewicki et al. (1992):

> Data indicate that as compared with consciously controlled cognition, the nonconscious information—acquisition processes are not only much faster but are also structurally more sophisticated, in that they are capable of efficient processing of multidimensional and interactive relations between variables. (p. 796)

They outline an impressive array of experiments in which complex conclusions, insights, and generalizations were derived from the unconscious processing of information. The data they present establish that under the right circumstances persons are capable of intricate unconscious evaluations and abstractions.

In addition, a number of investigators have shown that primary process, the presumed anlage of unconscious functioning, probably plays a role in creativity. Significant correlations have been described (e.g., Suler, 1980) between measures of primary process fantasy (e.g., as displayed in inkblot responses) and indexes of creativity. This is impressive because creativity represents one of the most complex and intricate forms of cognitive activity.

As already noted, the research literature reveals numerous examples of instances in which dreams contain information that would seem to have been derived from highly sophisticated (probably unconscious) analyses (Moffitt, Kramer, & Hoffmann, 1993). Dreams can be the source of new ideas and inventions. They have provided integration of important informational inputs; and revealed the presence of body feelings and sensations that were obscured at a conscious level. In short, a cognitive prowess is discernible in dream processes that parallels what has been detected in other observations of unconscious functioning. Freud simply did not appreciate that there is much more to dreaming than coping with an inner cauldron.

Psychoanalytic Psychotherapy: Data-Driven Observations, Extrapolations, and Speculations

Amid uncertainty about the relative merits of different brands of psychotherapy, treatment based on psychoanalytic principles has retained its place as a preferred orientation among practitioners. Surveys show that psychodynamic therapy is the single approach most favored by clinicians, second only to the undifferentiated designation "eclectic" (Sammons & Gravitz, 1990). Furthermore, the use of psychoanalytic theory is prominent even among those espousing an eclectic orientation. About three-quarters of "eclectic" clinicians indicate they employ psychodynamic concepts in their work (Jensen & Bergin, 1988). Therefore, our review of the research evidence pertaining to Freud's ideas has direct implications for the majority of psychotherapists.

Research indicates that devotees of the psychodynamic tradition should not be unduly alarmed by the trend toward briefer, more efficient forms of treatment. Despite decades of study, investigators have failed to demonstrate that orthodox psychoanalysis with its multi-session per week, multiyear format produces outcomes for most patients that are superior to those obtained by briefer variants of psychodynamic treatment. This result, which seems to have surprised some analysts as they examined both their own practices and that of their colleagues (e.g., Heilbrunn, 1963, 1966; Wallerstein, 1986a, 1989), might not have come as much of a surprise to Freud. Ironically, Freud's reported cases were seen for relatively brief periods compared with the standards of contemporary psychoanalyses (Fisher & Greenberg, 1985; Kardiner, 1977). In addition, Grinker (1974), speaking from experience as one of Freud's former patients, observed that Freud would have opposed the belief that treatments need to be lengthier or more frequent to be more effective. Other analysts have similarly documented that psychoanalytic treatment used to be of shorter duration (Coriat, 1917; Malan, 1963). It is oddly amusing that as psychoanalysis is supplanted by psychodynamically oriented therapy, the treatment is actually moving closer to Freud's original descriptions in terms of duration and innovation.

Our review highlights that individuals display characteristic patterns of relating to others (including therapists) just as Freud suggested. The patterns typically include defensive behaviors designed to protect the individual from perceived dangers that may not exist in the present. Presumably, these defenses were erected to deal with traumas and conflicts arising earlier in life. To the extent that they block an accurate assessment of current situations and limit behavioral options, these defenses can be maladaptive. As we have shown, Freud's general model of current experiences being tainted by and tested against past templates has received research support from a variety of quarters (e.g., the work emanating from Luborsky's group and that growing from the efforts of Weiss, Sampson, and their colleagues).

Freud, in claiming unique benefits for his treatment, placed a good deal of emphasis on the power of verbal interpretations to bring about insight. Insight or self-understanding was supposed to help the patient do away with the need for unnecessary self-protective maneuvers (symptoms). Freud's original supposition that insight would lead directly and automatically to change has been found to be deficient. We now know that Freud's early conception of treatment was too narrow in its consideration of therapeutic ingredients. Patients' awareness of their own motivations or dynamics has proven to be of more limited value in directly promoting change than Freud initially postulated. Alternative influence techniques (aside from verbal interpretations) have turned out to be helpful for many patients struggling with different types of problems. We also know now that changing behavior patterns can lead to insights as well as follow from them. Obviously, interpretations may sometimes be a useful element in psychotherapy. Our analysis of the evidence suggests that treatment potency may be increased for many when therapists can weave patient productions into consistent, well-focused explanatory stories concerning the underpinnings of patients' problems. Therapist interventions appear to be more effective when they are compatible with formulations based on the patient's narrative and experience.

We suspect that therapist understanding of patient dynamics will turn out to be more important than patient understanding. Therapist understanding can facilitate the presentation of a coherent explanatory scheme to the patient. It also allows the therapist to make educated choices about which techniques will best fit a patient's style and promote facing material (and situations) that may seem threatening. Therapists' conceptualizations of what they are dealing with should be helped by a reliance on research-supported ideas about personality development and psychopathology. We would speculate that therapists' awareness of such topics as validated aspects of theories of depression, paranoia, and personality types (all reviewed in this volume) are potentially translatable into more sophisticated treatments that are credible (and thus more persuasive) to patients.

Freud's depiction of his therapy was to some degree burdened by his desire to legitimize his personality and psychopathology theories. To conclude that his theories were sound, he needed to take the position that in-therapy patient creations were independent of analyst influence and suggestion. This is a position that we and others (e.g., Grunbaum, 1984, 1993) view as indefensible. Relatedly, Freud stated that analysts should not become too invested in expediting change (an outgrowth, we believe, of his desire to downplay the suggestive elements in his treatment). We feel that modern clinicians would be unnecessarily constrained if they take his comments about "furor therapeuticus" too literally. Indeed, Freud's writings and case descriptions show that he could be quite forceful in his attempts to influence the patients he was seeing. In short, what Freud said sometimes did not match what he actually did. Moreover, systematic observations of psychoanalytic practitioners have also documented the centrality of suggestion and persuasion (as well as relationship factors) to the treatment process (e.g., Eisenstein, Levy, & Marmor, 1994; Wallerstein, 1986a, 1989).

Freud's preoccupation with proving the correctness of his personality theories may have also detracted from the therapeutic potential of the approach because it led him to urge clinicians to remain "emotionally cold" and "opaque" in dealing with their patients (Freud, 1912a, 1912b). Research has demonstrated the powerful role that the therapy relationship or alliance plays in stimulating positive outcome (e.g., Beutler, Machado, & Allstetter Neufeldt, 1994; Horvath & Symonds, 1991; Lambert & Bergin, 1994). The instruction to remain distant from patients and remove the effects of the therapist's personality from the treatment process may often turn out to be antitherapeutic. Although therapist neutrality seems important, so do other factors like therapist empathy, warmth, and genuineness (Patterson, 1984). In addition, as we have documented, patients with differing personality styles may not be equally responsive to traditional psychodynamic therapy techniques. Evidence suggests the treatment process may be enhanced by tailoring the therapist's interpersonal style to match the relationship needs of individual patients (e.g., Beutler & Clarkin, 1990; Blatt & Felson, 1993). The trend toward stressing the interdependence of clinical techniques and therapeutic relationships is evident in a special section of the journal *Psychotherapy* edited by Norcross (1993). The articles in the section are devoted to exploring how relationships can be optimized to meet patient needs. The break with Freud's views about treatment relationships is reflected in the following comment made by Mahoney and Norcross (1993) after reviewing the articles submitted by the various contributing authors:

> Transference and counter-transference were preliminary scaffoldings for the interpersonal dynamics of professional services, but they were couched in a system of assumptions that dictated detachment and

emotional distance as the ideal posture of the service provider. It is, in fact, noteworthy that none of the contributors to this section endorsed the posture that was dominant in most psychotherapy for the first half of this century. (p. 423)

Overall, our review of the psychoanalytic therapy research literature has left us impressed with the intricacies of the treatment process and struck by the magnitude of Freud's contribution to our understanding of the psychotherapy framework. However, the explosion of modern psychotherapy research has also pinpointed the limits of Freud's vision. In the end, we are encouraged to believe, along with others (e.g., Castonguay & Goldfried, 1994), that the accumulating scientific evidence will move the field from a period of bitter debate about the relative merits of various schools of therapy into an era of rapprochement and respect for the research contributions coming from many different directions.

CONCLUSION

In returning again to the issue of why the available pool of scientific information pertinent to Freud's work is so often unappreciated, it is all too easy to fall back on the stereotype that psychoanalytic concepts are fading away and hardly worth the effort to investigate. As we noted earlier, Grunbaum (1984, 1993) has sent shock waves through psychoanalytic circles with his hard-hitting meticulous analyses of the defects in Freud's original assumptions and logic. Philip Holzman, in writing an introduction to one of Grunbaum's (1993) volumes, warned that the future viability of psychoanalysis depends on whether it can address the discrepancies Grunbaum grimly laid out. In essence, Grunbaum, discredited the whole domain of clinical data, specifically of the species harvested in psychoanalytic therapy sessions, and labeled it as an untrustworthy source for validating Freud's major propositions. However, he tempered his pessimism with the following comment:

I do *not* rule out the possibility that, granting the weakness of Freud's major clinical arguments, his brilliant theoretical imagination may nonetheless have led to correct insights in some important respects. Hence, I allow that a substantial vindication of some of his key ideas may perhaps yet come from well-designed extra-clinical investigations, be they epidemiological or experimental. (p. xi)

To the contrary, we would urge that what Grunbaum visualized as a remote future possibility is already substantially under way. A reservoir of experimental data pertinent to Freud's work currently exists and, as we have shown in detail, offers support for a respectable number of his major ideas and theories. The existence of such data has been, to varying degrees, documented by other previous publications (e.g., Kline, 1972, 1987; Masling, 1983, 1986, 1990; Masling & Schwartz, 1979). However, a sizable proportion of those observers who are presumably concerned with evaluating the standing of psychoanalysis have simply refused to acknowledge the existence, or accept the credibility of, such findings. Actually, this "shutting out" stance characterizes two extremes: (a) those who are conventional adherents of the psychoanalytic establishment and who regard any laboratory-based data as too artificial and simplistic to deserve serious attention; (b) those who identify with a scientific purity that will not touch the kinds of apparently fanciful metaphors and images in which Freud luxuriated. The rigidity of each of these positions is reinforced because at the one extreme are individuals who lack the interests necessary to appreciate research findings, and at the other extreme are individuals who are unwilling to assimilate Freud's work and acquire a functional understanding of its meaning.

Those who assume that laboratory-based tests of Freud's hypotheses are bound to be too simplistic do not realize the incredible amount of effort that has been invested in testing Freud's ideas fairly. Although the early attempts to subject Freud's ideas to experimental probing were often based on a narrow understanding and utilized procedures that ignored the presumed role of unconscious factors, there are now an abundance of studies that are reasonably complex and at times even ingenious. An impressive number of designs and technologies have been pressed into service. They include such examples as delivering subliminal Oedipal messages and measuring their impact on competitive performance; determining thresholds for accurately perceiving key words presented tachistoscopically; measuring latency of response in word association tasks; hypnotically implanting Oedipal fantasies and determining their impact on cognitive functioning; conditioning responses with oral versus anal reinforcers; ascertaining the effects of subliminal loss messages on food consumption; measuring the correlation between oral fantasy and readiness to touch others; quantifying oral and anal imagery in projective responses; identifying whether mate-choices conform to the Oedipal paradigm; quantifying the use of superego words in spontaneous verbalizations; determining the therapy themes that precede the occurrence of specific therapy behaviors (e.g., slips, complaints of pain); measuring the spatial placements of male versus female pictures by paranoid and nonparanoid individuals; detecting physiological responses to social isolation in individuals high and low in the production of oral imagery;

and correlating individuals' character classifications (e.g., oral, anal) with how they represent their parents in spontaneous descriptions. We have deliberately been redundant in providing such examples to dramatize their abundance and diversity. Many others could be cited. This is an armamentarium that signals serious interest in approaching Freud's work at a meaningful level.

The magnitude of the research effort that has been mobilized over the years to probe Freud's hypotheses is indicated too by the sheer volume of publications we have located that describe empirical studies dealing with various aspects of his work. If one combines the pertinent references from our previous book (Fisher & Greenberg, 1985) with those from our present enterprise, they total over 2500. Of course, they vary in quality, but overall they probably compare well with the accumulated studies relevant to any other major area of psychology. It is clearly not true that there has been a lack of research investment in what Freud had to say.

References

Abraham, K. (1968). The influence of oral erotism on character formation. In A. D. Bryan & A. Strachey (Eds.), In *Selected Papers on Psycho-Analysis* (pp. 383–406). New York: Basic Books.

Abramson, L. Y., Garber, J., & Seligman, M. E. P. (1980). Learned helplessness in humans: An attributional analysis. In J. Garber & M. E. P. Seligman (Eds.), *Human helplessness. Theory and applications* (pp. 3–34). New York: Academic Press.

Abramson, L. Y., Seligman, M. E. P., & Teasdale, J. (1978). Learned helplessness in humans: Critique and reformulation. *Journal of Abnormal Psychology, 87,* 49–74.

Abroms, G. M. (1968). Persuasion in psychotherapy. *American Journal of Psychiatry, 124,* 1212–1219.

Adelson, J., & Redmond, J. (1958). Personality differences in the capacity for verbal recall. *Journal of Abnormal and Social Psychology, 57,* 244–248.

Alexander, F. (1954). *Five year report of the Chicago Institute for Psychoanalysis, 1932–1937.*

Allen, L. S., & Gorski, R. A. (1992). Sexual orientation and the size of the anterior commissure in the human brain. *Proceedings of the National Academy of the United States of America, 89,* 199–202.

Alloy, L. B., & Abramson, L. Y. (1979). Judgment of contingency in depressed and nondepressed students: Sadder but wiser? *Journal of Experimental Psychology, 108,* 441–485.

Alloy, L. B., & Abramson, L. Y. (1988). Depressive realism: Four theoretical perspectives. In L. B. Alloy (Ed.), *Cognitive processes in depression* (pp. 223–265). New York: Guilford.

Alloy, L. B., Abramson, L. Y., & Viscusi, D. (1981). Induced mood and the illusion of control. *Journal of Personality and Social Psychology, 41,* 1129–1140.

Alloy, L. B., Albright, J. S., Abramson, L. Y., & Dykman, B. M. (1990). Depressive realism and nondepressive optimistic illusions: The role of the self. In R. E. Ingram (Ed.), *Contemporary psychological approaches to depression. Theory, research, and treatment* (pp. 71–87). New York: Plenum.

Alloy, L. B., & Clements, C. M. (1992). Illusion of control: Invulnerability to negative affect and depressive symptoms after laboratory and natural stressors. *Journal of Abnormal Psychology, 101,* 234–245.

Altman, J. H., & Wittenborn, J. R. (1980). Depression-prone personality in women. *Journal of Abnormal Psychology, 89,* 303–308.

American Psychiatric Association (1980). *Diagnostic and Statistical Manual of Mental Disorders* (3rd ed.). Washington, DC.

American Psychiatric Association (1987). *Diagnostic and Statistical Manual of Mental Disorders* (3rd ed. rev.). Washington, DC.

American Psychiatric Association (1994). *Diagnostic and Statistical Manual of Mental Disorders* (4th ed.). Washington, DC.

Andrews, B., & Brown, G. W. (1988). Social support, onset of depression and personality. *Social Psychiatry and Psychiatric Epidemiology, 23,* 99–108.

Antrobus, J. (1993). Dreaming. Could we do without it? In A. Moffitt, M. Kramer, & R. Hofmann (Eds.), *The functions of dreaming* (pp. 549–558). Albany: State University of New York Press.

Arndt, W. B., Jr., & Ladd, B. (1981). Sibling incest aversion as an index of Oedipal conflict. *Journal of Personality Assessment, 45,* 52–58.

Aron, A. (1974). Relationships with opposite-sexed parents and mate selection. *Human Relations, 27,* 18–24.

Asendorpf, J. B., & van Aken, M. (1991). Correlates of the temporal consistency of personality patterns in childhood. *Journal of Personality, 59,* 689–703.

Atkinson, C., & Polivy, J. (1976). Effects of delay, attack, and retaliation on state depression and anxiety. *Journal of Abnormal Psychology, 85,* 570–576.

Bachrach, H., Galatzer-Levy, R., Skolnikoff, A., & Waldron, S. (1991). On the efficacy of psychoanalysis. *Journal of the American Psychoanalytic Association, 39,* 871–916.

Bailey, J. M., & Pillard, R. C. (1991). A genetic study of male sexual orientation. *Archives of General Psychiatry, 48,* 2–9.

Baltes, P. B., & Schaie, K. W. (Eds.). (1973). *Life-span developmental psychology: Personality and socializations.* New York: Academic Press.

Bandura, A., & Walters, R. H. (1959). *Adolescent aggression.* New York: Ronald.

Barendregt, J. T., Bastiaans, J., & Vermeul-van Mullen, A. W. (1961). A psychological study of the effect of psychoanalysis and psychotherapy. In J. T. Barendregt (Ed.), *Research in psychodiagnostics* (pp. 157–183). The Hague and Paris: Mouton.

Barnett, P. A., & Gotlib, I. H. (1988). Psychosocial functioning and depression: Distinguishing among antecedents, concomitants, and consequences. *Psychological Bulletin, 104,* 97–126.

Barrett, D., & Loeffler, M. (1992). Comparison of dream content of depressed vs. nondepressed dreamers. *Psychological Reports, 70,* 403–406.

Barron, J. W., Eagle, M. N., & Wolitzky, D. L. (Eds.). (1992). *Interface of psychoanalysis and psychology.* Washington, DC: American Psychological Association.

Barry, H., III (1988). Psychoanalytic theory of alcoholism. In C. D. Chaudron & D. A. Wilkinson (Eds.), *Theories on alcoholism* (pp. 103–141). Toronto, Canada: Addiction Research Foundation.

Barth, K., Nielsen, G., Haver, B., Havik, O. E., Molstad, E., Rogge, H., & Skatun, M. (1988). Comprehensive assessment of change in patients treated with short-term dynamic psychotherapy: An overview. *Psychotherapy and Psychosomatics, 50,* 141–150.

Baudry, F. (1983). The evaluation of the concept of character in Freud's writings. *Journal of the American Psychoanalytic Association, 31,* 3–31.

Baumeister, R. E. (1991). *Meanings of life.* New York: Guilford.

Baumeister, R. F., Stillwell, A. M., & Heatherton, T. F. (1994). Guilt: An interpersonal approach. *Psychological Bulletin, 115,* 243–267.

Beck, A. T. (1967). *Depression: Causes and treatment.* Philadelphia: University of Pennsylvania Press.

Beck, A. T. (1983). Cognitive therapy of depression: New perspectives. In P. J. Clayton & J. E. Barrett (Eds.), *Treatment of depression: Old controversies and new approaches* (pp. 265–290). New York: Raven Press.

Beck, A. T., & Hurwich, M. S. (1959). Psychological correlates of depression. *Psychosomatic Medicine, 21,* 50–55.

Beck, A. T., Rush, A. J., Shaw, B. F., & Emery, G. (1979). *Cognitive therapy of depression.* New York: Guilford.

Becker, E. W., & Lesiak, W. J. (1977). Feelings of hostility and personal control as related to depression. *Journal of Clinical Psychology, 33,* 654–657.

Beckworth, J. B. (1986). Eating, drinking and smoking and their relationship in adult women. *Psychological Reports, 59,* 1089–1095.

Bell, A. P., Weinberg, M. S., & Hammersmith, S. K. (1981). *Sexual preference.* Bloomington, IN: Indiana University Press.

Beller, E. K. (1957). Dependency and autonomous achievement-striving related to orality and anality in early childhood. *Child Development, 29,* 287–315.

Bem, S. (1981). *Bem sex role inventory: Professional manual.* Palo Alto, CA: Consulting Psychologist Press.

Bem, S. (1993). *The lenses of gender: Transforming the debate on sexual inequality.* New Haven, CT: Yale University Press.

Benjaminsen, S., Jorgensen, J., Kragh-Hansen, L., & Pedersen, L. L. (1984). Memories of parental rearing practices and personality features. *Acta Psychiatrica Scandinavia, 69,* 426–434.

Berg, G., & Berg, R. (1983). Castration complex: Evidence from men operated for hypospadias. *Acta Psychiatrica Scandinavia, 68,* 143–153.

Berman, J. (1989, June). *Investigator allegiance and the findings from comparative outcome researchers.* Paper presented at the meeting of the Society for Psychotherapy Research, Toronto, Canada.

Berman, J., Miller, R., & Massman, P. (1985). Cognitive therapy vs. systematic desensitization: Is one treatment superior? *Psychological Bulletin, 97,* 451–461.

Beutler, L. E. (1991). Have all won and must all have prizes? Revisiting Luborsky et al.'s verdict. *Journal of Consulting and Clinical Psychology, 59,* 226–232.

Beutler, L. E., & Clarkin, J. F. (1990). *Systematic treatment selection: Toward targeted therapeutic interventions.* New York: Brunner/Mazel.

Beutler, L. E., Machado, P. P., & Allstetter Neufeldt, S. (1994). Therapist variables. In A. E. Bergin & S. L. Garfield (Eds.), *Handbook of psychotherapy and behavior change* (4th ed., pp. 229–269). New York: Wiley.

Beutler, L. E., Mitchell, R. (1981). Psychotherapy outcome in depressed and impulsive patients as a function of analytic and experiential treatment procedures. *Psychiatry, 44,* 297–306.

Biaggio, M. K., & Godwin, W. H. (1987). Relation of depression to anger and hostility constructs. *Psychological Reports, 61,* 87–90.

Bibring, E. (1954). Psychoanalysis and the dynamic psychotherapies. *Journal of the American Psychoanalytic Association, 2,* 745–770.

Biller, H. B. (1976). The father and personality development: Paternal deprivation and sex-role development. In M. E. Lamb (Ed.), *The role of the father in child development* (pp. 89–156). New York: Wiley.

Birtchnell, J., & Kennard, J. (1983). What does the MMPI Dependency Scale really measure? *Journal of Clinical Psychology, 39,* 532–543.

Blackburn, I. M. (1974). The pattern of hostility in affective illness. *British Journal of Psychiatry, 125,* 141–145.

Blackburn, I. M., & Eunson, K. M. (1989). A content analysis of thoughts and emotions elicited from depressed patients during cognitive therapy. *British Journal of Medical Psychology, 62,* 23–33.

Blackburn, I. M., Lyketsos, G., & Tsiantis, J. (1979). The temporal relationship between hostility and depressed mood. *British Journal of Social and Clinical Psychology, 18,* 227–235.

Blake, R. L., & Reimann, J. (1993). The pregnancy-related dreams of pregnant women. *Journal of the American Board of Family Practice, 6,* 117–122.

Blaney, P. H. (1985). Stress and depression in adults: A critical review. In T. Fields, P. McCabe, & N. Schneckerman (Eds.), *Stress and coping* (pp. 263–283). Hillsdale, NJ: Erlbaum.

Blatt, S. J. (1974). Levels of object representation in anaclitic and introjective depression. *Psychoanalytic Study of the Child, 29,* 107–157.

Blatt, S. J., D'Afflitti, P., & Quinlan, D. M. (1976). Experiences of depression in normal young adults. *Journal of Abnormal Psychology, 85,* 383–389.

Blatt, S. J., & Felsen, I. (1993). Different kinds of folks may need different kinds of strokes: The effect of patients' characteristics on therapeutic process and outcome. *Psychotherapy Research, 3,* 245–259.

Blatt, S. J., & Homann, E. (1992). Parent-child interactions in the etiology of dependent and self-critical depression. *Clinical Psychology Review, 12,* 47–91.

Blatt, S. J., Quinlan, D. M., Chevron, E. S., McDonald, C., & Zuroff, D. (1982). Dependency and self-criticism: Psychological dimensions of depression. *Journal of Consulting and Clinical Psychology, 50,* 113–124.

Blatt, S. J., Wein, S. J., Chevron, E., & Quinlan, D. M. (1979). Parental representations and depression in normal young adults. *Journal of Abnormal Psychology, 88,* 388–397.

Block, J. H. (with Haan, N.). (1971). *Lives through time.* Berkeley, CA: Bancroft Books.

Block, J. H., Gjerde, P. F., & Block, J. H. (1991). Personality antecedents of depressive tendencies in 18-year-olds: A prospective study. *Journal of Personality and Social Psychology, 60,* 726–738.

Blum, G. S. (1949). A study of the psychoanalytic theory of psychosexual development. *Genetic Psychology Monographs, 39,* 3–99.

Blum, H. P. (1980). Paranoia and beating fantasy: An inquiry into the psychoanalytic theory of paranoia. *Journal of the American Psychoanalytic Association, 28,* 331–361.

Blume, G. E. (1979). *A comparative study of dreams and related fantasies.* Unpublished doctoral dissertation, University of Florida, Gainesville.

Boldizar, J. P., Wilson, K. L., & Deemer, D. K. (1989). Gender, life experiences, and moral judgment development: A process-oriented approach. *Journal of Personality and Social Psychology, 57,* 229–238.

Bombard, J. A. (1969). *An experimental examination of penis envy.* Unpublished doctoral dissertation, Wayne State University, Detroit, MI.

Bornstein, R. F. (1990). Critical importance of stimulus unawareness for the production of subliminal psychodynamic activation effects: A meta-analytic review. *Journal of Clinical Psychology, 46,* 201–210.

Bornstein, R. F. (1993). *The dependent personality.* New York: Guilford.

Bornstein, R. F., Galley, D. J., & Leone, D. R. (1986). Parental representations and orality. *Journal of Personality Assessment, 50,* 80–89.

Bornstein, R. F., & Greenberg, R. P. (1991). Dependency and eating disorders in female psychiatric inpatients. *Journal of Nervous and Mental Disease, 179,* 148–152.

Bornstein, R. F., Greenberg, R. P., Leone, D. R., & Galley, D. J. (1990). Defense mechanism correlates of orality. *Journal of the American Academy of Psychoanalysis, 18,* 654–666.

Bornstein, R. F., Leone, D. R., & Galley, D. J. (1986). Rorschach measures of oral dependence and the internalized self-representation in normal college students. *Journal of Personality Assessment, 52,* 648–657.

Bornstein, R. F., Manning, K. A., Krukonis, A. B., Rossner, S. C., & Mastrosimone, C. C. (1993). Sex differences in dependency: A comparison of objective and projective measures. *Journal of Personality Assessment, 61,* 169–181.

Bornstein, R. F., & Masling, J. (1985). Orality and latency of volunteering to serve as experimental subjects: A replication. *Journal of Personality Assessment, 49,* 306–310.

Bornstein, R. F., Masling, J., & Poynton, F. G. (1987). Orality as a factor in interpersonal yielding. *Psychoanalytic Psychology, 4,* 161–170.

Bornstein, R. F., & O'Neill, R. M. (1992). Parental perceptions and psychopathology. *Journal of Nervous and Mental Disease, 180,* 475–483.

Bornstein, R. F., O'Neill, R. M., Galley, D. J., Leone, D. R., & Castrianno, L. M. (1988). Body image aberration and orality. *Journal of Personality Disorders, 2,* 315–322.

Bornstein, R. F., & Pittman, T. S. (Eds.). (1992). *Perception without awareness.* New York: Guilford.

Bornstein, R. F., Poynton, F. G., & Masling, J. (1985). Orality and depression: An empirical study. *Psychoanalytic Psychology, 2,* 241–249.

Bornstein, R. F., Scanlon, M. A., & Beardslee, L. A. (1989). The psychodynamics of paranoia: Anality, projection and suspiciousness. *Journal of Social Behavior and Personality, 4,* 275–284.

Bouchard, M. A., & Guerette, L. (1991). Psychotherapy as a hermeneutical experience. *Psychotherapy, 28,* 385–394.

Bowers, K., & Meichenbaum, D. (Eds.). (1984). *The unconscious reconsidered.* New York: Wiley.

Brady, J. P. (1967). Psychotherapy, learning theory, and insight. *Archives of General Psychiatry, 16,* 304–311.

Breger, L. (1967). Functions of dreams. *Journal of Abnormal Psychology Monographs, 72*(5), 1–28.

Breger, L. (1981). *Freud's unfinished journey.* London: Routledge & Kegan Paul.

Breger, L., Hunter, I., & Lane, R. W. (1971). The effect of stress on dreams. *Psychological Issues* (I, Monograph No. 27).

Brewin, C. R., Andrews, B., & Gotlib, I. H. (1993). Psychopathology and early experience: A reappraisal of retrospective reports. *Psychological Bulletin, 113,* 82–98.

Brewin, C. R., & Furnham, A. (1987). Dependency, self-criticism, and depressive attributional style. *British Journal of Clinical Psychology, 26,* 225–226.

Brim, O. G., & Kagan, J. (Eds.). (1980). *Constancy and change in human development.* Cambridge, MA: Harvard University Press.

Bromley, E., & Lewis, L. A. (1976). A factor analytic study of the Dynamic Personality Inventory using a psychiatric population. *British Journal of Medical Psychology, 49,* 325–328.

Brook, J. S., Whiteman, M., & Gordon, A. S. (1981). Maternal and personality determinants of adolescent smoking behavior. *Journal of Genetic Psychology, 139,* 185–193.

Broude, G. J. (1981). The cultural management of sexuality. In R. H. Munroe, R. L. Munroe, & B. B. Whiting (Eds.), *Handbook of cross-cultural human development* (pp. 633–673). New York: Garland.

Bruner, J. (1992). Another look at New Look 1. *American Psychologist, 47,* 780–783.

Bulatao, J. C. (1961). *The direction of aggression in clinically depressed women.* Unpublished doctoral dissertation, Fordham University, New York.

Burbach, D. J., & Borduin, C. M. (1986). Parent-child relations and the etiology of depression. *Clinical Psychology Review, 6,* 133–153.

Buss, A. H., & Durkee, A. (1957). An inventory for assessing different kinds of hostility. *Journal of Consulting Psychology, 21,* 343–349.

Byrne, W., & Parsons, B. (1993). Human sexual orientation. The biologic theories reappraised. *Archives of General Psychiatry, 50,* 228–239.

Caine, T. M. (1970). Personality and illness. In P. Mittler (Ed.), *The psychological assessment of mental and physical handicap* (pp. 781–817). London: Methuen.

Calvert, S. J., Beutler, L. E., & Crago, M. (1988). Psychotherapy outcome as a function of therapist–patient matching on selected variables. *Journal of Social and Clinical Psychology, 6,* 104–117.

Campbell, J. D., & Fehr, B. (1990). Self-esteem and perceptions of conveyed impressions: Is negative affectivity associated with greater realism? *Journal of Personality and Social Psychology, 58,* 122–133.

Cappon, D. (1964). Results of psychotherapy. *British Journal of Psychiatry, 110,* 35–45.

Carroll, L. (1962). *Alice's adventures in wonderland.* Harmondsworth, Middlesex: Penguin. (Original work published 1865)

Carroll, M. P. (1978a). Freud on homosexuality and the super-ego: Some cross-cultural tests. *Behavior Science Research, 13,* 255–271.

Carroll, M. P. (1978b). Levi-Strauss on the Oedipus myth: A reconsideration. *American Anthropologist, 80,* 805–814.

Carson, R. C. (1989). Personality. In M. R. Rosenzweig & L. W. Porter (Eds.), *Annual review of psychology* (Vol. 40, pp. 227–248). Palo Alto, CA: Annual Reviews.

Cartwright, R. D. (1966). A comparison of the response to psychoanalytic and client-centered psychotherapy. In L. A. Gottschalk & A. A. Auerbach (Eds.), *Methods of research in psychotherapy* (pp. 517–529). New York: Appleton-Century-Crofts.

Cash, T. F., & Pruzinsky, T. (1990). *Body images: Development, deviance, and change.* New York: Guilford.

Caspi, A., & Bem, D. J. (1990). Personality continuity and change across the life course. In L. A. Pervin (Ed.), *Handbook of personality: Theory and research* (pp. 549–575). New York: Guilford.

Caston, J. (1993). Can analysts agree? The problems of consensus and the psychoanalytic mannequin: I. A proposed solution. *Journal of the American Psychoanalytic Association, 41,* 493–511.

Caston, J., & Martin, E. (1993). Can analysts agree? The problems of consensus and the psychoanalytic mannequin: II. Empirical tests. *Journal of the American Psychoanalytic Association, 41,* 513–548.

Castonguay, L. G., & Goldfried, M. R. (1994). Psychotherapy integration: An idea whose time has come. *Applied & Preventive Psychology, 3,* 159–172.

Cavallero, C. (1987). Dream sources: Association mechanisms, and temporal dimension. *Sleep, 10,* 78–83.

Chapman, L. J., & Chapman, J. P. (1967). Genesis of popular but erroneous psychodiagnostic observations. *Journal of Abnormal Psychology, 72,* 193–204.

Chapman, L. J., Chapman, J. P., & Raulin, M. L. (1978). Body-image aberration in schizophrenia. *Journal of Abnormal Psychology, 87,* 399–407.

Chehrazi, S. (1986). Female psychology: A review. *Journal of the American Psychoanalytic Association, 34,* 141–162.

Cherry, E. F. (1977). *On success avoidance in women: A comparative study of psychoanalytic theories.* Unpublished doctoral dissertation, Adelphi University, New York, NY.

Cipolli, C., Fagioli, I., Maccolini, S., & Salzarulo, P. (1983). Associative relationships between presleep sentence stimuli and reports of mental sleep experience. *Perceptual and Motor Skills, 56,* 223–234.

Clayton, P. J., Halikas, J. A., & Maurice, W. L. (1972). The depression of widowhood. *British Journal of Psychiatry, 120,* 71–78.

Cochrane, N. (1975). The role of aggression in the psychogenesis of depressive illness. *British Journal of Medical Psychology, 48,* 113–130.

Cochrane, N., & Neilson, M. (1977). Depressive illness: The role of aggression further considered. *Psychological Medicine, 7,* 283–288.

Cofer, D. H., & Wittenborn, J. R. (1980). Personality characteristics of formerly depressed women. *Journal of Abnormal Psychology, 89,* 309–314.

Cohn, L. D. (1991). Sex differences in the course of personality development: A meta-analysis. *Psychological Bulletin, 109,* 252–266.

Colby, A., & Kohlberg, L. (1987). *The measurement of moral judgment.* Cambridge, MA: Cambridge University Press.

Colby, K. M. (1977). Appraisal of four psychological theories of paranoid phenomena. *Journal of Abnormal Psychology, 86,* 54–59.

Colby, K. M., & Stoller, R. J. (1988). *Cognitive science and psychoanalysis.* Hillsdale, NJ: Analytic Press.

Commins, W. D. (1932). The marriage-age of oldest sons. *Journal of Social Psychology, 3,* 487–489.

Coplin, J. D., & Gorman, J. M. (1990). Treatment of anxiety disorders in patients with mood disorders. *Journal of Clinical Psychiatry, 51*(Suppl. 10), 9–13.

Coriat, I. H. (1917). Some statistical results of the psycho-analytic treatment of the psychoneuroses. *Psychoanalytic Review, 4,* 209–216.

Costa, P. T., Fagan, P. J., Piedmont, R. L., Ponticas, Y., & Wise, T. N. (1992). The five-factor model of personality and sexual functioning in outpatient men and women. *Psychiatric Medicine, 10,* 199–215.

Cox, L. D. (1974). *Depressive symptoms as affected by aggressive stimuli subliminally and supraliminally presented.* Unpublished doctoral dissertation, Fordham University, New York.

Coyne, J. C. (1991). Social factors and psychopathology: Stress, social support, and coping processes. In M. R. Rosenzweig & L. W. Porter (Eds.), *Annual review of psychology* (Vol. 42, pp. 401–425). Palo Alto, CA: Annual Reviews.

Cramer, P. (1987). The development of defense mechanisms. *Journal of Personality, 55,* 597–614.

Cramer, P. (1988). The Defense Mechanism Inventory: A review of research and discussion of the scales. *Journal of Personality Assessment, 52,* 142–164.

Cremerius, J. (1962). *Die Beuteilung des Behandlungserfolges in der Psychotherapie.* Berlin: Springer-Verlag.

Crick, F., & Mitchison, G. (1986). REM sleep and neural networks. *Journal of Mind and Behavior, 7,* 229–250.

Critelli, J. W., & Neumann, K. F. (1984). The placebo: Conceptual analysis of a construct in transition. *American Psychologist, 39,* 32–39.

Crits-Christoph, P. (1992). The efficacy of brief dynamic psychotherapy: A meta-analysis. *American Journal of Psychiatry, 149,* 151–158.

Crits-Christoph, P., Barber, J. P., Baranackie, K., & Cooper, A. (1993). Assessing the therapist's interpretations. In N. E. Miller, L. Luborsky, J. P. Barber, & J. P. Docherty (Eds.), *Psychodynamic treatment research: A handbook for clinical practice* (pp. 361–386). New York: Basic Books.

Crits-Christoph, P., Barber, J., & Kurcias, J. S. (1993). The accuracy of therapists' interpretations and the development of the alliance. *Psychotherapy Research, 3,* 25–35.

Crits-Christoph, P., Barber, J. P., Miller, N. E., & Beebe, K. (1993). Evaluating insight. In N. E. Miller, L. Luborsky, J. P. Barberg, & J. P. Docherty (Eds.), *Psychodynamic treatment research: A handbook for clinical practice* (pp. 407–422). New York: Basic Books.

Crits-Christoph, P., Cooper, A., & Luborsky, L. (1988). The accuracy of therapists' interpretations and the outcome of dynamic psychotherapy. *Journal of Consulting and Clinical Psychology, 56*(4), 490–495.

Crits-Christoph, P., & Luborsky, L. (1990). The measurement of self-understanding. In L. Luborsky & P. Crits-Christoph (Eds.), *Understanding transference: The Core Conflictual Relationship Theme method.* New York: Basic Books.

Crocker, J., Alloy, L. B., & Kayne, N. T. (1988). Attributional style, depression, and perceptions of consensus for events. *Journal of Personality and Social Psychology, 54,* 840–846.

Crook, T., & Eliot, J. (1980). Parental death during childhood and adult depression: A critical review of the literature. *Psychological Bulletin, 87,* 252–259.

Crook, T., Raskin, A., & Eliot, J. (1981). Parent-child relationship and adult depression. *Child Development, 52,* 950–957.

Dahlstrom, W. G., & Welch, G. S. (1960). *An MMPI handbook.* Minneapolis: University of Minnesota Press.

Dammann, E. J. (1993). *Psychodynamic correlates of depression: Hostility and orality.* Unpublished Master's thesis, Michigan State University, East Lansing.

Dauber, R. B. (1984). Subliminal psychodynamic activation in depression: On the role of autonomy issues in depressed college women. *Journal of Abnormal Psychology, 93,* 9–18.

Davies, M. J. (1978). *The manifest content of initial dreams in psychotherapy: Their diagnostic and prognostic significance.* Unpublished doctoral dissertation, Fordham University, New York.

Davis, P. J., & Schwartz, G. E. (1987). Repression and the inaccessibility of affective memories. *Journal of Personality and Social Psychology, 52,* 155–162.

de Jong, M. A., & Visser, P. (1983). Mood, dream content and secondary revision after different presleep stimuli. *Sleep Research, 12,* 175.

Dement, W. C. (1960). The effect of dream deprivation. *Science, 131,* 1705–1707.

Dement, W. C. (1964). Experimental dream studies. In J. H. Masserman (Ed.), *Science and psychoanalysis. Scientific proceedings of the Academy of Psychoanalysis* (pp. 129–162). New York: Grune and Stratton.

Dement, W. C., & Fisher, C. (1963). Experimental interference with the sleep cycle. *Canadian Psychiatric Association Journal, 8,* 400–405.

Demos, E. V. (1992). The early organization of the psyche. In J. W. Barron, M. N. Eagle, & D. L. Wolitzky (Eds.), *Interface of psychoanalysis and psychology* (pp. 200–232). Washington, DC: American Psychological Association.

Depue, R. A., & Iacono, W. G. (1989). Neurobehavioral aspects of affective disorders. In M. R. Rosenzweig & L. W. Porter (Eds.), *Annual review of psychology* (Vol. 40, pp. 457–492). Palo Alto, CA: Annual Reviews.

Derry, P. A., & Kuiper, N. A. (1981). Schematic processing and self-reference in clinical depression. *Journal of Abnormal Psychology, 90,* 286–297.

Deutsch, H. (1944–1945). *Psychology of women* (2 Vols.). New York: Grune and Stratton.

Digman, J. M. (1990). Personality structure: Emergence of the five-factor model. In M. R. Rosenzweig & L. W. Porter (Eds.), *Annual review of psychology* (Vol. 40, pp. 417–440). Palo Alto, CA: Annual Reviews.

Dizinno, G. A. (1983). *An evolutionary analysis of male homosexual behavior.* Unpublished doctoral dissertation, Florida State University, Gainesville.

Dobson, K. S. (1985). The relationship between anxiety and depression. *Clinical Psychology Review, 5,* 307–324.

Dobson, K. S., & Shaw, B. F. (1986). Cognitive assessment with major depressive disorders. *Cognitive Therapy and Research, 10,* 13–29.

Domhoff, G. W. (1993). The repetition of dreams and dream elements: A possible clue to a function of dreams. In A. Moffit, M. Kramer, & R. Hoffmann (Eds.), *The functions of dreams* (pp. 293–320). Albany: State University of New York Press.

Douglas, M. (1970). *Natural symbols.* New York: Random House.

Douvan, E., & Adelson, J. (1966). *The adolescent experience.* New York: Wiley.

Duberstein, P. R. (1990). *Parental representations and behavioral modulation.* Unpublished doctoral dissertation, State University of New York, Buffalo.

Duberstein, P. R., & Talbot, N. L. (1992). Parental idealization and the absence of Rorschach oral imagery. *Journal of Personality Assessment, 50,* 50–58.

Duberstein, P. R., & Talbot, N. L. (1993). Rorschach oral imagery, attachment style, and interpersonal relatedness. *Journal of Personality Assessment, 61,* 294–310.

Dudek, S. Z. (1970). Effects of different types of therapy on the personality as a whole. *Journal of Nervous and Mental Disease, 150,* 329–345.

Duhrssen, A., & Jorswieck, E. (1965). An empirical-statistical investigation into the efficacy of psychoanalytic therapy. *Nervenarzt, 36,* 166–169.

Dunning, D., & Story, A. L. (1991). Depression, realism, and the overconfidence effect: Are the sadder wiser when predicting future actions and events? *Journal of Personality and Social Psychology, 61,* 521–532.

Dush, D. M. (1986). The placebo in psychosocial outcome evaluations. *Evaluation & the Health Professions, 9,* 421–438.

Duval, S., & Wicklund, R. A. (1972). *A theory of objective self awareness.* New York: Academic Press.

Eckardt, B. V. (1982). Why Freud's research methodology was unscientific. *Psychoanalysis and Contemporary Thought, 5,* 549–574.

Edelson, M. (1977). Psychoanalysis as science. *Journal of Nervous and Mental Disease, 165,* 1–28.

Edelson, M. (1984). *Hypothesis and evidence in psychoanalysis.* Chicago: University of Chicago Press.

Edwards, C. P. (1981). The comparative study of the development of moral judgment and reasoning. In R. H. Munroe, R. L. Munroe, & B. B. Whiting (Eds.), *Handbook of cross-cultural human development* (pp. 501–530). New York: Garland.

Eisenberg, N. (1988). The development of prosocial and aggressive behavior. In M. H. Bornstein & M. E. Lamb (Eds.), *Developmental psychology: An advanced textbook* (pp. 461–495). Hillsdale, NJ: Erlbaum.

Eisenstein, S., Levy, N. A., & Marmor, J. (1994). *The dyadic transaction: An investigation into the nature of the psycho-therapeutic process.* New Brunswick, NJ: Transaction.

Elliott, R., Barker, C. B., Caskey, N., & Pistrang, N. (1982). Differential helpfulness of counselor verbal response modes. *Journal of Counseling Psychology, 29,* 354–361.

Elliott, R., Hill, C. E., Stiles, W. R., Friedlander, M. L., Mahrer, A. R., & Margison, F. R. (1987). Primary therapist response modes: Comparison of six rating systems. *Journal of Consulting and Clinical Psychology, 55,* 218–223.

Ellis, A. (1957). Outcome of employing three techniques of psychotherapy. *Journal of Clinical Psychology, 13,* 344–350.

Ellman, C. S. (1970). *An experimental study of the female castration complex.* Unpublished doctoral dissertation, New York University.

Ellman, S. J. (1992). Psychoanalytic theory, dream formation, and REM sleep. In J. W. Barron, M. N. Eagle, & D. L. Wolitzky (Eds.), *Interface of psychoanalysis and psychology* (pp. 357–374). Washington, DC: American Psychological Association.

Epstein, S. (1994). Integration of the cognitive and the psychodynamic unconscious. *American Psychologist, 49,* 709–724.

Erdelyi, M. H. (1992). Psychodynamics and the unconscious. *American Psychologist, 47,* 784–787.

Erikson, B. E. D. (1977). *An examination of sexual behavior and of differences among women in patterns of emotional, cognitive, and physical change during the menstrual cycle.* Unpublished doctoral dissertation, University of North Carolina, Chapel Hill.

Erikson, E. H. (1954). The dream specimen of psychoanalysis. *Journal of the American Psychoanalytic Association, 2,* 5–56.

Erikson, E. H. (1963). *Childhood and society* (Rev. ed.). New York: Norton.

Erikson, E. H. (1968). *Identity, youth and crisis.* New York: Norton.

Eysenck, H. J., Wakefield, J. A., Jr., & Friedman, A. F. (1983). Diagnosis and clinical assessment. In M. R. Rosenzweig & L. W. Porter (Eds.), *Annual review of psychology* (Vol. 34, pp. 167–193). Palo Alto, CA: Annual Reviews.

Eysenck, H. J., & Wilson, G. D. (1973). *The experimental study of Freudian theories.* London: Methuen.

Fagan, P. J., Wise, T. N., Schmidt, C. W., Ponticas, Y., Marshall, R. D., & Costa, P. T. (1991). A comparison of five-factor personality dimensions in males with sexual dysfunction and males with paraphilia. *Journal of Personality Assessment, 57,* 434–448.

Fairbairn, W. R. D. (1952). *Psychoanalytic studies of the personality.* London: Routledge & Kegan Paul.

Farrell, B. A. (1981). *The standing of psychoanalysis.* New York, Oxford University Press.

Fava, G. A., Kellner, R., & Lisansky, J. (1986). Hostility and recovery from melancholia. *Journal of Nervous and Mental Disease, 174,* 414–417.

Fava, G. A., Kellner, R., Munari, F., Pavan, L., & Pesarin, F. (1982). Losses, hostility and depression. *Journal of Nervous and Mental Disease, 170,* 474–478.

Feiner, K. (1988). A test of a theory of anxiety about body integrity: Part 2. *Psychoanalytic Psychology, 5,* 71–79.

Feldman, F. (1968). Results of psychoanalysis in clinic case assignments. *Journal of American Psychoanalytic Association, 16,* 274–300.

Feldman, P. (1978). *Body type, oral imagery and group behavior.* Unpublished doctoral dissertation, State University of New York, Buffalo.

Fenichel, O. (1930). *Ten years of the Berlin Psychoanalytic Institute.* Vienna: International Psychoanalytic Publishers.

Fenigstein, A., & Vanable, P. A. (1992). Paranoia and self-consciousness. *Journal of Personality and Social Psychology, 62,* 129–138.

Fernando, S. J. (1977). Hostility, personality, and depression. *British Journal of Medical Psychology, 50,* 243–249.

Fiedler, F. E. (1950a). A comparison of therapeutic relationships in psychoanalytic, non-directive, and Adlerian therapy. *Journal of Consulting Psychology, 14,* 436–445.

Fiedler, F. E. (1950b). The concept of an ideal therapeutic relationship. *Journal of Consulting Psychology, 14,* 239–245.

Fiedler, F. E. (1951). Factor analysis of psychoanalytic, non-directive, and Adlerian therapeutic relationships. *Journal of Consulting Psychology, 15,* 32–38.

Finney, J. C. (1964). A factor analysis of mother-child influence. *Journal of Genetic Psychology, 103,* 351–367.

Fischer, K. W., & Pipp, S. L. (1984). Development of the structures of unconscious thought. In K. S. Bowers & D. Meichenbaum (Eds.), *The unconscious reconsidered* (pp. 88–148). New York: Wiley.

Fischer, K. W., & Silvern, L. (1985). Stages and individual differences in cognitive development. In M. R. Rosenzweig & L. W. Porter (Eds.), *Annual review of psychology* (Vol. 37, pp. 613–648). Palo Alto, CA: Annual Reviews.

Fischer, R. E., & Juni, S. (1982). The anal personality: Self-disclosure, negativism, self-esteem, and superego severity. *Journal of Personality Assessment, 46,* 50–58.

Fisher, J. M., & Fisher, S. (1975). Response to cigarette deprivation as a function of oral fantasy. *Journal of Personality Assessment, 39,* 381–385.

Fisher, S. (1970). *Body experience in fantasy and behavior.* New York: Appleton-Century-Crofts.

Fisher, S. (1973). *The female orgasm.* New York: Basic Books.

Fisher, S. (1978). Dirt-anality and attitudes toward Negroes: A test of Kubie's hypothesis. *Journal of Nervous and Mental Disease, 166,* 280–290.

Fisher, S. (1980). Personality correlates of sexual behavior in Black women. *Archives of Sexual Behavior, 9,* 27–35.

Fisher, S. (1986). *Development and structure of the body image* (Vols. 1 & 2). Hillsdale, NJ: Erlbaum.

Fisher, S. (1989). *Sexual images of the self: The psychology of erotic sensations and illusions.* Hillsdale, NJ: Erlbaum.

Fisher, S., & Fisher, R. L. (1993). *The psychology of adaptation to absurdity. Tactics of make-believe.* Hillsdale, NJ: Erlbaum.

Fisher, S., & Greenberg, R. P. (1977). *The scientific credibility of Freud's theories and therapy.* New York: Basic Books.

Fisher, S., & Greenberg, R. P. (1985). *The scientific credibility of Freud's theories and therapy.* New York: Columbia University Press.

Fisher, S., & Greenberg, R. P. (Eds.). (1989). *The limits of biological treatments for psychological distres: Comparisons with psychotherapy and placebo.* Hillsdale, NJ: Erlbaum.

Fisher, S., & Greenberg, R. P. (1993). Psychodynamics of spatial experience: Role in localization of somatic discomfort. In J. M. Masling & R. F. Bornstein (Eds.), *Psychoanalytic perspectives on psychopathology* (pp. 253–280). Washington, DC: American Psychological Association.

Fiss, H. (1993). The "Royal Road" to the unconscious revisited: A signal detection model of dream function. In A. Moffit, M. Kramer, & R. Hoffmann (Eds.), *The function of dreaming* (pp. 381–418). Albany: State University of New York Press.

Fiss, H., Klein, G. S., & Bokert, E. (1966). Waking fantasies following interruption of two types of sleep. *Archives of General Psychiatry, 14,* 543–551.

Flowerman, S. H. (1954). Psychoanalytic theory and science. *American Journal of Psychotherapy, 8,* 415–441.

Forrest, M. S., & Hokanson, J. E. (1975). Depression and autonomic arousal reduction accompanying self-punitive behavior. *Journal of Abnormal Psychology, 84,* 346–357.

Foster, R. P. (1981). *The effects of subliminal tachistoscopic presentation of drive-related stimuli on the cognitive functioning of paranoid and nonparanoid.* Unpublished doctoral dissertation, St. John's University, New York, NY.

Foulds, G. A. (1965). *Personality and personal illness.* London: Tavistock.

Foulkes, D. (1985). *Dreaming: A cognitive-psychological analysis.* Hillsdale, NJ: Erlbaum.

Foulkes, D. (1993). Data constraints on theorizing about dream function. In A. Moffit, M. Kramer, & R. Hoffmann (Eds.), *The functions of dreams* (pp. 11–20). Albany: State University of New York Press.

Fowles, D. C. (1992). Schizophrenia: Diathesis-stress revisited. In M. R. Rosenzweig & L. W. Porter (Eds.), *Annual review of psychology* (Vol. 43, pp. 303–336). Palo Alto, CA: Annual Reviews.

Franck, K., & Rosen, E. (1949). A projective test of masculinity-femininity. *Journal of Consulting Psychology, 13,* 247–256.

Frank, J. D. (1973). *Persuasion and healing* (Rev. ed.). Baltimore, MD: John Hopkins University Press.

Frank, J. D., & Frank, J. (1991). *Persuasion and healing: A comparative study of psychotherapy* (3rd ed.). Baltimore, MD: John Hopkins University Press.

Frank, S. J., Jacobson, S., & Tuer, M. (1990). Psychological predictors of young adults' drinking behaviors. *Journal of Personality and Social Psychology, 59,* 770–780.

Franz, C. E., McClelland, D. C., & Weinberger, J. (1991). Childhood antecedent of conventional social accomplishment in midlife adults: A 36-year prospective study. *Journal of Personality and Social Psychology, 60,* 586–595.

French, T., & Fromm, E. (1964). *Dream interpretation.* New York: Basic Books.

Fretter, P. B. (1984). The immediate effects of transference interpretations on patients' progress in brief, psychodynamic psychotherapy. *Dissertation Abstracts International, 46*(6). (University Microfilms No. 85–12, 112).

Fretter, P. B., Bucci, W., Broitman, J., Silberschatz, G., & Curtis, J. T. (1994). How the patient's plan relates to the concept of transference. *Psychotherapy Research, 4,* 58–72.

Freud, S. (1896). The aetiology of hysteria. In J. Strachey (Ed.), *The standard edition of the complete psychological works of Sigmund Freud* (Vol. 3, pp. 187–221). London: Hogarth.

Freud, S. (1898). Sexuality in the aetiology of the neurosis. In J. Strachey (Ed.), *The Standard edition of the complete psychological works of Sigmund Freud* (Vol. 3, pp. 259–285). London: Hogarth.

Freud, S. (1900). The interpretation of dreams. In J. Strachey (Ed.), *The standard edition of the complete psychological works of Sigmund Freud* (Vols. 4 & 5, pp. 1–678). London: Hogarth.

Freud, S. (1905). Three essays on the theory of sexuality. In J. Strachey (Ed.), *The standard edition of the complete psychological works of Sigmund Freud* (Vol. 7, pp. 135–243). London: Hogarth.

Freud, S. (1905a). Fragment of an analysis of a case of hysteria. In J. Strachey (Ed.), *The standard edition of the complete psychological works of Sigmund Freud* (Vol. 7, pp. 7–134). London: Hogarth.

Freud, S. (1905b). On psychotherapy. In J. Strachey (Ed.), *The standard edition of the complete psychological works of Sigmund Freud* (Vol. 7, pp. 255–268). London: Hogarth.

Freud, S. (1905c). Psychical (or mental) treatment. In J. Strachey (Ed.), *The standard edition of the complete psychological works of Sigmund Freud* (Vol. 7, pp. 281–302). London: Hogarth.

Freud, S. (1906). My views on the part played by sexuality in the aetiology of the neuroses. In J. Strachey (Ed.), *The standard edition of the complete psychological works of Sigmund Freud* (Vol.7, pp. 270–279). London: Hogarth.

Freud, S. (1908). Character and anal erotism. In J. Strachey (Ed.), *The standard edition of the complete psychological works of Sigmund Freud* (Vol. 9, pp. 169–175). London: Hogarth.

Freud, S. (1909a). Analysis of a phobia in a five-year-old boy. In J. Strachey (Ed.), *The standard edition of the complete psychological works of Sigmund Freud* (Vol. 10, pp. 3–149). London: Hogarth.

Freud, S. (1909b). Notes upon a case of obsessional neurosis. In J. Strachey (Ed.), *The standard edition of the complete psychological works of Sigmund Freud* (Vol. 10, pp. 151–320). London: Hogarth.

Freud, S. (1910a). Five lectures on psycho-analysis. Second lecture. In J. Strachey (Ed.), *The standard edition of the complete psychological works of Sigmund Freud* (Vol. 11, pp. 21–28). London: Hogarth.

Freud, S. (1910b). *Leonardo da Vinci and a memory of his childhood.* New York: Norton.

Freud, S. (1910c). The future prospects of psycho-analytic therapy. In J. Strachey (Ed.), *The standard edition of the complete psychological works of Sigmund Freud* (Vol. 11, pp. 139–151). London: Hogarth.

Freud, S. (1910d). "Wild" psycho-analysis. In J. Strachey (Ed.), *The standard edition of the complete psychological works of Sigmund Freud* (Vol. 11, pp. 219–227). London: Hogarth.

Freud, S. (1911). Psychoanalytic notes on an autobiographical account of a case of paranoia (dementia paranoids). In J. Strachey (Ed.), *The standard edition of the complete psychological works of Sigmund Freud* (Vol. 12, pp. 1–82). London: Hogarth.

Freud, S. (1912a). Recommendations to physicians practicing psycho-analysis. In J. Strachey (Ed.), *The standard edition of the complete psychological works of Sigmund Freud* (Vol. 12, pp. 109–120). London: Hogarth.

Freud, S. (1912b). The dynamics of transference. In J. Strachey (Ed.), *The standard edition of the complete psychological works of Sigmund Freud* (Vol. 12, pp. 97–108). London: Hogarth.

Freud, S. (1913a). On beginning the treatment. (Further recommendations on the technique of psychoanalysis I). In J. Strachey (Ed.), *The standard edition of the complete psychological works of Sigmund Freud* (Vol. 12, pp. 121–144). London: Hogarth.

Freud, S. (1913b). The disposition to obsessional neurosis. In J. Strachey (Ed.), *The standard edition of the complete psychological works of Sigmund Freud* (Vol. 12, pp. 311–326). London: Hogarth.

Freud, S. (1914a). On narcissism: An introduction. In J. Strachey (Ed.), *The standard edition of the complete psychological works of Sigmund Freud* (Vol. 14, pp. 67–102. London: Hogarth.

Freud, S. (1914b). On the history of the psychoanalytic movement. In J. Strachey (Ed.), *The standard edition of the complete psychological works of Sigmund Freud* (Vol. 14, pp. 3–66). London: Hogarth.

Freud, S. (1914c). Remembering, repeating, and working through. In J. Strachey (Ed.), *The standard edition of the complete psychological works of Sigmund Freud* (Vol. 12, pp. 145–156). London: Hogarth.

Freud, S. (1917). Mourning and melancholia. In J. Strachey (Ed.), *The standard edition of the complete psychological works of Sigmund Freud* (Vol. 14, pp. 237–242). London: Hogarth.

Freud, S. (1919). A child is being beaten: A contribution to the study of the origins of sexual perversions. In J. Strachey (Ed.), *The standard edition of the complete psychological works of Sigmund Freud* (Vol. 17, pp. 175–204). London: Hogarth.

Freud, S. (1922). Dreams and telepathy. In J. Strachey (Ed.), *The standard edition of the complete psychological works of Sigmund Freud* (Vol. 18, pp. 195–220). London: Hogarth.

Freud, S. (1923). The ego and the id. In J. Strachey (Ed.), *The standard edition of the complete works of Sigmund Freud* (Vol. 19, pp. 12–68). London: Hogarth.

Freud, S. (1924). The dissolution of the Oedipus Complex. In J. Strachey (Ed.), *The standard edition of the complete psychological works of Sigmund Freud* (Vol. 19, pp. 173–179). London: Hogarth.

Freud, S. (1925). An autobiographical study, In J. Strachey (Ed.), *The standard edition of the complete psychological works of Sigmund Freud* (Vol. 20, pp. 7–74). London: Hogarth.

Freud, S. (1926). Inhibitions, symptoms, and anxiety. In J. Strachey (Ed.), *The standard edition of the complete psychological works of Sigmund Freud* (Vol. 20, pp. 77–173). London: Hogarth.

Freud, S. (1927). The future of an illusion. In J. Strachey (Ed.), *The standard edition of the complete psychological works of Sigmund Freud* (Vol. 21, pp. 3–56). London: Hogarth.

Freud, S. (1930). Civilization and its discontents. In J. Strachey (Ed.), *The standard edition of the complete psychological works of Sigmund Freud* (Vol. 21, pp. 21–134). London: Hogarth.

Freud, S. (1933a). Femininity. In J. Strachey (Ed.), *The standard edition of the complete psychological works of Sigmund Freud* (Vol. 22, pp. 122–135). London: Hogarth.

Freud, S. (1933b). New introductory lectures on psychoanalysis. In J. Strachey (Ed.), *The standard edition of the complete psychological works of Sigmund Freud* (Vol. 22, pp. 3–182). London: Hogarth.

Freud, S. (1937a). Analysis terminable and interminable. In J. Strachey (Ed.), *The standard edition of the complete psychological works of Sigmund Freud* (Vol. 23, pp. 209–253). London: Hogarth.

Freud, S. (1937b). Construction in analysis. In J. Strachey (Ed.), *The standard edition of the complete psychological works of Sigmund Freud* (Vol. 23, pp. 255–269). London: Hogarth.

Freud, S. (1962). The aetiology of hysteria. In J. Strachey (Ed.), (in collaboration with A. Freud), *The standard edition of the complete psychological works of Sigmund Freud* (Vol. 3, pp. 187–221). London: Hogarth.

Friedman, A. S. (1970). Hostility factors and clinical improvement in depressed patients. *Archives of General Psychiatry, 23,* 524–537.

Friedman, H. S., Tucker, J. S., Tomlinson-Keasey, C., Schwartz, J. E., Wingard, D. L., & Criqui, M. H. (1993). Does childhood personality predict longevity? *Journal of Personality and Social Psychology, 65,* 176–185.

Friedman, R. C., & Downey, J. (1993). Neurobiology and sexual orientation: Current relationships. *Journal of Neuropsychiatry, 5,* 131–153.

Friedman, S. M. (1952). An empirical study of the castration and Oedipus complexes. *Genetic Psychology Monographs, 46,* 61–130.

Friman, P. C., Allen, K. D., Kerwin, M. L. E., & Larzelere, R. (1993). Changes in modern psychology. A citation analysis of the Kuhnian displacement thesis. *American Psychologist, 48,* 658–664.

Garamoni, G. L., & Schwartz, R. M. (1986). Type A behavior pattern and compulsive personality: Toward a psychodynamic-behavioral integration. *Clinical Psychology Review, 6,* 311–336.

Gartrell, N. K. (1982). Hormones and homosexuality. In W. Paul, J. D. Weinrich, J. C. Gonsiorek, & M. E. Hotnedt (Eds.), *Homosexuality: Social, psychological and biological issues* (pp. 169–182). Beverly Hills, CA: Sage.

Gaston, L., Piper, W. E., Debbane, E. G., Bienvenu, J. P., & Garant, J. (1994). Alliance and technique for predicting outcome in short- and long-term analytic psychotherapy. *Psychotherapy Research, 4,* 121–135.

Gelso, C. J., & Johnson, D. H. (1983). *Explorations in time-limited counseling and psychotherapy.* New York: Teachers College Press.

Georgaklis, C. C. (1987). Relationship between parental views and romantic happiness in college women. *Psychological Reports, 61,* 75–78.

Gershon, E. S., Cromer, M., & Klerman, G. L. (1968). Hostility and depression. *Psychiatry, 31,* 224–235.

Gibbons, F. X., Smith, T. W., Ingram, R. E., Pearce, K., Brehm, S. S., & Schroeder, D. J. (1985). Self awareness and self-confrontation: Effects of self-focused attention on members of a clinical population. *Journal of Personality and Social Psychology, 78,* 662–675.

Gill, H. S. (1986). Oedipal determinants in differential outcome of bereavement. *British Journal of Medical Psychology, 59,* 21–25.

Gill, M. (1943). Functional disturbance of menstruation. *Bulletin of the Menninger Clinic, 7,* 6–14.

Gill, M. M. (1982). Analysis of transference: Vol. I. Theory and technique. New York: International Universities Press.

Gilleard, E., Eskin, M., & Savasir, B. (1988). Nailbiting and oral aggression in a Turkish student population. *British Journal of Medical Psychology, 61,* 197–201.

Gilligan, C. (1982). *In a different voice.* Cambridge, MA: Harvard University Press.

Glass, D. C. (1977). *Behavior patterns, stress and coronary disease.* Hillsdale, NJ: Erlbaum.

Glaubman, H., Orbach, I., Aviram, O., Frieder, I., Frieman, M., Pelled, O., & Glaubman, R. (1978). REM deprivation and divergent thinking. *Psychophysiology, 15,* 75–79.

Gleser, C. G., & Sacks, M. (1973). Ego defenses and reaction to stress: A validation study of the Defense Mechanisms Inventory. *Journal of Consulting and Clinical Psychology, 40,* 181–187.

Glover, E. (1954). The indications for psychoanalysis. *Journal of Mental Science, 100,* 393–401.

Goldfried, M. R. (1980). Toward the delineation of therapeutic change principles. *American Psychologist, 35,* 991–999.

Goldfried, M. R., & Padawer, W. (1982). Current status and future directions in psychotherapy. In M. R. Goldfried (Ed.), *Converging themes in psychotherapy* (pp. 3–49). New York: Springer.

Goldfried, M. R., Stricker, G., & Weiner, L. B. (1971). *Rorschach handbooks of clinical and research applications.* Englewood Cliffs, NJ: Prentice-Hall.

Goldstein, A. P. (1962). *Therapist–patient expectancies in psychotherapy.* New York: Pergamon.

Goldstein, A. P., & Stein, N. (1976). *Prescriptive psychotherapies.* New York: Pergamon.

Gomez, E. A. (1982). The evaluation of psychosocial casework services to Chicanos: A study of process and outcome (Doctoral dissertation, 1983). *Dissertation Abstracts International, 43*(3A), 925.

Gordon, J. E. (1957). Leading and following psychotherapeutic techniques with hypnotically induced repression and hostility. *Journal of Abnormal and Social Psychology, 54,* 405–410.

Gordon, K. S., & Zax, M. (1981). Once more unto the breach dear friends . . . A reconsideration of the literature on symptom substitution. *Clinical Psychology Review, 1,* 33–47.

Gordon, M., & Tegtmeyer, P. F. (1983). Oral dependent content in children's Rorschach protocols. *Perceptual and Motor Skills, 57,* 1163–1168.

Gordon, N. G., & Brackney, B. E. (1979). Defense mechanism preference and dimensions of psychopathology. *Psychological Reports, 44,* 188–190.

Gotlib, I. H., Mount, J. H., Cordy, N. I., & Whiffen, V. E. (1988). Depression and perceptions of early parenting: A longitudinal investigation. *British Journal of Psychiatry, 152,* 24–27.

Gottschalk, L. A. (1968). Some applications of the psychoanalytic concept of object relatedness: Preliminary studies on a human relations content analysis scale applicable to verbal samples. *Comprehensive Psychiatry, 9,* 608–620.

Gottschalk, L. A., Gleser, G., & Springer, K. J. (1963). Three hostility scales applicable to verbal samples. *Archives of General Psychiatry, 9,* 254–279.

Gottschalk, L. A., Hoigaard, J. C., Birch, H., & Rickels, K. (1979). The measurement of psychological states: Relationships between Gottschalk–Gleser Content Analysis scores and Hamilton Anxiety Rating Scale scores, Physician Quesionnaire Rating Scale score and Hopkins Symptom Checklist scores. In L. A. Gottschalk (Ed.), *The content analysis of verbal behavior—Further studies* (pp. 41–94). New York: SP Medical and Scientific Books.

Graber, R. B. (1981). A psychocultural theory of male genital mutilation. *Journal of Psychoanalytic Anthropology, 4,* 413–434.

Grayson, H. T., Jr. (1967). *Psychosexual conflict in adolescent girls who experienced parental loss by death.* Unpublished doctoral dissertation, Boston University Graduate School.

Graziano, W. G., & Ward, D. (1992). Probing the big five in adolescence: Personality and adjustment during a developmental transition. *Journal of Personality, 60,* 425–439.

Greenberg, R. (1981). Dreams and REM sleep—An integrative approach. In W. Fishbein (Ed.), *Sleep, dreams and memory.* (pp. 125–133). New York: Spectrum.

Greenberg, R., & Pearlman, C. (1993). An integrated approach to dream theory: Contributions from sleep research and clinical practice. In A. Moffitt, M. Kramer, & R. Hoffman (Eds.), *The functions of dreaming* (pp. 363–380). Albany: State University of New York Press.

Greenberg, R. P., & Bornstein, R. (1988). The dependent personality: I. Risk for physical disorders. *Journal of Personality Disorders, 2,* 126–135.

Greenberg, R. P., & Fisher, S. (1980). Freud's penis–baby equation: Exploratory tests of a controversial theory. *British Journal of Medical Psychology, 53,* 333–342.

Greenberg, R. P., & Fisher, S. (1983). Freud and the female reproductive process: Test and issues. In J. Masling (Ed.), *Empirical studies of psychoanalytic theories* (Vol. 1, pp. 251–281). Hillsdale, NJ: Analytic Press.

Greenwald, A. G. (1992). New Look 3: Unconscious cognition reclaimed. *American Psychologist, 47,* 766–779.

Grinker, R. R. (1974). Two of his analysands recall the "real" Freud: Report on a meeting of the American Academy of Psychoanalysis. *Roche Report: Frontiers of Psychiatry, 4,* 3.

Grinker, R. R., Miller, J., Sabshin, M., Nunn, R., & Nunnally, J. (1961). *The phenomena of depressions.* New York: Hoeber.

Grunbaum, A. (1984). *The foundations of psychoanalysis: A philosophical critique.* Berkeley: University of California Press.

Grunbaum, A. (1993). *Validation in the clinical theory of psychoanalysis: A study in the philosophy of psychoanalysis.* Madison, CT: International Universities Press.

Grygier, T. G. (1961). *The Dynamic Personality Inventory.* London: NFER.

Guidano, V. S., & Liotti, G. (1983). *Cognitive processes and emotional disorders: A structural approach to psychotherapy.* New York: Guilford.

Habermas, J. (1971). *Knowledge and human interests.* (J. J. Shapiro, Trans.). Boston: Beacon Press.

Hall, C. S. (1963). Strangers in dreams: An experimental confirmation of the Oedipus complex. *Journal of Personality, 3,* 336–345.

Halperin, K. M., & Snyder, C. R. (1979). Effects of enhanced psychological test feedback on treatment outcome: Therapeutic implications of the Barnum Effect. *Journal of Consulting and Clinical Psychology, 47,* 140–146.

Hamburg, D. A., Bibring, G. L., Fisher, C., Stanton, A. H., Wallerstein, R. S., Weinstock, H. I., & Haggard, E. (1967). Report of the Ad Hoc Committee on central fact-gathering data of the American Psychoanalytic Association. *Journal of the American Psychoanalytic Association, 15,* 841–861.

Hamilton, M. (1967). Development of a rating scale for primary depressive illness. *British Journal of Social Psychology, 6,* 278–296.

Hammen, C., Ellicott, A., & Gitlin, M. (1989). Vulnerability to specific life events and prediction of course of disorder in unipolar depressed patients. *Canadian Journal of Behavioural Science, 21,* 377–388.

Hammen, C., Ellicott, A., Gitlin, M., & Jamison, K. R. (1989). Sociotropy/Autonomy and vulnerability to specific life events in patients with unipolar depression and bipolar disorders. *Journal of Abnormal Psychology, 98,* 154–160.

Hammen, C., Marks, T., Mayol, A., & deMayo, R. (1985). Depressive self-schemas, life stress, and vulnerability to depression. *Journal of Abnormal Psychology, 94,* 308–319.

Hammen, C., Mayol, A., deMayo, R., & Marks, T. (1986). Initial symptom levels and the life-event—depression relationship. *Journal of Abnormal Psychology, 95,* 114–122.

Hampel, R., & Selg, H. (1975). FAF: *Fragebogen zur Erfassung von Aggressivitats-fakoren.* Gottingen, Germany: Hogrefe.

Hardaway, R. A. (1990). Subliminally activated symbiotic fantasies: Facts and artifacts. *Psychological Bulletin, 107,* 177–195.

Hartmann, E. (1984). *The nightmare.* New York: Basic Books.

Haspel, K. C., & Harris, R. S. (1982). Effects of tachistoscopic stimulation of subconscious Oedipal wishes on competitive performance: A failure to replicate. *Journal of Abnormal Psychology, 91,* 437–443.

Hay, D. F. (1986). Infancy. In M. R. Rosenzweig & L. W. Porter (Eds.), *Annual review of psychology* (Vol. 37, pp. 135–161). Palo Alto, CA: Annual Reviews.

Hayworth, J., Little, B. C., Carter, S. B., Raptopoulos, P., Priest, R. G., & Sandler, M. (1980). A predictive study of post-partum depression: Some predisposing characteristics. *British Journal of Medical Psychology, 53,* 161–167.

Heilbrun, A. B., Blum, N., & Goldreyer, N. (1985). Defensive projection: An investigation of its role in paranoid conditions. *Journal of Nervous and Mental Disease, 173,* 17–25.

Heilbrun, K. S. (1982). Reply to Silverman. *Journal of Abnormal Psychology, 91,* 134–135.

Heilbrunn, G. (1963). Results with psychoanalytic therapy: Report of 241 cases. *American Journal of Psychotherapy, 17,* 427–435.

Heilbrunn, G. (1966). Results with psychoanalytic therapy and professional commitment. *American Journal of Psychotherapy, 20,* 89–99.

Heine, R. W. (1953). A comparison of patients' reports on psychotherapeutic experience with psychoanalytic, nondirective and Adlerian therapists. *American Journal of Psychotherapy, 7,* 16–23.

Henry, W. P., Schacht, T. E., Strupp, H. H., Butler, S. F., & Binder, J. L. (1993). Effects of training in time-limited dynamic psychotherapy: Mediators of therapists' responses to training. *Journal of Consulting and Clinical Psychology, 61,* 441–447.

Henry, W. P., Strupp, H. H., Butler, S. F., Schacht, T. E., & Binder, J. L. (1993). The effects of training in time-limited dynamic psychotherapy: Changes in therapist behavior. *Journal of Consulting and Clinical Psychology, 61,* 434–440.

Henry, W. P., Strupp, H. H., Schacht, T. E., & Gaston, L. (1994). Psychodynamic approaches. In A. E. Bergin & S. L. Garfield (Eds.), *Handbook of psychotherapy and behavior change* (4th ed., pp. 467–508). New York: Wiley.

Herdt, G. H. (1981). *Guardians of the flutes.* New York: McGraw-Hill.

Herdt, G. H. (Ed.). (1984). *Ritualized homosexuality in Melanesia.* Berkely: University of California Press.

Hetherington, E. M., Cox, M., & Cox, R. (1978). *Family interaction and social, emotional, and cognitive development of children following divorce.* Paper presented at the Symposium on the Family Setting Priorities. Sponsored by the Institute for Pediatric Service and Johnson Baby Company, Washington, DC.

Hewitt, P. L., & Flett, G. L. (1993). Dimensions of perfectionism, daily stress, and depression: A test of the specific vulnerability hypothesis. *Journal of Abnormal Psychology, 102,* 58–65.

Hewitt, P. L., & Genest, M. (1990). The ideal self: Schematic processing of perfectionistic content in dysphoric university students. *Journal of Personality and Social Psychology, 59,* 802–808.

Hilgard, E. R. (1952). Experimental approaches to psychoanalysis. In E. Pumpian-Minlin (Ed.), *Psyhoanalysis as science* (pp. 3–45). Stanford, CA: Stanford University Press.

Hill, A. B. (1978). *The differential susceptibility of oral and anal character types to hypnosis.* Unpublished doctoral dissertation, Rutgers University, New Brunswick, NJ.

Hill, A. B. (1979). Factor-analytic studies of the anal character: A rejoinder to Kline. *British Journal of Medical Psychology, 52,* 397–399.

Hill, C. E., Helms, J. E., Tichenor, V., Speigel, S. B., O'Grady, K. E., & Perry, E. S. (1988). Effects of therapist response modes in brief psychotherapy. *Journal of Counseling Psychology, 35,* 222–233.

Hirschfeld, R. M. A., & Klerman, G. L. (1979). Personality attributes and affective disorders. *American Journal of Psychiatry, 136,* 67–70.

Hirschfeld, R. M. A., Klerman, G. L., Clayton, P. J., & Keller, M. B. (1983). Personality and depression. Empirical findings. *Archives of General Psychiatry, 40,* 993–998.

Hirschfeld, R. M. A., Klerman, G. L., Clayton, P. J., Keller, M. B., McDonald-Scott, P., & Larkin, B. H. (1983). Assessing personality: Effects of the depressive state on trait measurement. *American Journal of Psychiatry, 140,* 695–699.

Hirschfeld, R. M. A., Klerman, G. L., Gough, H. G., Barrett, J., Korchin, S. J., & Chodoff, P. (1977). A measure of interpersonal dependency. *Journal of Personality Assessment, 41,* 610–618.

Hirschfeld, R. M. A., Klerman, G. L., Lavori, P., Keller, M. B., Griffith, P., & Coryell, W. (1989). Premorbid personality assessment of first onset major depression. *Archives of General Psychiatry, 46,* 345–350.

Hobson, J. A., & McCarley, R. W. (1977). The brain as a dream state generator: An activation-synthesis hypothesis of the dream process. *American Journal of Psychiatry, 134,* 1335–1348.

Hoelscher, T. J., Klinger, E., & Barta, S. G. (1981). Incorporation of concern- and nonconcern-related verbal stimuli into dream content. *Journal of Abnormal Psychology, 90,* 88–91.

Hoffman, A. J. (1975). *The Freudian theory of the relationship between paranoid and repressed homosexual wishes in women.* Unpublished doctoral dissertation, Case Western Reserve University, Cleveland, OH.

Hoglend, P., Engelstad, V., Sorbye, O., & Heyerdahl, O. (in press). The role of insight in exploratory dynamic psychotherapy. *British Journal of Medical Psychology.*

Hoglend, P., Sorbye, O., Sorlie, T., Fossum, A., & Engelstad, V. (1992). Selection criteria for brief dynamic psychotherapy: Reliability, factor structure and long-term predictive validity. *Psychotherapy and Psychosomatics, 57,* 67–74.

Hoglend, P., Sorlie, T., Heyerdahl, O., Sorbye, O., & Amlo, S. (1993). Brief dynamic psychotherapy: Patient suitability, treatment length, and outcome. *Journal of Psychotherapy Practice and Research, 2,* 230–241.

Hollander, M. H., Luborsky, L., & Harvey, R. B. (1970). Correlates of the desire to be held in women. *Journal of Psychosomatic Research, 14,* 387–390.

Holmes, D. (1968). Dimensions of projection. *Psychological Bulletin, 69,* 248–268.

Holmes, D. (1978). Projection as a defense mechanism. *Psychological Bulletin, 85,* 677–688.

Holmes, D. (1981). Existence of classical projection and the stress-reducing function of attributive projection: A reply to Sherwood. *Psychological Bulletin, 90,* 460–466.

Holt, R. R. (1975). Drive or wish? A reconsideration of the psychoanalytic theory of motivation. In M. M. Gill & P. S. Holtzman (Eds.), *Psychology vs. metapsychology: Psychoanalytic essays in honor of George S. Klein* (p. 182). New York: International Universities Press.

Holt, R. R. (1991). *Freud reappraised: A fresh look at psychoanalytic theory.* New York: Guilford.

Holtzman, W. H., Thorpe, J. S., Swartz, J. D., & Herron, E. W. (1961). *Inkblot perception and personality.* Austin: University of Texas Press.

Hooley, J. M., & Richters, J. E. (1992). Allure of self-confirmation. A comment on Swann, Wenzlaff, Krull, and Pelham. *Journal of Abnormal Psychology, 101,* 307–309.

Hornstein, G. A. (1992). Psychology's problematic relations with psychoanalysis, 1909–1960. *American Psychologist, 47,* 254–263.

Horowitz, L., Rosenberg, S. E., & Kalehzan, B. M. (1992). The capacity to describe other people clearly: A predictor of interpersonal problems in brief dynamic psychotherapy. *Psychotherapy Research, 2,* 37–51.

Horowitz, M. J., Marmar, C. R., Weiss, D. S., DeWitt, K. N., & Rosenbaum, R. (1984). Brief psychotherapy of bereavement reactions: The relationship of process to outcome. *Archives of General Psychiatry, 41,* 438–448.

Horvath, A. O., & Symonds, D. B. (1991). Relationship between working alliance and outcome in psychotherapy: A meta-analysis. *Journal of Counseling Psychology, 38,* 139–149.

Horvath, P. (1988). Placebos and common factors in two decades of psychotherapy research. *Psychological Bulletin, 104,* 214–225.

Hoult, T. F. (1984). Human sexuality in biological perspective: Theoretical and methodological considerations. *Journal of Homosexuality, 9,* 137–155.

Howard, K. I., Kopta, S. M., Krause, M. J., & Orlinsky, D. E. (1986). The dose-effect relationship in psychotherapy. *American Psychologist, 41,* 159–164.

Howarth, E. (1980). A test of some old concepts by means of some new scales: Anality or psychoticism, oral optimism or extraversion, oral pessimism or neuroticism. *Psychological Reports, 47,* 1039–1042.

Howarth, E. (1981). Comment on Kline's note on "A test of some old concepts by means of some new scales." *Psychological Reports, 49,* 178.

Howarth, E. (1982). Factor analytic examination of Kline's scales for psychoanalytic concepts. *Personality and Individual Differences, 3,* 89–92.

Howe, M., & Summerfield, A. B. (1979). Orality and smoking. *British Journal of Medical Psychology, 52,* 85–90.

Hoyt, M. F. (1979a). An experimental study of the thematic structure of primal-scene imagery. *Journal of Abnormal Psychology, 88,* 96–100.

Hoyt, M. F. (1979b). Primal-scene experiences: Quantitative assessment of an interview study. *Archives of Sexual Behavior, 8,* 225–245.

Hoyt, M. F. (1979c). Primal-scene reactions: Accounts of firsthand experiences. *Bulletin of the Menninger Clinic, 43,* 424–442.

Humphrey, L. L. (1986). Structural analysis of parent–child relationships in eating disorders. *Journal of Abnormal Psychology, 95,* 395–402.

Hunt, H. T. (1989). *The multiplicity of dreams: Memory, imagination, and consciousness.* New Haven, CT: Yale University Press.

Husby, R. (1985). Short-term dynamic psychotherapy: A 5-year follow-up of 36 neurotic patients. *Psychotherapy and Psychosomatics, 43,* 17–22.

Hyman, H. T. (1936). The value of psychoanalysis as a therapeutic procedure. *Journal of the American Medical Association, 107,* 326–329.

Ihilevich, D., & Gleser, G. C. (1986). *Defense mechanisms: Their classification, correlates, and measurement with the Defense Mechanism Inventory.* Owasco, MI: DMI Associates.

Imber, R. (1969). *An experimental study of the Oedipus complex.* Unpublished doctoral dissertation, Rutgers University, New Brunswick, NJ.

Ingram, R. E. (1990a). Depressive cognition: Models, mechanisms and methods. In R. E. Ingram (Ed.), *Contemporary psychological approaches to depression* (pp. 169–195). New York: Plenum.

Ingram, R. E. (1990b). Self-focused attention in clinical disorders: Review and conceptual model. *Psychological Bulletin, 107,* 156–176.

Jackson, J. (1983). *The effects of fantasies of oneness with mother and father on the ego functioning of male and female schizophrenics.* Unpublished doctoral dissertation, New York University.

Jacobs, M. A., & Warner, B. L. (1981). Interaction of therapeutic attitudes with severity of clinical diagnosis. *Journal of Clinical Psychology, 37,* 75–82.

Jacobsson, S., Fasman, J., & DiMascio, A. (1975). Deprivation in the childhood of depressed women. *Journal of Nervous and Mental Disease, 160,* 5–14.

Jacoby, L. L., Lindsay, D. S., & Toth, J. P. (1992). Unconscious influences revealed: Attention. *American Psychologist, 47,* 802–809.

Jamison, K., & Comrey, A. L. (1968). Further study of dependence as a personality factor. *Psychological Reports, 22,* 239–242.

Jedlicka, D. (1980). A test of the psychoanalytic theory of mate selection. *Journal of Social Psychology, 112,* 295–299.

Jedlicka, D. (1984). Indirect parental influence on mate selection: A test of the psychoanalytic theory. *Journal of Marriage and the Family, 46,* 65–70.

Jensen, J. P., & Bergin, A. E. (1988). Mental health values of professional therapists: A national interdisciplinary survey. *Professional Psychology: Research and Practice, 19,* 290–297.

Joffe, R. T., & Regan, J. J. (1988). Personality and depression. *Journal of Psychiatric Research, 22,* 279–286.

Johnson, C. P. (1973). *Oral dependence and its relationship to field dependence and dependent behavior in same and mixed sex pairs.* Unpublished doctoral dissertation, State University of New York, Buffalo.

Johnson, D. H., & Gelso, C. J. (1980). The effectiveness of time limits in counseling and psychotherapy. *The Counseling Psychologist, 9,* 70–83.

Johnson, J. A., & Ostendorf, F. (1993). Clarification of the five factor model with the abridged big five dimensional circumplex. *Journal of Personality and Social Psychology, 65,* 563–576.

Jones, E. (1926–1936). Report of the clinic work (London Clinic of Psychoanalysis). *The life and work of Sigmund Freud* (Vols. 1–3). New York: Basic Books.

Jones, E. E. (1993). Introduction to special section: Single-case research in psychotherapy. *Journal of Consulting and Clinical Psychology, 61,* 371–372.

Jones, R. L. (1989). *The empirical validity of psychoanalytic interpretations of premenstrual symptomatology.* Unpublished master's thesis, State University of New York, Buffalo.

Jones, R. L. (1991). *An empirical study of Freud's penis-baby equation and literal versus metaphorical interpretations of penis envy.* Unpublished doctoral dissertation, State University of New York, Buffalo.

Jones, R. L. (1994). An empirical study of Freud's penis–baby equation. *Journal of Nervous and Mental Disease, 182,* 127–135.

Joyce, A. S. (1991). *Concentration and correspondence of transference interpretations in short-term individual psychotherapy.* Paper presented at the annual meeting of the Society for Psychotherapy Research, Lyon, France.

Joyce, A. S. (1992). *Assessing the correspondence of interpretation with the therapist's initial problem formulation.* Paper presented at the annual convention of the Society for Psychotherapy Research, Berkeley, CA.

Juni, S. (1979). *Experimental studies of behavioral implications of oral and anal characterology.* Unpublished doctoral dissertation, State University of New York, Buffalo.

Juni, S. (1981a). Career choice and orality. *Journal of Vocational Behavior, 19,* 78–83.

Juni, S. (1981b). Maintaining anonymity vs. requesting feedback as a function of oral dependency. *Perceptual and Motor Skills, 52,* 239–242.

Juni, S. (1982). Humor preference as a function of preoedipal fixation. *Social Behavior and Personality, 10,* 63–64.

Juni, S. (1983). Food preference and orality. *Psychological Reports, 52,* 842.

Juni, S. (1984). The psychodynamics of disgust. *Journal of Genetic Psychology, 144,* 203–208.

Juni, S., & Fischer, R. E. (1986). Religiosity and preoedipal fixation. *Journal of Genetic Psychology, 146,* 27–35.

Juni, S., & Frenz, A. (1981). Psychosexual fixation and perceptual defense. *Perceptual and Motor Skills, 52,* 83–89.

Juni, S., & LoCascio, (1985). Preference for counseling and psychotherapy as related to preoedipal fixation. *Psychological Reports, 56,* 431–438.

Juni, S., Masling, J. M., & Brannon, R. (1979). Interpersonal touching and orality. *Journal of Personality Assessment, 43,* 235–237.

Juni, S., Nelson, S. P., & Brannon, R. (1987). Minor tonality music preference and oral dependency. *Journal of Psychology, 12,* 229–236.

Juni, S., Rahamin, E. L., & Brannon, R. (1984). Sex role development as a function of parent models and Oedipal fixation. *Journal of Genetic Psychology, 146,* 89–99.

Juni, S., & Rubenstein, V. (1982). Anality and routine. *Journal of Personality Assessment, 46,* 142.

Juni, S., & Semel, S. R. (1982). Person perception as a function of orality and anality. *Journal of Social Psychology, 118,* 99–103.

Kagan, J. (1980). Perspectives on continuity. In O. G. Brim & J. Kagan (Eds.), *Constancy and change in human development* (pp. 26–74). Cambridge, MA: Harvard University Press.

Kagan, J., & Moss, H. A. (1962). *Birth to maturity.* New York: Wiley.

Kardiner, A. (1977). *My analysis with Freud.* New York: Norton.

Karnilow, A. (1973). *A comparison of Oedipal and peer sex through the use of hypnotically implanted paramnesias.* Unpublished doctoral dissertation, Michigan State University, Lansing.

Karon, B. (1989). Psychotherapy versus medication for schizophrenia: Empirical comparisons. In S. Fisher & R. P. Greenberg (Eds.), *The limits of biological treatments for psychological distress* (pp. 105–150). Hillsdale, NJ: Erlbaum.

Katz, R., & McGuffin, P. (1987). Neuroticism in familial depression. *Psychological Medicine, 17,* 155–161.

Kay-Reczek, C. E. (1977). *The relationship between dominance and sexuality in college women.* Unpublished doctoral dissertation, University of Vermont and State Agricultural College, Burlington.

Kazdin, A., & Bass, D. (1989). Power to detect differences between alternate treatments in comparative psychotherapy outcome research. *Journal of Consulting and Clinical Psychology, 57,* 138–147.

Kehoe, P. (1977). *Psychological factors in the experience of premenstrual and menstrual symptomatology.* Unpublished doctoral dissertation, University of Texas, Austin.

Kendall, P. C., Kortlander, E., Chansky, T. E., & Brady, E. V. (1992). Comorbidity of anxiety and depression in youth: Treatment implications. *Journal of Consulting and Clinical Psychology, 60,* 869–880.

Kendell, R. E. (1970). Relationship between aggression and depression: Epidemiological implications of a hypothesis. *Archives of General Psychiatry, 22,* 308–318.

Kernberg, O. F., Burstein, E. D., Coyne, L., Appelbaum, A., Horwitz, L., & Voth, H. (1972). Psychotherapy and psychoanalysis. *Bulletin of the Menninger Clinic, 36,*(182), 1–178.

Kessel, L., & Hyman, H. T. (1933). The value of psychoanalysis as a therapeutic procedure. *Journal of the American Medical Association, 101,* 1612–1615.

Kihlstrom, J. F. (1987). The cognitive unconscious. *Science, 237,* 1445–1452.

Kihlstrom, J. F., Barnhardt, T. M., & Tataryn, D. J. (1992). The psychological unconscious: Found, lost, and regained. *American Psychologist, 47,* 788–791.

Kilner, L. A. (1988). Manifest content in dreams of Gussi and U.S. females: Social and sexual interactions, achievement and fortune. *Psychiatric Journal of the University of Ottawa, 13,* 79–84.

King, L. A., & Emmons, R. A. (1990). Conflict over emotional expression: Psychological and physical correlates. *Journal of Personality and Social Psychology, 58,* 864–877.

Kirk, S. A., & Kutchins, H. (1992). *The selling of DSM.* New York: Aldine de Gruyter.

Kirkpatrick, C. (1937). A statistical investigation of the psychoanalytic theory of mate selection. *Journal of Abnormal and Social Psychology, 32,* 427–430.

Kisch, J., & Kroll, J. (1980). Meaningfulness vs. effectiveness. *Psychotherapy: Theory, Research and Practice, 17,* 402–413.

Klein, D. N. (1989). The Depressive Experiences Questionnaire: A further evaluation. *Journal of Personality Assessment, 53,* 703–715.

Klein, D. N., Harding, K., Taylor, E. B., & Dickstein, S. (1988). Dependency and self-criticism in depression: Evaluation in a clinical population. *Journal of Abnormal Psychology, 97,* 399–404.

Klein, G. S. (1973). Two theories or one? *Bulletin of the Menninger Clinic, 37,* 102–132.

Klein, M. H., Kupfer, D. J., & Shea, M. T. (1993). *Personality and depression: A current view.* New York: Guilford.

Klein, M. H., Mathieu, P. L., Gendlin, E. T., & Kiesler, D. J. (1970). *The Experience Scale: A research and training manual.* Madison: Wisconsin Psychiatric Institute.

Klerman, G. L., & Gershon, E. S. (1970). Imipramine effects upon hostility in depression. *Journal of Nervous and Mental Disease, 150,* 127–132.

Klerman, G. L., Weissman, M. M., Rounsaville, B. J., & Chevron, E. S. (1984). *Interpersonal psychotherapy of depression.* New York: Basic Books.

Kline, P. (1969). The anal character: A cross-cultural study in Ghana. *British Journal of Social and Clinical Psychology, 8,* 201–210.

Kline, P. (1972). *Fact and fantasy in Freudian theory.* London: Methuen.

Kline, P. (1978). The status of the anal character: A methodological and empirical reply to Hill. *British Journal of Medical Psychology, 51,* 87–90.

Kline, P. (1979). Psychosexual personality traits, fixation, and neuroticism. *British Journal of Medical Psychology, 52,* 393–395.

Kline, P. (1981). *Fact and fantasy in Freudian theory* (2nd ed.). London: Methuen.

Kline, P. (1987). The experimental study of the psychoanalytic unconscious. *Personality and Social Psychological Bulletin, 13,* 363–378.

Kline, P., & Barrett, P. (1983). The factors in personality questionnaires among normal subjects. *Advances in Behavior Research and Therapy, 5,* 141–202.

Kline, P., & Storey, R. (1977). A factor analytic study of the oral character. *British Journal of Social and Clinical Psychology, 16,* 317–329.

Kline, P., & Storey, R. (1978a). The Dynamic Personality Inventory: What does it measure? *British Journal of Psychology, 69,* 375–383.

Kline, P., & Storey, R. (1978b). Oral personality traits and smoking. *Projective Psychology, 23,* 1–4.

Kline, P., & Storey, R. (1980). The etiology of the oral character. *Journal of Genetic Psychology, 136,* 85–94.

Knight, R. P. (1941). Evaluation of the results of psychoanalytic therapy. *American Journal of Psychotherapy, 98,* 434–446.

Kochanska, G. (1991). Socialization and temperament in the development of guilt and conscience. *Child Development, 62,* 1379–1392.

Kochanska, G. (1993). Toward a synthesis of parental socialization and child temperament in early development of conscience. *Child Development, 64,* 325–347.

Koestner, R., Franz, C. E., & Weinberger, J. (1990). The family origins of empathic concern: A 26-year longitudinal study. *Journal of Personality and Social Psychology, 58,* 709–717.

Koestner, R., Zuroff, D. C., & Powers, T. A. (1991). Family origins of adolescent self-criticism and its continuity into adulthood. *Journal of Abnormal Psychology, 100,* 191–197.

Kohlberg, L. (1966). A cognitive-developmental analysis of children's sex-role concepts and attitudes. In E. Maccoby (Ed.), *The development of sex differences* (pp. 82–173). Stanford, CA: Stanford University Press.

Kohlberg, L. (1984). *The psychology of moral development.* San Francisco: Harper & Row.

Kohut, H. (1977). *The restoration of the self.* New York: International Universities Press.

Kopta, S. M., Howard, K. I., Lowry, J. L., & Beutler, L. (1994). Patterns of symptomatic recovery in psychotherapy. *Journal of Consulting and Clinical Psychology, 62,* 1009–1016.

Koulack, D. (1993). Dreams and adaptation to contemporary stress. In A. Moffitt, M. Kramer, & R. Hoffmann (Eds.), *The functions of dreaming* (pp. 321–340). Albany: State University of New York Press.

Kramer, M. (1982). The psychology of the dream: Art or science? *Psychiatric Journal of the University of Ottawa, 7,* 87–100.

Kramer, M. (1993). The selective mood regulatory function of dreaming: An update and revision. In A. Moffit, M. Kramer, & R. Hoffman (Eds.), *The function of dreaming* (pp. 139–196). New York: State University of New York Press.

Krohn, A., & Mayman, M. (1974). Object representations in dreams and projective tests. *Bulletin of the Menninger Clinic, 38,* 445–460.

Kubie, L. S. (1965). The ontogeny of racial prejudice. *Journal of Nervous and Mental Disease, 141,* 265–273.

Kuiper, N. A., MacDonald, M. R., & Derry, P. A. (1983). Parameters of a depressive self-schema. In J. Suls & A. G. Greenwald (Eds.), *Psychological perspectives on the self* (Vol. 2, pp. 191–218). Hillsdale, NJ: Erlbaum.

Kumari, N., & Blackburn, I. M. (1992). How specific are negative automatic thoughts to a depressed population? An exploratory study. *British Journal of Medical Psychology, 65,* 167–176.

Lachmann, F. M., & Beebe, B. (1992). Reformulations of early development and transference: Implications for psychic structure formation. In J. W. Barron, M. N. Eagle, & D. L. Wolitzky (Eds.), *Interface of psychoanalysis and psychology* (pp. 133–153). Washington, DC: American Psychological Association.

Lambert, M. J., & Bergin, A. E. (1994). The effectiveness of psychotherapy. In S. L. Garfield & A. E. Bergin (Eds.), *Handbook of psychotherapy and behavior change: Fourth edition* (pp. 143–189). New York: Wiley.

Lambert, M. J., Shapiro, D. A., & Bergin, A. E. (1986). The effectiveness of psychotherapy. In S. L. Garfield & A. E. Bergin (Eds.), *Handbook of psychotherapy and behavior change: An empirical analysis* (pp. 157–212). New York: Wiley.

Landis, B. (1970). Ego boundaries. *Psychological Issues, 6*(Monograph No. 24).

Langer, E. J. (1975). The illusion of control. *Journal of Personality and Social Psychology, 32,* 311–328.

Lauer, C., Riemann, D., Lund, R., & Berger, M. (1987). Shortened REM latency: A consequence of psychological strain. *Psychophysiology, 24,* 263–271.

Layne, C. (1983). Painful truths about depressives' cognitions. *Journal of Clinical Psychology, 39,* 848–853.

Lazare, A., Klerman, G. L., & Armor, D. J. (1966). Oral, obsessive, and hysterical personality patterns. *Archives of General Psychiatry, 14,* 624–630.

Lazare, A., Klerman, G. L., & Armor, D. J. (1970). Oral, obsessive, and hysterical personality patterns: Replications of factor analysis in an independent sample. *Journal of Psychiatric Research, 7,* 275–279.

Lefcourt, H. M. (1982). *Locus of control: Current trends in theory and research.* Hillsdale, NJ: Erlbaum.

Lefkowitz, M. M., Eron, L. D., Walder, L. O., & Huesmann, L. R. (1977). Rejection and depression: Prospective and contemporaneous analyses. *Developmental Psychology, 20,* 776–785.

Lefkowitz, M. M., & Tesiny, E. P. (1984). Rejection and depression: Prospective and contemporaneous analyses. *Developmental Psychology, 20,* 776–785.

Lei, T. (1994). Being and becoming moral in a Chinese culture: Unique or universal. *Cross-Cultural Research, 28,* 58–91.

Lemaire, T. E., & Clopton, J. R. (1981). Expressions of hostility in mild depression. *Psychological Reports, 48,* 259–262.

Leon, G. R., Gillum, B., Gillum, R., & Gouze, M. (1979). Personality stability and change over a 30-year period—Middle age to old age. *Journal of Consulting and Clinical Psychotherapy, 47,* 517–524.

LeVay, S. (1993). *The sexual brain.* Cambridge, MA: MIT Press.

Levin, R. (1990). Psychoanalytic theories on the function of dreaming: A review of the empirical literature. In J. Masling (Ed.), *Empirical studies of psychoanalytic theories* (Vol. 3, pp. 1–53). Hillsdale, NJ: Analytic Press.

Levin, R. B. (1966). An empirical test of the female castration complex. *Journal of Abnormal Psychology, 71,* 181–188.

Levinson, D. (1977). What have we learned from cross-cultural surveys? *American Behavioral Scientist, 20,* 757–792.

Levit, D. B. (1991). Gender differences in ego defense in adolescence. *Journal of Personality and Social Psychology, 61,* 992–999.

Lewicki, P., Hill, T., & Czyzewska, M. (1992). Nonconscious acquisition of information. *American Psychologist, 47,* 796–801.

Lewin, I., & Glaubman, H. (1975). The effect of REM deprivation: Is it detrimental, beneficial, or neutral? *Psychophysiology, 12,* 349–353.

Lewinsohn, P. M., & Rosenbaum, M. (1987). Recall of parental behavior by acute depressives, remitted depressives, and nondepressives. *Journal of Personality and Social Psychology, 52,* 611–619.

Lewis, C. C. (1990). The effects of parental firm control: A reinterpretation of findings. *Psychological Bulletin, 90,* 547–563.

Lewis, H. B. (1987). Shame and the narcissistic personality. In D. L. Nathanson (Ed.), *The many faces of shame* (pp. 93–132). New York: Guilford.

Lewis, M., Feiring, C., McGuffog, C., & Jaskir, J. (1984). Predicting psychopathology in six-year-olds from early social relations. *Child Development, 55,* 123–136.

Lewis, S. A. (1969). *Experimental induction of castration anxiety and anxiety over loss of love.* Unpublished doctoral dissertation, Yeshiva University, New York, NY.

Lifton, P. D. (1985). Individual differences in moral development. *Journal of Personality, 53,* 306–334.

Lindzey, G., Tehessy, C., & Zamansky, H. S. (1958). Thematic Apperception Test: An empirical examination of some ideas of homosexuality. *Journal of Abnormal Psychology, 57,* 67–75.

Loch, W. (1977). Some comments on the subject of psychoanalysis and truth. In J. Smith (Ed.), *Thought, consciousness and reality* (pp. 217–255). New Haven, CT: Yale University Press.

Loftus, E. F. (1993). The reality of repressed memories. *American Psychologist, 5,* 518–537.

Loftus, E. F., & Klinger, M. R. (1992). Is the unconscious smart or dumb? *American Psychologist, 47,* 761–765.

Londerville, S., & Martin, M. (1981). Security of attachment, compliance, and maternal training methods in the second year of life. *Developmental Psychology, 17,* 289–299.

London, P. (1964). *The modes and morals of psychotherapy.* New York: Holt, Rinehart & Winston.

Luborsky, L. (1977). Measuring a pervasive psychic structure in psychotherapy: The Core Conflictual Relationship Theme. In N. Freedman & S. Grand (Eds.), *Communicative structures and psychic structures.* New York: Plenum.

Luborsky, L. (1984). *Principles of psychoanalytic psychotherapy: A manual for supportive-expressive treatment.* New York: Basic Books.

Luborsky, L., & Auerbach, A. H. (1969). The symptom–context method. *Journal of the American Psychoanalytic Association, 17,* 68–99.

Luborsky, L., Bachrach, H., Graff, H., Pulver, S., & Christoph, P. (1979). Preconditions and consequences of transference interpretations: A clinical-quantitative investigation. *Journal of Nervous and Mental Disease, 169,* 391–401.

Luborsky, L., & Barber, J. P. (1993). Benefits of adherence to psychotherapy manuals, and where to get them. In N. E. Miller, L. Luborsky, J. P. Barber, & J. P. Docherty (Eds.), *Psychodynamic treatment research: A handbook for clinical practice* (pp. 211–226). New York: Basic Books.

Luborsky, L., Barber, J. P., & Crits-Christoph, P. (1990). Theory-based research for understanding the process of dynamic psychotherapy. *Journal of Consulting and Clinical Psychology, 58,* 281–287.

Luborsky, L., & Crits-Christoph, P. (1990). *Understanding transference. The Core Conflictual Relationship Theme method.* New York: Basic Books.

Luborsky, L., Crits-Christoph, P., Alexander, L., Margolis, M., & Cohen, M. (1983). Two helping alliance methods for predicting outcomes of psychotherapy. *Journal of Nervous and Mental Disease, 17,* 480–491.

Luborsky, L., Crits-Christoph, P., Mintz, J., & Auerbach, A. (1988). *Who will benefit from psychotherapy? Predicting therapeutic outcome.* New York: Basic Books.

Luborsky, L., Diguer, L., Luborsky, E., Singer, B., Dickter, D., & Schmidt, K. A. (1993). The efficacy of dynamic psychotherapies: Is it true that "Everyone has won and all must have prizes"? In N. E. Miller, L. Luborsky, J. P. Barber, & J. P. Docherty (Eds.), *Psychodynamic treatment research* (pp. 497–516). New York: Basic Books.

Luborsky, L., & Mintz, J. (1974). What sets off momentary forgetting during a psychoanalysis? *Psychoanalysis and Contemporary Science, 3,* 233–268.

Luborsky, L., Singer, B., & Luborsky, E. (1975). Comparative studies of psychotherapies: Is it true that "Everybody has won and all must have prizes"? *Archives of General Psychiatry, 32,* 995–1008.

Luborsky, L., & Spence, D. P. (1978). Quantitative research on psychoanalytic therapy. In S. L. Garfield & A. E. Bergin (Eds.), *Handbook of psychotherapy and behavioral change: An empirical analysis* (pp. 331–368). New York: Wiley.

Lund, D. A., Caserta, M. S., & Dimond, M. F. (1986). Gender differences through two years of bereavement among the elderly. *The Gerontologist, 26,* 314–319.

Lyketsos, G. C., Blackburn, I. M., & Tsiantis, J. (1978). The movement of hostility during recovery from depression. *Psychological Medicine, 8,* 145–149.

Lyness, S. A. (1993). Predictors of differences between Type A and B individuals in heart rate and blood pressure reactivity. *Psychological Bulletin, 114,* 266–295.

Maccoby, E. E., & Martin, J. (1983). Socialization in the context of the family. Parent–child interaction. In E. M. Hetherington (Ed.), *Handbook of child psychology: Socialization, personality, and social development* (Vol. 4, pp. 1–101). New York: Wiley.

MacEvoy, B., Lambert, W. W., Karlberg, P., Karlberg, J., Klackenberg-Larsson, I., & Klackenberg, G. (1988). Early affective antecedents of adult Type A behavior. *Journal of Abnormal and Social Psychology, 54,* 108–116.

Macmillan, M. (1991). *Freud evaluated: The completed arc.* Amsterdam: North-Holland.

Mahoney, M. J. (1991). *Human change processes: Theoretical bases for psychotherapy.* New York: Basic Books.

Mahoney, M. J., & Norcross, J. C. (1993). Relationship styles and therapeutic choices: A commentary. *Psychotherapy, 3,* 423–426.

Maiman, J. B. (1977). *Response to humor stimuli as a function of the obsessional defense.* Unpublished doctoral dissertation, California School of Professional Psychology, Los Angeles.

Malan, D. M. (1963). *A study of brief psychotherapy.* Springfield, IL: Thomas.

Malan, D. M. (1976). *Toward the validation of dynamic psychotherapy.* New York: Plenum.

Malinowski, B. (1927). *Sex and repression in savage society.* New York: Meridian Books.

Malinowski, B. (1929). *The sexual life of savages in North-Western Melanesia.* New York: Eugenic.

Mangus, A. R. (1936). Relationships between the young woman's conception of her intimate male associates and of her ideal husband. *Journal of Social Psychology, 7,* 403–420.

Marziali, E. (1984). Prediction of outcome of brief psychotherapy from therapist interpretive interventions. *Archives of General Psychiatry, 41,* 301–304.

Marziali, E., & Sullivan, J. (1980). Methodological issues in the content analysis of brief psychotherapy. *British Journal of Medical Psychology, 53,* 19–27.

Maser, J. D., & Cloninger, C. R. (Eds.). (1990). *Comorbidity of mood and anxiety disorders.* Washington, DC: American Psychiatric Press.

Masling, J. (Ed.). (1983a). *Empirical studies of psychoanalytic theories* (Vol. 1). Hillsdale, NJ: Erlbaum.

Masling, J. (1983b). Orality, pathology, and interpersonal behavior. In J. Masling (Ed.), *Empirical studies of psychoanalytic theories* (Vol. 2, pp. 73–106). Hillsdale, NJ: Erlbaum.

Masling, J. (Ed.). (1986). *Empirical studies of psychoanalytic theories* (Vol. 2). Hillsdale, NJ: Erlbaum.

Masling, J. (Ed.). (1990). *Empirical studies of psychoanalytic theories* (Vol. 3). Hillsdale, NJ: Erlbaum.

Masling, J., Johnson, C., & Saturansky, C. (1974). Oral imagery, accuracy of perceiving others, and performance in Peace Corps training. *Journal of Personality and Social Psychology, 30*, 414–419.

Masling, J., O'Neill, R., & Jayne, C. (1981). Orality and latency of volunteering to serve as experimental subjects. *Journal of Personality Assessment, 45*, 20–22.

Masling, J., O'Neill, R. M., & Katkin, E. S. (1982). Autonomic arousal, interpersonal climate and orality. *Journal of Personality and Social Psychology, 42*, 529–534.

Masling, J., Price, J., Goldband, S., & Katkin, E. S. (1981). Oral imagery and autonomic arousal in social isolation. *Journal of Personality and Social Psychology, 40*, 395–400.

Masling, J., Rabie, L., & Blondheim, S. H. (1967). Obesity, level of aspiration, and Rorschach and TAT measures of oral dependence. *Journal of Consulting Psychology, 31*, 233–239.

Masling, J., & Schwartz, M. (1979). A critique of research in psychoanalytic theory. *Genetic Psychology Monographs, 100*, 257–307.

Masling, J., Shiffner, J., & Shenfeld, M. (1980). Client perception of the counselor and orality. *Journal of Counseling Psychology, 27*, 294–298.

Masling, J., Weiss, L., & Rothschild, B. (1968). Relationships of oral imagery to yielding behavior and birth order. *Journal of Consulting and Clinical Psychology, 32*, 89–91.

Mathews, K. A. (1977). Caretaker-child interactions and the Type A coronary prone behavior patterns. *Child Development, 48*, 1752–1756.

Matussek, P., & Feil, W. B. (1983). Personality attributes of depressive patients. *Archives of General Psychiatry, 40*, 783–790.

Matussek, P., Molitor, G. A., & Seibt, G. (1985). Childhood experiences of endogenous and neurotic depressives. *European Archives of Psychiatry and Neurological Sciences, 235*, 12–20.

Mayman, M. (1967). Object-representation and object relationships in Rorschach responses. *Journal of Projective Techniques and Personality Assessment, 31*, 17–24.

Mayman, M. (1968). Early memories and character structure. *Journal of Projective Techniques and Personality Assessment, 32*, 303–306.

Mayo, P. R. (1967). Some psychological changes associated with improvement in depression. *British Journal of Social and Clinical Psychology, 6*, 63–68.

McAdams, D. P. (1992). The five-factor model in personality: A critical appraisal. *Journal of Personality, 60*, 329–361.

McClelland, D. (1961). *The achieving society.* Princeton, NJ: Van Nostrand.

McCrae, R. R., & John, O. P. (1992). An introduction to the five-factor model and its applications. *Journal of Personality, 60*, 175–215.

McCranie, E. W., & Bass, J. D. (1984). Childhood family antecedents of dependency and self-criticism: Implications for depression. *Journal of Abnormal Psychology, 93*, 3–8.

McCullough, L., Winston, A., Farber, B. A., Porter, F., Pollack, J., Laikin, M., Vingiano, W., & Trujillo, M. (1991). The relationship of patient–therapist interaction to outcome in brief psychotherapy. *Psychotherapy, 28*, 525–533.

McGrath, M. J., & Cohen, D. B. (1978). REM sleep facilitation of adaptive waking behavior. *Psychological Bulletin, 85,* 24–57.

McGrath, M. J., & Cohen, D. B. (1980). REM drive and function: A study of the interactive effects of personality and presleep condition. *Journal of Abnormal Psychology, 89,* 737–743.

McGuire, W. J., & McGuire, C. V. (1982). Significant others in self-space: Sex differences and developmental trends in the social self. In J. Suls (Ed.), *Psychological perspectives on the self* (Vol. 1, pp. 71–125). Hillsdale, NJ: Erlbaum.

McManus, J., Laughlin, C. D., & Shearer, J. (1993). In A. Moffit, M. Kramer, & R. Hoffmann (Eds.), *The functions of dreaming.* (pp. 21–50). Albany: State University of New York Press.

McNeilly, C. L., & Howard, K. I. (1991). The effects of psychotherapy: A reevaluation based on dosage. *Psychotherapy Research, 1,* 74–78.

Meehl, P. E. (1956). Wanted—A good cookbook. *American Psychologist, 11,* 262–272.

Meehl, P. E. (1962). Schizotaxia, schizotypy, schizophrenia. *American Psychologist, 17,* 827–838.

Melstrom, M. A., & Cartwright, R. D. (1983). Effects of successful vs. unsuccessful psychotherapy outcome on some dream dimensions. *Psychiatry, 46,* 51–64.

Meltzoff, J., & Kornreich, M. (1970). *Research in psychotherapy.* New York: Atherton Press.

Mendell, W. (1964). The phenomenon of interpretation. *American Journal of Psychoanalysis, 24,* 184–189.

Merikle, P. M. (1992). Perception without awareness: Critical issues. *American Psychologist, 47,* 792–795.

Miller, A. R. (1969). Analysis of the Oedipal complex. *Psychological Reports, 24,* 781–782.

Miller, J. G. (1994). Cultural diversity in the morality of caring: Individually oriented versus duty-based interpersonal moral codes. *Cross-Cultural Research, 28,* 3–39.

Miller, J. M. (1973). *The effects of aggressive stimulation upon young adults who have experienced the death of a parent during childhood and adolescence.* Unpublished doctoral dissertation, New York University.

Miller, R. C., & Berman, J. S. (1983). The efficacy of cognitive behavior therapies: A quantitative review of the research literature. *Psychological Bulletin, 94,* 39–53.

Miller, T. R. (1991). The psychotherapeutic utility of the five-factor model of personality: A clinician's experience. *Journal of Personality Assessment, 57,* 415–433.

Miller, W. B., & Smith, P. J. (1975). Elimination of the menses: Psychosocial aspects. *Journal of Psychiatric Research, 12,* 153–166.

Mills, J. K., & Cunningham, J. (1988). Oral character and attitude and behavior related to food and eating. *Psychological Reports, 63,* 15–18.

Minkowich, A. (1959). *Correlates of superego functions.* Unpublished doctoral dissertations, University of Michigan, Ann Arbor.

Mirowsky, J., & Ross, C. E. (1983). Paranoia and the structure of powerlessness. *American Sociological Review, 48*, 228–239.

Mischel, W., Shoda, Y., & Peake, P. K. (1988). The nature of adolescent competencies predicted by preschool delay of gratification. *Journal of Personality and Social Psychology, 54*, 687–696.

Modell, A. H., & Sacks, M. H. (1985). The Oedipus complex: A reevaluation. *Journal of the American Psychoanalytic Association, 33*, 201–216.

Moffitt, A., Kramer, M., & Hoffmann, R. (1993). *The functions of dreaming.* Albany: State University of New York Press.

Mongrain, M., & Zuroff, D. C. (1989). Cognitive vulnerability to depressed affect in dependent and self-critical college women. *Journal of Personality Disorders, 3*, 240–251.

Monroe, S. M., & Simms, A. D. (1991). Diathesis—stress theories in the context of life stress research: Implications for the depressive disorders. *Psychological Bulletin, 110*, 406–425.

Moore, B. E., & Fine, B. D. (Eds.). (1990). *Psychoanalytic terms and concepts.* New Haven, CT: American Psychoanalytic Association and Yale University Press.

Moore, T. W., & Paolillo, J. G. (1984). Depression: Influence of hopelessness, focus of control, hostility, and length of treatment. *Psychological Reports, 54*, 875–881.

Moreno, J. K., Fuhriman, A., & Selby, M. J. (1993). Measurement of hostility, anger, and depression in depressed and nondepressed subjects. *Journal of Personality Assessment, 61*, 511–523.

Morgan, R. W. (1977). *The relationships among therapeutic alliance, therapist facilitative behaviors, patient insight, patient resistance, and treatment outcome in psychoanalytically oriented psychotherapy.* Unpublished doctoral dissertation, University of Miami, Florida.

Morgan, R. W., Luborsky, L., Crits-Christoph, P., Curtis, H., & Solomon, J. (1982). Predicting the outcomes of psychotherapy using the Penn Helping Alliance rating method. *Archives of General Psychiatry, 39*, 397–402.

Motley, M. T. (1980). Verification of "Freudian slips" and semantic prearticulatory editing via laboratory-induced spoonerisms. In V. A. Fromkin (Ed.), *Errors in linguistic performance: Slips of the tongue, ear, pen, and hand* (pp. 133–147). New York: Academic Press.

Motley, M. T., & Baars, B. J. (1976). Semantic bias effects on the outcome of verbal slips. *Cognition, 4*, 177–187.

Murdock, G. P., & White, D. (1969). Standard cross-cultural sample. *Ethnology, 8*, 329–369.

Nasrillah, H. A., & Weinberger, D. R. (1986). *The neurology of schizophrenia.* New York: Elsevier.

Nathan, S. G. (1978). *Penis envy in cross-cultural perspective.* Unpublished doctoral dissertation, New York University.

Nathan, S. G. (1981). Cross-cultural perspectives on penis envy. *Psychiatry, 44*, 39–44.

Nelson, R. E., & Craighead, E. (1977). Selective recall of positive and negative feedback, self-control behaviors and depression. *Journal of Abnormal Psychology, 86*, 379–388.

Newcomb, M. D. (1984). Sexual behavior, responsiveness, and attitudes among women: A test of two theories. *Journal of Sex and Marital Therapy, 10*, 272–286.

Newman, R. S., & Hirt, M. (1983). The psychoanalytic theory of depression: Symptoms as a function of aggressive wishes and level of field articulation. *Journal of Abnormal Psychology, 92*, 42–48.

Newton, T. L., & Contrada, R. J. (1992). Repressive coping and verbal-autonomic response dissociation: The influence of social context. *Journal of Personality and Social Psychology, 62*, 159–167.

Nietzel, M. T., & Harris, M. J. (1990). Relationship of dependency and achievement/autonomy to depression. *Clinical Psychology Review, 10*, 279–297.

Noblin, C. D. (1962). *Experimental analysis of psychoanalytic character types through the operant conditioning of verbal responses*. Unpublished doctoral dissertation, Louisiana State University, Baton Rouge.

Noblin, C. D., Timmons, E. O., & Kael, H. C. (1966). Differential effects of positive and negative verbal reinforcement on psychoanalytic character types. *Journal of Personality and Social Psychology, 4*, 224–228.

Nolen-Hoeksema, S. (1987). Sex differences in unipolar depression: Evidence and theory. *Psychological Bulletin, 101*, 259–282.

Norcross, J. C. (1993). Tailoring relationship stances to client needs: An introduction. *Psychotherapy, 3*, 402–403.

Oberndorf, C. P., Greenacre, P., & Kubie, L. (1949). Symposium on the evaluation of therapeutic results. *Yearbook of Psychoanalysis, 5*, 9–34.

O'Connor, J. F., Daniels, G., Karush, A., Moses, L., Flood, C., & Stern, O. (1964). The effects of psychotherapy on the course of ulcerative colitis: A preliminary report. *American Journal of Psychiatry, 20*, 738–742.

O'Connor, L. E., Edelstein, S., Berry, J. W., & Weiss, J. (1994). Changes in the patients' level of insight in brief psychotherapy: Two pilot studies. *Psychotherapy, 31*, 533–544.

O'Dell, J. W. (1980). A re-examination of Finney's oral and anal characters. *Journal of General Psychology, 102*, 143–146.

Olds, D. E., & Schaver, P. (1980). Masculinity, femininity, academic performance, and health: Further evidence concerning the androgeny controversy. *Journal of Personality, 48*, 323–341.

Olinger, L. J., Kuiper, N. A., & Shaw, B. F. (1987). Dysfunctional attitudes and stressful life events: An interactive model of depression. *Cognitive Therapy and Research, 11*, 25–40.

Oliver, J. M., & Burkham, R. (1982). Subliminal psychodynamic activation in depression: A failure to replicate. *Journal of Abnormal Psychology, 91*, 337–342.

O'Malley, S. S., Chong, S. S., & Strupp, H. H. (1983). The Vanderbilt Psychotherapy Process Scale: A report on the scale development and process-outcome study. *Journal of Consulting and Clinical Psychology, 51*, 581–586.

Omer, H., & Dar, R. (1992). Changing trends in three decades of psychotherapy research: The flight from theory into pragmatics. *Journal of Consulting and Clinical Psychology, 60*, 88–93.

Omer, H., & London, P. (1988). Metamorphosis in psychotherapy: End of the systems era. *Psychotherapy, 25*, 171–180.

Omer, H., & London, P. (1989). Signal and noise in psychotherapy. The role and control of non-specific factors. *British Journal of Psychiatry, 155,* 239–245.

O'Neill, M. K., Lancee, W. J., & Freeman, S. J. (1987). Loss and depression. A controversial link. *Journal of Nervous and Mental Disease, 175,* 354–357.

O'Neill, R. M. (1984). Anality and Type A coronary-prone behavior pattern. *Journal of Personality Assessment, 48,* 627–628.

O'Neill, R. M., & Bornstein, R. F. (1990). Oral-dependence and gender: Factors in help-seeking response set and self-reported psychopathology in psychiatric inpatients. *Journal of Personality Assessment, 55,* 28–40.

O'Neill, R. M., & Bornstein, R. F. (1993). Orality and depression in psychiatric inpatients. *Journal of Personality Disorders, 5,* 1–7.

O'Neill, R. M., Greenberg, R. P., & Fisher, S. (1984). Orality and field dependence. *Psychoanalytic Psychology, 1,* 335–344.

O'Neill, R. M., Greenberg, R. P., & Fisher, S. (1992). Humor and anality. *Humor, 5,* 283–291.

Orgel, S. Z. (1958). Effect of psychoanalysis on the course of peptic ulcer. *Psychosomatic Medicine, 20,* 117–123.

Orlinsky, D. E., Grawe, K., & Parks, B. K. (1994). Process and outcome in psychotherapy—Noch einmal. In A. E. Bergin & S. L. Garfield (Eds.), *Handbook of psychotherapy and behavior change* (4th ed., pp. 270–376). New York: Wiley.

Orlinsky, D. E., & Howard, K. I. (1986). Process and outcome in psychotherapy. In S. L. Garfield & A. E. Bergin (Eds.), *Handbook of psychotherapy and behavior change* (pp. 311–384). New York: Wiley.

Osgood, C., Suci, G., & Tannenbaum, P. (1957). *The measurement of meaning.* Urbana: University of Illinois Press.

Ouimette, P. C., & Klein, D. N. (1993). Convergence of psychoanalytic and cognitive-behavioral theories of depression. In J. M. Masling & R. F. Bornstein (Eds.), *Psychoanalytic perspectives on psychopathology* (pp. 191–223). Hillsdale, NJ: Erlbaum.

Overholser, J., Kabakoff, R., & Norman, W. H. (1989). The assessment of personality characteristics in depressed and dependent psychiatric inpatients. *Journal of Personality Assessment, 53,* 40–50.

Palombo, S. (1978). *Dreaming and memory.* New York: Basic Books.

Palumbo, R., & Gillman, I. (1984). Effects of subliminal activation of Oedipal fantasies on competitive performance. *Journal of Nervous and Mental Disease, 172,* 737–741.

Parens, H. (1990). On the girl's psychosexual development: Reconsiderations suggested from direct observation. *Journal of the American Psychoanalytic Association, 38,* 743–772.

Parens, H., Polleck, L., Stern, J., & Kramer, S. (1976). On the girl's entry into the Oedipus complex. *Journal of the American Psychoanalytic Association, 24*(Suppl.), 79–107.

Parker, G. (1979). Parental characteristics in relation to depressive disorders. *British Journal of Psychiatry, 134,* 138–147.

Parker, G. (1984). The measurement of pathogenic parental style and its relevance to psychiatric disorder. *Social Psychiatry, 19,* 75–81.

Parker, G., Tripling, H., & Brown, L. B. (1979). A parental bonding instrument. *British Journal of Medical Psychology, 52*, 1–10.

Parloff, M. B. (1986). Placebo controls in psychotherapy research. A sine qua non or a placebo for research problems? *Journal of Consulting and Clinical Psychology, 54*, 79–87.

Patterson, C. H. (1984). Empathy, warmth, and genuiness in psychotherapy: A review of reviews. *Psychotherapy, 21*, 431–438.

Patton, C. J. (1992). Fear of abandonment and binge eating. A subliminal psychodynamic activation investigation. *Journal of Nervous and Mental Disease, 180*, 484–490.

Paul, G. L. (1967). Strategy of outcome research in psychotherapy. *Journal of Consulting Psychology, 31*, 109–119.

Paxton, A. L., & Turner, E. J. (1978). Self-actualization and sexual permissiveness, satisfaction, prudishness, and drive among female undergraduates. *Journal of Sex Research, 14*, 65–80.

Paykel, E. S., Klerman, G. L., & Prusoff, B. A. (1976). Personality and symptoms pattern in depression. *British Journal of Psychiatry, 129*, 327–334.

Paykel, E. S., Weissman, M., Prusoff, B. A., & Tonks, C. M. (1971). Dimensions of social adjustment in depressed women. *Journal of Nervous and Mental Disease, 152*, 158–172.

Pearlman, C. (1982). Sleep structure variation. In W. Webb (Ed.), *Biological rhythms, sleep, and performance* (pp. 143–173). London: Wiley.

Perris, C., Eisemann, M., von Knorring, L., & Perris, H. (1984). Personality traits in former depressed patients and in healthy subjects without past history of depression. *Psychopathology, 17*, 178–186.

Perry, J. C., & Cooper, S. H. (1989). An empirical study of defense mechanisms. *Archives of General Psychiatry, 46*, 444–452.

Peskin, H. (1973). Influence of the developmental schedule of puberty on learning and ego functioning. *Journal of Youth and Adolescence, 2*, 273–290.

Peterson, C., Luborsky, L., & Seligman, M. E. P. (1983). Attributions and depressive mood shifts: A case study using the symptom–context method. *Journal of Abnormal Psychology, 92*, 96–103.

Petty, R. E., & Brock, T. C. (1979). Effects of Barnum personality assessments on cognitive behavior. *Journal of Consulting and Clinical Psychology, 47*, 201–203.

Philip, A. E. (1971). Psychometric changes associated with response to drug treatment. *British Journal of Social and Clinical Psychology, 10*, 138–143.

Piaget, J. (1965). *The moral judgment of the child*. New York: Free Press.

Pilowsky, I. (1979). Personality and depressive illness. *Acta Psychiatrica Scandinavia, 60*, 170–176.

Pilowsky, I., & Katsikitis, M. (1983). Depressive illness and dependency. *Acta Psychiatrica Scandinavia, 68*, 11–14.

Pilowsky, I., & Spence, N. D. (1975). Hostility and depressive illness. *Archives of General Psychiatry, 32*, 1154–1165.

Piper, W. E. (1991). *Concentration, correspondence, therapeutic alliance, and therapy outcome*. Paper presented at the annual meeting of the Society for Psychotherapy Research, Lyon, France.

Piper, W. E., Azim, F. A., Joyce, S. A., & McCallum, M. (1991). Transference interpretations, therapeutic alliance and outcome in short-term individual psychotherapy. *Archives of General Psychiatry, 48,* 946–953.

Piper, W. E., Debbane, E. G., Bienvenu, J., Carufel, F., & Garant, J. (1986). Relationships between the object focus of therapist interpretations and outcome in short-term individual psychotherapy. *British Journal of Medical Psychology, 59,* 1–11.

Piper, W. E., Joyce, A. S., McCallum, M., & Azim, H. F. (1993). Concentration and correspondence of transference interpretations in short-term psychotherapy. *Journal of Consulting and Clinical Psychology, 61,* 586–595.

Piper, W. E., McCallum, M., Azim, H. F., & Joyce, A. S. (1993). Understanding of the relationship between transference interpretation and outcome in the context of other variables. *American Journal of Psychotherapy, 47,* 479–493.

Pledger, R. H., Jr. (1977). *Early parent-child relationships of male homosexuals and heterosexuals.* Unpublished doctoral dissertation, University of Texas, Austin.

Pollak, J. M. (1978). Relationships between psychoanalytic personality pattern, death anxiety, and self-actualization. *Perceptual and Motor Skills, 46,* 846.

Pollak, J. M. (1979). Obsessive–compulsive personality: A review. *Psychological Bulletin, 86,* 225–241.

Polombo, S. (1978). *Dreaming and memory.* New York: Basic Books.

Porter, F. A. (1987). *The immediate effects of interpretation on patient response in short-term dynamic psychotherapy.* Unpublished doctoral dissertation, Columbia University, New York.

Purcell, S., Moffitt, A., & Hoffman, R. (1993). Waking, dreaming, and self-regulation. In A. Moffitt, M. Kramer, & R. Hoffman (Eds.), *The functions of dreams* (pp. 197–260). Albany: State University of New York Press.

Pyszczynski, T., & Greenberg, J. (1987). Self-regulatory perseveration and the depressive self-focusing style: A self-awareness theory of reactive depression. *Psychological Bulletin, 102,* 122–138.

Pyszczynski, T., Hamilton, J. C., Herring, F. H., & Greenberg, J. (1989). Depression, self-focused attention, and the negative memory bias. *Journal of Personality and Social Psychology, 57,* 351–357.

Pyszczynski, T., Holt, K., & Greenberg, J. (1987). Depression, self-focused attention, and expectancies for positive and negative future life events for self and others. *Journal of Personality and Social Psychology, 52,* 994–1001.

Rabin, A. I. (1958). The Israeli kibbutz (collective settlement) as a laboratory for testing psychodynamic hypotheses. *Psychological Record, 7,* 111–115.

Radke-Yarrow, M., Zahn-Waxler, C., & Chapman, M. (1983). Children's prosocial dispositions and behavior. In E. M. Hetherington (Ed.), *Handbook of child psychology: Socialization, personality, and social development* (Vol. 4, pp. 775–912). New York: Wiley.

Rados, R., & Cartwright, R. D. (1982). Where do dreams come from? A comparison of presleep and REM sleep thematic content. *Journal of Abnormal Psychology, 91,* 433–436.

Rangell, L. (1954). Similarities and differences between psychoanalysis and dynamic psychotherapy. *Journal of the American Psychoanalytic Association, 2,* 734–744.

Rangell, L. (1981). Psychoanalysis and dynamic psychotherapy: Similarities and differences twenty-five years later. *Psychoanalytic Quarterly, 50,* 665–693.

Rapaport, C. (1963). *Character, anxiety, and social affiliation.* Unpublished doctoral dissertation, New York University.

Raulin, M. L. (1984). Development of a scale to measure intense ambivalence. *Journal of Consulting and Clinical Psychology, 52,* 63–72.

Reich, J., Noyes, R., Hirschfeld, R., Coryell, W., & O'Gorman, T. (1987). State and personality in depressed and panic patients. *American Journal of Psychiatry, 144,* 181–187.

Reid, J., & Finesinger, J. (1952). The role of insight in psychotherapy. *American Journal of Psychiatry, 108,* 726–734.

Rest, J. R. (1979). *Development in judging moral issues.* Minneapolis: University of Minnesota.

Reyher, J. (1958). *Hypnotically induced conflict in relation to subception, repression, antisocial behavior and psychosomatic reactions.* Unpublished doctoral dissertation, University of Illinois, Urbana.

Richman, J. A., & Flaherty, J. (1985). Coping and depression. The relative contribution of internal and external resources during a life cycle transition. *Journal of Nervous and Mental Disease, 173,* 590–595.

Richman, J. A., & Flaherty, J. A. (1986). Childhood relationships, adult coping resources and depression. *Social Science and Medicine, 23,* 709–716.

Richman, J. A., & Flaherty, J. A. (1987). Adult psychosocial assets and depressive mood over time. Effects of internalized childhood attachments. *Journal of Nervous and Mental Disease, 175,* 703–712.

Ricoeur, P. (1974). *Hermeneutics and the human sciences.* (J. B. Thompson, Trans.) New York: Cambridge University Press.

Riley, W. T., & Treiber, F. A. (1989). The validity of multidimensional self-report anger and hostility measures. *Journal of Clinical Psychology, 45,* 397–404.

Riley, W. T., Treiber, F. A., & Woods, M. G. (1989). Anger and hostility in depression. *Journal of Nervous and Mental Disease, 177,* 668–674.

Rizley, R. (1978). Depression and distortion in the attribution of causality. *Journal of Abnormal Psychology, 87,* 32–48.

Roback, H. B. (1974). Insight: A bridging of the theoretical and research literatures. *Canadian Psychologist, 15,* 61–88.

Robbins, P. R., & Tanck, R. H. (1978). The dream incident technique as a measure of unresolved problems. *Journal of Personality Assessment, 42,* 583–591.

Robbins, P. R., Tanck, R. H., & Farzaneh, H. (1985). Anxiety and dream symbolism. *Journal of Personality, 53,* 18–22.

Robins, C. J. (1990). Congruence of personality and life events in depression. *Journal of Abnormal Psychology, 99,* 393–397.

Robins, C. J., & Block, P. (1988). Personal vulnerability, life events, and depressive symptoms: A test of a specific interactional model. *Journal of Personality and Social Psychology, 54,* 847–852.

Robinson, L. A., Berman, J. S., & Neimeyer, R. A. (1990). Psychotherapy for the treatment of depression: A comprehensive review of controlled outcome research. *Psychological Bulletin, 108,* 30–49.

Rogers, R., & Wright, E. W. (1975). Behavioral rigidity and its relationship to authoritarianism. *Perceptual & Motor Skills, 40,* 802.

Rohner, R. P. (1975). *They love me, they love me not.* Human Relations Area Files, Inc.

Rosenberg, H. (1993). Prediction of controlled drinking by alcoholics and problem drinkers. *Psychological Bulletin, 113,* 129–139.

Rosenfarb, I. S., Becker, J., Khan, A., & Mintz, J. (1994). Dependency, self-criticism, and perceptions of socialization experiences. *Journal of Abnormal Psychiatry, 103,* 669–675.

Rosenthal, R. (1966). *Experimenter effects in behavioral research.* New York: Appleton-Century-Crofts.

Rosenwald, G. C. (1972). Effectiveness of defenses against anal impulse arousal. *Journal of Consulting and Clinical Psychology, 39,* 292–298.

Rosenzweig, S. (1936). Some implicit common factors in diverse methods of psychotherapy. *American Journal of Orthopsychiatry, 6,* 412–415.

Ross, M., & Conway, M. (1986). Remembering one's own past: The construction of personal histories. In R. M. Sorrentino & E. T. Higgins (Eds.), *Handbook of motivation and cognition: Foundations of social behavior* (pp. 122–144). New York: Wiley.

Rossi, A. S., & Rossi, P. E. (1977). Body time and social time: Mood patterns by menstrual cycle phase and day of the week. *Social Science Research, 6,* 273–308.

Rotenberg, V. S. (1993). REM sleep and dreams as mechanisms of the recovery of search activity. In A. Moffit, M. Kramer, & R. Hoffmann (Eds.), *The function of dreaming* (pp. 261–292). Albany: State University of New York Press.

Rubin, D. M. (1986). *Client expression of hostility in psychotherapy.* Unpublished doctoral dissertation, Michigan State University, East Lansing.

Ruse, M. (1981). Medicine as social science: The case of Freud on homosexuality. *Journal of Medicine and Philosophy, 6,* 361–386.

Rutstein, E. H., & Goldberger, L. (1973). The effects of aggressive stimulation on suicidal patients. An experimental study of the psychoanalytic theory of suicide. In B. B. Rubenstein (Ed.), *Psychoanalysis and contemporary science* (pp. 157–174). New York: Macmillan.

Ryle, A. (1984). How can we compare different psychotherapies? Why are they all effective? *British Journal of Medical Psychology, 57,* 261–264.

Sackeim, H. A., & Gur, R. C. (1979). Self-deception, other-deception, and self-reported psychopathology. *Journal of Consulting and Clinical Psychology, 47,* 213–215.

Sadeh, A., Rubin, S. S., & Berman, E. (1993). Parental and relationship representations and experiences of depression in college students. *Journal of Personality Assessment, 60,* 192–204.

Sammons, M. T., & Gravitz, M. A. (1990). Theoretical orientations of professional psychologists and their former professors. *Professional Psychology: Research and Practice, 21*, 131–134.

Sandler, J., & Hazari, A. (1960). The "Obsessional":On the psychological classification of obsessional character traits and symptoms. *British Journal of Medical Psychology, 33*, 113–122.

Sands, S. H. (1981). *Child-rearing styles of parents of paranoid and nonparanoid schizophrenic patients.* Unpublished doctoral dissertation, University of California, Berkely.

Schafer, R. (1976). *A new language for psychoanalysis.* New Haven, CT: Yale University Press.

Schaie, K. W. (1955). A test of behavioral rigidity. *Journal of Abnormal and Social Psychology, 51*, 604–610.

Schaie, K. W. (Ed.). (1983). *Longitudinal studies of adult psychological development.* New York: Guilford.

Schick, J., Arnold, J. D., & Tomedi, J. (1984, March). *Anality and the Type A behavior pattern: A suggestion for research and intervention programs.* Paper presented at the annual meeting of the Eastern Psychological Association.

Schless, A. P., Mendels, J., Kipperman, A., & Cochrane, C. (1974). Depression and hostility. *Journal of Nervous and Mental Disease, 159*, 91–100.

Schill, T. (1966). Sex differences in identification of the castrating agent on the Blacky Test. *Journal of Clinical Psychology, 22*, 324–325.

Schiller, B. (1932). A quantitative analysis of marriage selection in a small group. *Journal of Social Psychology, 3*, 297–318.

Schjelderup, H. (1955). Lasting effects of psychoanalytic treatment. *Psychiatry, 18*, 103–133.

Schless, A. P., Mendels, J., Kipperman, A., & Cochrane, C. (1974). Depression and hostility. *Journal of Nervous and Mental Disease, 159*, 91–100.

Schneider, S. C. S. (1960). *An analysis of presurgical anxiety in boys and girls.* Unpublished doctoral dissertation, University of Michigan, Ann Arbor.

Schofer, G., Koch, U., & Balck, F. (1979). The Gottschalk-Gleser content analysis of speech: A normative study. In L. A. Gottschalk (Ed.), *The content analysis of verbal behavior—Further studies* (pp. 95–118). New York: SP Medical and Scientific Books.

Schumacher, C. M. (1988). *An empirical exploration of the Oedipus complex.* Unpublished doctoral dissertation, University of Detroit, Detroit.

Schwartz, J. C., & Zuroff, D. C. (1979). Family structure and depression in female college students: Effects of parental conflict, decision-making power, and inconsistency of love. *Journal of Abnormal Psychology, 88*, 398–406.

Sears, R. R. (1943). *Survey of objective studies of psychoanalytic concepts.* New York: Social Science Research Council.

Sears, R. R., Maccoby, E. E., & Levin, H. (1957). *Patterns of child rearing.* Evanston, IL: Row-Peterson.

Segal, Z. V., Shaw, B. F., & Vella, D. D. (1989). Life stress and depression: A test of the congruency hypothesis for life event content and depressive subtype. *Canadian Journal of Behavioral Science, 21,* 389–400.

Segal, Z. V., Shaw, B. F., Vella, D. D., & Katz, R. (1992). Cognitive and life stress predictors of relapse in remitted unipolar depressed patients: Test of the congruency hypothesis. *Journal of Abnormal Psychology, 101,* 26–36.

Seligman, M. E. (1975). Helplessness: *On depression, development, and death.* San Francisco: Freeman.

Senger, H. L. (1987). The "placebo" effect of psychotherapy: A moose in the rabbit stew. *American Journal of Psychotherapy, 41,* 68–95.

Sethi, B. B. (1964). Relationship of separation to depression. *Archives of General Psychiatry, 110,* 486–496.

Shadish, W., & Sweeney, R. (1991). Mediators and moderations and meta-analysis: There's a reason we don't let Dodo birds tell us which psychotherapies should have prizes. *Journal of Consulting and Clinical Psychology, 59,* 883–893.

Shakow, D., & Rapaport, D. (1964). *The influence of Freud on American psychology.* (*Psychological Issues, 4,* Monograph No. 13). New York: International Universities Press.

Shapiro, D. A. (1985). Recent applications of meta-analysis in clinical research. *Clinical Psychological Review, 5,* 13–34.

Shapiro, D. A., & Shapiro, D. (1982). Meta-analysis of comparative therapy outcome studies: A replication and refinement. *Psychological Bulletin, 92,* 581–604.

Sherwood, G. (1979). Classical and attributive projection: Some new evidence. *Journal of Abnormal Psychology, 88,* 635–640.

Sherwood, G. (1982). Consciousness and stress reduction in defensive projection: A reply to Holmes. *Psychological Bulletin, 91,* 372–375.

Shevrin, H. (1984). The fate of the five metapsychological principles. *Psychoanalytic Inquiry, 4,* 33–58.

Shevrin, H., & Dickman, S. (1980). The psychological unconscious: A necessary assumption for all psychological theory. *American Psychologist, 35,* 421–434.

Shilkret, C. J., & Masling, J. (1981). Oral dependence and dependent behavior. *Journal of Personality Assessment, 45,* 125–129.

Shill, M. (1981a). Castration fantasies and assertiveness in father-absent males. *Psychiatry, 44,* 263–272.

Shill, M. (1981b). TAT measures of gender identity (castration anxiety) in father-absent males. *Journal of Personality Assessment, 45,* 136–146.

Siegel, J. S. (1985). The measurement of anger as a multidimensional construct. In M. A. Chesney & R. H. Rosemman (Eds.), *Anger and hostility in cardiovascular and behavioral disorders* (pp. 59–82). New York: Hemisphere.

Silberschatz, G., Fretter, P. B., & Curtis, J. T. (1986). How do interpretations influence the process of psychotherapy? *Journal of Consulting and Clinical Psychology, 54,* 646–652.

Silver, R. L., & Wortman, C. B. (1980). Coping with undesirable life events. In J. Garber & M. E. P. Seligman (Eds.), *Human helplessness: Theory and applications* (pp. 279–340). New York: Academic Press.

Silverman, D. K. (1986). Some proposed modifications of psychoanalytic theories of early child development. In J. Masling (Ed.), *Empirical studies of psychoanalytic theories* (pp. 49–72). Hillsdale, NJ: Analytic Press.

Silverman, L. H. (1982). A comment on two subliminal psychodynamic activation studies. *Journal of Abnormal Psychology, 91,* 126–130.

Silverman, L. H. (1983). The psychodynamic activation method: Overview and comprehensive listing of studies. In J. Masling (Ed.), *Empirical studies of psychoanalytic theories* (Vol. 1, pp. 69–100). Hillsdale, NJ: Erlbaum.

Silverman, L. H., Bronstein, A., & Mendelsohn, E. (1976). The further use of the psychodynamic activation method for the experimental study of the clinical theory of psychoanalysis: On the specificity of the relationship between symptoms and unconscious conflicts. *Psychotherapy: Theory, Research and Practice, 13,* 2–16.

Silverman, L. H., Kwawer, J. S., Wolitzky, C., & Coron, M. (1973). An experimental study of aspects of the psychoanalytic theory of male homosexuality. *Journal of Abnormal Psychology, 82,* 178–188.

Silverman, L. H., Lachman, F. M., & Milich, R. H. (1982). *The search for oneness.* New York: International Universities Press.

Silverman, L. H., Ross, D. L., Adler, J. M., & Lustig, D. A. (1978). Simple research paradigm for demonstrating subliminal activation effects: Effects of Oedipal stimuli on dart-throwing accuracy in college males. *Journal of Abnormal Psychology, 87,* 341–357.

Singer, J. L. (1990). *Repression and dissociation.* Chicago: University of Chicago Press.

Sjoback, H. (1988). *The Freudian learning hypotheses.* Lund, Sweden: Lund University Press.

Slade, A., & Aber, J. L. (1992). Attachments, drives, and development: Conflicts and convergences in theory. In J. W. Barron, M. N. Eagle, & D. L. Wolitzky (Eds.), *Interface of psychoanalysis and psychology* (pp. 154–185). Washington, DC: American Psychological Association.

Slipp, S., & Nissenfeld, S. (1981). An experimental study of psychoanalytic theories of depression. *Journal of the American Academy of Psychoanalysis, 9,* 583–600.

Smith, M. L., & Glass, G. V. (1977). Meta-analysis of psychotherapy outcome studies. *American Psychologist, 32,* 752–760.

Smith, M. L., Glass, G. V., & Miller, T. I. (1980). *The benefits of psychotherapy.* Baltimore, MD: Johns Hopkins Press.

Smith, R. C. (1986). Studying the meaning of dreams: Accurate definition of the independent variable. *Biological Psychiatry, 21,* 989–996.

Smith, R. C. (1987). Do dreams reflect a biological state? *Journal of Nervous and Mental Disease, 75,* 201–207.

Smith, T. W., O'Keefe, J. L., & Jenkins, M. (1988). Dependency and self-criticism: Correlates of depression or moderators of the effects of stressful events? *Journal of Personality Disorders, 2,* 160–169.

Smyth, L. D. (1982). Psychopathology as a function of neuroticism and a hypnotically implanted aggressive conflict. *Journal of Personality and Social Psychology, 43,* 555–564.

Snyder, C. R., Shenkel, R. J., & Lowery, C. R. (1977). Acceptance of personality interpretations: The "Barnum Effect" and beyond. *Journal of Consulting and Clinical Psychology, 45,* 104–114.

Sommerschield, H., & Reyher, J. (1973). Post-hypnotic conflict, repression and psychopathology. *Journal of Abnormal Psychology, 82,* 278–290.

Spence, D. P. (1970). Human and computer attempts to decode symptom language. *Psychosomatic Medicine, 32,* 615–625.

Spence, D. P. (1982a). Narrative truth and historical truth. *Psychoanalytic Quarterly, 51,* 43–59.

Spence, D. P. (1982b). *Narrative truth and historical truth: Meaning and interpretation in psychoanalysis.* New York: Norton.

Spero, M. H. (1987). Qualities of object relations and field dependence in alcoholic and recovered alcoholic males. *International Journal of the Addictions, 22,* 1019–1032.

Spielberger, C. D., Jacobs, G., Russell, S., & Crane, R. (1983). Assessment of anger: The State-Trait Anger Scale. In J. N. Butcher & C. D. Spielberger (Eds.), *Advances in personality assessment* (Vol. 2, pp. 159–177). Hillsdale, NJ: Erlbaum.

Spiro, M. E. (1982). *Oedipus in the Trobriands.* Chicago: University of Chicago Press.

Steenbarger, B. N. (1992). Toward science–practice integration in brief counseling and therapy. *The Counseling Psychologist, 20,* 403–450.

Steenbarger, B. N. (1994). Duration and outcome in psychotherapy: An integrative review. *Professional Psychology: Research and Practice, 25*(2), 111–119.

Steinberg, L. (1985). Early temperamental antecedents of adult Type A behaviors. *Developmental Psychology, 21,* 1171–1180.

Stephens, W. N. (1962). *The Oedipus complex: Cross-cultural evidence.* New York: Free Press of Glencoe.

Stern, D. N. (1977). *The first relationship.* Cambridge, MA: Harvard University Press.

Stern, D. N. (1985). *The interpersonal world of the infant: A view from psychoanalysis and developmental psychology.* New York: Basic Books.

Stiles, W. B., & Shapiro, D. A. (1994). Disabuse of the drug metaphor: Psychotherapy process-outcome correlations. *Journal of Consulting and Clinical Psychology, 62,* 942–948.

Stiles, W. B., Shapiro, D. A., & Elliot, R. (1986). "Are all psychotherapies equivalent?" *American Psychologist, 41,* 165–180.

Stone, G. C., & Gottheil, E. (1975). Factor analysis of orality and anality in selected patient groups. *Journal of Nervous and Mental Disease, 160,* 311–323.

Stone, L. J. (1967). The psychoanalytic situation and transference: Postscript to an earlier communication. *Journal of American Psychoanalytic Association, 15,* 3–58.

Stone, L. J., & Hokanson, J. E. (1969). Arousal reduction via self-punitive behavior. *Journal of Personality and Social Psychology, 12,* 72–79.

Strachey, J. (1934). The nature of the therapeutic action of psychoanalysis. *International Journal of Psychoanalysis, 15,* 127–159.

Strachey, J. (1958). Papers on technique (1911–1915): Editor's Introduction. In J. Strachey (Ed.), *The standard edition of the complete psychological works of Sigmund Freud* (Vol. 12, pp. 85–88). London: Hogarth.

Strachey, J. (1969). The nature of the therapeutic action of psycho-analysis. *International Journal of Psycho-Analysis, 50,* 275–292.

Staub, E. (1979). *Positive social behavior and morality. Socialization and development* (Vol. 2). New York: Academic Press.

Straube, E. R., & Oades, R. D. (1992). *Schizophrenia.* New York: Academic Press.

Strauss, A. (1946). The influence of parent-images upon marital choice. *American Sociological Review, 11,* 554–559.

Stroebe, M., Gergen, M. M., Gergen, K. J., & Stroebe, W. (1992). Broken hearts or broken bonds. Love and death in historical perspective. *American Psychologist, 47,* 1205–1212.

Strupp, H. H., & Binder, J. L. (1984). *Psychotherapy in a new key: A guide to time-limited psychotherapy.* New York: Basic Books.

Strupp, H. H., & Hadley, S. (1979). Specific vs. non-specific factors in psychotherapy. *Archives of General Psychiatry, 36,* 1125–1136.

Stubbs, J. P., & Bozarth, J. D. (1994). The Dodo bird revisited: A qualitative study of psychotherapy efficacy research. *Applied and Preventive Psychology, 3,* 109–120.

Sturman, P. A. (1980). *Derivatives of the castration complex in normal adults.* Unpublished doctoral dissertation, St. John's University, New York, NY.

Suler, J. R. (1980). Primary process thinking and creativity. *Psychological Bulletin, 88,* 144–165.

Sulloway, F. J. (1979). *Freud, biologist of the mind.* New York: Basic Books.

Suls, J., & Fletcher, B. (1985). The relative efficacy of avoidant and nonavoidant coping strategies: A meta-analysis. *Health Psychology, 4,* 249–288.

Surtees, P. (1984). Kith, kin and psychiatric health: A Scottish survey. *Social Psychiatry, 19,* 63–67.

Svartberg, M., & Stiles, T. (1991). Comparative effects of short-term psychodynamic psychotherapy: A meta-analysis. *Journal of Consulting and Clinical Psychology, 59,* 704–714.

Swann, W. B., Wenzlaff, R. M., Krull, D. S., & Pelham, B. W. (1992). Allure of negative feedback: Self-verification strivings among depressed persons. *Journal of Abnormal Psychology, 101,* 293–306.

Talbot, N., Duberstein, P. R., & Scott, P. (1991). Subliminal psychodynamic activation, food consumption and self-confidence. *Journal of Clinical Psychology, 47,* 813–823.

Taylor, S. E. (1989). *Positive illusions. Creative self-deception and the healthy mind.* New York: Basic Books.

Taylor, S. E., & Brown, J. D. (1988). Illusion and well-being: A social psychological perspective on mental health. *Psychological Bulletin, 103,* 193–210.

Tennant, C., Bebbington, P., & Hurry, J. (1980). Parent death in childhood and risk of adult depressive disorders: A review. *Psychological Medicine, 10,* 289–299.

Tennant, C., Smith, A., Bebbington, P., & Hurry, J. (1981). Parental loss in childhood. *Archives of General Psychiatry, 38,* 309–314.

Tennen, H., & Herzberger, S. (1987). Depression, self-esteem, and the absence of self-protective attributional biases. *Journal of Personality and Social Psychology, 52,* 72–80.

Terman, L. M. (1938). *Psychological factors in marital happiness.* New York:-McGraw-Hill.

Thoma, S. (1986). Estimating gender differences in the comprehension and preference of moral issues. *Developmental Review, 6,* 165–180.

Torgersen, S. (1980). The oral, obsessive, and hysterical personality syndromes. *Archives of General Psychiatry, 37,* 1272–1277.

Torrey, E. F. (1992). *Freudian fraud: The malignant effect of Freud's theory on American thought and culture.* New York: HarperCollins.

Touhey, J. C. (1977). "Penis envy" and attitudes toward castration-like punishment of sexual aggression. *Journal of Research in Personality, 11,* 1–9.

Trachtman, R. S. (1978). *Father absence during the Oedipal phase of development.* Unpublished doctoral dissertation, Smith School for Social Work, New York, NY.

Tribich, D., & Messer, S. (1974). Psychoanalytic character type and status of authority as determiners of suggestibility. *Journal of Consulting and Clinical Psychology, 42,* 842–848.

Trijsburg, R. W., & Duivenvoorden, H. J. (1987). Reactive-narcissistic character, obsessional personality and obsessive-compulsive behavior: A study of the validity of Sandler and Hazari's typology. *British Journal of Medical Psychology, 60,* 271–278.

Urist, J. (1980). Object relations. In R. W. Woody (Ed.), *Encyclopedias of clinical assessment* (Vol. 2, pp. 821–833). San Francisco, CA: Jossey-Bass.

Vaillant, G. E. (1977). *Adaptation to life.* New York: Little, Brown.

Vaillant, G. E. (Ed.). (1986). *Empirical studies of ego mechanisms of defense.* Washington, DC: American Psychiatric Press.

Van den Berg, P. J., & Helstone, F. S. (1975). Oral, obsessive, and hysterical personality patterns: A Dutch replication. *Journal of Psychiatric Research, 12,* 319–327.

Varga, M. P. (1973). *An experimental study of aspects of the psychoanalytic theory of elation.* Unpublished doctoral dissertation, New York University.

Viderman, S. (1979). The analytic space: Meaning and problems. *Psychoanalytic Quarterly, 48,* 257–291.

Vinck, J. (1979). Body awareness and personality. *Psychotherapy and Psychosomatics, 32,* 170–179.

Vitiello, M. V., Carlin, A. S., Becker, J., Barris, B. P., & Dutton, J. (1989). The effect of subliminal Oedipal and competitive stimulation on dart throwing: Another miss. *Journal of Abnormal Psychology, 98,* 54–56.

Vogel, W., Vogel, F., McAbee, R., Barker, R., & Thurmond, A. J. (1980). Improvement of depression by REM sleep deprivation. New findings and a theory. *Archives of General Psychiatry, 37,* 247–253.

Volans, P. J. (1976). Style of decision-making and probability appraisal in selected obsessional and phobic patients. *British Journal of Clinical Psychology, 15*, 305–317.

Von der Lippe, A., & Torgersen, S. (1984). Character and defense: Relationships between oral, obsessive, and hysterical character traits and defensive mechanisms. *Scandinavian Journal of Psychology, 25*, 258–264.

Wachtel, P. (1977). *Psychoanalysis and behavior therapy: Toward one integration.* New York: Basic Books.

Walker, L. J. (1984). Sex differences in the development of moral reasoning: A critical review. *Child Development, 55*, 677–691.

Wallace, E. R., IV (1988). What is truth? Some philosophical contributions to psychiatric issues. *American Journal of Psychiatry, 145*, 137–147.

Waller, N. G., & Ben-Porath, Y. S. (1987). Is it time for clinical psychology to embrace the five-factor model of personality? *American Psychologist, 42*, 887–889.

Wallerstein, R. S. (1965). The goals of psychoanalysis: A survey of analytic viewpoints. *Journal of the American Psychoanalytic Association, 13*, 748–770.

Wallerstein, R. S. (1986a). *Forty-lives in treatment: A study of psychoanalysis and psychotherapy.* New York: Guilford.

Wallerstein, R. S. (1986b). Psychoanalysis as a science: A response to new challenges. *Psychoanalytic Quarterly, 55*, 414–451.

Wallerstein, R. S. (1989). The psychotherapy research project of the Menninger Foundation: An overview. *Journal of Consulting and Clinical Psychology, 57*, 195–205.

Warren, L. W., & McEachren, L. (1983). Psychosocial correlates of depressive symptomatology in adult women. *Journal of Abnormal Psychology, 92*, 151–160.

Watson, C. G., & Clark, L. A. (1984). Negative affectivity: The disposition to experience aversive emotional states. *Psychological Bulletin, 96*, 465–490.

Watson, D., & Clark, L. A. (1992). On traits and temperament: General and specific factors of emotional experience and their relation to the five-factor model. *Journal of Personality, 60*, 441–446.

Watson, M. W., & Getz, K. (1990). The relationship between Oedipal behaviors and children's family role concepts. *Merrill-Palmer Quarterly, 36*, 487–505.

Weber, J. J., Elinson, J., & Moss, L. M. (1966). The application of ego strength scales to psychoanalytic clinic records. In G. Goldman & S. Shapiro (Eds.), *Developments in psychoanalysis at Columbia University* (pp. 215–281). New York: Hafner.

Weber, J. J., Elinson, J., & Moss, L. M. (1967). Psychoanalysis and change: A study of psychoanalytic clinic records utilizing electronic data-processing techniques. *Archives of General Psychiatry, 17*, 687–709.

Weinberger, J., & Silverman, L. H. (1990). Testability and empirical verification of psychoanalytic dynamic propositions through subliminal psychodynamic activation. *Psychoanalytic Psychology, 7*, 299–339.

Weiss, J., Sampson, H., & the Mount Zion Psychotherapy Research Group. (1986). *The psychoanalytic process: Theory, clinical observation, and empirical research.* New York: Guilford.

Weiss, L. R. (1969). Effects of subject, experimenter and task variables in compliance with the experimenter's expectation. *Journal of Projective Techniques and Personality Assessment, 33,* 247–256.

Weiss, L. R., & Masling, J. (1970). Further validation of a Rorschach measure of oral imagery: A study of six clinical groups. *Journal of Abnormal Psychology, 76,* 83–87.

Weissman, A. N., & Beck, A. T. (1978). *Development and validation of the dysfunctional attitude scale: A preliminary investigation.* Paper presented at the annual meeting of the American Educational Research Association, Toronto, Canada.

Weissman, M. (1992). The changing rate of major depression: Cross National comparison. *Journal of the American Medical Association, 268,* 3098–3105.

Weissman, M., Fox, K., & Klerman, G. L. (1973). Hostility and depression associated with suicide attempts. *American Journal of Psychiatry, 130,* 450–455.

Weissman, M. M., Klerman, G. L., & Paykel, E. S. (1971). Clinical evaluation of hostility in depression. *American Journal of Psychiatry, 128,* 261–266.

Wenzlaff, R. M., & Grozier, S. A. (1988). Depression and the magnification of failure. *Journal of Abnormal Psychology, 97,* 90–93.

Werner, H. (1957). *Comparative psychology of mental development.* New York: International Universities Press.

Wessman, A. E., Ricks, D. F., & Tyl, M. M. (1960). Characteristics and concomitants of mood fluctuation in college women. *Journal of Abnormal and Social Psychology, 60,* 117–126.

Westen, D. (1990). Psychoanalytic approaches to personality. In L. Pervin (Ed.), *Handbook of personality theory and research* (pp. 21–65). New York: Guilford.

Wetzler, S. (1985). The historical truth of psychoanalytic reconstructions. *International Review of Psycho-Analysis, 12,* 187–197.

Wheeler, W. M. (1949). An analysis of Rorschach indices of male homosexuality. *Journal of Projective Techniques, 13,* 29–42.

Whiffen, V. E., & Sasseville, T. M. (1991). Dependency, self-criticism and recollection of parenting: Sex differences and the role of depressive affect. *Journal of Social and Clinical Psychology, 10,* 121–133.

Whitbeck, L. B., Hoyt, D. R., Simons, R. L., Conger, R. D., Elder, G. H., Lorenz, F. O., & Huck, S. (1992). Intergenerational continuity of parental rejection and depressed affect. *Journal of Personality and Social Psychology, 63,* 1036–1045.

Whitbourne, S. K., Zuschlag, M. K., Elliot, L. B., & Waterman, A. S. (1992). Psychosocial development in adulthood: A 22-year sequential study. *Journal of Personality and Social Psychology, 63,* 260–271.

Wilkins, W. (1984). Psychotherapy: The powerful placebo. *Journal of Consulting and Clinical Psychology, 52,* 570–573.

Winch, R. F. (1946). Interrelations between certain social background and parent–son factors in a study of courtship among college men. *American Sociological Review, 11,* 333–343.

Winch, R. F. (1950). Some data bearing on the Oedipus hypothesis. *Journal of Abnormal and Social Psychology, 45,* 481–489.

Winch, R. F. (1951). Further data and observations on the Oedipus hypothesis: The consequence of an inadequate hypothesis. *American Sociological Review, 16,* 784–795.

Winget, C., & Kramer, M. (1979). *Dimensions of dreams.* Gainesville: University Presses of Florida.

Winson, J. (1992). The function of REM sleep and the meaning of dreams. In J. W. Barron, M. N. Eagle, & D. L. Wolitzky (Eds.), *Interface of psychoanalysis and psychology* (pp. 347–356). Washington, DC: American Psychological Association.

Winter, W. D., & Prescott, J. W. (1957). A cross-validation of Storer's test of cultural symbolism. *Journal of Consulting Psychology, 21,* 22.

Witkin, H. A., Dyk, A. B., Faterson, H. F., Goodenough, D. R., & Karp, S. A. (1962). *Psychological differentiation.* New York: Wiley.

Witkin, H. A., Lewis, H. B., Hertzman, M., Machover, K., Meissner, P., & Wapner, S. (1954). *Personality through perception.* New York: Harper and Brothers.

Wittenborn, J. R., & Maurer, H. S. (1977). Persisting personalities among depressed women. *Archives of General Psychiatry, 34,* 968–971.

Wood, J. M., Bootzin, R. R., Rosenhan, D., Nolen-Hoeksema, S., & Jourden, F. (1992). Effects of the 1989 San Francisco earthquake on frequency and content of nightmares. *Journal of Abnormal Psychology, 101,* 219–224.

Wortman, C. B., & Silver, R. C. (1992). Reconsidering assumptions about coping with loss: An overview of current research. In L. Fillipp & M. J. Lerner (Eds.), *Life crisis and experiences of loss in adulthood* (pp. 341–365). Hillsdale, NJ: Erlbaum.

Yesavage, J. A. (1983). Direct and indirect hostility and self-destructive behavior by hospitalized depressives. *Acta Psychiatrica Scandinavia, 68,* 345–350.

Zepelin, H. (1980–1981). Age differences in dreams: 1. Men's dreams and thematic apperceptive fantasy. *International Journal of Aging and Human Development, 12,* 171–183.

Zuckerman, M., Persky, H., Echman, C. M., & Hopkins, T. R. (1967). A multitrait multimethod measurement approach to the traits (or states) of anxiety, depression and hostility. *Journal of Projective Techniques, 31,* 39–48.

Zuroff, D. C., & Mongrain, M. (1987). Dependency and self-criticism: Vulnerability factors for depressive affective states. *Journal of Abnormal Psychology, 96,* 14–22.

Author Index

Subject Index